"I knew how to race. Carroll Smith taught me to drive race cars."
- Danny Ongais

DRIVE TO WIN

The essential guide to RACE DRIVING

CARROLL SMITH

First Published in 1996 by Carroll Smith Consulting, Inc.
1236 Via Landeta, Palos Verdes Estates, CA 90274

© 1996 Carroll Smith

Edited by Ian Bamsey
Graphic Layout and Cover by Eugene Ball, GBL

Library of Congress Catalogue Card Number: 96-092204
ISBN 0-9651600-0-9

Printed and bound in the United States of America

Cover photo: Michael Schumacher driving a 1996 Ferrari 310 Formula 1 car.
Photo courtesy of Ferrari and **Pan Images**

STATEMENT OF NON-LIABILITY

Our society has reached the point where I am advised that, in order to protect myself from possible lawsuits, I should include a statement of non-liability in this book. Since I believe that the human being is wholly responsible for his own actions, I strongly object to this necessity and to the morality that has spawned it. However, I would object even more strongly to being sued - so here it is.

The price of man in motion is the occasional collision. Motor racing is dangerous. In order to be competitive in this business it is necessary to operate at the outer edges of the performance envelope. The closer we come to the edge, the greater the risk of falling off.

This book is about improving the performance of the racing car and its driver - particularly with respect to the roadholding department. It deals with the deliberate exploration of the outer limits of traction. The closer the racing car approaches its potential in this department, the less forgiving it becomes - and the greater the chances of paying a sudden stop-type penalty when an error in judgement occurs.

If, while attempting to apply any of the ideas, procedures or advice contained in this book you should come unstuck, you will have done so through your own conscious decision. I disclaim responsibility for your actions – and for your accident.

Carroll Smith

DEDICATION

I had intended to dedicate this one to the memories of two fine racing drivers and close friends who had to leave the party early - Ken Miles and Peter Revson. They were extraordinary men and we shall not see their like again.

However, on Saturday, October 15, 1994, Jane, my wife and partner in all things, mother of Dana and Christopher, friend and surrogate mother to generations of racers and students died instantly as the result of a fall from the balcony of our home.

She went doing what she liked best, enjoying the ocean view and gardening on the balcony of the home that she loved. She departed secure in the love of her family and friends and in the respect of her co-workers and students. Our last words to each other were, "It just doesn't get any better than this."

At her request there was no funeral as such. Our closest friends gathered with us for an informal celebration of her life. She touched each of our lives in special ways. Each of us will remember her in our own ways and at our own times.

I have been blessed by a lifetime of love, of challenge and of adventure shared with a most remarkable woman. This book is dedicated to the inspiration of that love and to the Lady Jane.

FOREWORD

For more than thirty years now I have spent a large portion of my waking hours with racing drivers. At first racing against them and, more recently, working with them but always in their company and talking with them, both the ones I was working with and the ones that I was working against. I have been extremely fortunate in that I have spent a lot of time with some very talented and successful drivers. I have also spent a lot of time with very talented but less than successful drivers and not much time at all with untalented ones. From each of them I have learned something. From many of them I have learned a lot.

In my own way I have tried to give as much of this education back as I have been able. Because I can only work with a few drivers in any given season, I get more than I give. It is time for this one-on-one information sharing to stop. What follows is two things:

(1) An attempt by me to formalize my thinking on a great many aspects of the art and science of driving the racing car and the relationship between the racing driver and the development engineer.

(2) An attempt to pass on what I have learned about the subjects to those aspiring drivers who may be both interested enough to read through it and brave enough to try things my way.

There never was a lot of contention about my qualifications to write Prepare To Win, Tune To Win or Engineer To Win and those books filled an obvious void. People are now going to ask two questions:

(1) Does the world need another book on how to drive a racing car?

(2) Where do I, an Engineer and a Team Manager (from the days when Team Managers were something more than travel agents/purchasing agents), get off writing a driving book? Driving books are written by drivers! My justifications have very little to do with the fact that I was a driver for a long time before I was either a Team Manager or an active Engineer. Rather, they have to do with the nature of existing driving books and the changing role of the racing driver.

The existing good books are all written from the point of view of the driver. This book is not. Here we are going to look at what the driver does (or should do) from the point of view of the racing car, the Engineer, the Team Manager, the car owner and the sponsor.

Why? Because both the role and the tasks of the racing driver in the overall scheme of professional motor racing have gone through a subtle change in the past decade or so. The day of the virtuoso driver who used his skill, his experience and his daring to overcome, or to drive around, the deficiencies of his machine and defeat his rivals with sheer driving brilliance has passed into the history books. Pity!

The modern racing car is a sophisticated and almost infinitely adjustable device. Properly adjusted and set up, it should exhibit no vices and very few deficiencies (except, of course, for every driver's age old lament about lack of power). However, if the car's set up on any given day does not closely approach the ideal, no man on earth can win races with it. The only man available to set the car up is the racing driver.

Now and forever more, a very large portion of the driver's professional life consists of working with his ever faithful and dedicated crew in developing and setting up his machine so that, come Sunday, he will have a suitable and competitive tool with which to practice his art. If he performs this task well enough - and if he drives the race itself well enough - he may win on Sunday. If he fails in development and set up, he will spend Sunday trying to pound nails with a rock. No matter how much skill and daring he may exhibit, he will not win - except by chance.

The modern racing driver (except on IROC weekends) is almost as much technician, data gatherer/filter and feedback device as he is racer. While no one can teach another person how to race, the ground rules, techniques and procedure of perception and evaluation can be and must be taught. That is what we are going to try to do. An added attraction will be the possible benefits of learning how the Engineer and the Team Manager look at the role of the driver and their interaction with him - if for no other reason than to enable you to more effectively snivel at and con those worthies with whom you work!

CONTENTS

SECTION ONE: THE DRIVER
Chapter One: The Yellow Brick Road · · · · · · · · · · · · · · · · · · ·1–3
Chapter Two: Fitness, Mental and Physical · · · · · · · · · · · · · ·1–17

SECTION TWO: VEHICLE DYNAMICS
Introduction ·2–3
Chapter Three: The Driver's Best Friend: You & Your Tires · · · · · ·2–5
Chapter Four: Braking ·2–21
Chapter Five: The Cornering Sequence · · · · · · · · · · · · · · · · ·2–31
Chapter Six: Shifting Gears, Gearing and Using the Gearbox · · · ·2–39

SECTION THREE: LEARN TO WIN
Chapter Seven: Training Aids ·3–3

SECTION FOUR: ENVIRONMENTS
Chapter Eight: Permanent Circuits · · · · · · · · · · · · · · · · · · ·4–3
Chapter Nine: Oval Track Hints ·4–7
Chapter Ten: Street Fighting ·4–13
Chapter Eleven: Racing in the Rain · · · · · · · · · · · · · · · · · ·4–17

SECTION FIVE: ON TRACK
Chapter Twelve: Testing ·5–3
Chapter Thirteen: Practice Time ·5–13
Chapter Fourteen: The Race ·5–19

SECTION SIX: AT THE OFFICE
Chapter Fifteen: Safety and Cockpit Controls · · · · · · · · · · · · ·6–3
Chapter Sixteen: Don't Burn the Hands that Support You · · · · · ·6–13

SECTION SEVEN: ADVANCED DRIVE TO WIN
Chapter Seventeen: The Old Rules Change · · · · · · · · · · · · · · ·7–3
Chapter Eighteen: The Racing Shock Absorber · · · · · · · · · · · ·7–13
Chapter Nineteen: The Racing Differential · · · · · · · · · · · · · ·7–23

SECTION ONE

THE DRIVER

1

"Winners do what losers aren't willing to do." Anon.

THE YELLOW BRICK ROAD, OR HOW TO GET THERE FROM HERE

When our son, Christopher, announced his serious intent to become a racing driver I pointed out that, having grown up in a racing family, he of all youngsters should realize the odds against success (say 10,000:1). Why didn't he take up golf or tennis? The cost of the necessary equipment is minuscule and the cost of travel is the same as that in racing - except that the equipment flies free and the maximum support crew is one coach. I pointed out that his family could afford the best golf or tennis equipment and instruction in the world and an airline credit card - all of which would cost less than one season of Formula Ford racing.

After all, for the cost of a set of Formula Atlantic tires you would have a year's supply of the best tennis rackets and balls in the world. The cost of one Atlantic engine would take care of all of the golf equipment that there is. I further pointed out that if he were to devote a fraction of the time and energy to perfecting either game that he would have to devote to racing in order to get to the point where he could honestly win a Formula Ford National Race, he would be a teenage millionaire and able to support his aging father in some style.

No such luck! Ten years later he is driving, not playing golf or tennis. He is winning, and making some money - but not supporting his still aging parent. Maybe soon?

MONEY MATTERS

The basic problem with motor racing as a profession is that it costs too much money to get good enough at it to get paid for doing it. Ours is the only sport in the world where the participants routinely have more money invested in any single event than the guy who owns the stadium. There is, of course, a perfectly logical reason for this - driving racing cars is the single most challenging and rewarding activity that man has yet come up with, so, to the participants, income is a secondary consideration.

Every so often TV commentators or journalists ask the Grand Prix or Indy Car stars what they like best about their profession. Almost always the answer has to do with money and/or lifestyle. Don't believe it for a minute - those guys drive racing cars because driving racing cars is their whole life. Sure, they like the money and the perks. But, make no mistake, if the money went away today, almost all of them would still be driving racing cars tomorrow.

This premise is borne out by three facts. First, the vast majority of the racing drivers of this world (and I mean racing drivers, as opposed to men who drive racing cars) don't make a living at it and have to do something else to support their racing - let alone their families. Second, racing has always been a cyclical business; at the moment we are ending a "golden age" and the peak of the driver pyramid, worldwide, is very well paid indeed. It has not always been so and during the periods when no one was making any real money, every racing car still had a bunch of would-be drivers standing in line waiting for the chance to drive it - just like now. Third, it is difficult for me to believe that the "old guard" - Berger, Earnhardt, Fittipaldi (E.), etc. - feel that they need (or can use) any more money than they already have earned. This sport is addictive.

THE LEARNING PROCESS

It has been said that the only way in which the human being is capable of learning is through experience. It has also been said that experience is the sum of our past mistakes. There are actually two ways to learn anything - from our own mistakes or from someone else's. The easy (and cheap) way to learn is from other people's mistakes. It takes too much time and costs too much money to make our own. It can also hurt. But don't worry about missing out on the experience; no matter how diligently you attempt to use other people's mistakes as a learning springboard, you'll make plenty of your own. And, make no mistake about it, race driving is something you learn. No matter how much talent and determination you have been born with, there is a long and difficult learning process involved before you can even think about making a living at it.

The first major step toward becoming a racing driver is taken when the Acolyte finally realizes that those wondrous and unique talents for driving racing cars that he always believed God gave to him alone were also given to just about everyone else on the track. And that he had best forget about getting anywhere on unassisted talent.

WHAT DOES IT TAKE?

I am often asked what personal attributes are necessary to make a successful racing driver. There are several. We read that the racing driver must have abnormal reflexes, hand-eye coordination and eyesight; that he cannot have much imagination (or intelligence); that he must be absolutely fearless and finally that he must be blessed with huge amounts of money. Wrong on all counts!

There have been, are and will be very successful racing drivers who cannot see worth a damn without corrective lenses. Try the story on Tom Sneva, Bobby Rahal, Paul Tracy, Jacques Villeneuve or Brian Herta. What is required in the vision department is an exceptional ability to focus one's vision on the whole picture rather than on one particular object. This is more than peripheral vision - it is more on the line of awareness.

Really good racing drivers are acutely aware of everything that is going on around them - just like really good fighter pilots. You notice it when riding with them on the highway - they see things that other people do not and not just good looking ladies. Some of this ability is inborn and some of it is developed. It is crucial so develop it.

Excellent reflexes and hand-eye coordination are necessary, but they need not be awesome. Of course, awesome reflexes and hand-eye coordination cannot hurt and the "great" drivers are blessed with them. Both can be improved by training. As a matter of fact, good racing drivers pick up things like juggling and tennis very quickly.

The racing driver's reflexes seem abnormal because, like all athletes, they have been trained and conditioned. The truth of the reflex bit is that the successful racing driver does not react to what the car does - he anticipates what the car is going to do and makes the car do what he wants it to do. The driver's speed comes from anticipation. Reflexes are what saves his life when the anticipation (or the car) fails.

For some obscure reason we seldom read that the racing driver requires an abnormal sense of balance. He does. It has been said that the Earnhardts, Ervans, Kinsers, Mears, Prosts, Sennas, Schumachers, Swindells and Unsers of the world could walk high wires - I don't doubt it. Good racing drivers are usually good skiers and they can all ride skateboards right away. In the immortal words of the late, great Denny Hulme, "It's all a question of balance."

To my mind "lack of imagination" implies a certain lack of intelligence - and I have never known a successful racing driver who did not possess a high degree of intelligence (although I have worked with a few drivers who will probably never believe I made that statement). The (non-racing) journalists who have propagated this particular old saw seem to feel that a person of normal imagination is just not going to allow himself to do anything that he, the journalist, considers to be abnormally dangerous. Again, rubbish! The racing driver, like the fighter pilot, the downhill skier, the rock climber - or for that matter, the policeman or the surgeon - has simply trained himself to block out contraproductive worry at times when it can serve no useful purpose. This is a trait that each of us should cultivate. On the other hand, all of these people get a real high from operating on the edge of fear. There is no doubt in my mind that the successful racing driver, like the successful fighter pilot, must be a risk taker - but the risks must be calculated ones.

So far as the money end of things goes, this argument is usually advanced by the wannabees, the could-have-beens and the should-have-beens - those who didn't make it and those who were afraid to even try. I consider it to be just another form of poor mouthing. Try the argument on Mario Andretti, Scott Pruett, Brian Till, Jimmy Vasser or, for that matter, Nigel Mansell. Mind you, I am not saying that anyone is going to make it from the relief rolls or that great heaps of money are not necessary to advance beyond Formula Ford. What I am saying is that, if a driver has the ability, the discipline, the determination and the political acumen to make it in racing, then he will find a way.

I don't think that good drivers are fearless. There are people born without fear. They are, thankfully, rare, and they don't last very long in this business. Courage is the ability to force yourself to do something that you know can well and truly frighten you. Since racing drivers frighten themselves to varying degrees on a daily basis, they possess courage by definition. The great ones have maybe a little more of it - an ability to push themselves just a little bit further - than the good ones.

Determination, combined with discipline, is what enables one to drive the racing car to the limit of one's ability, after one has just succeeded in well and truly frightening (or even injuring) one's self. And those to me are the definitive words in describing the successful racing driver - discipline and determination.

What is required is a level of discipline usually found only in Saints - which is admirable - together with a level of self confidence usually found only in very good con men - which is only partially admirable - and an inner selfishness that, in many ways, is not very admirable at all. In order to be successful at his chosen profession, the racing driver must be a truly selfish human being - willing to subordinate and sacrifice anything and anybody to further his career. The saving grace is that he must be at least as selfish with himself as with everyone else.

I am not saying that racing drivers do not make good and loyal friends - they do. Most of my friends are or have been racing drivers. They even make good and loyal mates. It is just that the racing driver's friends and mates must realize, going in, that the driver will sell them down the river for a chance at a better ride. They may regret doing it, fleetingly, but do it they will - and they will not expect the act to materially affect the friendship. This is a way of life in which hard cuts soft.

Whether through cause or effect, successful drivers are very hard men. Their friends and lovers who are new to racing sometimes have a lot of trouble understanding their single minded behavior at the track - friends and lovers are left out of that part of their lives. The rest of us are fully aware of it, we joke about it all the time. This factor does not bother me. It never has. If it ever does, it will be time for me to leave.

The bottom line here is that exceptional talent, by itself, won't get it done. What will get it done is perseverance and a bottomless determination to succeed - an absolute refusal to quit or to be beaten. There have been lots of young drivers with the God given driving talents of Prost, or Senna, or Schumacher, or Unser. There have been very few with the mental toughness, dedication, determination and perseverance. The driver whose proudest claim is that he used to beat the current champion when they were both in Formula Fords is a "might have been". He is also a loser.

THE GOOD BOOKS

There have been dozens of books written purporting to describe the art of driving racing cars. Most of them are simple biographies and, while entertaining, are of little value to the aspiring driver. Those that are of value are of enormous value and should be read and re-read - preferably before you read this one. They include, more or less in order of merit:

THE RACING DRIVER by Denis Jenkinson

A TWIST OF THE WRIST and THE SOFT SCIENCE OF MOTORCYCLE ROAD RACING by Keith Code

TECHNIQUES OF MOTOR CYCLE ROAD RACING by Kenny Roberts

THE ART OF MOTOR RACING by Emerson Fittipaldi and Gordon Kirby

AYRTON SENNA'S PRINCIPLES OF RACE DRIVING by Ayrton Senna

COMPETITION DRIVING by Alain Prost and Pierre-Francois Rousselot

THE ART AND SCIENCE OF GRAND PRIX DRIVING by Niki Lauda

THE ACE FACTOR by Mike Spick

THE ART OF WINNING by Dennis Conner

Many of these books are available at your local library. All except the last two are available from my good friends at Motorbooks International (see the Appendix).

None of these books will teach you how to drive a racing car - or to race. As Wilbur Wright once said: "Sitting on a fence and watching birds doesn't teach you a thing about learning how to fly; you've got to get in there and do it."

In each case what the author has to say about the physical act of driving the car is of nowhere near as much value as what he has to say - either directly or between the lines - about the discipline, dedication and attitude required to win motor races at the highest level of the sport. Without exception, the champions take their racing very seriously indeed. Also virtually without exception, they gave up most of the normal "good things in life" for a period of several years in order to get there.

THE FACTS OF LIFE

One of things that I point out to the legion of aspiring driver who approach me every year is that in order to get to the top in motor racing, except for brief moments, you have to be willing to give up almost everything else in life, until you have advanced to the point at which a living can be made driving.

If you are uncomfortable with this concept, it is time to seriously reconsider your career options.

The second thing that I stress is that speed, by itself, is not enough. Even speed combined with consistency and intelligence is not enough. You must win!

Niki Lauda once pointed out that all of the good

drivers, given the same car, would produce very similar lap times. But only a few drivers in each series, from Club Formula Ford to Formula One, honestly win races. Odd, isn't it? What's more, with a few exceptions, most of the "winning" drivers started winning very early in their careers and continued winning as they moved up.

The third thing that I point out on this subject is that winning races, by itself, will not necessarily advance your career. I have just returned from the last CART race of 1995. There were at least three drivers with proven winning records wandering around on foot while several others who have never won a race and who show no sign of ever winning one were being paid to drive Indy Cars - as well as several more who will never win another one. We all start out firmly believing that if we win enough races, the Big Time will come and find us. It will not. You have to go and find it. The inescapable fact of racing life is that the driver himself must get out there and find the rides/sponsorship that will advance his career.

The last thing I point out is that the business is so demanding and the competition so fierce that you cannot afford to give anything away.

This means no drugs whatsoever. The long and short term effects of even "recreational usage" of drugs as supposedly benign as marijuana on the workings of the brain are medical fact, not conjecture. For the same reason it means damned little if any alcohol.

It also means getting yourself into peak physical condition and keeping yourself there. This, by the way, is not because driving the racing car takes much in the way of strength - it is because of two of the basic facts of driving.

The first is that the driver spends his working life in a very debilitating environment - even in open cockpit, mid-engined racing cars, it is hot, debilitatingly hot. Even the air you breathe is hot. To compound this, the driver is encased in at least three layers of Nomex. What we need is physical and mental endurance, not physical strength.

The second fact is that, as we become physically tired, our brain slows down and our decision making capacity deteriorates. The racing driver needs none of this. The driver needs an optimum diet and an optimum training program - more about this later.

My attitude towards all this is the same as that of every professional racing team manager (as opposed to the rent-a-ride team manager, who is liable to have different standards and to be after different results). I am simply not interested in any driver who doesn't care enough (or isn't intelligent enough) to get himself in shape. Except at the end of a long day of testing I do not

ever want to hear a driver say, "because I was (or am) tired". I will not hear it three times from the same driver.

Sometimes I feel my attitude toward many of the young drivers in our sport is at least approaching that of a crusty old curmudgeon. I have been accused, frequently, of demanding too much. I don't, most of the time, think that either of the above is valid. I make the same demands of the drivers I work with that I always have - and that I make of myself and of every member of the team. Those who have whatever it is that it takes to climb to the top of the heap have never said that my demands on them were excessive - quite the opposite in fact.

I don't mind seeing my drivers at the cocktail parties or in the bar but they had better be drinking what they are chasing - virgin Marys.

My point is simple. If you can be happy without driving racing cars, then you should not drive them. However, if drive them you must, then you might as well learn to do it properly. As George Harrison once said, "If you're going to be born and be in a rock band, you may as well be in the Beatles."

THE RISE OF TECHNOLOGY

For some years we have been reading that advancing technology has changed everything in motor racing and, specifically, has reduced the driver's role virtually to that of a spectator. To this I say; "Rubbish, the driver has always been somewhere between 60% and 80% of the performance equation - and he always will be! They don't pay Berger, Earnhardt, Mansell, Schumacher, and Unser that kind of money because they like them".

I will also say that, should this ever change, I will leave the sport. Motor racing, as I have lived it, is meant to be a contest between men in machines, not between the machines themselves. The machines are merely tools for the men. The way that I look at it, the racing car is to the racing driver as the hammer is to the carpenter. The difference is that the carpenter buys his hammer while the racing driver develops his racing car.

That statement leads us to what actually has changed in the last decade or so. What has changed is the driver's role in the great scheme of things. Once upon a time - when I was young and for the sixty odd years of motor racing before that time - very little on the racing car was adjustable. The driver pretty much drove what the team gave him and there wasn't much sense in bitching about the car because there wasn't much that could be done about it.

As late as the legendary Mercedes domination of Grand Prix racing in the Fifties, Ing. Uhlenhaut was astonished (and pleased, I am glad to say) that Fangio and Moss were able to drive the W 196 hard enough to both find and utilize the final oversteer characteristic he had designed into the car. It wasn't until Cooper, Chapman, Broadley and Tauranac made everything on the car adjustable in the 1960s that the "whinging driver" syndrome came into being.

Time was that the driver's job was mainly done on Sundays. Testing and practice were for determining final drive ratio (for the straight(s), not the corners - that option wasn't there) optimum tires and pressures for the circuit, how much front toe-in to run and what jets to put in the carburetors. Now, if the driver does his job properly during testing and practice, Sunday is liable to come as a reward.

Not only is everything on the car adjustable, but the day when a superior driver could carry a mediocre car on his shoulders into the winner's circle are long gone (except on street circuits in the lower classes of professional racing, about which more later). Not only can the superior driver not carry a mediocre car into the winner's circle, unless the car is pretty close to right, he cannot even push it onto the podium.

With all of the electronic data gathering equipment - both on board and telemetered - in use, the most sensitive and accurate data gathering device at our command is still the racing driver. In all probability this will always be so. The driver is the only instrument which can feel the "balance" of the racing car under the endless variety of track and traffic conditions - and relate what he feels to us poor engineers in some comprehensible form.

An often overlooked aspect of on board data gathering is that unless the driver involved is able to drive the car to its limits - and to do so consistently - the data gathered will only serve to confuse everyone concerned.

So what has actually changed is not the driver's importance in the performance equation, but part of his role in it. He is now almost as much of a data gatherer/filter/interpreter as he is a racer.

Mind you, the best and most sensitive test driver in the world would be useless unless he were also a highly skilled, aggressive and intelligent racing driver. This is why Prost and Senna got the big bucks - they, more than anyone in this generation, combined the attributes of test driver and racing driver into one man. Between the two of them they won 92 Grands Prix.

On the other hand, Mansell, World Champion, winningest Brit of all time and a less than brilliant development driver, dominated CART - for one year. Some people can seemingly break the rules - but only with a very experienced team who employ a good development driver (Andretti Sr. - awesome).

McLaren's 1989 mistake was not in choosing Senna over Prost, but in allowing Prost to revitalize Ferrari. They should have either shot him or paid him the national debt to go to CART! Fortunately for the Brits, Enzo Ferrari died and the traditional Italian disorganizational genius did the rest.

Further, while I decry the arrival of such technological marvels as active suspension, anti-lock brakes, active differentials and automatic mechanical gearboxes, their advent was inevitable and they will not change the driver contribution to the equation. The genius driver will merely have fewer distractions (housekeeping chores someone called them) and more time to devote to his art.

Anyway, while this book has a lot to do with the driving of the racing car, it has as much to do with the relationship between the racing driver, the racing car, the engineer, the crew, the sponsors and the road to the top.

STARTING OUT

I get a lot of questioning (as well as questionable) letters. I also get a lot of questioning phone calls and a lot of in-person questions. The technical questions are fun. They get my brain working and lead to a certain amount of consulting work. Unfortunately the most popular question has no real answer. Every aspiring driver in the world seems to feel that there is some sort of yellow brick road that leads to the opportunity to drive someone else's racing car(s). Further, a large percentage of these worthies seem to think that I am the custodian of the road map. I am not.

As a point of interest, I also do not hold the key to entry level racing car design jobs. My answer there has always been, "Fly to England; hang a digitizer pick around your neck and start knocking on doors." Both of the young engineers who took that advice were hired within two weeks of their arrival.

So far as the race track engineer position is concerned, the entry level job is data geek and electronics guy - both in CART and IMSA. One friend got hired by a leading CART team by the simple expedient of asking Pi Research to train him in England. Clever man, Barry O'Toole - well done!

The question that I hear most is, "I don't have the money to buy and run a car, but I know that I have the talent and the determination to succeed - how do I get started?"

You get started, my friend, any way that you can. It is highly unlikely that you are going to earn enough money to finance your racing while you are young enough to still have a career in racing. This leaves convincing someone to provide either a ride or a car and the money to run it, selling the family whatever, robbing a bank or renting your sister/girlfriend/wife by the hour, day, week or month. Again, if you are not comfortable with this concept, reconsider your career options.

I don't think that I have changed much in the past 40 years. I am certain that there has been no fundamental change in the nature of motor racing. What I believe has happened, however, is that changes in our society have brought into motor racing (and into the world in general) a previously unthinkable amount of money - along with a generation of relatively affluent young people, many of whom are unfamiliar with the concepts of 'struggle', 'determination', 'dedication' and 'earn your way'.

I am not talking here about personal wealth. Worldwide, the top ranks of road racing have always contained a healthy percentage of men born to wealth - and they always will. The kind of hunger that gets a man to the top is not physical.

The percentage of drivers on a Grand Prix grid who are being paid, bringing sponsorship money with them or paying for the ride has been remarkably constant for almost a century. There has never, however, been a time when wealth - by itself or even combined with natural talent - could get one to the top of professional motor racing. That takes enormous amounts of ruthless determination and single minded dedication.

It must be admitted, of course, that, given the requisite amounts of talent, dedication and determination, dollars accelerate the learning curve a whole lot. Again, the basic thing to remember here is the old rule that, no matter what aspect of engineering or of human performance is being discussed, hard cuts soft - every time.

This is a brutally competitive business which must be played with other people's money. It takes a hard man to get to the apex of the pyramid. He will use people to get where he wants to go - but he will be as hard on himself as he is on anyone else or he will simply not get there. Period. End of story.

One last time: if you are not comfortable with this concept, reconsider your choice of profession. Of course, the old saying that, "You had better be nice to people on your way up because you are going to meet the same people on your way back down" is absolutely true. It is not necessary to be anal to get ahead. So far as I know, Dan Gurney and Phil Hill still have all of their surviving old friends. If we were to query the top twenty professional road racing drivers in the world at any given time, we would find that they got to where they are by twenty different routes. The routes would have a lot in common (Karts, Formula Ford, Formula Three or Atlantic and conning people out of money/rides). What's worse, getting started is only the beginning. The better you get at it, the more you develop whatever talent

and determination you turn out to have, the more it is going to cost to keep going - let alone to advance your career.

No matter how much talent you may have and no matter how many races you may win, there are damned few free rides in the minor leagues and, with the exception of a few all-too-rare patrons of the sport, no one is going to pay you to drive a road racing car until you get to the big time. This is one of the great problems with motor racing - you don't get paid at all until you get to the big leagues.

Worldwide, two basic problems face the masses of young people who think that they are ready to kill in order to become professional road racing drivers:

1) There are maybe 1000 people in the world making any kind of a decent living driving any kind of racing car. There are maybe 100 doing so in road racing cars. There are at least hundreds of thousands who think that they both want to and can. Each and every one of the hundreds of thousands is absolutely convinced that he (she) has the talent and determination required to reach the top.

2) The capital outlay required to reach the level of skill and experience where someone might be willing to pay you to drive any racing car is silly. That required to get you to the point where someone might pay you to drive a road racing car in the USA is awesome.

In the United States of America these problems are compounded by the simple fact that there exists no logical road to professional status. It's not like the stick and ball games where the progression from the sand lot to the big leagues is almost as formalized as the progression from grammar school to a University degree. With the exception of Skip Barber's munificent $100,000 bonus to the winner of the Barber/Dodge series (which is still not enough to move up with), there are no scholarships for students of motor racing, no matter how worthy or how needy they may be.

In Europe, Japan, and even in Canada, the road to Formula One or Indianapolis, for the determined few, leads from Sprint Karts to Formula Ford (or Formula Renault or Formula Fiat) through Vauxhall/Lotus to Formula Three or 3000. Any of the steps along the way may be skipped (Formula 3000, supposedly the last hurdle before F1, is often bypassed) but the path is there.

Corporations, national sanctioning bodies and racing teams are actually looking for outstanding talent. In many cases they are willing and able - assuming that the talent is matched by at least equal amounts of political and business acumen - to nurture and, to some extent, to financially support outstanding talent. As an example, in 1993 there were four drivers being paid to drive Toyota Formula Atlantic cars in the US and Canada. All four were Canadians, sponsored by Canadian corporations. Just to make things more emphatic, the opening CART, Indy Lights and Formula Atlantic races of 1995 were all won by Canadians.

Not so here in the USA. Our sanctioning bodies couldn't care less about supporting developing talent and the same is true of almost all of the professional teams and corporate sponsors. Those innocents who are convinced that Rick Galles, Chip Ganassi, Carl Haas, Carl Hogan, Bruce McCraw and Derek Walker spend any part of their weekends looking for their next generation of drivers by watching Atlantic or Indy Lights drivers are smoking some pretty optimistic stuff.

The laudable exceptions are Roger Penske (Rick Mears, Kevin Cogan, and Paul Tracy), Chip Ganassi (Bryan Herta and Jimmy Vasser), A.J. Foyt (Mike Groff and Bryan Herta) and Carl Hogan/Bobby Rahal (Mike Groff) and were Steve Horne at Truesports (Scott Pruett), Bruce Levin (Dominic Dobson) and Rob Dyson (Drake Olson, James Weaver and Price Cobb). Unfortunately the last two are gone from the scene.

Horne, thankfully, has returned and will doubtless give fresh talent a chance when his circumstances permit. Penske may do the same. The rest seem to prefer hiring established stars - often going to Europe to do so - or allowing wealthy young men of varying levels of talent to pay to drive their cars.

One of the problems facing young American drivers is that the current crop of foreigners are not only arriving with foreign sponsorship money (due largely to CART's marketing of TV in South America), they are arriving with both experience and talent. No less an authority than A.J. Foyt recently said; "There's a lot of talent out there, but they'll probably never get a chance to move up. I was fortunate to come along when I did because I didn't have a pot to piss in. If, like today, a lot of guys had come in with money, I'd have never made it!"

This from the man who has done it all - and who (reluctantly) taught me as much as anyone ever has. Of course, he currently has Mr. Cheever driving his car...

Maybe the forthcoming civil war between Indianapolis Motor Speedway (IRL) and Indy Car (CART) will give rise to some testing rides...

While I do not approve of this state of affairs, there is defensible logic behind the situation. First and foremost is the simple fact that, while road racing is a major professional sport in the UK, Europe, Japan and even in Mexico, in this country it is neither major nor professional.

A major sport is one which regularly commands big time television audiences on prime time. A professional sport is one in which at least the majority of the team owners, as well as the players and supporting cast, normally make money - by some method other than renting their sports equipment to the players. Sure, NASCAR runs at Sears Point and Watkins Glen - but you would hardly call NASCAR a road racing operation. CART's 16 race series currently includes 11 road racing circuits - but how many of CART's team owners are making money? And, except for Indianapolis, how many CART events rate high in the Neilson ratings?

Trans Am and IMSA are professional only for a few teams in each series and their television audience approaches the media's definition of zero (possibly because ESPN doesn't very often stick to its printed schedule of coverage). No, in this country, ours is a lunatic fringe sport. For confirmation take a look at the racing coverage in your daily newspaper, television sports news or weekly news magazine - and then compare it with equivalent European or Canadian coverage (or Mexican, for that matter).

Major industries, of any nature, require constant influxes of fresh talent. Any major professional sport will, of necessity, develop its own farm system. The farm system will develop the fresh talent by natural selection. This is exactly what has happened in UK and European road racing. It has not happened here (except in Stock Car Racing, the only truly professional arm of American Motor Racing), and it will not happen until (and if) we become a major sport - by which time it will be too late for anyone who is reading this now. In this business, you cannot wait for it to happen - you have to make it happen. Now!

For this reason alone, the major road racing teams tend to get their new drivers from the foreign talent pool. The driver who has several seasons of Formula Three, 3000 and maybe some good years of Formula One behind him, but is not going to be a Formula One Star (say Mr. Cheever or Mr. Johansson) is perceived to be better qualified to drive an Indy Car competitively and safely than a young American with a couple of years of Atlantic and maybe a year of Indy Lights - at twelve races per year.

Of course, that particular class of import has never won a Formula One race and, as I expected, neither have they yet won an Indy Car race. They are journeymen, not stars. Better yet is a genuine Formula One star who isn't up for the commitment any more - say Mr. Fittipaldi (E.) or Mr. Mansell. The point is that the team does not have to pay for the learning curve.

Another point that helps the foreign drivers is the fact that many of the Indy Car Team Managers and mechanics are from the UK and are familiar with the abilities of UK and European drivers. This is not an old boy network as such - just a question of familiarity with the school and the schoolmasters that produce the talent.

Anyway, those are the ground rules. The bottom line is that if you intend to become a professional road racing driver, the best way is to get yourself to Europe and learn your profession. The only way to get really good at anything is to do a lot of it.

If you equate learning this job to earning a university degree, it takes, say, 160 semester hours to qualify for an engineering degree. A young driver in the US drives at the most fourteen races a year. If he is lucky he might get another ten test days. The British Formula Three Championship comprises 20 races, the German 24. Those guys test two days a week, every week. The top five in each country get to do Macau and Fuji at the end of the season. It takes a lot less time to amass the semester hours over there - and the quality of instruction (i.e. competition) is better. What's more, regardless of the horror stories, it doesn't cost any more.

There are other reasons why the drivers with European experience are better than our home grown products:

1) The top teams are truly professional and will bring out the best in deserving drivers. The driver will also learn proper procedures.

2) Formula Three cars have lots of stick and very little horsepower. They stop and corner very well. However, they hardly accelerate at all. Every mile per hour lost takes forever to get back. Therefore, in order to be really quick, the drivers must learn to carry maximum speed through every corner. This is especially true because the majority of the corners are very fast.

3) There are not a lot of circuits. Each is visited several times. The top teams know the circuits and the set ups very well. The driver arrives with a car that is 95% there and spends almost all of the time honing his driving rather than trying to figure out a set up.

4) The driver learns all about the importance of qualifying up front and of truly racing from the fall of the green flag. More than in any other series, he who hesitates is left behind - and there is no such thing as catching up.

The major problem, of course, is that motor racing is the second most expensive sport on this planet (America's Cup sailboat racing takes the grand prize).

There are people in this world who simply cannot be content with pastel colors. These people drive racing cars (or bikes), fly fighter aircraft, climb mountains, race downhill on skis, surf the big waves or fight bulls. They may also play golf (Prost, Mansell and Rahal do) - but only for relaxation.

Nothing in life is a smooth curve. Even the most talented and dedicated drivers go through stages in their development. Typically they start out with a, "Wow, this is fun!" attitude - and they are right. Driving a racing car at the limit is more fun than anything else that people do with their clothes on. The trouble is that the driver who remains at the "fun" level will probably never become consistent and will certainly never become fast - he will remain a club driver forever. To get fast enough, consistent enough and good enough at setting up a car so that someone will pay you to drive a racing car is really hard mental work and requires a somewhat higher degree of self discipline than the priesthood - although, thank God, not the same sort of denials.

GETTING STARTED

Anyway, at the risk of alienating virtually every rent-a-ride team in the country, I am going to put forth on the printed page (i.e. cast in stone) my advice to the young would be road racing driver on how to get there.

First off, unless you want a career in sedans, don't waste your time with sedans or sedan derivatives until you are really good. Open wheel cars will teach you how to drive and how to race. Once you have progressed to where you are winning at something like the Toyota Atlantic or Indy Lights level, you can turn to sedans to make money.

The reason has nothing to do with the technology of the cars or the quality of the racing. It has to do with the response time of the cars. Learn to drive and to race in a car with instantaneous response and a lot of stick and you will be able to transition to the more predictable sedans immediately. Learn on sedans and you may never successfully transition to open wheeled cars. Any F-16 jockey can fly a Cessna. The other way around doesn't work.

I live in a relatively real world, so my advice is broken into two similar but not identical channels which, for lack of better terms, we will call "funded" and "under-funded". For the purpose of this discussion funded means that one is able to spend at least US $250,000 (1995) per annum of someone's money on racing.(Twice that would be a lot more realistic.).

In either case, the only place to start is in Sprint Karts. Not in Enduro or "lie down" Karts which will teach you a lot about engines but very little about either driving or racing, nor in Super Karts which scare a novice away from the race track before he learns anything at all. Pick the stock engine class that is most competitive in your area and race every chance that you get. Don't tell me that you cannot afford to race Karts. Go get a job.

The outlay is modest and the learning curve very steep. Run both dirt and pavement. You will for sure learn whether you really want to race or not. If you do, you will also learn how. Don't do anything more until you are winning in Sprint Karts. The concept of, "I can't win in this class, so I'll move up" is beyond my comprehension. It is also popular. When you are winning at the national level in stock engined Sprint Karts, graduate to the gearbox Karts and find out if you are really any good at it.

After Karts, both the funded and the underfunded should start out at one of the better racing (as opposed to high performance driving) schools. Neither Bob Earl nor Richard Spenard are now teaching, so my current favorites are the Skip Barber, Bob Bondurant and Jim Russell Schools in the US and the Jim Russell school at Mount Tremblant in Canada. Overseas, the Elf Winfield school in France is in a class of its own and offers a free season of Formula Renault Racing for the annual school champion pupil. One would think that the chances of a non-French student getting that plum are remote indeed, but Americans have done it twice in the past six years.

The funded driver should go through the school, do a few of the school Formula Ford races and then go to Elf Winfield. Most people who think that they want to be racing drivers find out quickly that the reality is a bit different from the dream. What it is actually about is not "being" a racing driver but teaching one's self to "become" a racing driver.

If you are not very quickly running up front in the school races, the Barber instructors have a term, "OSB" which stands for "Other Sports Beckon". This is nothing to be ashamed of and, if you fall into the "funded" category, it doesn't even mean that you cannot enjoy motor racing. There are thousands of drivers enjoying racing at their own level - from Club Formula Ford to World Sports Cars - fully aware that they are never going to make a living at it. Only the very tip of the pyramid ever gets good enough to do this full time - and they pay in other ways.

The funded driver who is winning at the school level should take himself instantly to England. He should present himself at the door of Van Diemen, Swift or Vector, arrange for a season of Formula Ford racing in the UK and go about learning how to drive racing cars properly. If he succeeds at that, Formula Vauxhall Lotus is the next step, followed by the British Formula Three Championship.

There is no sense in a funded driver going with a team less than the best. There are charlatans in every business in every country and UK Formula Vauxhall and Formula Three are not exceptions. There are a lot of teams who will be only too happy to take your money. There are only a few who are capable of doing a good job. (It is up to you to inspire them to do it.) A year in the UK doing Formula Ford will show anyone

smart enough to deserve success which Vauxhall Lotus and Formula Three teams to go with. The rest are to be avoided.

Assuming success in Formula Three, the logical next step is the latest single-engine, single-chassis version of Formula 3000 or Indy Lights. The same precautions apply - even more so because more money is involved and the difference between competitive and non-competitive teams is even greater.

If, at any time after some success has been achieved in Formula Three, the aspirant runs out of talent, determination or money, he may well have established sufficient credentials and absorbed enough political acumen to arrange a paid ride in Touring Cars, Sports Cars or maybe even CART (there are virtually no paid rides in Formula Three, 3000, Atlantic or Indy Lights).

Even if money is not a major problem, there are no viable alternatives to this route because I am convinced that you should eventually do Formula Three in the UK (or Germany or Italy or Japan if you happen to be European or Japanese) and it is best to learn your way around before you jump into that particular rat race.

That takes care of the 1% of my readers who have this kind of dollar to spend. How about the "underfunded" masses? It's a hell of a lot more difficult! It is going to take longer - but it is not impossible.

Current members of the exclusive "made it in road racing in the USA without big time family funding" club include (in alphabetical order) Jack Baldwin, Geoff Brabham, Price Cobb, Robbie Gordon, Rick Mears, Scott Pruett, Danny Sullivan and Jimmy Vasser. In Canada we have Scott Goodyear in the big time with David Empringham,and possibly Patrick Carpentier, on the way.

It takes one hell of a lot of work and even more persistence. It also requires a detailed but flexible master plan. I should point out right now that if you are underfunded to the extent that you cannot afford a good driving school and a school race series, you have only two choices - get funded or modify your ambitions. This is not a sport for poor people.

The object is to move through the ranks really quickly - not staying in any one class any longer than it takes to start running consistently at the front. The trick is getting the rides to start with - and making sure that they are the right rides.

Again, the only place to start is at a school - you have to learn the basics and the schools offer the most economical way to learn the basics. Go to the best and do at least your first few races in a school series - it may not look it at first, but it really is cheaper. The concept of working at one of the schools that offers driving instruction and school races in return for mechanical work is tempting. It is almost essential if you intend to do something like the Barber Dodge series or any of the school "pro" series.

The easiest way to win a race is to drive the best car. The surest way to lose a race is to drive a bad car. There is no way on God's green earth to prepare a bunch of cars so that they will be identical. The way to find out which are the best cars and the best mechanics is to work with them for a while and to cultivate relationships with the people who run the series and those who prepare the cars. If this sounds a little Machiavellian, then so be it - it's a Machiavellian world.

Assuming that reality keeps you from going to the UK at this point, currently the best learning series for an impecunious young driver are the Barber School Formula Ford series (which offers a free season of Barber Dodge to the Champion) and the Formula Ford 2000 series.

In FF2000 one has to arrange access to a competitive car and engines - but one man, the driver, can perform all of the maintenance and do the major share of the engine rebuilds. For the top three, prize money is damned near enough to keep going on. This is not a series that offers a lot of recognition but it is probably the best junior high school in the hemisphere. If you can afford it, the Barber Dodge series is outstanding.

If you can win in either of these series, you are ready to go to Europe and do Vauxhall Lotus - which can still be done with an open trailer and minimum staff. How you do it, I don't know, but do it you should. The $100,000 from the Barber Dodge Championship would do it - my way.

Do not fall into any of the SCCA traps. Formula Ford 1600 in this country is dead. Sport 2000 and Olds Pro are "doctor/lawyer" classes and Olds Pro is a cheater's paradise. The spec racer classes are a complete waste of time. Toyota Atlantic requires a budget that would allow you to do a competitive year in the British Formula Three Championship. The same is true of Indy Lights, but at least the media coverage and the Indy Car connection are good.

Of course, if you are so fortunate as to arrange realistic sponsorship for any of these series, the whole picture changes. Do not, however, make the mistake of trying to do a competitive pro series without sufficient equipment, dollars and crew to be competitive. At this stage in your career it is more important to be running up front than it is to be running. Your job is to get people's attention. When you arrive at your first event in a series new to you, you had better qualify somewhere in the first three rows. If you are not certain that you can do this, don't go. Wait until you are.

By the same token, it is better to do a few races competitively than a whole series uncompetitively. It is also imperative to move through the lower series as rapidly as possible. If, after a move up, you are not winning - or at least consistently running up front - at the end of the season, it is time for a brutally honest re-evaluation - of your talents, your judgement, your determination or any combination thereof.

This is probably the time to mention the ladder. We usually think of the young driver's progress from sandlot to World Champion as a smoothly ascending curve. It seldom is. Instead of a curve the path is very liable to be a series of hills - with relatively flat (or even downward) areas between the slopes. This is natural. Young drivers who are going to get anywhere instantly win at the entry levels of motor racing, say Regional Formula Ford. They then move up to National Formula Ford and, naturally, expect to keep on winning. Sometimes it even happens that way - especially in a year and/or a geographic region where the national competition is weak.

However, sooner or later the aspirant moves up to a level where he not only doesn't win - he isn't even competitive. In other words, natural talent reaches its Peter Principle level and reality strikes. No matter how much natural talent a driver has, it will only carry him to the level where he comes up against the people who not only have as much natural talent as he has but have added intelligence and experience to that talent. It hurts. Anyway, the progress of the young driver after he reaches his talent level is not a smooth curve but a series of steps. Just as in Europe, dominance in Formula Three seldom produces instant competitiveness in Formula 3000 and dominance in 3000 does not guarantee competitiveness in Formula One, so in the US, the star Toyota Atlantic driver does not instantly win at Indy Lights and the Indy Lights champions have not been instantly competitive in Indy Cars. Similarly the NASCAR Winston West and Busch Grand National drivers take a couple of seasons to fight their way to the front of the Winston Cup, and the typical CRA or Pennsylvania Sprint Car driver meets with little success on his first Outlaw tour.

There are a lot of reasons for this. Some of them have to do with budgets, equipment and crews - the top CART and Formula One teams do not hire rookies and the usual Atlantic graduate cannot afford a top Indy Lights team, etc. But a lot of it has to do with the increased level of skill and experience faced by the new driver on his way up. It is tough to realize, after you have fought your way to the top of your particular mountain and graduated to a higher level of professional competition that your mountain was only a foothill. And that you are not starting your climb of the next mountain from anywhere near the top.

This destroys a lot of young drivers (and football players, and basketball players, etc.) - their spirit (or their ego) simply cannot take it and they do not progress. Others - the Alesis, Cobbs, Kulwickis, Luyendyks, Tracys and Vassers of the world - put their heads down, carry on, learn fast and get the job done. This is called determination. It is also called intelligence.

Anyway, the major goal of the young driver is obviously to win races and to advance his career. It is equally important to keep honing skills and building real experience so that, regardless of the win record, the driver is ready in all respects to take advantage of his "break" when he finally makes it happen. As a case in point I offer Mssr. Alesi whose Formula Three career and his first year in Formula 3000 were not exactly blazingly successful. When Eddie Jordan gave him his break in Formula 3000 and even more so when Tyrrell gave him his break in the 1989 French Grand Prix, he was ready. The rest is history. I predict that the same will be true of Mika Salo and Tyrrell.

Funded or not, one of the situations that must be avoided is winding up driving a racing car either prepared or set up by someone who doesn't know what he is doing. Badly prepared cars can get you hurt. Badly set up cars will get you confused and discouraged. Choose the people that you work with very carefully. This business is full of wannabees and charlatans.

There are a couple of fundamental problems with climbing the ladder to road racing success in the USA. The first is that there is virtually no way to get there from here. The logical road to success passes through England. This is unfortunate indeed but it is absolutely necessary to realize that it is the way things are. The only professional road racing cars in the US are Indy Cars, three or four Trans Am and GTO cars and a very few IMSA WSC cars. Virtually no one gets paid for driving Atlantic cars (except in Canada), Indy Lights or WSC.

Let's look at the paid drivers: 1992's stars in IMSA were Geoff Brabham, Price Cobb, Juan Manuel Fangio II, Pete Halsmer, Davy Jones, and P.J. Jones. Fangio is foreign born and trained. Brabham is foreign born but resident in the US and might as well be one of us. He was trained in Formula Three and arrived as an accomplished driver and as a friend of Ralt. Of the natives, D. Jones served his apprenticeship in Formula Three in the UK. Only the Joneses came to their paid rides relatively young.

Cobb was an absolute standout in Atlantic and Super Vee for years and years before anyone recognized his talents. With the demise of GTP only Fangio and P.J. Jones had rides in 1993 and they were each mainly testing in 1994 and 95. The same sort of thing was true of Camel Lights - a "doctor/lawyer" class with damned

few (dominant) professionals. At the time of writing (1995) WSC has yet to produce paid drivers on a consistent basis. Hopefully this will change. The situation is even worse in CART. The Great American Race at Indianapolis is dominated by English chassis, English and Japanese engines (some with American names), English mechanics, engineers, team managers and foreign drivers.

If we look at 1995 paid Indy Car drivers, we see Michael Andretti, Raul Boesel, Eddie Cheever, Gil de Ferran, Christian Fittipaldi, Emerson Fittipaldi, Teo Fabi, Adrian Fernandez, Scott Goodyear, Robbie Gordon, Mauricio Gugelmin, Bryan Herta, Stefan Johansson, Arie Luyendyk, Scott Pruett, Bobby Rahal, Danny Sullivan, Paul Tracy, Al Unser Jr., Jimmy Vasser and Jacques Villeneuve. Nine Americans vs ten foreign borns - sad state of affairs, right? The real picture is, however, worse than that.

Of the US born drivers, Cheever is American by birth only, Rahal and Sullivan both learned their trade in Europe (as did Canadian Villeneuve). So, effectively, 13 of the 19 are foreign born and/or foreign trained. Further, Unser and Michael Andretti had big time backing related to the family name. They would each have made it anyway, but the backing certainly accelerated their progress.

This leaves Herta and Vasser as the only ones who got there in this country without big time backing (Michael Kranefuss put Gordon where he is). As I said, the high road to Indianapolis leads through England. This is OK, so long as we realize it and are not led astray by the claims of Toyota Atlantic and Indy Lights to be the training grounds for Indy.

It is a hell of a lot easier to make a living driving race cars with roofs and fenders than it is to make a living driving open wheelers. The sensible aiming point for any American wannabee race driver is NASCAR's Winston Cup. If you feel that you must specialize in road racing, IMSA GTO/GTU offers valid and well paid but rare possibilities. Trans Am offers the same, but fewer. I'll wager that there are more people making a living driving fendered road racing cars in the US than there are doing the same in CART.

The dollars at the peak of the pyramid are a lot less, but the opportunities for employment are a lot more - and it is possible to graduate to Indy Cars from tin tops (rare, but possible). Scott Pruett and Robbie Gordon did it successfully and Willy T. Ribbs and Wally Dallenbach at least got to drive Indy Cars. It took Willy and Wally a long time, but Pruett, (probably the most impressive combination of ability, intelligence, and political awareness of the past decade) made it very quickly. So did Gordon.

Another advantage is that the top closed wheel teams have historically searched for and employed talented and politically astute young drivers - a complete change from the open wheel scene. Enough hanging around and grovelling has often produced good rides in entry level road racing sedans - currently SCCA's Escort World Challenge and IMSA'S Firehawk. Again, unlike the open wheeled series, consistently brilliant results at the lower levels can produce factory tryouts in the tin tops.

Anyway, if tin tops are your bag, the scene is a lot more cheerful. The paid Trans Am and IMSA GTO/GTU drivers are almost exclusively home grown products. The exception is Steve Millen, but he arrived on these shores a total unknown Kiwi (undeservedly - he had really good credentials) and got where he is by ability and chutzpah. In fact, his route is really strange - it leads through off road trucks which I designed and in which he dominated. As with all successful drivers, Steve's success is also the result of a lot of "being there, visible, and audible, with helmet in hand."

I am fully aware that all young drivers hate being around race tracks when they don't have a ride. I am also aware that one of the bottom lines in this business is that, if you're not physically present when drivers are needed or even being discussed, your name will not come up. It is absolutely essential to be visible - highly visible. It can be done without losing either self respect or dignity.

My own thoughts on the matter are that, if you want to make a good living driving racing cars in this country, you should set your sights on NASCAR's Winston Cup Series. In my opinion, NASCAR is the only truly professional sanctioning body in the USA. Further, there is a road - a hard road, but a feasible one. I give you Ernie Irvan - who was welding bleachers at Charlotte Motor Speedway when he first ventured south.

I would suggest starting out in either Legends or Dwarf cars. If you can win at that level and have any promotional skills, you should be able to get a good short track ride - or even a Pick Up Truck ride. Winning there can lead to Busch and winning at Busch is almost a guarantee of a Cup ride. Of course, as always, if you cannot win at any of the intermediate levels, it's time to think of something else to do with your life. It is true that Niki Lauda didn't win until Formula One and that Jean Alesi didn't win until Formula 3000 but these are extreme exceptions.

THE DRIVER TRY OUT

It is about as difficult to convince the owner of an expensive and delicate racing car that he should turn you loose in it as it would be to convince him to turn you loose in his daughter's bedroom. Still, with enough talent, determination and dogged perseverance, the young racing driver may eventually get a "try out" for a real racing team (i.e., one that does not require him to bring bags of gold to the party).

Invariably the Team Manager will say something along these lines. "Now, we realize that you have never driven anything remotely resembling this car and that you have never seen the circuit before. We don't expect you to go fast today - just take your time, settle in and get used to the car." He is lying. If he wanted a steady driver, there are literally thousands of them around - lots of them with bags of gold to bring to the party. What the professional is looking for is a quick driver. The rest can be taught. Speed, real speed, is either there or it is not - and you had better demonstrate it right away. You may or may not be forgiven for damaging the car during a driver evaluation. You will not be forgiven for going slow.

Don't be afraid to let your enthusiasm show.

FINDING A SPONSOR.

The second most frequently asked question is, "How do I go about finding a sponsor?" It's as if people think that finding a sponsor is like finding a drugstore. The usual whine is, "I know that I have the talent, dedication and balls to get to Formula One or Indianapolis or Winston Cup - but I don't have any money and no one will sponsor me (or my son/boyfriend/husband)".

The first thing you have to realize is that there is no valid commercial reason for any corporation to sponsor anyone in the lower levels of motor racing. There are only two valid reasons for commercial sponsorship - product recognition/ identification/ advertising and Research and Development.

We can pretty much forget about R & D until you get to Indy or Winston Cup cars and even there the validity issue is pretty shaky. So far as product recognition, etc, goes, the reality is equally grim - the real media coverage is so minimal as to be non-existent. The second thing you have to realize is that the only person who is going to find sponsorship for you is you. Once you get these two facts through your head you can concentrate your energies and abilities on those who might actually be willing to help.

The only reason that anyone is going to sponsor your Formula Ford (through and including Indy Lights) car is because he or she likes racing and/or being associated with racing and cannot afford to sponsor an Indy Car. It helps a lot if they believe in, respect and like you. Once you have realized this simple fact you will stop spending money on "press kits" which are actually given away to kids and on "sponsorship proposals" which are actually money makers for the so called sponsor finders who charge you for making them up and distributing them.

So how do you find a sponsor? I don't really know - I have never found one. Over the years a few have found me but I have never found a sponsor. This is indicative of a gap in my personality. This is not a sponsor finding book. There are, however, a few basic rules that are worth discussing.

The first rule is that you ask! You ask a great many potential sponsors for support and you do not get discouraged when prospect after prospect turns you down. It's a bit like the apocryphal guy wandering down the beach and asking each lady to go to bed. Sooner or later you're going to score - if only because you finally run across a prospect whose curiosity and/or sense of adventure outweighs their common sense.

The second rule is that you will get nowhere by telling a prospective sponsor what he can do for you - that's obvious. Spend your efforts telling him what you and your program can do for him. The object, of course, is to narrow the odds of success. There are a lot of possible ways of doing just that. There are also two methods that historically have always failed. We'll talk about the guaranteed failure modes first:

1) Don't pay someone else to find sponsorship for you. They will take your money. They will be "on the verge" of a really big deal forever. They will need "just a little more" expense money or promotional money to close the deal. The deal will never come through. Even the ones who do it for "expenses and a percentage of the money I find" never find anything. They collect expenses from several clients for the same trip/proposal and live (badly) on that. Make no mistake, there is no altruism out there. The only way that a young driver is going to find sponsorship is to do it himself.

2) Don't pay out a lot of money for "press kits" or "sponsorship proposals" to be mailed blind to corporations or other prospective sponsors. The press kits wind up being given to kids at the track and the sponsorship proposals end up in the circular file at however many corporations they get mailed to.

The rules for success are less simple. There are no guarantees - and we are not going into any detail here. When it comes to looking for sponsors, there is no sense at all in looking for them in your living room or at the beach. There is even less sense in sitting by your telephone waiting for it to ring - it won't. You have to go where they are - and you have to do it in person.

The basic idea is to make a list of corporations or individuals that you think might be interested in sponsoring your effort and a list of the benefits to them of that sponsorship. If you cannot list meaningful benefits on paper, forget it - you sure as hell won't be able to do it in person.

The trick is to approach any corporation from the CEO level. Don't even think about the ad agencies. None of the money that a corporation spends on the running of a race team is billable through the agency. Ad agencies hate us because they see us as taking bread from their mouths.

First of all, you have to find a CEO who can be convinced that he wants to go racing and that he wants to go racing with you. This man is highly unlikely to be the CEO of a Fortune 500 company. If the Fortune 500 CEO wants to go racing he will go with Al Unser. You need to find the CEO of a local company that can afford to take a flyer with a little money.

There are two ways to find them. One is through stories that you plant in the local media. The other is through personal research. Don't even think about hiring someone to do this for you - they will do a bad job. The personal approach works best and, besides, at this point in your career you need the experience.

The way to plant a newspaper story is simple: go to the local newspaper, find the sports editor and make your pitch. If you do it often enough the story will get printed - even if you have to write it yourself. Make very certain that the local media knows about any success you may achieve and make sure that your search for local sponsorship is subtly mentioned in each story.

Then you have to get out there and meet the people who can help you. How you do this is up to you - just don't do it in torn Levis and a tee shirt. Once you have identified them and arranged to meet them, go in with a solid proposal, not a vague dream. Don't make the common error of pitching the proposal on the benefits to you and your career - concentrate on the benefits of your proposal to the seductee.

Every young driver should learn to play golf - well. Aside from the relaxation and social aspect of the game you can meet a lot of people on the golf course and a great many sponsorship deals have been put together on the links. I even know one legendary team owner who has, with malice aforethought, made a practice of arranging to socially meet CEOs at the 19th hole. To a lesser extent, the same is true of tennis.

If this whole thing sounds too much like prostitution to you, or if you are now saying to yourself, "I could never sell myself like that, it's just too cold blooded," then find another line of work. Motor racing is not for you.

We should perhaps note that aspiring touring golf pros have been syndicating themselves for decades. The basic idea is that a "syndicate" of enthusiasts puts up some affordable amount of money each in return for a possible future reward - a percentage of earnings being the most popular. A couple of drivers have arranged this sort of thing with some success.

Another approach is that, in return for limited support at the beginning of a driver's career, a corporation obtains the right to his services if and when he makes the big time.

At any rate, I have never been a successful sponsor finder and this is not a "how to find a sponsor" book. I am simply tired of hearing and reading about how racing has changed and it is now a rich man's sport, talent does not matter any more, only those who can buy the ride get to go to Indianapolis, etc, - ad nauseum. Not only has nothing basic changed during my time in motor racing, nothing ever will. This has always been a business that very few could afford to get started in, let alone progress to the higher levels. Most successful drivers have always had to find sponsorship in order to get beyond the local level and those who have found it have found it themselves.

After you become a star, Mark McCormack or Jack Nicklaus will make you wealthy. But their profession is the marketing of stars, not the making of them. The only person who is going to make you a star is reading these words right now. If you really believe that you have the talent, the toughness, the dedication and the determination to become a professional racing driver, then get off your butt and get on with it.

WHAT "OVERNIGHT" STARS WERE DOING TEN YEARS AGO:

MICHAEL ANDRETTI - SUPER VEE

PATRICK CARPENTIER - SNOWMOBILES

ROBBIE GORDON - OFF ROAD

SCOTT GOODYEAR - FF2000

MICHAEL SCHUMACHER - KARTS

JEAN ALESI - KARTS

JACQUES VILLENEUVE - GRAMMAR SCHOOL

CHRISTOPHER SMITH - KARTS

DAVID EMPRINGHAM - SKI RACING

RUBENS BARICHELLO - KARTS

JOS VERSTAPPEN - KARTS

JIMMY VASSER - 1/4 MIDGETS

2

"The day that you take complete responsibility for yourself - the day that you stop-making any excuses - is the day that you start for the top." O.J. Simpson.

FITNESS, MENTAL AND PHYSICAL

A century of superficial evidence to the contrary, the business of being a successful racing driver is very much a mental endeavor. In fact, after a reasonable amount of physical skill and racing experience has been deposited in one's personal bank account (hopefully to draw interest), achieving excellence as a racing driver is about 98 percent cerebral and two percent physical.

Of course, the same is true of tennis, golf, baseball, etc. They don't count because they are merely pleasant and sometimes profitable pastimes for people less driven (and perhaps in some ways more fortunate) than racers.

A large part of the mental acuity necessary for success has to do with attitude - perhaps confidence is a better word. Racing drivers are exactly the same people as fighter pilots - the major difference is that it is easier to become a fighter pilot and the governments of the earth have spent a lot of money trying to define the personal characteristics that combine to make a good fighter pilot. Despite all the money that has been spent, I feel that Col. Robin Olds (USAF, Ret.), one of the best fighter pilots who ever lived, summed it up best.

"The fighter pilot has an attitude. It is aggressiveness - cockiness - if you like. Take self confidence and add a measure of rebellion. Add competitiveness to this and you've got a fighter pilot. There is a huge spark that drives him to be good, to be better than anybody ever was. And, although you probably wouldn't believe it, he is highly disciplined. "

"A good fighter pilot has to be willing to take risks. It is not like simply flying. It must be inborn - you can't teach it. And independence is one of his main traits. You have to have the basic skills - situational awareness coupled with personal characteristics - and you have to have a mind that can grasp a rapidly evolving situation and react to it almost instinctively." Sound familiar?

Motor racing is a very difficult thing to do well. Perhaps a valid measure of the degree of difficulty of prop-

erly driving a racing car is to compare the age at which the practitioners of the art attain prominence. The youngest Formula One World Champion was Jim Clark at 25. Next on the list are Ayrton Senna and Michael Schumacher at 26. Typical is late 20s. In most sports, the athlete is on his way downhill by 28. It takes a long time, a lot of seat time and a lot of racing to learn to do this well...

Another scale would be the age at which the successful practitioners begin to make a living at it. That age in tennis seems to be in the mid teens. All other sports seem to begin in the late teens or the very early 20s. It is an exceptional racing driver who is making a living at it by 25 - an age by which other athletes have either made it or quit trying to. It takes a long time to learn to do this well...

FITNESS, MENTAL

Success at motor racing demands a level of self confidence that is simply not found in more "normal" fields of endeavor. All successful racing drivers have one characteristic in common - absolute confidence in their ability, given almost equal equipment, to out-race every other driver present on the day. End of discussion!

A lesser attitude will not result in the consistent winning of motor races. There is exactly one absolute truth in motor racing. If you do not believe - deep down truly believe - that you can win any given race, you will do so only through divine intervention.

The kind of confidence that I am talking about shows - and it shows in everything that the winners do. Watch a group of racing drivers walking to the grid. If you are at all perceptive it will be pretty obvious which of them came to win the motor race and which came merely to drive in a motor race.

To illustrate the level of confidence and commitment that we are talking about, listen to Stirling Moss. After the big accident that ended his driving career he

THE RACING DRIVER AND THE FIGHTER PILOT

Some years ago a military researcher discovered that in the entire history of air to air combat between fighter aircraft (leaving out ground fire, fighter to bomber combat, operational accidents, etc) about 80% of recorded kills had been scored by about 5% of all fighter pilots. The information available covered the period from 1914 through the Korean Conflict and the beginning of Vietnam. This was of great interest to the powers that be and a considerable amount of further research was done in an attempt to find a practical and reliable way to preselect the winning 5%.

The end results included the establishment of the Navy's Top Gun School, The Air Force's Fighter Weapons Schools and an excellent book by Mike Spick entitled, "The Ace Factor". The book is available from my good friends at Motorbooks International and should be read and re-read by everyone contemplating a competitive career. There is another military aviation publication, "No Guts, No Glory" by Major General Frederick C. Blesse which is also required reading - although, outside of the Air Force, I don't know where to find it. The research uncovered a few common denominators among the successful pilots:

1) An exceptionally high degree of "situational awareness" - they were all constantly tuned in to everything that was going on around them.

2 They were all dedicated to their craft and spent virtually all of their "free" time thinking about how to do it better.

Fighter Pilots are the same people as Racing Drivers - it is just easier to become one. As a point of interest, the much celebrated fighter pilot motion pictures have about as much to do with reality as do the racing flicks - there is just no way that a director/producer/studio could ever sell the reality to an audience. Flying has been defined as hours and hours of sheer boredom relieved only by seconds of stark terror.

The life of the racing driver, at most levels, is largely one of worry and drudgery. He worries about his ride, present or future - or lack of a ride (no fun at all). He goes through the drudgery of staying in shape (very little fun) and the seemingly endless rounds of sponsor negotiations and sponsor related appearances (seldom fun).

Visualizing the race track and situations that might arise thereon is fun. The real fun part, driving the racing car, requires such intense concentration that there is all too little time and too little capacity left in the brain to enjoy the brightness of the colors. In the days when Trans Am cars were basically production carts with race tires, Peter Revson used to say that he drove Trans Am in order to get all the fun stuff - tossing and sliding - out of his system so that he could drive real racing cars properly.

wrote in 'All But My Life': "I believe that I could run the four minute mile (at that time no one had) - I would have to give up everything in life to train for it; but I could do it". He meant it. Knowing Stirling, I almost think that he could have...

On another level, the story is told of how the legendary Ted Horn would arrive at the scene of the day's festivities and ask the simple question: "Alright, which one of you ———s is going to finish second today?" Horn went a whole season on the half mile dirt ovals without being beaten. It would be nice to think that today's "more sophisticated" generation of drivers would not be affected by such an attitude - but we would be wrong. In a more polished manner, this is exactly what Senna did - and Earnhardt does.

It is not necessary to be anal about this attitude thing - indeed, it is almost certainly a good idea not to be. Look at the personalities of the great drivers of my lifetime. Andretti (Mario), Brabham (J.), Clark, Earnhardt, Fangio, Foyt, Gurney, Hill (G.), Hill (P.), Johnson (J.), Jones (Parnelli), Kinser, Mears (Rick), Moss, Petty (R.), Piquet, Senna, Stewart (J.), Swindell (S.), Villeneuve (G.), Wolfgang, Yarborough (and others). In all you will find enormous amounts of confidence - even some cockiness.

You will also find lots and lots of mind games, but, with some notable exceptions (usually by the same men), only a few outbursts of anal behavior. Gerhard Berger said of Senna, "When he is eighty years old he will have the same 'nobility' as Fangio." I think that we could call this an ideal - and it is truly unfortunate that we will not see it come to pass. Every so often this business has to kill the King just to remind us how very serious a business it really is.

I am not a psychiatrist nor a psychologist - in fact, I have little time for either. I do not know why some people have this level of self confidence and some do not. I do know, however, two things:

1) Some portion of it is inborn - genetic in origin. Some other portion has to do with the environment in which one has been raised. Still another portion of it is developed through accomplishment and retroflection.

2) Some of it is misplaced. In my opinion, most of the misplaced sort seems to be environmental. The Little League Father is, in general, an overall negative influence on the development of the child.

As I have said already (and will say again throughout this book) it is not the physical attributes that separate the great drivers from the herd, but the mental ones. The real road to success as a racing driver begins when we finally realize that our talents are not unique - that God gave us pretty much the same natural talents that he gave to a whole lot of other people and that is up to us to develop those talents.

THE RACE FACE

The driver must be in the right state of mind - which is relaxed. The correct feeling is one of confident infallibility combined with anticipation. Every successful driver has his own way of putting on his race face. Develop your method - it's crucial.

FITNESS, PHYSICAL

"There are no fat tigers.." Sign over US Navy fighter squadron ready room door, 1958.

In the early days the racing driver had to be strong like Arnold Schwarzenegger just to drive the thing. Those early racers were giants among men. They sat close to the steering wheel so they could get their shoulders into it and wrestle the damned thing. That's what it took in those days. It really doesn't take much physical strength to drive today's cars - at least most cars - and there is a school of thought that holds that physical fitness is not a necessity for the modern racing driver.

Wrong! If you think Formula One drivers - as well as all of the serious Formula Three, 3000, Indianapolis, and WSC drivers - go through their regime of physical training and diet because they enjoy it, you are seriously misguided. The lunatic fringe of body builders and marathon runners might not be lying when they say that they enjoy it. I have never heard anyone else say that they enjoy it - the results, yes, the act, no (rather like the old "close your eyes and think of the Empire" days in England).

If the driver no longer needs brute strength, he damned well needs a lot of endurance. He spends his working lifetime in a truly enervating environment. The cockpit is hot, really hot - particularly if the car features a roof and/or a front engine and/or front radiator - and he is covered in layers of insulating safety clothing. His body is constantly being subjected to pretty brutal and sudden "g" forces - from four different directions.

Mentally, the driver is in about as stressful a situation as can be imagined. It's not a lot different from flying onto a carrier deck - except that you get to do it continuously, for the duration of the race.

Virtually every top line racing driver with whom I have ever worked has been in really good physical shape. Further, the older they got, the better shape they were in, even though they had to work at it harder. I have also worked with several drivers who could have been a lot better if they had been willing to make the (considerable) effort to get themselves into shape.

Over the years I have succeeded in convincing a lot of drivers of a lot of things. I have seldom, however, managed to convince a young driver of the necessity of getting himself into really good physical condition.

My current attitude is simple. If a driver - any driver - is not intelligent enough to understand the need for physical conditioning and dedicated enough to get himself into shape and to maintain himself there, I am not going to waste my time on him. I do not have enough years left to throw any of them away on someone who is not serious about his (or her) racing. Anyone who is not in superb physical shape is simply not serious enough to succeed at this business. How's that for a typically pragmatic Smith statement? Let's see if I can back it up.

The usual retort to my demand for fitness goes like this; "Why? I don't get tired during a race!" Wrong! You may not arrive at the point where you feel physically tired during a 30 minute Formula Ford race. In fact, if you do, you shouldn't be driving at all. But that isn't the point. I am not a physician, a dietician or a psychologist. I have, in fact, no background in any branch of sports medicine. I have, however, been racing for a long time and I have a pretty good idea of what it takes to win at this game - both physically and mentally. What it takes has little, if anything to do with muscle power or physical strength (except for the neck muscles). It has, however, a great deal to do with physical endurance.

Part of this requirement is because the environment is debilitating, but most of it is because the one thing that the racing driver needs above all things is to stay mentally alert, fresh and capable of instant optimum decisions and extreme concentration. Physiologically it is simply not possible to be mentally acute while physically tired. The better the physical conditioning of the human body, the better the mind works - and the faster and more consistent are the communications and commands between mind and body. This is not some cockamamie notion of mine. It is physiological fact.

Dr Kenneth Cooper is a U.S. Air Force flight surgeon who specializes in endurance fitness. In his milestone book, "Aerobics", the good doctor points out that, although military pilots spend all of their working time 'sitting down' without much physical exertion, they have a great need to be physically fit. Further, the more demanding the aircraft and/or the mission is to fly, the greater is the need for the pilot to be fit. There is a definite, and measurable, correlation between physical fitness, mental alertness, reaction time and g-force tolerance.

Dr. Cooper's testing programs have proven that, compared to his normal level of performance, the pilot who is physically fatigued - even though he may not be fatigued to the point where he realizes that the condition exists - will accept lower standards of performance, will make more errors in judgement and will not only have slower reaction times in normal circumstances but will be slower in reacting to emergency situations. Not an acceptable condition for either a pilot or a racing driver - and completely preventable.

I have neither the background nor the desire to write a book on physical conditioning for endurance. Dr. Cooper, among others, has already done that very well and you should read him. He is in every public library. His latest book is 'The New Aerobics'. What I do want to do is to point out, as emphatically as I can, that the driver who is not in top physical condition is giving himself a handicap in this business.

If the driver has immense natural talent he may achieve success at the lower levels of the sport; he will not reach his full potential. It is highly unlikely that he will make a living at driving. Don't bother telling me about A.J.'s gut or the fact that Nelson Piquet refused for years to get himself in shape, Piquet saw the light and A.J. wasn't human. Instead, let me tell a couple of war stories.

In the years when the Australian Grand Prix was for Formula Atlantic cars, Bob Jane usually imported a couple of the lesser Grand Prix stars to give the event some stature. The year that I have in mind the race was held at Calder in 120 degree F. heat. The locals, born to the climate, wilted and faded. The imports, Mssrs. Prost and Pironi (if I recall correctly) finished first and second and jumped out of their cars laughing, scratching and ready to go another hundred miles.

Mind you, the imports would probably been first and second no matter what, simply because they were better racing drivers (although Alan Jones was there). However, in this case they didn't even have to work at it. They walked the event simply by being in shape. Peter Halsmer damned near did the same thing at the Cleveland CART race in 1983 and he was by no means the best driver there.

I also recall Ray Wardell trying, unsuccessfully, to convince Gilles Villeneuve that he was not in good enough shape for Formula One - and Gilles later admitting that his biggest surprise was how tired he became during his first Formula One race. Naturally, it didn't happen again.

What we are talking about here is not a Mr. Universe contest. Weight training will do the race driver no good at all - in fact the bulging muscle bit would be harmful. What we are talking about here is "endurance training" or "aerobic exercise" - designed to increase the capacity of the body to use oxygen efficiently - and stretching-type exercises. The very best way to get into and stay in shape would be a personal program developed for the individual by a specialist in sports medicine. In almost all cases this will be beyond the financial reach of the aspiring racing driver.

What the aspirant needs to do is to read the good books and then design his own program. He should design the program based on what he can do every day - no matter where he may be. Playing golf or "health walking" will not get it done. Unfortunately "no pain, no gain" is pretty much true. For most of us this means a program based on running, swimming and/or calisthenics.

Swimming does nothing bad to the human body. It develops endurance and long, limber muscles - just what we want. It is pleasant, can be done almost anywhere (although motel pools tend to be both small and crowded) and might even give an opportunity to make new acquaintances of the opposite sex.

Running, on the other hand, can do a lot of bad things to the human framework. While it builds endurance and the right kind of muscles, done on pavement it is hell on feet, knees, hips and things. Anyone who runs on pavement is asking for trouble - from automobile exhaust fumes, if nothing else. People with legs full of stainless pins (endemic among racers) have trouble enough in this department. If you are going to run, run on the beach, on grass (like a golf course), or on the local school cinder track - and spend the money for proper shock absorbing running shoes. Don't jog, run. Buy a book and learn how to do it properly.

Cycling is very good, but dangerous on public roads. It also requires a bicycle. Mountain biking is excellent - and fun, which is more than you can say for most types of exercise. It does, of course, require a bike and somewhere to ride it - and you can bust your butt.

I don't think that the actual nature of the exercise program is particularly important (as long as it builds neck strength and endurance rather than muscular strength) so long as it is regular and strenuous enough to get the job done. If tennis is your bag, then by all means play tennis but play it hard and play it regularly - or squash, or racquet ball, or handball. They are all good for reflexes and hand/eye coordination. Or do whatever, as long as it extends your body, gets rid of excess fat and builds endurance.

You are aiming at long and limber muscles (as in swimmers/long distance runners) which do not cramp - as opposed to the short muscles of sprinters, weight lifters and such, which do. There is nothing more useless than a racing driver, in a racing car, with a leg cramp. What we need is endurance and flexibility.

I do not believe in dirt bike riding as exercise, although it is probably the best of all exercise programs - no other group short of triathletes matches the physical condition of the pro moto cross rider. It can be done alone (although it shouldn't) and is good for a lot of things other than conditioning. But done at a beneficial level, it's just too dangerous to the body for serious consideration.

Nautilus type programs, when not carried to extremes, are good, but require equipment. The important thing is to realize that your training program is going to be at least a five times a week appointment for the rest of your working life - so choose a program which you will not hate.

The other important thing to realize is that, no matter how broke you may be, fitness is one aspect of preparing yourself for a career in racing that you can afford. In fact, you cannot afford not to do it.

Unless you are wealthy, your early career is unlikely to feature an equipment advantage over your rivals - in fact, parity will probably be an unattainable dream.

Regardless of what you think, I know that you are not going to have a talent advantage over your rivals once you rise beyond Formula Atlantic or Formula Three. There are, however, a few career-long advantages that you can give yourself at no cost and physical and mental fitness is one of them.

As a point of interest the other advantages are:

1) A knowledge of vehicle dynamics as it applies to the racing car.

2) Enough mechanical knowledge to ensure that your car is properly prepared.

3) The development of an excellent relationship with your crew.

If you do not give yourself all four, there is only one word for you. That word is stupid.

EAT TO WIN

"The racing driver needs to be fed a diet of other racing drivers." Anon.

The other side of the physical conditioning coin is diet. Without a reasonable diet, you simply cannot be in proper condition to go motor racing. Racers tend to live on the road and to eat in an endless (and joyless) succession of junk and fast food restaurants. This is really dumb - and unnecessary. I will admit that it is not easy to eat well on the road. But it can (and must) be done.

I'm not advocating becoming a health food fanatic - although it would probably pay off. Alain Prost claims that he ate meat once a week; raw vegetables, fish, salads and dairy products the rest of the time. He also ran a minimum of four kilometers (maximum 15) 300 days per year - along with lots of cycling, rowing and golf. That's part of what it takes to win 52 Grands Prix.

I'm just talking about avoiding McDonalds and eating a sensible, balanced diet with minimum plastic and saturated fats. It's also cheaper. What we are actually looking for is a diet in which our daily caloric intake will consist of 60-80% complex carbohydrates (i.e. starches), 5-10% simple carbohydrates (i.e. sweets), 10-15% protein (animal and vegetable) and 5-20% animal and vegetable fats with a minimum of the saturated (i.e. animal) fats.

Something as simple as stopping at the fruit stand and the deli on the way to the track for a decent do-it-yourself lunch; turkey - not roast beef - on wheat - not wonder - sandwiches, for example. This will also save a bunch of money over the course of a season.

Avoiding fried food, most red meats, as much fat as practical and all junk food. Eating a real breakfast (like oatmeal or one of the good dry cereals) and a real dinner (like non-hormoned skinless chicken, pasta or fish) with lots of salads and vegetables. That will pretty much get it done.

Find out which poultry suppliers don't use hormones (Foster and Zacky farms are two I know of) and ask the restaurant who supplies their birds. Most of the commercial salad dressings are pure saturated fats - use olive oil and vinegar on your salads. Unless you have access to a good sports medicine specialist, read 'Eat to Win' (as listed in the Appendix) and live by it.

One thing that every sports medicine specialist does agree on is carbohydrate loading before an event, for endurance. Pasta and potatoes are the driver's best friends on the nights before work (including testing). Watching Bob Earl carbohydrate load on pasta was about as impressive as watching him drive.

REST

The body also needs rest. While the rest requirement varies quite a bit from one individual to another, it is very real. The driver who stays up all night working on the race car - or worrying about it - is not going to be able to give his best. Period.

I am fully aware that, particularly in the early stages of the driving career (when the driver is liable to be the entire organization and the equipment is liable to need a certain amount of fixing), long nights before the race cannot always be avoided. Most all nighters are, however, the result of bad organization, not dire necessity. Most of the drivers whom I have known are sleep hounds anyway, so this one is painless.

ALCOHOL

Alcohol, in real moderation, will probably not hurt you. On the other hand, for sure it will not help you. It takes a finite amount of time for any alcohol to work its way out of the bloodstream and body tissues, so serious drivers abstain completely for a couple of days before testing or driving. That being the case, it would seem that one might as well abstain completely - except for victory champagne, which obviously doesn't count. Actually, the only good thing that happened when I stopped driving was that I could, with a clear conscience, enjoy a reasonable amount of good wine.

TOBACCO

Don't be silly. Take their money. Do the job. I don't consider tobacco advertising immoral. Every human being has the right to choose whether or not to smoke tobacco - and no right whatsoever to bitch about it when it kills them. No serious athlete can afford the stuff.

SEX

If abstaining from alcohol is a good idea, it is more than balanced by the certain knowledge that abstaining from sex is a bad idea. Who says racers don't have their priorities right?

In the days when Stirling Moss was every young driver's role model (he still should be) he once did the sport a great dis-service by announcing that he refrained from sex for several days before each race. I personally think he lied, possibly in order to better his own odds with the birds of the weekend. After his retirement he did admit that he had recanted fairly early in his career. He now says, "I'm too old to play the game, so I'll keep score." He lies again, but it's a great line.

What is beneficial on the weekend is not the thrill of the chase but the comfort of the act - with a friend, not a conquest. Everyone in his/her right mind knows that good sex is therapeutic. Saturday night orgies will result in Sunday debilitation, but good therapeutic sex can do nothing but improve the tone of one's body and the state of one's mind. It also helps one sleep. Besides, the profession has a reputation to maintain.

PILLS AND SUCH

Nothing that comes in a pill or a needle is going to help you on the race track. In fact, any drug that I know of is going to result in a net reduction in your personal performance. I strongly believe that the sanctioning bodies should require drug tests as a matter of course. I will, if pressed, admit to being both square and straight - but reasonably broad minded.

I have sought competent medical opinion regarding the use of stimulants, uppers and "slow the world down" additives. Without exception the doctors have told me that they know of no additive that will enhance the overall performance of a racing driver. I am willing to admit that a case can be made for certain "slow the world down" pills in the case of older drivers in short events - but only under the direction of a competent physician. Even in that case the reward is liable to be more psychological than physiological and is most unlikely to apply to my young readers.

THE GREAT GATORADE GAME

Peter Revson and I first heard of Gatorade in the late 1960s - long before Stokley Van Kamp got on that particular bandwagon. We obtained some from the LA Rams and used it in the heat of Riverside. It seemed to work. My doctor friends said, "Bullshit!". They still do. What the athlete needs is water - clear, cool water - and lots of it. Everyone agrees that what we do not need is any form of "soft drink". Water is cheap and readily available. Gatorade is neither. Water has no bad side effects.

All of the "sports drinks" are about the same, Gatorade, Staminade, Glucosade, ERG, etc. The idea is that they replace the "salts and minerals" that the body loses through perspiration. They also contain sizeable doses of glucose and they claim to get whatever they contain into the bloodstream right away. That they do - try Gatorade as a mix with vodka sometime! Anyway, the driver needs lots and lots of fluid intake. I suggest water. If you believe in - or are sponsored by - one of the sports drinks, go ahead.

THE GREAT ENERGY BAR GAME

There are lots of ultra-hyped "energy bars" on the market - even "Official Energy Bar of the U.S. Olympic Team". If you must use such things, pick the ones with the lowest fat content. My advisors say that four fig newtons give the same amount of energy, less fat, taste better and for sure cost less.

THE GREAT SALT PILL GAME

There are those who insist that we need to take salt supplements when we are losing body fluids through perspiration. To my knowledge none of these advocates are either MDs or sports medicine specialists. If there is any single item that we Americans get enough of in our daily intake of foods and fluids, it is sodium. When you are sweating, drink lots of water. Period.

We do not need to increase our sodium intake - we need to decrease it. For almost half a century I was a mild salt junkie. A few years ago my doctor gave me some alternatives. The one that I found acceptable was to stop adding salt to anything at all. I quit, cold. It turns out that, like tobacco, salt is an acquired taste and that, unlike tobacco, it is not really hard to quit. You just have to convince yourself that you really want to.

Like tobacco, I hardly ever miss the stuff. Once in a while someone wanders by smoking my old brand of pipe tobacco (usually Lee Gaug) and I get a nostalgic twinge and once in a while I am eating something like a real tomato and I think, "This thing needs some salt." I resist the tobacco temptation.

DRESS, APPEARANCE AND DEMEANOR

Young racing drivers live in constant hope of finding sponsorship. In the early stages of a career this sponsorship, if it comes at all, is probably going to come from a private individual rather than from a corporation or racing team. Private individuals pay the bills for motor racing efforts for a variety of reasons - few of which I understand and all of which I applaud. These individuals have one thing in common. Excess disposable income.

Although the scene is changing, most really affluent people tend to be fairly conservative. They enjoy bringing their family, friends, clients and associates to the race track. They are unlikely to enjoy showing off a driver who either dresses or acts like an animal. This is even more true when one advances to the level of real corporate sponsorship. Use your head - a pin striped suit and a haircut like mine is totally unnecessary but so are torn jeans and rock'n'roll tee shirts.

There is a place for clean, pressed jeans and sport shirts. There is a place for a blazer, slacks, a shirt and a tie. And there is a place for a suit. There is even a place for a tuxedo. Clean, conservative dress and demeanor are both expected and respected in most moneyed circles. There are not many Ted Fields, Alexander Heskeths or Vic Siftons in motor racing (pity!). Drivers are, or at least hope to be, in the public and corporate eye. The higher up the pyramid you get, the more important this bit becomes - the big corporations who sponsor motor racing are really conservative.

This also extends to driving uniforms and the scattering about of same. I have known a few young drivers who ruined their big chance by carrying the free spirit bit too far. One by changing into his driving uniform in front of the sponsor's 12 year old daughter. She may have enjoyed the scene. Her father did not and the driver was gone. He deserved it.

There is no need to be subservient in any sense of the word - just be reasonable and be socially acceptable. Culture shock has no value in this business. What the driver, and the race team, is really doing is selling - themselves - to the people or corporations with money to spend. Take a good look at the appearance and deportment of the drivers, in any branch of racing, who have attracted big time sponsorship.

You will find few exceptions - and none that have lasted very long. Better yet, pay some attention to the way that Danny Sullivan and Emerson Fittipaldi conduct themselves in public. Last word on the subject: "There is no conceivable excuse for being late to an appointment with a sponsor or a prospective sponsor. And there are very few things with a stronger guarantee to turn the prospect off.

SECTION TWO

VEHICLE DYNAMICS

VEHICLE DYNAMICS. WHAT'S IT ALL ABOUT?

"Most people, particularly English speaking people, dislike theory and usually do not think much of theoreticians." – J.E. Gordon

Some years ago I was introduced to a British Formula Three Champion. He acknowledged the introduction with something like; "Oh yes, you're the chap who writes books. Very interesting, I'm sure - but I don't pay any attention to that technical stuff."

Unlike almost all British Formula Three Champions before and since, this worthy didn't go much farther and is no longer driving. Coincidence?

What this section of this book is about is vehicle dynamics from the driver's seat - how to tell what your car is doing badly and how to help your crew do something constructive about it. How to get the most out of what you have.

What this section is not about is where to place your hand on the steering wheel and lines to take through corners. If you need someone to tell you how to hold the wheel, God help us all. With regard to line, I pretty much agree with Niki Lauda's statement that the track, the tactical situation and the race car set up determine the optimum line through any corner or series of corners. Further, line is, or at least should be, almost instinctive to the driver.

There was a time, in living memory - mine - when the racing driver did not have to know much, if anything, about vehicle dynamics. That time is gone forever.

The driver has no need to be an engineer. In fact an engineering education would almost certainly be contra productive if only because those years would be better spent driving (obviously I do not go along with the idea that engineers have too much respect for machinery to mete out the required amount of punishment).

The modern driver, however, must effectively communicate with engineers. Occasionally he must over rule an engineer's technical decision. In order to do so the driver must understand the basics - and the language. He must also keep up to date. It is no big deal. Since everything in vehicle dynamics starts and ends where the rubber meets the road, we will start with the tires. We shall continue through braking, cornering and gear shifting and at the back of the book, in the 'Advanced Drive to Win' section, you will find more in-depth material on car set up, shock absorbers and differentials.

3

"The footprints of your tires are all that lie between you and Saint Peter"
– Mark Donohue

THE DRIVER'S BEST FRIEND: YOU AND YOUR TIRES

Grip is what our business is all about. Grip comes from tires, period. The racing driver's best friend is the racing tire - followed closely by the sponsor. If you want to get anywhere in this business you will learn to take care of both.

Everything that you hope to achieve with a racing car will be realized through the good offices of your tires. Your racing car is connected to the track only by the contact patches - or "footprints" - of its four tires. Through these tenuous interfaces are transmitted all of the accelerations and thrusts that propel the car, decelerate it and change its direction. Through them also are reacted all of your control actions and from them comes most of the sensory information which allows you to maintain - or to regain - control at the limit of adhesion.

Mario Andretti, Alain Prost and Ayrton Senna achieved legendary status among tire engineers because of their sensitivity and their ability to extract the most their tires had to give without abusing them. They also achieved success unmatched in modern racing. It behooves every racing driver to learn all that he can about the care, feeding and inner workings of the racing tire - and to then assiduously practice what he has learned.

With a total lack of modesty, may I suggest that you start by reading (or re-reading) my earlier tome 'Tune to Win', Chapter Two.

TIRE STICK REVISITED

In Tune to Win, while trying to explain how the pneumatic tire works, I talked, a lot, about the curves of slip angle, vertical load and percent slip vs cornering force and tractive effort. I am not going to repeat very much of the information (Tune to Win is still in print). I am, however, going to use the same curves to explain how to use your tires efficiently.

Slip angle is the angular displacement between the tire's plane of rotation and its actual path over the ground (Figure 1 illustrates). Slip angle is the key to the tire's lateral performance - cornering force increases with slip angle up to some maximum value, peaks and then falls off.

Looking at the idealized graph of FIGURE 2, we find that peak cornering force is reached at a slip angle of about six degrees. No surprise. There is, however, a point of diminishing returns. In the slip angle range from five degrees to six degrees the increase in cornering force is relatively minor - about 5%. However, in that same range, temperature, wear, tear and stress on the tire increase markedly.

In FIGURE 3, the curve is divided into separate areas or slip angle envelopes. The steeply increasing portion of the curve is the entry phase of the corner and, for purposes of this discussion, will be ignored.

Area one, labeled "talent", encompasses the entire portion of the curve on both sides of the peak and is the broad envelope of the average competent racing driver.

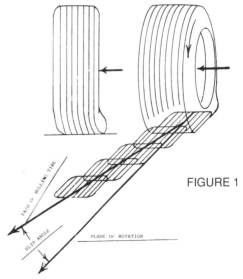

FIGURE 1

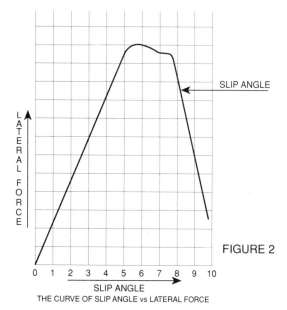

SLIP ANGLE

FIGURE 2

THE CURVE OF SLIP ANGLE vs LATERAL FORCE

Area two, "excellence", which I will call the Prost, Fittipaldi (E.) and Unser, A. (either one) portion of the curve is where the racing driver should be operating most of the time. In this area the tire is delivering something like 95% of its theoretical maximum cornering force, but it is not being tortured.

Area three, where Jean Alesi, Robbie Gordon and Paul Tracy live, is a wider band with about the same amount of average cornering force, but significantly more stress on the tire.

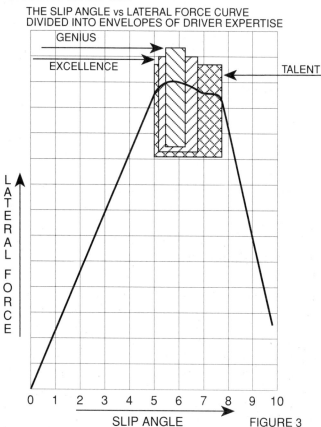

THE SLIP ANGLE vs LATERAL FORCE CURVE
DIVIDED INTO ENVELOPES OF DRIVER EXPERTISE

GENIUS

EXCELLENCE

TALENT

FIGURE 3

Area four labeled "genius" is where the gifted group from area two ventures, with malice aforethought, in qualifying or diceing.

Note in particular how thin is the line between excellence and genius. If Mr. Gordon's development continues, he will move from area three to areas two and four (as will Mr. Tracy if he ever develops the concentration to match his talent). It is probable that there is also an area five - the property of Schumacher, Senna, Gurney, Moss and J.M. Fangio the first. I have no other way of explaining their genius.

FIGURE 4 shows the wide envelopes of both the talented novice and the beginner who is going to be a star - if and when he (or she) develops the discipline that stardom requires. This is where the driver waits for the tires to break loose and then corrects for the loss of traction - an area full of sound and fury signifying an impressed crowd, wasted time and wasted tires. This is also the territory of the experienced idiot who has no idea of what it is all about and is incapable of learning.

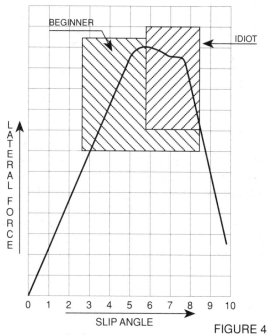

BEGINNERS AND IDIOTS SLIP ANGLE ENVELOPES

BEGINNER

IDIOT

FIGURE 4

The sensitive driver can feel the difference between these areas because of the relationship between the slip angle curve and curve of self aligning torque. Self aligning torque is the force generated by elastic deformation of the tread rubber as it rolls through the footprint. The distortion builds from a minimum value at the leading edge to a maximum value at the trailing edge of the footprint.

Since the rubber tries to "snap back" with a force proportional to the amount of distortion and since the center of pressure of the footprint is behind its (the footprint's) geometric center, the self aligning torque tries to return the tire to its straight ahead position - it is one of the two main reason reasons why the steering wheel snaps back to center when you let go of it (the other is castor).

Self aligning torque, reacted through the steering, is one of the factors which allows the driver to "feel" what his (front) tires are doing. Reacted through the chassis and the seat of his pants it is one of the factors which tells him what the rear tires are doing.

Referring to FIGURE 5, we find that either providence or Akron genius has arranged things so that the

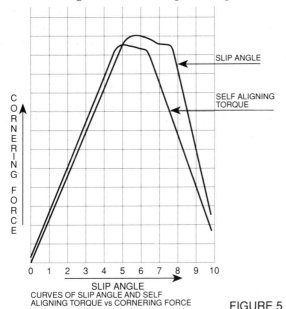

CURVES OF SLIP ANGLE AND SELF
ALIGNING TORQUE vs CORNERING FORCE

FIGURE 5

self aligning torque generated by slip angle peaks slightly before the cornering force generated by slip angle does. This allows the exceptionally sensitive driver to operate in the area where self aligning torque is just starting to fall off - before "it goes all light and funny". The placement and width of the operating band depends upon the sensitivity and discipline of the driver. Simple, heh?

THE FOOTPRINT

The only area of the tire that we are really interested in is the footprint. The size and shape of the footprint, the load imposed on it by mass, load transfer and aerodynamics and the distribution of pressure within it pretty much determine the lateral and longitudinal acceleration performance of the car.

The basics are simple. The length of the footprint has a major effect on longitudinal traction - acceleration and braking - which is why drag racing tires are huge in diameter. The width has a major effect on lateral acceleration - cornering force - which is why Formula One tires are as wide as the rules allow. The area of the footprint effects both and, in terms of stick, bigger is better.

THE VALUE OF EXPERIENCE

After forty years of this nonsense I still get revelations several times a year. I received one recently. For a very long time I have been aware that there is a tie in between driver experience, vehicle balance, driver confidence, lap speed and consistency. Like most of the people in this business I had never formalized the relationship(s) in my mind. This past week the fog lifted and it all became clear in my mind. The result is yet another of Smith's Laws of Motor Racing.

"The ability of the racing driver to go fast in any given racing car is directly proportional to his confidence in how the car will react to his control inputs. This confidence is directly related to his perception of the width of the slip angle threshold between ,"I've got it", and "it's got me". The perception is directly proportional to the amount of valid time under the driver's helmet."

What happened was that I took a car which, after a day of development testing at Road America with a talented, serious, intelligent but inexperienced middle aged driver, was predictable, well balanced and reasonably fast but pretty sloppy and rolling/squatting off its little (and inadequate) camber curves. I stiffened it about half of what I thought it needed, lost the balance, the driver's confidence and a mere six seconds per lap.

Unfortunately it took me a considerable time to realize what was going on and we wasted a lot of expensive track time until I finally caught on, softened the car in ride to give the driver some feel and stuck on a stiff front bar to transfer some load back onto the inside rear wheel during corner exit to keep the outside rear wheel from going nuts and causing corner exit oversteer.

We were then able to get on with the job and ended up with a fast car and a good weekend. Had I been dealing with an experienced test driver we would have balanced the car with its increased ride rate and probably have ended up faster yet. Had I realized what was going on earlier the same would have been true.

So what am I saying here? I'm simply saying that we have to be careful not to ask the driver to figure out more than he is capable of at any stage in his learning curve. When the tightrope gets too thin or starts to sway, the normal (i.e. intelligent) driver doesn't charge harder, he backs off.

It is up to us, the development engineers/driver coaches to realize when we are about to reach this point in our testing and to back down a bit - or explore a different road - or bite off smaller chunks. We can unbalance the car any old time and when we do, the smart thing is to go right back to the last good set up and start over. Occasionally this will entail putting on the last set of known good tires. Akron's quality control, while very good, is not perfect and I still get caught out by a bad tire now and again.

We really want to keep the whole footprint flat on the road and we want to keep the pressure developed by vertical load evenly distributed throughout its area - at least in the transverse sense. These last two factors are where we come unstuck. With independent suspension we cannot keep it flat and with any suspension system at all we cannot keep the unit pressure evenly distributed.

MOUNTING AND BALANCING

Taking care of tires starts with mounting and balancing. Away from CART and NASCAR, the tire busting crew is very liable to be minimum wage kids with little experience and only a dim realization of the importance of their work. Depending upon my personal opinion of the tire manufacturer's crew present on the day, I often prefer to mount and balance my own tires.

The very least that this accomplishes is doing away with the usual and inescapable wait for the tires to be done. It also ensures that I am not going to end up with a damaged rim, an out of round or out of balance tire, a tire inadvertently stretched oversize by being left for a long period of time with the 40 psi that it took to seat the beads, an oversized tire bead that is not safe on the rim (unlikely, but not unknown) or a tire full of moist air that will build up 10 psi when it is hot. It also makes it easier for me to select matched sets of tires with regard to diameter.

After mounting, drop the pressure immediately to what you intend to run hot. Static balance is almost always good enough - although I usually spend the money for a good dynamic balance once the tire has been broken in. When static balancing, try to get the weights near the axial center of the rim. If caliper clearance prevents this, split the weights between the outboard and inboard edges. I put an oil pen mark on the tire opposite the valve stem so that I can see if the tire has a tendency to creep on the rim.

INITIAL INSPECTION

Racing tires are handmade by very skilled people. These people are human. Every so often something goes wrong and a tire does not assume the proper shape when it is inflated. Usually the anomaly is a more pronounced than normal "dip" in the center of a bias ply tire (there should be no "dip" in a radial tire). More rarely it will be out of round or the tread will not be on straight. FIGURE 6 shows what can go wrong.

Every tire should be inspected for shape when it is first mounted and again after it has first been run. If it's bad, take it back - this is a lot easier sell if the tire has not been run. Before you attack the tire company for out of round or out of true, make sure that the problem isn't your rim rather than their tire.

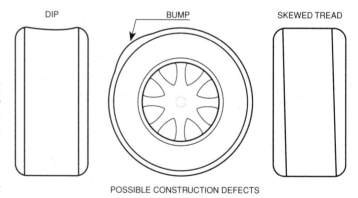

POSSIBLE CONSTRUCTION DEFECTS

FIGURE 6

TIRE BREAK IN

There are a lot of questions about the proper break in procedure for the racing tire. Some years ago Reed Kryder (now retired and running his own race team) at Goodyear Race Tire Engineering defined the process. Nothing has changed.

I quote: "The proper procedure of 'breaking-in' a race tire consists of running a few miles of warm-up, a few miles as hard as possible, and then letting the tire cool."

"There are several basic reasons for this method. Running a few miles of warm-up allows the new tire's internal construction to adjust to the forces acting on the tire. Tire irregularities from storage and shipping are reshaped into the desired size and contour for racing. The tread surface is scuffed and cleaned of dust, oil (and mould release agents - CS). Improper tire balance can also be discovered at this time."

"Speed should gradually be increased during these few miles of warm-up until the driver feels comfortable with the tires and is ready to go as hard as possible. Running the next few (three to five) miles as hard as possible completes the tire's adjustment to its new life style. This adjusting process results in extra heat (compared to a previously broken in tire) and the tire may actually overheat if hard running is continued. "

"A common complaint from drivers who start a race on new tires is that they worked great for the first few laps and then 'went away' or 'gave up'. What actually happened was that the tires were overheated due to the extra heat produced when a new tire is first run hard - and were never given a chance to cool down."

"As the tread and under-tread temperature went through its optimum range the tire felt as good as a tire ever does. When the temperature continued to climb above the optimum range the compound changed and the tire got slightly 'greasy'. Once this has happened the tire can never return to its optimum condition. Running a new tire through its optimum temperature range is great for qualifying, but not for racing."

"Letting the tire cool can be accomplished in several ways. It is best to allow it to cool naturally to ambient. If stopping to cool or to change tires is not practical, a couple of slow laps will be of some benefit. So will artificially cooling the tires (after a couple of slow laps) with wet towels."

"The best approach for a weekend when new tires are going to be used is to practice and set the car up on good used tires and then break in the new tires with a short qualifying attempt (very short - CS). Save this set for the race and you should have a predictable set of tires with a minimum of problems."

The facts of tire life and therefore the procedures to follow for non-abuse are the same regardless of who manufactured the tire and regardless of whether the construction is bias ply or radial. Somehow nobody wants to believe this basic truth - even when it has been promulgated in writing by Goodyear itself.

If you think that this means that changing to 'sticker' tires during a race is not a real good idea, you are right - regardless of how many 'name' teams you see doing so. If you aren't well enough organized to scrub all of your race tires, you shouldn't be there.

If you also think that you can get a little extra qualifying performance by going out on stickers, warming them up for a lap and going for it, you are also right. Just don't expect the tires to ever be really fast again. They will be perfectly OK to test and practice on, but not to race with. Of course, if you don't get it done in two or three laps, your dreams of the pole may evaporate in overheated and greasy rubber.

TIRE PRESSURE

The racing tire is designed, constructed and moulded to assume a specific shape when inflated. Since the tire is manufactured from rubber and fabric, it will deflect under load. Inflation pressure is the only method of ensuring proper dynamic shape.

Most of us realize that the pneumatic tire is, in actuality, a spring. Many of us are aware that this particular spring is underdamped. (Due to the nature of cords, rubber and sidewall construction it isn't undamped - just underdamped - but that is beyond the scope of this book as well as of my knowledge). Not enough of us have, however, made the next connection - that the spring rate of a tire is largely dependent upon its inflation pressure. This is not as simple as it might appear.

Aerodynamic download is a square function of road speed - ie, doubling road speed multiplies download by four times (two squared). Download at very high speed can be measured in tons and can profoundly alter the inflated shape of the tire. The optimum tire spring rate and therefore the optimum inflation pressure for a given tire on a specific car should be expressed as a function of the road speed of the crucial corners on the racing circuit in question. Tire pressure largely determines:

1) The spring rate of the tire.
2) The size and the shape of the actual dynamic footprint of the tire.
3) The dynamic pressure pattern within the footprint of the tire.
4) The height and shape of the sidewall of the tire.

These four factors profoundly influence both the tractive capacity and the transient response of the tire. There are certain self evident truths here:

1) Depending upon its construction, every tire has an envelope of dynamic pressures within which it can and will assume its optimum shape and operate efficiently - and outside of which it cannot and will not.
2) The optimum dynamic pressure is a function of the dynamic vertical load on the tire. The dynamic vertical load is a function of vehicle weight and

download. If either increases, so should the static pressure.

3) The manufacturers of racing tires and their field engineers know - or at least should know - what this pressure range is.

4) When a manufacturer has a stranglehold on a given racing series, his engineers are going to recommend a safe tire pressure.

5) When it is tire wars time, the engineers are still going to recommend safe pressures to all but those few cars that can either sit on the pole or win the race. Nobody likes to stick his (her) neck out.

6) The "safe" tire pressure is unlikely to be the hot ticket tire pressure for any given race track on any given day.

7) The only way to determine the optimum pressure is to try different pressures while testing on similar circuits. The chances are very good that the leading teams have done just that.

8) You can figure out the optimum pressure just as well as they can - or almost as well.

The guidelines are deceptively simple:

1) Within design limits, higher than suggested dynamic tire pressures give reduced rolling resistance, reduced scrub in corners and, with constant vertical load, reduced traction - both lateral and longitudinal. Dynamic pressures above the design envelope will also cause the center of the tire to overheat resulting in loss of tractive capacity or 'give up' and, in extreme cases, in center-line blistering.

2) Within the same design limits, lower dynamic tire pressures give improved compliance with road surface irregularities, increased rolling resistance, increased scrub and enhanced traction. Too low a dynamic pressure allows over-deflection of the carcass resulting in overheating of the tire's shoulders and, eventually, in blistering of the shoulders and possible air loss from carcass fatigue followed by catastrophic failure.

3) Vertical load is a function of the static load on a given tire, the effects of lateral and longitudinal load transfer and aerodynamic download.

4) Load transfers are functions of center of gravity (eg) heights, lateral and longitudinal accelerations (or 'g') and of track and wheelbase dimensions. Aerodynamic download, on the other hand, is independent of all of these and is dependent upon wing and tunnel characteristics and is the square function of road speed.

Another way of stating the same thing is to say that the critical factor in the determination of optimum tire pressure is the speed of the critical corners. Basically, the most that you need to determine is the optimum pressure for five types of circuits:

Short ovals

Long ovals

Street circuits

'Normal' road racing circuits - like Mid-Ohio or Sears Point where the majority of the corners are medium speed and the straights are not overly long.

'Fast' road racing circuits - like Road America or Road Atlanta, where the majority of the corners are fast and the straights are long.

The wizards of Akron fully realize this - which is why Indianapolis Motor Speedway tires have spring rates in the range of 2500 to 3000 pounds of force per inch of deflection while Indy Car road racing tires tend to have spring rates in the 1000 to 1500lb.in. range. The smooth-as-a-baby's-bottom corners of Indy are taken at 220mph-plus with literally tons of download and the washboarded corners at Long Beach are taken at 60mph with a few hundred pounds of download. Tire pressures at Indy tend to be in the thirty something range and at Long Beach in the someteen area.

Shocks come into this - a lot - but that is a different subject for another long flight. As near as I can determine, the wizards of Tokyo know very little about any of this.

I can hear the cries of dissent now - although probably not from Akron. "If you pump the tire up, it will become round like a motorcycle tire, crown in the middle and chunk". Wrong!

Think about it! If the road speed is up and the download is up, a tire with relatively high pressure will assume its designed shape as the footprint rolls into contact and is pushed, hard, onto the road surface. If, on the other hand, the tire is inflated towards the low end of the envelope and the road speed and download are up, the tire will be pushed down just as hard, but the push will be on the edges of the tire and we will end up with an inefficient pressure distribution within the footprint, and overheated tire edges.

We will also be slow - even before the compound degrades and we chunk the tire. We will be slow because the tire will be squashed down onto the race track, mis-shaped and will scrub instead of rolling free.. FIGURE 7 exaggerates the idea.

Of course, an underinflated tire gives a lot more warning of impending topping out of the slip angle curve and loss of lateral traction. (It operates at higher

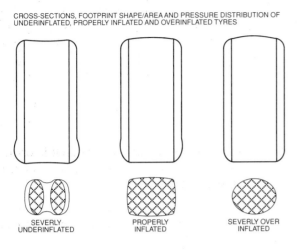

CROSS-SECTIONS, FOOTPRINT SHAPE/AREA AND PRESSURE DISTRIBUTION OF UNDERINFLATED, PROPERLY INFLATED AND OVERINFLATED TYRES

SEVERLY UNDERINFLATED   PROPERLY INFLATED   SEVERLY OVER INFLATED

FIGURE 7

slip angles with a broader slip angle threshold and so is easier to drive - slower!) There is no easy way to go really fast.

On the other hand, if we try to run Phoenix or Road America tire pressures at Long Beach or Des Moines, the front tires are going to slip and slide both under the brakes and when we try to turn the car in. The rears are not only going to slide, they are going to bound, pogo stick and hop on corner exit. It is very much "horses for courses"!

A sensitive driver, on board instrumentation and/ or a lot of valid test time helps a lot. The obvious optimum is all three but this is seldom realized. Typically the young driver, even with the incentive to learn sensitivity, doesn't command the capital resources that allow test time and instrumentation. Given the necessity to decide, I'll opt for the sensitive and thinking driver every time. Test time and instrumentation with insensitive and unthinking drivers can be very frustrating. Dragging the answers out of sensitive, thinking but uninformed drivers is both challenging and fun.

So, if the pneumatic tire is a spring, is it feasible to determine whether or not an increase in suspension spring rate will be a good thing by increasing tire pressure? Yes and no! If you are pretty sure that a stiffer car would be better in the corners but are worried about the effect of the increased ride rate over the critical bumps, increasing the tire pressure will tell you - at least about the bumps. But any increase in tire pressure over the optimum for the circuit will lead to a decrease in traction and a corresponding increase in lap time.

Along these lines, the optimum inflation pressure for street cars (and showroom stock and derivative racing cars) is very much a function of vehicle weight. A 205-15 tire on a 2800lb car requires more pressure than the same tire on a 2200lb car.

My last words on high tire pressures should be permanently engraved on every racer's brain. Do not use tire pressure as a substitute for spring rate. The purpose of the spring is to support the sprung mass and to control ride height. The function of the air pressure in the tire is to correctly shape the footprint of the tire. Attempts to quickly add spring by raising tire pressure above the design maximum will only lead to chunked tires. There is no room for error on an oval. Listen to Goodyear!

PRESSURE BUILD UP

We pressurize our tires with compressed air. Inevitably the air has a certain moisture content. Therefore, as the tires heat, the moist air expands and the tire pressure increases. We call this 'pressure build up'. Depending upon the moisture content of the air and the energy input into the tire (tire temperature), build up can be from two to eight psi - a significant percentage of the total pressure. This is a serious pain as we not only have to determine the optimum pressure for each track but also have to go through the exercise of figuring out what cold pressure corresponds to the hot pressure that we want - and the cold pressure will be different for each tire.

To digress for a moment, on road racing circuits I like to keep the left and right side hot pressures the same - it makes for better braking and makes it easier to set corner weights. Many operations ignore this factor. I think that they are wrong.

Some of the tire companies don't seem to worry much about moisture content in their compressors. To reduce pressure build up to manageable amounts, mount your own tires and use only dry compressed air. This means draining the water from the compressor at frequent intervals and using a dryer in the air line.

You can also use nitrogen. To get the full benefit of nitrogen, mount the tire (ie initial inflation) with it. To get about half the benefit of the inert gas, mount the tire with air, deflate the tire and reinflate with nitrogen. To get 90% of the benefit, evacuate the mounted tire with a vacuum cleaner and re-inflate with Nitrogen. It works (FIGURE 8).

Whatever method you use, use it consistently. Along these lines, exactly why we super-sophisticated road racers don't use pre-set blow off valves - which bleed off pressure as the tire heats up until a pre-set running, or hot pressure is reached and maintained - (like sprint car drivers do) is beyond me. It seems a simple solution to a vexing problem. God knows that if the valves can reliably survive the World of Outlaws treatment, we can't hurt them. Make sure however, that the brand you select will withstand the centrifugal force at your wheel rpm (sprint car wheel rpm is pretty low compared to, say, Formula Atlantic).

FIGURE 8

Of course, sprint car races are very short and the contained air volume of a sprint car tire is much greater than that of a conventional tire so an inaccurate or stuck valve will create less of a problem. Be that as it may, some of the current generation of bleeder valves are being used very successfully in road racing - especially if the wheel construction allows the bleeder valve to be mounted axially rather than radially

Be sure to keep your valves clean and to maintain them per the manufacturer's instructions. As an aside, at the time of writing Goodyear does not feel that the available valves are reliable enough to warrant their approval and so does not condone their use.

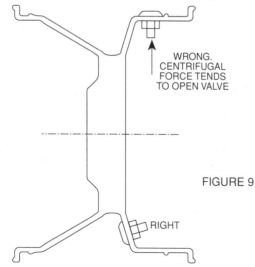

WRONG. CENTRIFUGAL FORCE TENDS TO OPEN VALVE

RIGHT

FIGURE 9

AXIALLY AND RADIALLY MOUNTED TYRE BLEEDER VALVES

PRESSURE IN THE WET

As nearly as I can determine, the construction of most racing rain tires is very similar to that of the equivalent dry tire. The difference seems to be in the compound and the tread pattern (or lack of it). The tire companies invariably recommend that we set the wet tire cold pressures slightly (2-3psi) higher than those of the dry tires. The reason is that, since the rain tires will run cooler than the dries, there will be less pressure build up and therefore, we should start higher in order to arrive at the optimum dynamic pressure.

My experience has been that, unless we are trying to cut through inches of solid water, we want the same dynamic pressure in the wets as we do in the dries, or, if anything, very slightly less. One of the problems that arises here is that, should the track dry, or even start to dry, the soft wet compound will generate more heat than the equivalent dry tire. Under these conditions the wet tire that started out with more pressure than the dry will end up with a significantly higher dynamic tire pressure than was intended - leading to more overheating, etc, etc, etc... Since we never know how wet it is going to be, this makes the blow off valves even more of a natural for wets than for dries.

STAGGER

The best demonstration of the effect of tire diameter stagger that I know of consists of rolling a tapered water glass over a smooth surface. The cylinder naturally turns toward its small end (FIGURE 10).

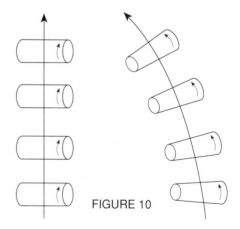

FIGURE 10

STAGGER EFFECT USING CYLINDRICAL AND TAPERED WATER GLASSES

Two of the objectives in setting up a car for an oval track are to get the car to turn in almost by itself and to minimize tire scrub and drag - to allow the car to roll free in the corners. We can go a long way toward these objectives by running a locked differential and staggering the rear tire diameters so that the outside rear is some percentage greater in circumference than the inside rear - in effect creating the tapered cylinder of the water glass demonstration. If the car's balance through ride rates, roll resistance, damping, wheel alignment and aero balance is close to perfect, and we get the stagger just right, two good things will happen. We will not have to force the car into the corner with steering lock (which creates tire drag) and both rear tires will be rolling at their natural rotational speed for the corner radius (the track width of the vehicle means that the outside tire turns about a greater radius and so requires a greater diameter to achieve the same rotational speed as the inner tire with its smaller radius of curvature (FIGURE 11).

TIRE STAGGER AS A FUNCTION OF TURN RADIUS

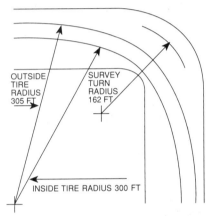

OUTSIDE TIRE RADIUS 305 FT

SURVEY TURN RADIUS 162 FT

INSIDE TIRE RADIUS 300 FT

IN A 90 DEGREE CORNER OF CONSTANT RADIUS THE INSIDE TYRE MUST COVER A DISTANCE OF (300x3.1416/4) OR 236 FEET. IF THE INSIDE TYRE DIAMETER IS 25.2", IT WILL COMPLETE 112 REVOLUTIONS IN THE CORNER. THE OUTSIDE TYRE WILL TRAVEL 239.5 FEET. TO COMPLETE 112 REVOLUTIONS (ZERO DRAG AND ZERO STEER) THE OUTSIDE TYRE DIAMETER MUST BE 25.6".

FIGURE 11

If the balance of the car is less than perfect, we can adjust it with stagger - but only in the pits. More outside stagger will reduce understeer (or increase oversteer) - but, in either case, departing from the natural amount of stagger with a locked rear end will produce tire drag in the corners. With a limited slip, it will produce diff drag. With an open diff, the effect is barely noticeable but then, so is the effect of stagger.

One of the problems with stagger lies in the very nature of bias ply tires - they are often not consistent in diameter. Further, their inflated diameter when new may not be an accurate indication of their hot diameter after break in. This makes playing with stagger on bias ply tires a bit of a guessing game - particularly when you are going to change tires during the race meeting. Sometimes you keep the vehicle balance and sometimes you do not. Radial tires are, by nature, very consistent in diameter and that particular problem almost goes away.

We adjust the diameter of a bias ply tire by over-inflating it and putting it in the sun for a few hours - stretching it to size, as it were. I don't like doing this because the center of the tire invariably stretches more than the edges and the result is a final shape that features more 'crown' than was designed into the inflated shape. The result can be a slightly inefficient footprint. I prefer to pick tires of naturally different diameters - which is usually inconvenient, if not impossible. It's a problem and I usually wind up stretching tires whether I want to or not.

The savior in this situation is that I only use stagger on ovals (if it turns by itself then God tells us that it cannot brake in a straight line and I consider braking performance to be critical on virtually any road circuit). On an oval the combination of high download, high lateral load transfer and banking is going to squash the outside rear abnormally flat anyway - so a slight increase in crown might even be a good thing.

Unfortunately, even on the ovals with radials there is a performance disadvantage to stagger. With the outside rear tire larger in diameter than the inside, when the car is going straight, (by definition under high engine torque loading) we have a problem - the car wants to turn left. With anything other than an open diff, the driver is going to have to hold right lock on the car. This isn't so bad - he will probably have to do so anyway because of the castor lead we use on ovals.

The problem is that with either a spool, an effective limited slip or a locking diff, one of the driven tires is going to be, to some extent, dragging. This isn't real good for the tire, the halfshafts or the acceleration. For this reason, among others, several of the leading CART teams have experimented with open differentials and with 80/80 Salisbury diffs - at least on the big ovals where the cars are never wheelspin limited.

And what, you may well ask is my opinion of all this? I feel that, given sufficient test and practice time, there are better and more efficient ways of making a car behave on a paved oval than tire stagger. If I were running a car that was not wheelspin limited on paved ovals I would certainly try an open diff or an almost open plate diff, or better yet, a viscous diff. I would also not let my ego get in the way if it didn't work or if I ran out of time. Oval track racers have been using stagger for a long time and there is an extensive body of knowledge available. What works is a hell of a lot more valuable on the day than what would theoretically be better.

TIRE SLIP - OR WHEELSPIN

From time to time I run across some sincere but misinformed soul who truly believes that some corner exit inside (unladen wheel) wheelspin is a good thing. "It helps to keep the engine rpm up and the tire is unloaded anyway". Wrong! Keeping the rpm up is what gear ratios are for. I have even, recently, had a semi-successful professional racer tell me that, in a Formula Three car, wheelspin on a 160mph straight on a circuit which features a lot of medium speed bumpy corners is of no consequence. Real wrong!

Wheelspin is never a good thing. Looking at the traction circle (sidebar), if 50% of a driving tire's tractive capacity is being used to generate forward traction, we still have 50% left to generate cornering force. If 90% of the tire is generating forward acceleration, we will have only 10% left for cornering force.

When all of the tire's ability is being used to go forward, we are wheelspin limited and there is nothing left for cornering force. Notice on the traction circle that on corner exit we lose the last bit of side bite in a big hurry - the last 10% increase in acceleration costs a quick 30% of cornering force. Regardless of tire size, cars with a serious power to weight ratio can bite you hard on corner exit - and that most definitely includes high powered street cars (which is why the manufacturers are putting traction control on the hot numbers).

Another way of stating this ultimate truth is that, no matter how lightly loaded it may be, until the inside tire is spinning it still has some lateral capacity left. The minute that it crosses over to the wheelspin side, there is no lateral capacity left at all. Even if a tire is completely unloaded at the time of throttle application, (which it should never be) it will load very soon afterward.

If, when the vertical load is re-applied, the tire is spinning, while it will generate some forward traction, the traction circle ensures us that it will generate no lateral traction until such time as it stops spinning - which it is unlikely to do until the driver takes his foot out of the throttle. To paraphrase Mr. Newton, "A spinning tire tends to continue spinning until acted upon by an outside force." The outside force can be either enough vertical load to stop the spin or a reduction in torque - either by less throttle or by waiting for the road speed to increase.

If we wait for the vertical load to stop the embarrassment, we will have to wait for the car to be going in a straight, or almost straight, line before it hooks up. Not good! If the driver takes his foot out of the throttle to stop the wheelspin, the car stops accelerating. If we wait for increasing road speed to reduce the available torque, we have seriously compromised our acceleration. Also not good. For a graphic example, try it on snow.

What all this means in practical terms is that, should the car be perfectly balanced on corner exit, wheelspin will cause both power on oversteer and a reduction in

THE TRACTION CIRCLE

The racing tire is capable of generating almost equal force in acceleration, deceleration or cornering. If we plot the maximum forces that a given tire can develop in each of these directions we end up with this diagram, often referred to as the "traction circle". Mark Donahue used to call it the wheel of life.

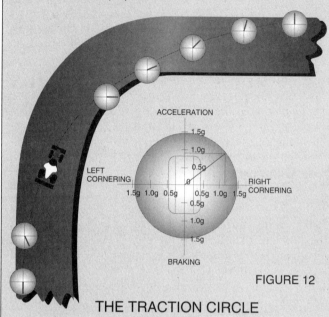

FIGURE 12

THE TRACTION CIRCLE

Contrary to current opinion, neither the concept nor the visualization is new. Because a tire's longitudinal capacity is slightly greater than its lateral capacity, it is not actually a circle. We will consider it to be a circle anyway.

The diagram represents a single tire at a constant level of vertical load. To be accurate, we would have to use four circles whose diameters would constantly change with dynamic load transfer and varying aero loads. We will leave this to Bill Mitchell's "Vehicle Dynamics Simulation" program (which I highly recommend) - and to the feedback system of the racing driver. The single diagram will do just fine for our purposes. Looking at the diagram, two things become obvious:

1) *The tire can generate either 1.4-g of acceleration thrust or 1.4-g of cornering force (we can substitute braking thrust for accelerative thrust). It cannot, however, develop 1.4-g of both at the same time. In fact, if it is generating 1.4-g of either, it can generate exactly 0.0-g of the other.*

   If a tire is generating both a lateral and a longitudinal force, it must develop a lesser amount of each than it could of either one singly. This is illustrated by the vector marked FT which shows the tire generating a cornering force of 1.1-g while accelerating at 0.8-g - with a resultant force vector of 1.4-g.

Continued...

Due to the geometry of the traction circle and the resolution of the vectors, the tire can and does generate forces in each direction the sum of which is greater than the total g-force capacity of the tire. In this case 1.1 + 0.8 = 1.9-g. In other words, the tire can simultaneously generate an amount of braking thrust and an amount of cornering force which, added together, will total more force than the tire is capable of generating in any one direction.

2) If we are going to utilize all of the performance potential designed and built into our tires, then we must keep the tire operating at a very high level of combined forces at all times while the car is turning. We must "ride the rim" of the traction circle by balancing the brakes, cornering force and throttle so as to keep the tires' resultant line of force just inside the boundary of the circle.

the car's rate of of acceleration. Another way of looking at the same situation is that if we can get rid of the wheelspin, we can increase the corner exit speed simply because we will have more rear tire lateral capacity earlier in the corner and so can begin to accelerate earlier.

We could say the same thing about dialing in a little more neutral throttle understeer - but that would reduce both the corner entry and corner apex speed. Getting rid of the inside wheelspin will not. There are a number of ways to reduce the tendency of a car to spin its wheels. The very first, and one of the most effective, is to teach the driver to control the throttle like a rifle trigger rather than a sledgehammer. Squeeze the power on over a tenth of a second or so rather than banging it on as hard as you can. It works - and it will prepare you for Indy Cars on the ovals where immediately after you bang the throttle, you bang the wall.

We must realize that the hot set up for circuits which feature fast corners and smooth surfaces will not be the hot ticket for circuits that feature slow corners and/or bumpy surfaces in those corners. This is very much a business of "horses for courses". Think about it!

In fast smooth corners, a ton of download is being generated - regardless of wing size and/ or angle, and regardless of whether we are talking spoilers, wings or ground effects. The car will not only tolerate high ride rates and roll resistance, it will demand them - to stabilize both the pitch and roll angles lest we lose the downforce. The more ground effects and the higher the road speed, the more critical a stable pitch attitude becomes.

This is even more critical with flat bottoms than with tunnel cars and becomes super critical with any car on the two and a half mile speedways. Due to the limited torque available at those speeds and to the large amounts of download, wheelspin will not be a problem. However, when we reduce the corner speed, the torque available for acceleration increases while the download decreases with the square of the speed reduction. Depending upon the power - to - weight ratio of the car, the amount of download generated, and the tire characteristics, pretty soon we switch over from torque limited corner exit acceleration to wheelspin limited corner exit acceleration - and the rules change. All of a sudden, tire compliance comes back into the picture. If the road surface becomes bumpy at the same time, tire compliance becomes critical.

So how do we increase tire compliance? Let me count the ways:

1) Increase rear droop travel (this may also require an increase in both front and rear ride height).

2) Design the rear springs properly so that they do not uncouple at droop.

3) Reduce rear lateral load transfer by reducing the rate of the rear anti-roll bar (must compensate by increasing rear spring rate).

4) Reduce the high piston speed bump control and/or valving characteristics of the rear shocks.

5) Reduce the rear anti-squat (or increase it if the camber curves are very steep).

6) Reduce the rear tire pressure.

7) Load the inside rear tire on acceleration by:

   a) Increasing the front roll resistance from the anti-roll bar (must either increase the rear wheel rate or decrease front to compensate).

   b) Increasing front track width (or decreasing rear).

8) Increase download (by increasing wing size/angle or spoiler size).

Which of the available bandaids will be feasible, let alone most effective, in any given situation depends on the time and equipment available, the amount of knowledge gained through previous testing and the characteristics of car, circuit, driver and crew - and is beyond the scope of this book. You must be aware, however, that you do not have to put up with an evil car under any circumstances and what range of cures is available for any given ill or ills.

TEMPERATURE

Every racing tire compound is designed to operate best in a specific and relatively narrow range of tread and under-tread temperature. While this optimum temperature range may vary somewhat from manufacturer to manufacturer and from compound to compound, it is pretty safe to say that if your temperatures as read in the pits are under 180 degrees F. you will be slow. On the other hand, if they are over 250 degrees F. you are about to be in serious trouble.

The temperature read in the pits is only an indication of the maximum temperature reached on the race track. One of the biggest surprises that sophisticated instrumentation provided was the speed with which tire temperature changed under varying conditions of load. It is just flat amazing.

I am often asked how to get the tire temperatures up into the operating range. Under normal operating conditions there is only one logical answer - drive the car faster. This is not the answer the driver wants to hear but, usually, the problem really is that simple - the driver simply isn't driving the thing hard enough to get temperature into the tires.

But I did say, "under normal conditions". When it is morning at Mosport and the air temperature is 35 degrees F, anyone silly enough to run a racing car is going to have to do something to get the tire temperatures up. Don't do it with camber unless you absolutely have to. Excessive negative camber will indeed increase tire temperature - but only at the inside edge of the tire. It will also have a seriously detrimental effect on your performance under braking and acceleration.

The best solution, if it is available, is a softer tire compound. Failing that, drop the tire pressures to the low end of the safe operating scale. Throwing the car around a bit more than is normally fast works very well - and every driver loves doing that. Softer wheel rates and shock forces will also help - even when it means raising the ride height. My last resort is to increase the toe at each end of the car. I don't like doing this because it may make the car a bit darty - but it does bring the temperatures up.

For God's sake, don't forget to put everything back to normal when the sun comes out. When you are in a situation where the ambient is colder than usual at the start of a session - or a race - but the tires will eventually come up to some reasonable temperature, remember Indianapolis 1992 and wait for the tires. In fact, always wait for the tires. You will note that none of the experienced star quality drivers got in trouble at that freezing 500...

CAMBER

Some racers try to set optimum camber by measuring tire temperature in the pits, adjusting camber until they

achieve an even temperature distribution across the surface of the tire. This does not work. A properly inflated bias ply tire will give its best performance when it measures 10 to 15 degrees F. hot on the inside. Radial tires will show relatively more inside temperature.

With bias ply tires, we have to compromise between cornering performance (more static camber or more camber change) and braking and accelerating performance (less static camber or less camber change). One of the nice features of racing radial tires is that they don't lose as much longitudinal performance with camber - so we can set the camber for maximum cornering performance and not lose much under the brakes.

READING THE TIRES

There are two methods of 'reading' the tires in order to optimize their performance. The first (and most common) is by use of a pyrometer to measure the temperature profile across the tread surface. I have already pointed out the folly of trying to achieve even temperature distribution - but there is another reason why I don't use a pyrometer much.

The speed of change of a racing tire's tread temperature with load has to be seen (either real time or on data logging) to be believed. For an indication watch the color change on the in-car cameras from acceleration to braking to cornering to acceleration. What we read in the pits is a not very accurate evidence of what the temperature was during the last load cycle before the car stopped.

I don't use a pyrometer very much except as a warning that I may be getting near the compound limit or that I have an oversteer/understeer imbalance. (On a well balanced car the front and rear temperatures should be close to equal.) The pyrometer will also tell me if the dynamic pressure is way off. As a point of interest, I do not believe in the use of infra-red surface temperature readers - getting under the surface with the needle gives a much truer picture. I spend a lot of time looking at the surface of my tires. A tire that is working at its optimum will show an even, finely "grained" surface across the width of the tire as shown by FIGURE 13A.

A heavily grained, deep rooted pattern all the way across the tire as shown in FIGURE 13B is evidence that the tire is being overworked, either due to too soft a compound or a chassis or aero imbalance.

Heavy graining on one side of the tire (FIGURE 13C) tells us that either camber or toe is extreme at that end of the car.

A portion of the tire that is ungrained - or, in extreme cases, not touching the track - indicates way too much camber. An ungrained or polished surface tells

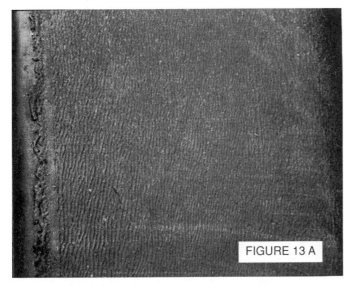

FIGURE 13 A

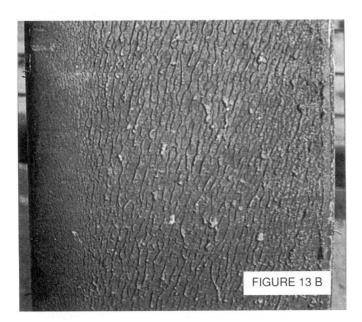

FIGURE 13 B

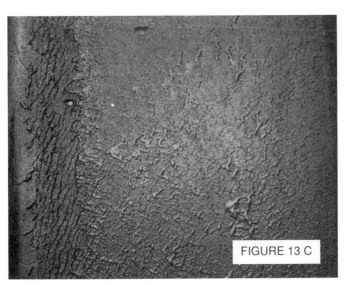

FIGURE 13 C

us that the compound is too hard or that the car is not being driven hard enough to get the tire working.

To my mind this is one of the many areas where the experienced human eyeball is an invaluable tuning tool - it's sort of like reading spark plugs.

WARMING TIRES

One of the more amazing sights I get to watch on most any Sunday is the sight of two conga lines of very expensive race cars. Driven by supposedly experienced, intelligent and cool-headed professional racing drivers, these cars are wiggling and squirming their way around the race track looking for all the world like something out of a retired strippers' convention in Atlantic City.

This nonsense is supposed to warm the tires prior to the start of the race. What all of this unchoreographed and undignified butt wiggling actually accomplishes (besides the odd accident) is to satisfy the drivers' need to do something constructive during the pace lap. What is does not do is effectively warm the tires.

A simple test with a tire pyrometer will quickly prove my point. What will warm the tires on the pace lap is the judicious use of the brakes and the accelerator. Actually the best method that I know of is 'The Bob Earl Tire Warming Procedure' (Bob is pretty smart).

Bob's procedure goes like this. During the pace lap(s), in addition to the accelerating and braking bit, on alternate slow corners, kick the front end and the back end loose (with steering wheel and throttle respectively). Not at the same time! You will arrive at the start with nicely warmed tires and will not have hit (or been hit by) any of the squirmers. Besides, the Earl procedure can be done with dignity.

Just to drive home my point (pun intended), last week two very experienced CART drivers had a nonsexual coming together while squirming tires on the pace lap for the race at Toronto. This week I witnessed a new high (or low) in this department when two less experienced Formula Atlantic drivers managed to get upside down on top of each other while doing the same thing!

TIRE WARMERS

Just about every sanctioning body on this side of the great waters has now outlawed tire warming blankets. Since I usually run low budget teams, I agree. I also agree that the warmers work and that anyone who doesn't use them where they are allowed is making a big mistake. The thought of having hot tires when you leave the pits to qualify should make you drool. So should the thought of having hot tires on the first lap after a pit stop.

TRACTION ENHANCERS

'Traction enhancing' fluids have been around for a long time. Basically, they soften the surface of the tread rubber. Obviously, to some extent, they soften the rubber immediately under the surface. The tire companies do not want to know about these fluids. Neither do the sanctioning bodies. Their use is forbidden in every racing series that I know of. The question, however, is not, "are they legal?" but, "do they work?"

Yes, they do - at least for a short time. They are sort of like qualifying tires in that they will make the car faster for a lap or so. What happens after that depends on a multitude of factors. I have friends who claim that they are a big advantage for qualifying and for the first lap until the tires get hot and that there is no disadvantage. Other friends, equally qualified, say that the tires "go off" noticeably after a couple of laps. I don't go directly against the tire companies' wishes so I don't know.

TIRE LIFE

When I was a young driver we measured the life of the racing tire by tread depth. We expected the tires to last for at least two race meetings and then we sold them to the back markers. Current race tires "give up" or get "greasy" long before they are worn out. Now we measure tire life in heat cycles.

After a while you will learn what the tires feel like when they "go off" and will figure out how many heat cycles a given compound and construction tire is good for. To keep track I make an oil pen hash mark on the sidewall for each heat cycle.

Don't even think about trying to do any development testing on tires that have gone off - you will only confuse yourself and everyone else. You can increase effective life by putting the heat into the tires for each cycle gradually and giving them a cool down lap.

THE UNDER-TIRED CAR

Many of the big sedans - Trans Am, GTO and so forth - are, by modern standards, under-tired. The cars are heavy, they have lots of power and not much download. It is easy to burn the tires off the things - usually the rears. We have already seen that wheelspin is detrimental to performance. It is also detrimental to tire life. So is excessive sliding. So don't slide. Set the car up properly and drive it properly (go back and re-read the self aligning torque section of this chapter).

THE RADIAL TIRE

Most serious racing is now done on radial tires. The difference between a bias ply tire and a radial tire is in the orientation of the carcass plies. FIGURE 14 applies.

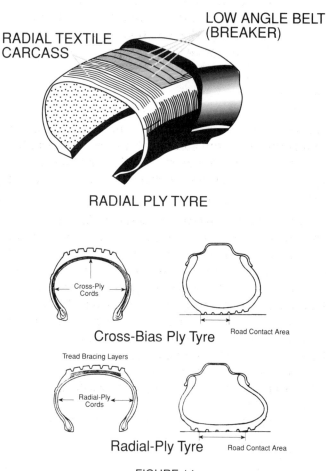

RADIAL TEXTILE CARCASS   LOW ANGLE BELT (BREAKER)

RADIAL PLY TYRE

Cross-Ply Cords

Cross-Bias Ply Tyre   Road Contact Area

Tread Bracing Layers

Radial-Ply Cords

Radial-Ply Tyre   Road Contact Area

FIGURE 14

Virtually everything I have said about racing tires applies directly to the radial racing tire. The advantages of the radial tire are:

1) Better accuracy and quality control in manufacture - radials are more round than bias ply tires and their diameters are more consistent.

2) Better compliance with the road surface.

3) Increased camber tolerance and (maybe) better use of camber thrust.

4) Radials are less sensitive to changing race track conditions than bias plies and so tend to be more consistent over the length of the race or the life of the tire.

The disadvantages are:

1) Radials are less tolerant of change in vehicle track width with vertical wheel movement than bias plies.

2) The original racing radials exhibited a momentary feeling of instability during turn in to fast corners as the sidewalls deflected and the car moved over on the footprints - the "windshield

wiper" effect of FIGURE 15. Development has resulted in a marked reduction in the sensation - to the point where experienced drivers don't even take notice of it. The sensation still exists, however - particularly with solid axle cars - and it takes some getting used to at first.

3) The slip angle threshold is liable to be less wide than that of a bias ply.

To take advantage of the radial's camber tolerance and camber thrust, we run considerably more static camber than we can with bias ply tires. At the same time the designers are able to use less camber gain in the suspension system.

Assuming that the car was designed for radial tires, when determining the optimum static front camber with radials, we can concentrate on cornering force and virtually ignore what the tire will do under braking. The suspension linkage will keep the tires at virtually their static camber setting under the brakes. What little camber gain does take place under the brakes will be accommodated by the tires. So, at the front of the car, the optimum camber setting for cornering will also produce very close to optimum braking. Again, this will not be true for cars designed for bias ply tires.

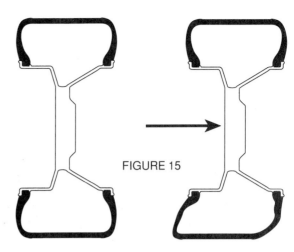

FIGURE 15

THE "WINDSHIELD WIPER" AXIAL DEFLECTION OF RADIAL TYRES UNDER TRANSVERSE LOAD

At the rear of the car, as with bias plies, the optimum static camber will be less than at the front (the tire is usually wider and so can tolerate less camber). Again, but to a lesser extent, we can pretty much concentrate on lateral capacity and let the tractive capacity on acceleration take care of itself.

If all of this sounds as if best we can hope for is to minimize the abuse we give our tires, I have succeeded. Take care of your tires and they will take care of you.

4

"Most passing is done under the brakes." Christopher Smith

BRAKING

In 'Bull Durham' (yes, I do occasionally see a movie!) the hero states at one point that baseball is a simple game; "You throw the ball, you hit the ball and you catch the ball - how simple can it get?" Well, motor racing is similarly deceptive. You accelerate the car, you stop the car and you turn the car. Period! Now we are going to talk about the simplest exercise of the three - stopping the car.

Jackie Stewart once said that the last thing that the racing driver learns how to do really well is to use the brakes. I agree. Sometime later the good Mr. Stewart modified his statement by saying that the last thing that he learned to do properly was to take his foot off the brake pedal correctly. I strongly suspect that he was actually talking about trail braking - about which, more later.

It is interesting that one of the finest drivers and certainly the most astute student of the game in history, feels that the very last step on the road to success has to do with what, on the surface of things, looks to be the most simple act in the play - stopping the car. In racing, as in many things, looks can be deceiving.

On the face of things, the whole problem of braking would appear to lie in figuring out just how deep you can go before you switch your right foot from the right hand pedal to the one in the middle (we'll get into left foot braking later). The actual technique of straight line braking is pretty simple - you push on the pedal until the tires are not quite locked. You modulate the pedal pressure to keep them in that state as the car loses speed (and download, and download-produced grip) and reacts to road surface irregularities. When you have slowed down enough to enter the corner, you take your foot off the brake pedal and get on with the business of cornering - right?

Wrong! The scenario we have just described will indeed get you slowed down enough to get through the corner - but you are very liable to be passed somewhere during the process. There is, in fact, a lot of technique involved in optimal braking.

The basic idea here is to build up braking force as rapidly as practical, to maintain maximum straight line retardation for as long as necessary and then to smoothly transition into either trail braking or cornering - all without upsetting the car. "Easy," you say, "I've been

doing that for as long as I have been driving racing cars." "I doubt it," say I. "In all probability you are too busy thinking about the upcoming corner - the one that has caused the braking in the first place - to concentrate properly on the braking itself".

Simple test: take your race car, on old tires, to a race track - any race track - a drag strip is perfect. At a convenient place on a straight mark a line across the track - use tape, chalk, or anything - just so you can see it from the cockpit. Choose the location so that you will be going at least 80 mph (100 is better) when you get there and so that you have plenty of distance to come to a full stop before you arrive at a corner (or something to hit).

Warm the car up and then, as you hit the line, bring the car to a full stop in the shortest possible distance - without downshifting and without intentionally locking a wheel. Have a crew member mark the place where you stopped with a pylon or something. Now, giving the brakes and the tires a chance to cool down between runs, repeat the exercise 10 times - without changing the brake bias. Then do it again downshifting. You will learn several things:

1) The last pylons to be placed will be noticeably closer to the starting line than the first ones were and, even after you have improved, the pylons will still be somewhat scattered longitudinally - proving that:

2) You didn't know how to stop the car anywhere near as well or as consistently as you thought that you did.

3) In all probability you stopped in less distance when you didn't downshift - telling you that you don't do that as well as you thought you did either.

4) Locking a wheel or wheels does terrible things to your stopping distance - not because of decreased friction, but because of what you have to do to unlock the wheel and regain control of the car.

5) Downshifting is not the big help you thought it would be.

6) Even under these conditions, with no corner to worry about and no traffic to bedevil you, it is not easy to stop the car at its maximum rate of retardation with precision and consistency.

7) If you can't do it here, under artificially ideal conditions, there is no hope at all under real world conditions.

So practice! As you get better and more consistent at it, add rear brake bias.

MECHANICS

We will look at the mechanics of the situation first. To begin with, it isn't the brakes that slow the car down - the rolling resistance of the vehicle, the aerodynamic drag of the vehicle as a whole and the friction between the contact patches of the four tires and the surface of the road do that. What the brakes do is decelerate the wheels so that the tires can generate decelerative thrust. The driver has no direct control over either the aerodynamic drag or the rolling resistance of the vehicle. Hopefully he has complete control over the braking system.

The people who study such things tell me what my own body told me decades ago - the human control loop wants to work through force, not through displacement. In this case, for the driver to properly modulate the brakes, we want the brake pedal itself to be hard like a rock and to move virtually not at all - like the control sticks in the latest fighter aircraft. We want the braking force to vary directly with the amount of force we put on the pedal - not with the amount of pedal movement. Pedal movement will merely confuse our body, our mind and the tenuous link between the two.

There are excellent racing drivers with truly distinguished records who will tell you that, in order for the driver to "feel" the brakes, a relatively "long" pedal is required. Like those who will tell you that the car has to roll so that the driver can feel it, they are wrong!

Pedal movement has no more to do with sensing brake lock up than body roll has to do with sensing the slip angle threshold of the tires. What a long pedal does do is make brake modulation imprecise and downshifts difficult. The modulation is imprecise because it is difficult to feel how far you are pushing your foot into a bucket of mush. The downshift is difficult because the brake pedal doesn't stay put in relation to the gas pedal. This means that while the driver is hunting around for the throttle in order to downshift, he cannot modulate the brakes properly.

This is, of course, why many drivers do not row the car down through all the gears in the braking area - moving the braking foot around, no matter how skilful the driver may be, upsets the modulation. These drivers brake and then, when the car has been slowed sufficiently to select the gear that they intend to go through the corner in, they downshift once and get on with it. For years this was an American technique ridiculed by the "sophisticated Europeans". More on this subject in just a bit.

I digress (again!) Drivers make several consistent mistakes while learning to slow the racing car just enough:

1) They take too long to build braking force (don't get on the pedal hard enough). This obviously wastes time.

2) They jump on the pedal too hard. This can compress the front tires and set up a pogo stick series of events which makes it impossible to modulate the brakes efficiently.

3) They brake too early - in extreme cases having to accelerate again before reaching the corner. This phase of the learning curve usually doesn't last very long at all. If it does, other sports beckon.

4) They brake too late, arriving at the turn in point:

   a) Too fast and,

   b) With the front tires on fire and the car refusing to turn. This phase can go on forever and, if it does, other sports beckon strongly.

Often the learning driver goes through all of these phases on the same lap - at different corners - and then again, in a different sequence, on the next lap. It's not easy. It's not meant to be.

So what do we really want to do? We want to change from maximum acceleration to maximum deceleration in the shortest practical time - without upsetting the car. FIGURE 16, taken from actual on board data, shows braking force being built up about as quickly as I think is humanly possible - from full acceleration to full braking in about 0.4 seconds (left foot braking, of course).

In a straight line and on a smooth surface this is neither particularly difficult to do nor to learn. It is simply a matter of learning how hard to make the initial push on the pedal and to quickly build up braking force (note the "knee point" in the brake line pressure curve).

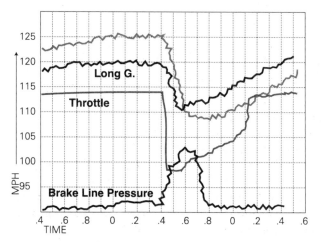

FULL ACCELERATION TO FULL BRAKING IN 0.4 SECONDS
FIGURE 16

Of course you must modulate the pedal pressure to keep the tires at the edge of traction as the car slows (and loses download) - but, so long as you are aware that the process is not automatic, the imperfectly understood human biofeedback system seems perfectly capable of handling that.

The difficult parts are learning to judge where the optimum braking point is - especially under changing track conditions and car/tire states - how to really modulate the pedal to maintain maximum retardation without locking a wheel as the car skips over the bumps and surface changes and when and how much to start easing off the pedal so as to balance the car before turning in. It is also real easy to fall mentally asleep in the braking area, even if the exercise only lasts a couple of seconds.

Some experts maintain that, after a certain level of skill and experience has been reached, there simply isn't much time to be gained under the brakes. They maintain that, since the modern braking systems are so good and the braking distances and times are so short, there are no longer advantages to be gained under the brakes. The time simply isn't there. It is important to realize that they are wrong.

Think about it. Instrumentation tells us that the modern download-generating, cast iron-braked racing car spends about 10% of its time braking on the "average" U.S. road racing circuit. Therefore a 2.5% improvement in braking performance (based on time, not distance) would net about 0.25% improvement in lap time on a 1 minute 30 second lap - or 0.225 seconds.

Any self respecting race driver would sell his mother for that kind of time. I should, however, point out that 2.5% difference in time is about the difference between your great aunt and Michael Schumacher. These approximations are for download cars - for sedans and stock cars the potential gains are significantly greater. This is, however, only a part of what Mr. Stewart was talking about - and not the most important part.

So what is the big deal that Mr. Stewart was talking about? Efficient corner entry and balance! Remember Denny Hulme's, "It is all a question of balance."

Remember that the point at which you get on the brakes determines both the turn in point for the corner and the corner entry speed. The secret of truly efficient braking in the racing car is not who can brake deeper - or even who can enter the corner faster. It is who can brake later and still enter the corner with the car in a balanced condition at the entry speed calculated to combine minimum elapsed time from turn in to apex, optimum apex speed (and location) and maximum acceleration out of the corner - along with minimum loss of speed going in.

"Keeping the momentum up" is what the good Formula Ford drivers used to call it. Carrying speed through the corner is what I call it. It requires a great deal of hard working practice combined with a lot of thought. And it has little to do with the outbraking manoeuver - which is another question altogether and, between experienced drivers in more or less equal cars, is usually an intrusion measure helped by semi consciousness on the part of the overtaken.

So, facing these facts, the question remains, "Is there anything practical that you, the driver, can do to give yourself an advantage in braking?" And the answer is, as always, "Of course!" The accompanying sidebar explains.

THE DOWNSHIFT - TO ROW OR NOT TO ROW [OTHER TIMES - OTHER CIRCUMSTANCES]

Mr. Senna was once called to task by Mr. Stewart for what Mr. Stewart (and most of the rest of the world) regarded as conduct unbecoming a great champion. Mr. Senna replied that critics should take into account the mental stress associated with being a three time World Champion. Mr. Stewart politely pointed out that, being a three time World Champion himself, he felt that he had a pretty good understanding of just about everything involved. Mr. Senna then diminished himself more than somewhat by pointing out that, "Those were different times". Downshifting one gear at a time is fine so long as we are going to be satisfied with great sounds, sublime smoothness (a good downshift should be heard, but not felt) and less than optimum brake modulation - or if we are only going down one gear. The technique is not difficult to master and is a source of great satisfaction to the purists among us.

Unfortunately, until the advent of the "semi-automatic mechanical gearbox" and the re-invention of the sequential shifting gearbox, in professional racing the glorious sound of a high revving multi-cylindered racing engine being rowed down through the gears was fast becoming a part of history. Some of the scribes would have us believe that so is the manly art of passing under the brakes. They must not watch the same races that I do.

Semi-automatic and sequential gearboxes aside, there is still considerable diversity of opinion as to whether one should downshift one at a time through all of the gears when approaching a corner or whether one should skip gears. Rowing down through each gear in turn is the "traditional" way of things.

In the heroic age (my day - the older we get, the faster we were) there was good reason for this procedure - the brakes were often woefully inadequate and one used the friction of the engine (not, as is commonly believed, the compression) to slow the car. Properly

CARBON - CARBON BRAKES

Anyone who watches Formula One on television (all of us) is familiar with the oft repeated statement that the carbon disc/carbon pad stops the cars faster than any iron disc system could. It is true that cars with carbon brake rotors enjoy shorter braking distances than those with iron discs in some circumstances - but, as often happens, the reasons are a lot more complex than the commentators realize.

Part of the advantage does not have to do with any difference in coefficient of friction between carbon/carbon brakes and cast iron/non-carbon pads. In fact, the carbon/carbon coefficient is about the same as that of Carbon Metallic pads on cast iron rotors (there are no steel rotor in serious auto racing).

Decelerating a racing car with the brakes converts the kinetic energy of motion (mass x velocity squared) into heat - lots and lots of heat. This heat is generated by the friction of the pads against the brake discs. The discs themselves serve as heat sinks from which the heat is transferred into the airstream. The discs must be capable both of storing the heat until it can be dissipated into the airstream and of mechanically surviving the repeated thermal shocks involved. This requires a finite mass of material.

The disk itself will be as large in diameter as can fit inside the wheel and will have a thickness and mass sufficient to do the job. The four discs are effective flywheels which must themselves be decelerated. The carbon/carbon material allows the use of significantly less mass for the same thermal capacity - resulting in a notable reduction in rotational inertia. This is the real reason why the cars stop sooner.

Remember that it is the tires that stop the car - not the brakes. The carbon/carbon system gives the tires less inertia to get rid of. Carbon/carbon also reacts more quickly to driver inputs and the rotors are physically and thermally more stable at elevated temperatures. As a point of interest, the glowing rotor syndrome is not unique to carbon/carbon - cast iron rotors also glow red (and sometimes almost white) and have for decades.

It is interesting to note that the use of carbon/carbon discs also has a significant effect on the fast corner turn in characteristics of the car. The brake discs are not only flywheels - they are gyroscopes. Gyroscopic precession resists any effort to turn in the plane of rotation of the gyroscope wheel - and in the case of the racing car, the road wheel and tire to which it is attached. When USAC allowed carbon discs at Indianapolis, the more sensitive drivers immediately reported that the steering was lighter, the car turned in smoother, easier and more predictably - interesting, what?

done by skilled praticioners, the technique was known as "saving the brakes" and it endeared generations of drivers to engineers and team managers. It also produced a lovely sound which endeared these same drivers to generations of spectators. Improperly done the result was damaged gearboxes, blown-up engines and spun out racing cars.

Today, thanks to the likes of Mssrs. Alcon, Automotive Products, Brembo, Castrol, Carbon Industrie, Hitco and Performance Friction, there should be no such thing as inadequate brakes on any racing car. Not only is the retarding force of engine friction no longer needed, its use may now be a detriment. Before the traditionalists (and the non-traditionalist drivers who lie about how they do things) start looking for the hanging rope, lets explore this statement a bit.

Once upon a time, braking distances (and times) were several times greater than they are now. This is due to a number of factors:

1) Great gobs of aerodynamic download have increased the stopping power of the modern racing car by orders of magnitude.

2) The coefficient of friction of the racing tire has increased dramatically - as has the area of their footprints.

3) Racing cars are a lot lighter than they used to be.

4) Racing brakes are a lot more powerful, fade resistant, long lived and reliable than they used to be.

5) Race tracks are a lot smoother than they used to be.

6) All of the above have allowed the drivers to become more skilled at the techniques of braking.

For example, in my day we could develop (probably) about 1-g retardation on a good track. At a constant 1-g of retardation, to stop from 160mph requires 855 feet and 7.3 seconds. At 2-g it requires 427.5 feet and 3.65 seconds. At 3.0-g it requires 285 feet and 2.44 seconds.

Admittedly there is no such thing in racing as a constant rate of deceleration - download and aero drag both decrease dramatically with decreasing road speed and God ensures that possible retardation decreases linearly with it. However, we are not quibbling over tenths of a second here. My point is that it is one thing to efficiently downshift from fourth to third to second in 7.3 seconds and quite another to downshift from sixth to fifth to fourth to third to second in 2.44 seconds. This assumes that the driver is modulating braking pressure to the maximum that the tires will accept and blipping the throttle almost perfectly to match the revs and not either snatching the rear tires or over-revving the engine.

What I am saying is that, to me, it seems that rowing down through all of the gears with a "standard", non sequential, gearbox is both a waste of time and effort and a detriment to efficient braking. To me the engine is for making the car go forward and the brakes are for slowing it down.

Concentrate your efforts on braking efficiently and, when the car has slowed sufficiently, downshift into the required gear (taking care to properly synch the revs) - and get on with the job. Mark Donohue is generally given credit for "inventing" the technique - just as Stirling Moss is supposed to have invented trail braking. Nonsense. With all due respect to two fine drivers (and splendid human beings), racing drivers have been trail braking at least since four wheel brakes were put on racing cars and skipping gears since gearboxes were developed.

For many years European scribes decried the "American practice" of skipping gears as an un-natural act fit only for colonials who didn't understand what proper motor racing was all about. The Mr. Prost let slip that he had been doing it for years and that all the throttle blipping the scribes heard in the braking areas was only to keep the revs up and the turbo spooled. Sometimes it's tough being a scribe. It's a lot easier when they leave the pits and wander around the race track to find out what's really going on.

I do not advocate shifting directly from top to first - partially because the downshift to first is usually difficult (often due to the flexibility of the first/reverse shift rail) partially because first is usually a pretty damned delicate gear and partially because doing so will drop the engine revs too far. So, before dropping into first from any gear other than second, it is a good idea to select third or second first - whichever will not require a cross gate shift.

This way you can concentrate all of your abilities on braking properly without worrying about rocking your foot back and forth between pedals, synching revs, missing shifts, etc. If you are using your left foot on the brake pedal, so much the better. If the revs get too low (very long braking area), shove the clutch in or move the stick to neutral and blip the engine.

Don't get me wrong - you must still learn to downshift properly. The penalties for hamfisted and/or mistimed downshifts are just what they have always been.

Don't blip the engine enough and you will not only hurt the gear and the dog, you will snatch the rear tires when the gear is engaged. The result is instantaneous dynamic oversteer - just about when you need it least. Blip too much and the gear still gets hurt and the engine is over-revved - unless the rev limiter saves you.

OPTIMIZING THE BRAKE SYSTEM

You can start the process of optimizing your brake system by making damned sure that your pedal geometry is correct (see 'Tune to Win' - Page 109), that your calipers are properly aligned, that your rotors are true, balanced and properly floated on the bells or top hats, that the master cylinder bores vs caliper piston sizes are somewhere near optimum and that the brake bias is correctly adjusted. This is pretty basic stuff - and it is often ignored.

You can insist that the rotating inertia of the vehicle be reduced to the maximum extent practical - light wheel rims, drilled discs, lightened CV joint outers, lightened diff carriers, ring gears and flywheels, clutches with minimum moments of inertia, etc. Anything in this line that contributes to increased acceleration will also contribute to increased deceleration.

By the way, I consider rifle drilling of half shafts to be a waste of money - it just doesn't reduce the rotational inertia of the part enough to warrant the expense and , if the shaft was designed properly to start with, the OD will have to be increased slightly to make up for the loss of (admittedly ineffective) material from the center. With an unlimited budget I would run hollow shafts - assuming that the OD didn't get so large as to make the transition to the spline into a weak point. With the budgets I am liable to see for the rest of my career I won't even consider it.

But you will probably get the most results by choosing the right brake pads. Those people out there still running Ferodo DS11 are living in the stone age. What we want is a pad with the maximum possible coefficient of friction combined with sufficient temperature capability for the vehicle and the circuit. We also want the coefficient of friction to be constant (or virtually so) from ambient temperature to maximum. Lastly, it would be nice if the pads didn't chew the discs up too badly.

This used to be an impossible dream. Then along came Mintex 171. This compound, while it chewed the hell out of discs, came pretty close to meeting the above impossible criteria - except that the coefficient fell off at the high end of the temperature scale. This required increased pedal pressure toward the end of long braking areas and planted the seeds of doubt in drivers' minds at a time and place when doubt is not what they wanted. Ferodo 2459 does almost the same thing and is easier on discs. Alcon 600 is better yet.

No matter - all that stuff is ancient history now. No, I'm not talking about carbon/carbon brakes. First of all, I have no experience with them and secondly, they aren't allowed in the forms of racing I am currently engaged in. No, I'm talking about Carbon Metallic pads from the Performance Friction Corporation.

Continued...

OPTIMIZING THE BRAKE SYSTEM, cont.

Carbon Metallic '90-series' pads (PFC90/93) offer a co-efficient of friction significantly higher than any other pads and that coefficient is virtually independent of temperature. This allows the use of larger master cylinders which produce a firmer pedal and thus allow better modulation. In the beginning they required a fairly elaborate burnishing procedure. They now come pre-burnished. The only disadvantage of these Carbon Metallic pads is that they do have a faster than 'normal' heat rise and they do transfer more heat into the calipers than 'normal' pads. This is easily overcome by attention to caliper cooling, caliper piston insulation and/or the use of the best non-silicon brake fluid available. They are more expensive than most other pads and they are 'aggressive' toward discs. It is my opinion that, in every type of open wheeled racing car where carbon/carbon is not allowed, and on heavy closed wheel cars with real racing tires (NASCAR, Trans-Am, GTO, etc.) they are worth the expense and the disc wear.

However, just because something like a brake pad works very well on one type of car doesn't mean that it is necessarily the best for all types. For example, in the smaller sedan classes where (due to lack of download and tire) the rate of retardation (and therefore the rate of heat generation) is less, Hawk's 'Carbotic' pads offer performance and consistency almost as good as Performance Friction, and are less aggressive toward the discs. They are, deservedly, the most popular pad in small sedan racing.

BEDDING IN

Everyone knows that most brake pads must be laboriously bedded in (or 'burnished'). The procedure is simple enough - medium stops followed by cooling off periods (usually following your normal driving pattern but braking early and moderately) until you feel the pads 'come in' - followed by a really hard stop from high speed and a cooling off period to ambient. To my mind this is an expensive waste of time. Performance Friction and Hawk pads are pre-burnished - which more than makes up for the difference in cost.

Many racers do not realize that cast iron rotors, regardless of pad material, should also be broken in. Although racing discs are normalized and stress relieved during manufacture, there is no practical way to simulate the thermal shock experienced on the race track.

The ideal procedure is to run a new set of discs (with old pads) through a few gentle stops, followed by a few moderate stops and finally (after the discs are evenly discolored) a few hard stops. They should then be dismounted and blanchard ground. They are then ready to be re-burnished and used seriously. This ideal is seldom realized.

Continued...

Throw the shift too early and the rear wheels will drag the engine into over-rev. In this not unusual case, no rev limiter can save you and you had best hope that there is no onboard recorder or that your engine builder/car owner didn't hear your crime (and they don't find it on the data system). The number of supposedly competent drivers I have seen habitually downshift before braking is almost as astounding to me as the number of engines that survive this sort of treatment - at least for a while.

THE OTHER SIDE OF THE COIN

A large number of exceedingly competent and accomplished drivers disagree with the idea of skipping gears. Their numbers include Mario and Michael Andretti and, for a while, our son, Christopher. They feel that, particularly in long braking areas - from very high speed to very low speed - the retardation of the rear wheels by the friction of the engine exerts a stabilizing influence on the back of the car (somewhat like a sea anchor) and gives them both better control and more retardation.

This diversity of opinion among the very best practitioners of the art merely confirms that there are no absolutes in motor racing. My job is to point out the options and their possible advantage. It is up to you to determine what is best for you. Bear in mind that what proves best in one situation may not be best in all situations.

BRAKING AND THE NEW GENERATION GEARBOXES

It will probably be some time before the majority of my readers will be exposed to the "semi automatic manual gearbox". The shift on these devices is triggered by switches on the steering wheel. They are therefore sequential shifters and there is no skipping of gears. Since these boxes almost demand left foot braking, there is no problem blipping the throttle with the right foot while modulating the brakes with the left - just a technique to learn for those who have been accustomed to braking with the right foot. If they don't already, it won't be long before some of the on board microprocessors do the blipping for you.

Many current generation racing cars use a motorcycle-type sequential shift mechanism for the simple reason that they shift faster - and it is harder for the driver to miss a shift. The lever is moved forward a few millimeters for the upshift and backwards the same distance for the downshift. There are no cross gate motions to confuse the driver and take up room in the cockpit. These boxes can, indeed, be shifted too fast - to the detriment of the dogs which have, in extreme cases, been sheared completely off.

In fact, some of the "automatic shifting" boxes are programmed to shift somewhat slower than a manual sequential shift. At any rate, one cannot skip gears with the sequential shift so the glorious sound has returned. Among the many things that I do not understand is why some clever young engineer has not come up with a way to skip a gear with the manual sequential box (a button on top of the lever, for instance).

ROWING WITH THE LEFT FOOT

We will discuss left foot braking in Chapter 6.. Modulating the brakes while downshifting is not a problem when using this technique, so one of the major reasons for skipping gears loses a lot of validity. At least when learning to brake with the left foot, I suggest that you not skip gears - the chance of missing one is just too great. After you become proficient at it, to skip or not to skip is up to you.

TRAIL BRAKING

Trail braking is one of the more popular buzzwords. Some racing schools (rightly) brag that they teach trail braking. Others (wrongly) brag that they do not. What's going on here?

It comes back to the 'Traction Circle'. As we saw in the last chapter, for maximum performance we must "ride the rim" of the traction circle. If we follow the prehistoric dictum of, "Do all the braking in a straight line, go through the corner at maximum cornering force and then accelerate in a straight line," we are going to waste a lot of tire and a lot of time. It is probable that no racing driver ever drove that way. It is certain that no successful driver has driven that way in the memory of living man.

Much of the technique of driving a racing car is either instinctive or intuitive. (Intuition is defined as instinct tempered by experience.) Just as correcting an oversteer slide is instinctive, so is driving the car so as to utilize all the tire that is available.

What we need to do - and what every racing driver instinctively does - is to continue our (reduced and trailing off) braking well into the corner entry phase so that, while the tires are in the process of building up cornering force, they are contributing to braking thrust. We don't have to give up much cornering force in order to develop meaningful amounts of braking thrust - and the resultant line of force follows the boundary of the traction circle.

We must also start to open up our exit line from the corner - or "release the car" early - so that we will have excess rear tire capacity available for early and hard acceleration. Never forget that he who gets the power down first - and is able to keep it down with the car straight - will arrive first at the other end. If you are using all of the rear tire capacity in cornering force, there is none left for acceleration. It is that simple.

OPTIMIZING THE BRAKE SYSTEM, cont.

The practical method is the same, with the substitution of a cool off period to near ambient temperature for the grinding process.

All of the Carbon Metallic and Carbotic pads require that an even coating of pad material be deposited on the disc prior to hard use. This layer should be left on and never attacked with sandpaper or the like. In fact, sandpaper should never be used on a disc. If, through overheating, you have organic pick up on your discs, remove it by grinding or with garnet paper - and change your pad compound.

BRAKE FADE

Brake fade should be of historic interest only. Unfortunately, it still occurs, but only through ignorance or misapplication. There are three possible types of fade: "Green Fade", "Pad Fade" and "Fluid Fade".

Green Fade occurs due to non-existent or inadequate pad bedding and sees the car heading for the boondocks without warning, the pedal remaining high and firm - and pumping does not help. Pad Fade is similar in feel and result. It occurs when the temperature generated by the brakes exceeds the upper temperature limit of the pad material.

Uncommon in racing, Pad Fade can easily be generated in a road car. The inexperienced driver is well advised to deliberately fade the pads in a road car so that he will know what it feels like and not confuse it with Fluid Fade. Do not do this on the public road - or anywhere you could get hurt!

Fluid Fade occurs when heat passed from the caliper causes the fluid to reach boiling point. Tiny bubbles of compressible gas form in and are diffused through the previously incompressible fluid - and the pedal goes to the floor. Frantic pumping of both the pedal and the driver's heart ensue. Upon arrival back at the pits the message invariably is, "The brakes faded and scared the hell out of me!".

After I get done explaining to the driver that if he really did experience a partial loss of braking effectiveness and stayed on the road, he wasn't using the brakes as hard as he should have been (!), I gently point out that he had better be able to differential between Pad and Fluid Fade. Not only are the symptoms diametrically opposite, so are the cures.

If the pedal goes all soft and horrible, you have boiled the fluid. The only cure is to upgrade the fluid or keep it cooler - which can be done by increasing the cooling to the caliper or by insulating the pistons. Additional disc cooling or going to a harder pad compound are not remedies.

On the other hand, assuming the pads have been properly bedded, the only way you are going to cure Pad

Continued...

OPTIMIZING THE BRAKE SYSTEM, cont.

Fade is by going to a harder (more temperature resistant) pad, by better cooling or by increasing the effective heat sink of the disc. This means increasing its mass, its surface area and/or the effectiveness of its cooling. A harder pad can only do so much - but, if necessary, cooling can be enhanced by a water spray system, or perhaps a water cooled caliper (which will also guard against Fluid Fade).

BRAKE BIAS

Most racing cars feature adjustable fore and aft brake bias. Most inexperienced drivers have no idea how to even approximate the optimum brake bias and often end up with it truly screwed up - an unpleasant and unnecessary experience. It is not necessary to lock up the wheels in front of observers. The truth of the matter is that, at least with mid engined cars, the brake ratio can be adjusted very closely with the car on stands.

Place a 'driver' in the car and have him hold the steering wheel firmly in the straight ahead position. Explain to him, in detail, what the two of you are about to do and why.

With an open wheeled car, straddle a front tire and start turning it - with your hands pulling up. Try real hard not to pinch a finger between the rim and the brake caliper. Have the driver gradually apply brake pressure until you can just not turn the wheel. Have the driver hold the exact same pressure on the pedal while you run to a rear wheel. If the bias is correct, you should just barely be able to turn it. If not, adjust the bias until it is right.

Done properly, this method will get you within one turn of the adjuster every time. Done improperly, it will confuse you. Do not attempt to determine bias with less force than required to lock a wheel - it simply will not work. Do not attempt the method with unbedded pads or discs. Do not accept your first attempt - repeat the exercise until you get consistent results. Fixed fenders make this exercise is difficult at best - use pressure taps.

BRAKE BIAS ADJUSTMENT ON TRACK

Using a set of tires of the same size, construction and compound that you will race on, but which you do not value highly, have the driver brake very hard on a smooth, level and clean surface where you - or someone else who is capable of telling which end locks up first - can observe at a safe close range. It helps to have an observer on each side of the car.

Adjust the bias until the fronts lock first - but just barely. The more experienced and sensitive the driver

Continued...

All of this calls for some pretty artful choices of lines and some reasonably delicate control on the part of the driver. The task is not simplified by dynamic load transfer, changing aerodynamic loads, gobs of available torque, variations in road surface and condition - or by traffic...

The truth of the matter is that racing drivers have been trail braking at least since four wheel brakes arrived on the scene. Those scribes and PR men who claim that Al Unser Jr. drives in the classic manner, braking in a straight line, while Michael Andretti trail brakes simply don't know what they are watching. Every successful driver trail brakes at some corners. No successful driver trail brakes at every corner.

Whether or not to trail brake depends on a number of factors. They include:

1) How much time is available for Barishnikov-type footwork - remembering that taking your foot off the brake pedal properly is almost certainly the last thing that you will learn to do well.

2) How much front lateral tractive capacity will be necessary for turn in - and how much of it will be provided by aerodynamic download.

3) How large and how abrupt the initial steering wheel movement will be (how tight the corner).

4) How bad the understeer is at this moment in time and space.

5) How fast the corner is.

Trail braking basically works in medium and low speed corners. It doesn't work well in bumpy corners. Unless it is done with the left foot against partial power, it doesn't (usually) work in very fast corners because it changes the pitch attitude of the car.

Done properly, trail braking can significantly reduce corner entry understeer by a combination of degrading the rear tires' lateral capacity and increasing the vertical load on the front tires. It takes some very artful juggling to make it work consistently. One of the problems with this sort of thing is that, if you have set the car up to use trail braking to kill understeer at 10-tenths, when you get into the fortunate situation where you can back off a bit, the understeer returns.

There ain't no free lunch but, since this problem is mechanical rather than aerodynamic, driver adjustable anti-roll bars can be a wonderful thing...

There is another theory that says the way to cure initial understeer is to set up excessive rear brake bias and trail brake into the corner. This will also work - but consistency is real hard to come by and it is a really dumb way to cure understeer.

Three last words on trail braking:

1) Trail braking does not include braking hard into the corner. It means just what it says - trailing off the brakes as you enter the corner. Braking hard in-

to the corner is for when you have overcooked things and are concentrating on getting the thing slowed down without hitting something. Then you brake, hard, in a straight line toward the fence, ignoring the corner itself, until you have slowed enough to turn and get on with things. Trail braking saves lap time. This manoeuver costs time but saves the car.

2) Don't try it with front tires on fire - ease off first.

3) While you are learning the technique, during the race, if in doubt don't.. Slow in and fast out beats fast in and slow out.

LEFT FOOT BRAKING

For twenty years I have been asked two related questions:

1) Do I recommend using the clutch for shifting gears or not?

2) Do I recommend left foot braking or not?

So far as clutch use goes, I have always said that, if you are going to use your right foot on the brake pedal, you may as well use the clutch. Used properly, it doesn't slow the shift - much. Racers don't actually release the thing anyway, they just sort of dab at it. And dabbing at it does cushion the shock of gear engagement and reduce the danger of a missed shift.

I have been a bit ambivalent about which foot to use on the center pedal. While I have always advocated left foot braking on ovals - and on selected corners where you need to lose just a little bit of speed and no downshift is involved - I have not actually come out and recommended left foot braking everywhere.

What I have said is that if a driver is skilled enough and confident at shifting without the clutch, there are significant advantages to be gained by left foot braking - once the technique is developed. The advantages are:

1) Better brake modulation and control- no more heel and toe, no more rocking of the braking foot to blip the engine for downshifts. The left foot concentrates on braking and the right blips the throttle every so often.

2) No loss of time while the traditional right foot shifts from one pedal to the other - the transition from power to braking and back is instantaneous and smooth.

3) With left foot braking, when just a little speed needs to be taken off, the pitch attitude of the car and the related aero balance can be kept constant by braking against partial engine power. This can be a big deal - especially on fast corners.

To make things even more interesting, braking against engine power will keep the exhaust gases "blowing" the tunnels (or diffusers as the case may

OPTIMIZING THE BRAKE SYSTEM, cont.

becomes, the less he is going to flat spot the tires doing this. Eventually he will arrive at a point where he can do it by himself - on race tires. Remember that fuel load may have a lot to do with optimum bias and that a car set up with a light fuel load may well have a rearward bias on full tanks. That is what the cockpit adjustor is for. Find out about this sort of thing and make sure that the driver remembers - even if the crew chief has to remind him on the radio.

It is as well to start a rookie out with a slight excess of forward bias and work toward the optimum as his (or her) skill, judgement and sensitivity increase. The better and more experienced the driver, the more rear brake will be required for optimum results. When it rains, several turns to the rear is in order. Again it is as well to figure out how much beforehand - and to record the required adjustment.

Once the proper bias is established (on the race track, not on the jack stands), it is important to be able to quickly and conveniently re-establish it so that you can get back there after somebody screws with the adjuster or the assembly is taken apart for maintenance. There are three ways of accomplishing this. You can measure and record relative front to rear line pressure levels. You can measure and record torque wrench break loose settings or you can measure the position of the bias bar itself.

I prefer line pressure because it is the most accurate method - even though it usually adds more potential leak points in the system. Automotive Products has very recently introduced a gauge system which screws into the caliper bleed screw ports - obviating this problem. I don't do torque wrench readings because it is almost impossible to be accurate (the radius is too small). I do carefully measure and record the position of the balance bar.

So far as I am concerned, only the driver ever touches the bias adjusting knob - no mistakes and no misunderstandings. Still, it is a wise precaution to check the measurement before each session. I also check the static bias (by turning wheels as described above) every morning.

INSTABILITY UNDER THE BRAKES

Once upon a time, in the days of my youth, instability under the brakes was a fact of life. Actually it didn't matter that much because the brakes, if used hard enough to cause instability, were unlikely to last long enough for the instability to become a major problem.

Things have changed - for the better. The brakes are now probably the most reliable and fool proof part of the racing car. It takes dedicated effort to screw them up to the point where they cause a problem. Racers being determined people, it can be done.

Continued...

be) and will prevent the download interruption associated with "normal" off throttle braking.

Left foot braking also allows you to alter the mechanical balance of the car in corners by working the pedals against each other.

4) And most important. Current high downforce racing cars are capable of developing so much retardation at high speed that the time required to move the right foot from the throttle to the brake and develop the considerable pressure necessary to take advantage of the available retardation is significant - especially in a passing situation. With left foot braking, the left foot is already poised over the brake pedal, there is no lag, the car goes from full acceleration to full braking just as fast as you can slam your foot down.

And make no mistake about it, slamming your foot down is exactly what you are going to do. It is difficult to lock the brakes on a modern high downforce car at speed - there is simply too much download generated traction. Modulation comes as speed decreases later in the braking zone.

Consider: 180mph is 264 feet per second. The fastest foot in the world is going to take at least 0.3 seconds to shift pedals and develop maximum pressure. That translates to 79.2 feet of race track. Admittedly the improvements in tires and download generation over the past few years have markedly shortened braking distances. But, among competitive cars, most passing is still done under the brakes.

Think about it. The accomplished left foot braker can go 80 feet deeper into a corner that is approached at 180 mph. Of course, this advantage decreases with decreasing approach speed, but it will always be worthwhile.

Most of the traditional drivers, and all of the schools, are against left foot braking. The technique takes time to develop. Every driver should learn to downshift without the clutch and if you are going to left foot brake you had better learn it damned well. Further, those of you who have not driven Karts have not developed braking sensitivity with the off side leg and foot. You need to.

Buy an old clunker floor shift street car and practice a lot. Any cone type synchro box can be shifted without the clutch so long as the revs are properly synchronized (the synchros exist only for the clutzes who can't shift). Don't worry about hurting the synchros - that's why you buy a clunker and, when you are not using the synchros, it doesn't matter whether they are worn out or not. Go for it.

As automatic-manual gearboxes become the rage, left foot braking will become a necessity - so the younger one learns it, the better.

One of the big mistakes that beginning left foot brakers make is pulling too much speed off the car - it is really easy to do without realizing it. Another common mistake is to not take your right foot all the way off the throttle when you are not braking against partial power - the data recorder will show this one.

Far and away the cheapest way to learn the braking end of things is to go Sprint Kart racing. It is also the cheapest way to learn how to race. And it is fun.

The bottom line is that - even in this day of decreased stopping distances and times - between equal (or almost equal) cars, most passing for position is still done under the brakes. One thing is very certain - if you can be outbraked, you will be. So learn!

<u>5</u>

"Side bite is fine - but you have to be going forward to win." *Danny Ongais*

THE CORNERING SEQUENCE

Any fool can drive a modern racing car as fast as it will go in a straight line. Most fools can be taught to brake or to accelerate (also in a straight line) at very near the limit of tire adhesion. This has little to do with the driving of the racing car.

The driving of the racing car is about two things - racing and cornering. Racing is a question of courage, of disciplined and controlled aggression and of judgement. The racing driver, like the fighter pilot, must be willing to take risks - but they must be calculated risks. While the courage and aggression are inborn, the judgement, control and calculation must be learned - largely through experience. The same is true of the sequence of events that we refer to as "cornering" - but, in this case, we can examine the physics and techniques involved as a basis for the learning experience.

To my way of thinking the physical cornering sequence begins when the driver starts to decelerate for the approaching corner - after all, when things are done correctly, the braking point determines the turn in point and, therefore, the turn in speed. The turn in point and speed determine virtually everything else.

However, since we have already covered braking in detail, for the purpose of this discussion we will consider the cornering sequence to start when the driver begins to reduce the braking pressure preparatory to turning the steering wheel for the first time. The mental sequence begins when he spots or picks up the braking reference point.

PHASES

The Gods of physics have arranged things so that most corners are made up of four distinct but interconnected sections or phases:

1) Phase One - initial turn in
2) Phase Two - from turn in to apex (or throttle on point)
3) Phase Three - neutral throttle period
4) Phase Four - corner exit

All drivers in some corners and some drivers in all corners skip Phase Three.

PHASE ONE

Phase One would appear to be pretty simple - you turn the wheel, right? Not exactly! I mentioned earlier that Jackie Stewart once said that the last thing a really good driver learns how to do well is to take his foot off the brake pedal properly. I think his actual meaning was two fold:

1) If you remove your foot from the center pedal suddenly, the nose of the car will come up, load will be transferred from the front tires onto the rear, and almost as suddenly. If you ask the car to turn as you are doing this, it won't. Watch the stars at some corner where they are not trail braking - the nose comes up gradually just as the car turns in. This is hard to see with current open wheeled cars but easy to see in Trans Am and the like. As a point of interest, the same thing happens when they are trail braking - it's just harder to see because the vertical displacement is less.

2) If you are trail braking, the maximum amount of braking that will allow the car to turn in at the speed you have chosen is a finely judged thing - and it had better be arrived at before the turn in point.

The other part of the equation has to do with corner speed and should be pretty obvious. In slow corners you turn the car in a very positive fashion. In very fast corners you do not - you sort of "wish" the car into the corner. No two drivers do this in exactly the same way.

Some great drivers, Mssrs. Prost, Senna and Mansell for instance, turn the car in, even at high speed, more positively than others. In every case, assuming that the driver isn't doing something to prevent it, the car should turn in willingly and positively. If it won't, you and your crew have some work to do.

PHASE TWO

Phase Two is, to my mind, the most critical and important part of the corner. For decades I have preached the over-riding importance of corner exit speed. What I have not preached in print (because I have not before written a driving book) is that corner exit speed is determined by the corner entrance.

Get ready for heresy. The most important part of any corner is the slowest part - from turn in to the point where making the chosen apex is a certainty. If the corner entrance is done properly - with the maximum speed carried through each portion, the minimum elapsed time and the optimum throttle on point - the exit speed is predetermined.

Watch Schumacher, Unser, Villeneuve, etc. closely on tape as compared to lesser mortals. The difference between the great drivers and the very good ones is how fast and how hard they can hustle or squirm the car down into the corner while retaining enough control to allow early throttle application. Mansell sometimes carried this to extremes, but (usually) got away with it.

PHASE THREE

Phase Three may seem strange to you. Many racers believe that the foot should be hard on either the brake or the throttle at all times. I do not - and not just because of trail braking. I believe that it is essential to have a neutral throttle or pure cornering phase in almost every corner. The period may be very short - as in a standard 90 degree boulevard corner on a street course - or it may be quite lengthy - as in very long 180 degree corners like the Carousel at Road America or the Keyhole at Mid-Ohio. Neutral throttle should not be confused with off throttle. I most emphatically do not believe in "coasting" - ever. By neutral throttle I mean enough throttle to maintain speed or to accelerate slightly. This period allows the driver to balance the car properly prior to hard acceleration. My reasons have to do with both carrying speed through the corner and accelerating out of it.

Let's use some simplistic numbers and graphics to illustrate the point. Referring to FIGURE 17, on the straight approaching the braking area, the car is accelerating at its maximum rate. Cornering force and braking force are at zero. When we reach the braking point, acceleration drops to zero and braking almost instantly reaches maximum. Cornering remains at zero.

Just before the turn-in point, the braking begins to diminish.(Remember, if all of the tires' tractive capacity is being used in braking, the car cannot turn.) At the turn-in point braking continues to diminish as cornering force builds.

At some point prior to the apex, braking is reduced to zero, enough throttle is added to maintain speed and cornering force reaches its maximum value. This period of "pure cornering" blends into the corner exit phase as the throttle is increased - cornering falls off as acceleration builds until the car is straight and under pure acceleration.

NAVIGATING THE RACE TRACK

Consciously or subconsciously, the racing driver navigates by the point to point system. The thinking ones choose the points consciously even if they will react to them subconsciously. Whether you realize it or not, you actually proceed around the race track from reference point to reference point in a sort of connect-the-dots exercise. Your reference points are landmarks that tell you both where you are on the track and where you want to go. The way that the human eye/brain/nerve/muscle system works is such that the car tends to go where the driver is looking. So you need to look where you want the car to go - the reference points are actually "aiming points".

Some of the reference points are obvious - braking points, turn in points, apex points, corner exit points, the place on the race track where you want to be when you crest the blind hill, and so forth. The points can be anything immovable; a discolored spot on the pavement, a clump of grass, a curb (preferably not a cone), a break in or a spot on the Armco, or what-have-you. What these landmarks do is remind you of where you are on the race track and what your next response should be.

"I have to get on the brakes at that point, so I had better get my foot programmed."

"I'm going to turn in at that clump of grass, so I had better start looking for my apex point."

"I need to stay to the left of that crack or I'm going to hit a big bump."

And so on. I don't mean that your mind should focus on these points - or that you should stare at them (that could lead to target fixation). Once you have learned the track, in a particular car, all of these reference points are resident in your personal RAM and you stop thinking about them - you just use them. Once the reference points have been established, your eye and your brain will almost automatically focus on the next point.

In fact, if we ask most drivers what they look at on the race track they are very liable to say something like; "I don't know, nothing in particular, I guess". If we can sit them down and make them visualize the track we will find that they use literally hundreds of visual reference points. They just don't think about it - it's almost a ballistic response.

I am not, by the way, suggesting that anyone drive geographically - far from it. The landmarks merely tell you where you are and where you want to go. To be really fast you must drive the footprints of your tires. For instance, you will normally detect changing levels of grip - either of your car or of the race track - in the braking areas. When you suspect that grip is deteriorating, brake a little early.

...continued

NAVIGATING THE RACE TRACK, cont.

When you brake too late you spend the first phases of the corner trying to regain control and you lose a lot of time - at best. When you brake a little early you lose very little time and you have time to analyze the situation.

MORE IS BETTER

Although the navigational exercise can be carried to non-productive extremes, in general the more reference points you identify, the better off you are going to be. If you have just a few, the scene unfolding in front of you will be nervous and jerky like the old movies - before they increased the number of frames per second - and so will your driving. With lots of landmarks the scene flows smoothly and so do you.

WHERE TO LOOK

We all know that you want to be looking where you want the car to go. But there is more to it than that. You need to look ahead - far ahead.

At anywhere near the limit of tire adhesion, you have very little influence over where the car is going to be in the next twenty feet - so you may as well be looking at something useful. If you focus on the road directly ahead of you it will rush at you at warp speed - too fast to recognize landmarks and too fast for your brain to process information - (try it as a passenger in a street car at speed). The further ahead you look, the slower you seem to be going and the more time your brain has to process information.

Of course, if you are looking too far ahead, you can loose the detail sense of where you are on the race track. Actually, where you should be looking is a function of road speed, the nature of that particular portion of the track, what the car is doing at the time and the traffic situation. On ovals you must be looking at least one turn ahead of yourself or you are eventually going to drive right into someone else's accident. We saw the results of that, big time, at the Phoenix CART race in the spring of 1994.

REFERENCE POINTS AND VISUALIZATION

The quickest way to determine if you are picking up and using enough valid reference points is to try visualizing the race track. If you cannot drive the track with your eyes closed - without hesitation and pretty darn close to your actual lap time - the chances are that you haven't picked up enough reference points. Your mental map is incomplete.

If your mental map of the circuit is incomplete, there is no way that you are approaching your potential performance on that race track. Remember, after a certain amount of skill and experience has been attained, 98% of this business is mental.

Continued...

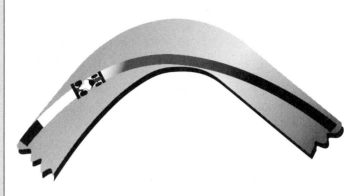

THE PHASES OF A CORNER
FIGURE 17

The transitions are smooth. Once again it is all a question of balance. Notice that the "line" on our diagram is not a constant curve, but opens on corner exit. This is, of course, just another way of looking at the Traction Circle.

The object here is to keep the platform stable as car and driver negotiate the corner. With ground effect cars the reason is obvious. Download is of overwhelming importance, so, in order to achieve maximum performance and linear response, we need a vehicle with a constant aerodynamic center of pressure location and a level of download dependent only upon road speed. Slamming from brakes to power and stabbing at the throttle upsets the pitch attitude of the car which, in turn, changes both the level of download and the location of the center of pressure - resulting in non linear response due to upsets in aerodynamics, roll axis inclination and load transfers.

With non ground effect cars, the results are similar, if less pronounced. Smooth transitions produce smooth changes in dynamic load transfer and vertical load on the individual tires. Abrupt transitions produce abrupt changes in load transfer and vertical load. Abrupt changes in vertical load produce sudden changes in tire camber and footprint size, shape and pressure pattern - all of which upset the tractive capacity of the individual tires.

Throwing the car around never was a very good idea. Watch the videos of the likes of Clark, Fangio, Gurney and Moss - they were just as smooth as anyone today. Jackie Stewart has said that the driver should never feel the end of a corner - the transition from cornering to acceleration should be so smooth as to be imperceptible. Of course, none of the above denies the necessity, validity and usefulness of "rough" techniques when they are required to modify the behavior of a recalcitrant race car.

NAVIGATING THE RACE TRACK, cont.

LAST WORDS

I'm not going any deeper into this subject simply because it has already been covered as well as I think that it can be - by Keith Code in his outstanding book, "A Twist of the Wrist". The Appendix tells more about this landmark effort. Find it, buy it, read it and learn from it.

PHASE FOUR

Phase Four, the corner exit, is where the payoff lives. The indescribable feeling of driving out of a corner under full power with the car drifting right up to the wall just barely under control is the reward for having done Phases One, Two and Three correctly.

This is when you have done it all just right and the car carries you out to the wall under full song. It is a different thing altogether to fake it by driving the car out to the wall after you are sure that you aren't going to need that last foot of race track at the exit.

The object here, of course, is to be going just as fast (or faster) than the other guy and still get the power down - and keep it down - earlier than he can. It's like red lighting at the drag strip and getting away with it.

All other things being equal, he who gets the power down first will get to the next corner first. It really is that simple - in concept. Of course, the reality of carrying as much speed into the corner and through Phases Two and Three as the other guy did and getting the chassis and the driver tuned to the point where it all happens is a bit more difficult than the concept.

LINE

As I promised in the Introduction, there isn't going to be much talk about lines through the various types of corner in this book. The best treatment of lines that I have seen in print is contained in Alain Prost's 'Competition Driving' with Pierre-Francois Rousselot. Me, I go along with Mr. Lauda. If the combination of God, your intelligence, the race track, the race car and the competition do not tell you the proper line for the situation and conditions, there is no way that I can, and you had best give serious thought to another type of endeavor.

I have never understood why drivers ask each other about the line through a given corner. Each of them is driving at least a slightly different car; each has at least a slightly different driving technique and each of them should damned well be capable of figuring out the line for himself. The same is true of gears, wing settings, etc...

However, I will mention that each and every corner in the whole world has not one but several optimum lines - under different circumstances. Quite obviously there is the fast line (which may well leave the door open for your opponents to come down the inside), the passing line and the blocking line. Less obvious (until you think about them) are the off-camber line, the crowned road (as in street courses) line, the banked corner line, the rain line, the "front/rear tires or brakes are going away and need to be nursed" lines and the "this damned race track is breaking up (or getting slick and greasy)" lines. The optimum line through any given corner is a matter of circumstance, corner configuration, track, car and tire conditions.

THE FUNDAMENTAL TRUTHS

By now you are beginning to understand that, when I stated that I wasn't going to talk much about lines through corners, I lied. Throughout the rest of the book there will be talk about lines - spotted in with other topics in a non-random fashion. There are, however, a few fundamental truths about line that might take a long time to learn by yourself - it surely took me a long time to learn the second of them.

FUNDAMENTAL TRUTH # 1 - THE LATE APEX

Every thinking racer knows that the ideal apex point for virtually every corner of constant or decreasing radius lies somewhere past the geometric apex. There are two reasons:

1) A late apex (FIGURE 18) allows you to increase the exit radius which, in turn, lets you put the power down geographically early in the corner. This increases corner exit speed which is a good thing.

2) A late apex gives you a bigger insurance policy at the corner exit. This is also a good thing, especially when you are learning the race track, driving on unfamiliar or public roads (as in rallying or off road racing) or when the car is less than predictable.

There are, however, downsides to this late apex bit:

1) The car must cover a slightly greater linear distance (FIGURE 19).

2) The turn in must be more abrupt (FIGURE 19) and the radius of curvature from turn in to apex (Phase Two) will be less.

3) Because of (2) you will be slower in Phase Two and cannot carry as much speed through the corner.

4) The wide entry leaves the door open, making late apexes dodgy at best when you are trying to hold an aggressive opponent at bay.

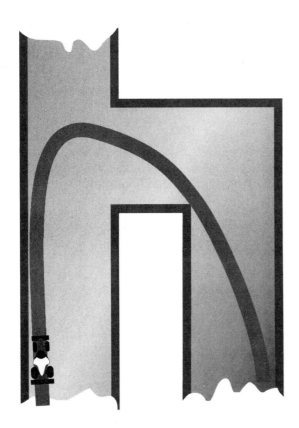

FIGURE 18

THE LATE APEX

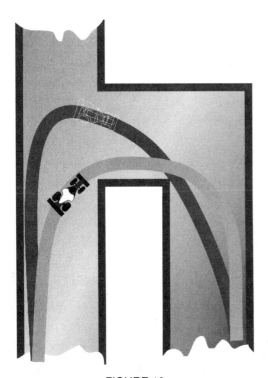

FIGURE 19

IMPLICATIONS OF A LATE APEX

5) In FIGURE 19, it looks as if late apexes allow later braking. Unfortunately this is largely a misconception. While the car is travelling in a straight line for a longer time, the slower Phase Two of the corner dictates that the braking points will be pretty much the same.

This is fine at hairpins and slow corners. By opening the exit radius, a late apex in effect converts the exit phase of the slow corner into a faster corner. Getting the power down early takes precedence over both the increase of distance travelled and the necessarily slower Phases One and Two. The abrupt turn in, done cleverly, may even rotate the car and kill the inevitable slow corner entry understeer (although you don't often see the big boys doing it that way). However, the technique, while spectacular, is not a good one for fast corners. It is time to look at root causes.

FUNDAMENTAL TRUTH # 2
THE FASTER THE CORNER THE EARLIER THE APEX

The gospel according to Smith has always taught that all that we road and circle track racers really do is drag race between corners and that getting the throttle down early - and keeping it down without wheelspin or sideways motoring - is the key to lap time. This is absolutely true and always will be - but there is a sliding scale of paybacks involved. The benefits of getting the power down early are in direct proportion to the accelerative capacity of the car at the road speed involved.

Driving an Indy Lights car at 25mph through the Queen's Hairpin at Long Beach, or a Formula One car through the Lowes Hairpin at Monaco, you have a lot more torque available than you have tire to hold it. The car is wheelspin limited, and you had damned well better open up the radius at the exit of the corner so that you can release the car early. Because of the rate of acceleration from very low speed, the extra few feet that you cover and the upsetting effect of the abrupt turn in just don't matter when compared to the advantage of getting the power down early.

The kink at Road America, or any corner at Indianapolis Motor Speedway presents an entirely different set of circumstances. The road speed is high, the available torque is low, the download induced grip is high and the accelerative capacity of the car is limited at best.

Where we could accelerate out of the hairpin at 1.0-g plus, we can now accelerate at 0.25-g. The car is traction limited and every mile per hour of entry and apex speed that we sacrifice will take forever to get back. Every foot of extra distance that we travel will be lost forever. Finally, the last thing that we want to do is to upset the car (which is on tip toe to begin with) with an abrupt turn in - not because of the risk of losing control

A FAST CORNER LINE

FIGURE 20A

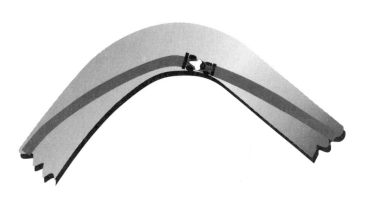

TURNING AT THE APEX

FIGURE 20B

but because it will inevitably cost us speed. As a point of interest, the same is true of trail braking in very fast corners

So, in slow corners we take a late apex in order to open out the corner exit radius and improve our linear acceleration because we can accelerate hard enough to win the trade off between carrying speed through the corner, lower apex speed, greater distance travelled and accelerative capacity. We sand our buns and our finger tips and finesse the fast corners with relatively early apexes (FIGURE 20A). Carrying the speed through the corner will pay a higher dividend than putting the power down earlier simply because we don't have any excess power to put down.

There is another side to this question of line. The optimum line through low and medium speed corners is also a function of what your car does best. If your car brakes and accelerates better than it corners, it may well pay you to brake hard right down to the apex, rotate the car abruptly and accelerate hard rather than carrying

more speed through the corner. FIGURE 20B illustrates. Mansell did this, a lot - especially when passing. So does Michael Andretti. When they do it right it is beautiful. When they do it wrong in traffic, they often hit someone. It is a valid if unforgiving technique.

These are not simple equations. The ideal line (and technique) varies with power to weight ratio, torque characteristics, tire capacity, download and track conditions. If you understand the basics involved, the car and the race track will teach you the details. Keep your brain functioning and your receptors open.

FUNDAMENTAL TRUTH # 3
YOU MUST RELEASE THE CAR

On corner exit, you must release the car in order to accelerate. In any corner, if after your chosen apex you are consistently doing anything with the steering wheel other than unwinding lock, you have done something wrong. Obviously this does not apply to corrective steering measures. Perhaps the most common cornering error is "choking" the corner exit - usually as a result of turning in too early (FIGURE 21).

After the apex (or sometimes before it) the object of the exercise is to "release" the car so that it can accelerate freely. Adding steering lock - or even retaining the required amount of lock prior to the apex - will inevitably lead to understeer tire drag and reduced acceleration. Of course, it may also save your life. This is the sort of thing that we expect to see with inexperienced drivers and with middle-aged businessmen. I am continuously amazed to see it with experienced drivers with reasonable reputations. You don't see it with the legitimate stars - or super stars.

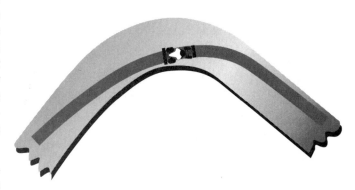

CHOKING THE CORNER EXIT

FIGURE 21

FUNDAMENTAL TRUTH # 4
SOME CORNER ENTRY UNDERSTEER IS A NECESSITY

In order to be able to accelerate in Phase Four while still cornering, in Phases Two and Three the car must have reserve rear tire capacity. This means that every fast car will have a certain amount of Phase One, Two and Three understeer.

Think about it. If you are using up all the available traction of all four tires in the generation of cornering force, there is nothing left to accelerate with - applying power will produce instant oversteer. Rearward load transfer and opening the line to release the car will help some, but in the case of powerful cars and slow-to-medium speed corners, not enough. There are ways to reduce the understeer - see the section on trail braking, for example.

Tape the Formula One and Indy Cars on TV and watch the leading cars closely in slow motion. All of the fast cars exhibit Phase Two and Three understeer - and they put the power down out of slow and medium speed corners unbelievably well (and smoothly). The day of fast visible oversteer on paved race tracks, if it was ever really here, is gone. Corner exit oversteer thrills the spectators and makes the inexperienced (or ignorant) driver feel heroically fast. In some ways it's a pity that it isn't the fast way around the race track.

Of course, on the other hand we can carry this early power application too far. If you put the power down too early and too hard one of two things will happen. If you have lots of excess available torque, the back end will jump into oversteer. If you do not have much torque, you will cause power-on understeer. In either case you will have to come off the throttle. It would have been a lot better to wait!

THE LIMIT

In the early stages of one's career it may seem that the limits of tire adhesion are pretty easy to detect - the understeer limit is reached when the front loses traction and heads for the fence and the oversteer limit is reached when the rear escapes your grasp and only your superhuman skill prevents the car from spinning. Too simple by half!

What the inexperienced driver often describes as terminal corner entry understeer is often driver induced simply by trying to turn the car when it is going too fast, with the brakes on too hard (or with excessive front brake bias) - or even by turning the steering wheel too abruptly. Conversely, what is often described as power on oversteer is often caused by the apprentice hero driver attempting to overcome severe entry understeer by hurling the car at the corner and stabbing the throttle too hard.

Self analysis is the key here - as is an experienced independent eye watching the antics on the race track and/or analyzing overlays of steering angle, lateral g., engine rpm and road speed from the data logger.

One of the signs that alerts the experienced race engineer to the progress of a young driver is that, one day, said driver will come in moaning about understeer as usual but with a new twist:, "This is different, winding more steering lock on doesn't help - it just keeps pushing". What the driver is actually reporting is that he (or she) has finally found the understeer limit of adhesion rather than the limit of his own driving ability. We are seldom able to convince the apprentice hero of this, but that is beside the point - the learning curve has steepened and progress is being made.

6

"Mr. Gleason wrote the book on gears in the 1920s
All we've learned since is metallurgy." – Mike Hewland.

SHIFTING GEARS, USING THE GEARBOX AND GEARING

There are two separate discussions here - the physical shifting of gears so as to neither waste time nor hurt the gearbox and the selection of the most efficient gears for any given circuit. We will attack the physical end of things first.

SHIFTING AS AN ART

Most people now learn to drive in cars with automatic transmissions. Therefore most beginning racers don't know how to shift - even badly. So, if you want to be a racing driver, drive a manual shift car on the street and learn how to shift - properly. It's not difficult - although, to efficiently downshift a street car while braking, you will probably have to re-organize the pedals somewhat. It's real easy to tell if you are doing it right. A good shift (either up or down) should be heard but not felt. It should also be fast - very fast.

Many racers (including those who do it well) do not believe that there is an art to shifting gears - "Just move the stick". I disagree. I have known World Champions who were very hard on gearboxes - one in particular required a whole new set of dog rings every session. I have known other, equally accomplished, and equally successful drivers - who shifted gears with equal speed - and whose dog rings were replaced because they were cracked, not worn out. Believe me, there is an art to shifting.

Unfortunately, having said that, I'll be damned if I can describe the art of the shift. One definition of the term "art" is something that we do not understand - and maybe that is valid here. I am absolutely certain that the "power shift" so beloved of teenagers and drag racers is not the answer in road racing.

Yes, the power shift does use the kinetic energy of the rotating engine, flywheel and clutch masses to give a boost to the car's acceleration on each shift. And, yes,

some of the automatic transmissions in Formula One probably did that very thing (or were about to when they were, thankfully, banned).

For those of us in less exalted spheres of racing, the damage done to shift linkage, gears, dogs, synchros, driveshafts, etc that were not designed for this kind of punishment more than counterbalances the gain in acceleration. There is a time for this sort of thing - the Thursday night "grudge races" at your local drag strip (or even the dash from the last corner to the finish line).

I am equally certain that the elegantly precise upshift during which the driver waits for the engine revs to drop far enough for a perfectly synchronized shift is not the answer. Perish the thought - even though the popular belief that time in neutral is somehow added to the time required to accelerate through the gears is mistaken.

First of all, with the racing car, the time in neutral is almost infinitesimal. What we are actually talking about here is the time when you are not at full throttle. Secondly, the car doesn't stop during a shift, it merely doesn't accelerate during the time between gears. So, if it takes 5.2 seconds to accelerate from 50mph to 120mph with two shifts at 0.4 seconds each, reducing the shift time to 0.2 seconds each will not result in a 4.8 second ET - or anything like it.

The difference will, however, be measurable. It is also calculable, given a whole bunch of factors, but, like a lot of things in racing, the calculation isn't worth the effort. It is enough to know that the faster you shift, the better your acceleration will be.

Every current manual gearbox that I know of is a "constant mesh box" - that is, all of the gears on both shafts are spinning whenever the clutch is engaged (although only one pair of gears is engaged). Every current manual box uses some sort of face gears for engagement - synchros in a street box and face dogs on almost all racing gearboxes (except for Porsche, who no longer manufactures racing cars). It dawns upon me that many drivers do not understand the workings of the gearbox. If you are one that does, you have my permission to skip the accompanying sidebar. If you do not, read it.

THE ACT OF THE SHIFT

Any mechanical shift is actually a play in three separate acts:

1) Disengagement of the current gear.

2) A period in neutral.

3) Engagement of the next gear.

Many drivers (and engineers, for that matter) don't consider the second phase - neutral - to be a distinct event. It is, otherwise the box would be in two gears at once - with the attendant mechanical catastrophe.

There is a widely held opinion that in the "perfect upshift", the engine slows down enough in neutral so that engine revs and gear revs are matched when the next gear is engaged. This would indeed be smooth and elegant. It would also be slow.

With the typical racing car, the gear splits on a five useable speed box will be from 800 to 1500 rpm. Typical "fast" manual racing upshift elapsed time is 0.2 seconds. Racing engines decelerate pretty quickly off throttle - but not that quickly. Fortunately, complete synchronization is not necessary - all that is needed is for the opposing dogs to fall into their "windows" and engage without damaging each other.

Since the actual rotational rpm of the dog ring and the gear to be engaged will seldom be more than a few hundred rpm apart and the "windows" are reasonably wide, the driver who develops the knack of shifting properly can shift about as fast as he can move his hand - without wearing the dogs very much. So, in reality, on every racing shift (or even every reasonably fast street shift) the engine will be going somewhat faster than the rear wheels when the gear is engaged - sort of a partial "power shift".

The exercise is confirmed (and assisted) by the fact that you don't come completely out of the throttle - you just let up a bit while you move the stick. Because you are not achieving complete synchronization, you have to be real positive (as opposed to brutal) with your movements.

Part of the art of shifting lies in timing and in rhythm - about which more later. Another part of the art lies in using the wrist rather than the arm to shift with. The throw of the racing gear lever is very short. If things are set up properly the effort involved in shifting is not

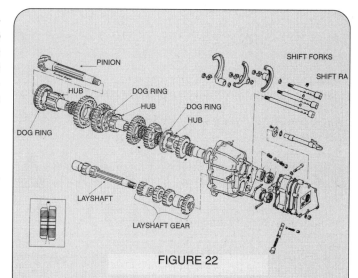

FIGURE 22

GEARBOX TECHNICALS

FIGURE 22 is an exploded view of a Hewland FT200 transaxle - a standard, every day, two shaft face dog box. Engine torque is transmitted through the clutch to the input shaft which is splined into the ID of the constant motion shaft (often termed the "layshaft"). One half of each change gear set is splined directly onto the constant motion shaft. Any time that the clutch is engaged, the constant motion shaft, and all of its gears, will spin at engine rpm.

This is a "constant mesh" gearbox. The matching gears on the pinion shaft are constantly in mesh with their opposite numbers on the layshaft, so they must also spin - at the rpm corresponding to the ratio involved. So all of the gears in the transaxle are spinning whenever the clutch is engaged.

The gears on the pinion shaft are bearing-mounted on "hubs" which are in turn ID-splined onto the pinion shaft. The pinion shaft gears, therefore, spin freely (but at speeds determined by engine rpm and individual gear ratio) on their hubs - and no torque is transmitted to the pinion shaft until one of the gears is "engaged" by the shifter.

Each pinion shaft gear is equipped with a series of undercut face dogs (at least road racing boxes are undercut). Between each pair of gears a corresponding "dog ring" is splined onto the OD of the hub on which the gear spins. The dog rings are located radially and axially by "shift forks" which can be moved by the shift rails and linkage.

When a shift fork moves a dog ring into engagement with a pinion shaft gear, the matching dogs engage and the pinion shaft gear is effectively splined to the pinion shaft by the dog ring and the hub. Torque is then transmitted from the constant motion shaft gear through the pinion shaft gear, the dog ring and the hub to the pinion shaft and the pinion gear.

Continued..

FIGURE 23 (see main text) shows the gearbox with gears engaged and in neutral. The pinion gear drives the ring gear which in turn drives the axles and, therefore, the wheels and tires. The overall gear ratio is determined by the ratios between constant motion and pinion shaft gears and the ratio between the pinion and the ring gear. All manual racing gearboxes, including the transverse and three-shaft units, function in the same way - only the layouts are different.

When a dog is engaged with a gear, the matching dogs do not completely fill the annular space available to them. The clearance is called the "window". The larger the window, the easier it is to engage the gear when the revs are not matched. The downside is that the larger the window, the more room there is for the dogs to accelerate before they come into contact and the greater the force of impact. Large windows and small dogs lead to sheared dogs and disaster. Large dogs and small windows are difficult to engage. As always, compromise is the name of the game.

great. The racing car should be shifted with a very precise, very positive, very controlled and very fast flick of the wrist.

With a face dog box, it is not easy to engage first gear with the car at rest. Some drivers can feel the engagement windows on the dogs and snick into first without a sound - and some cannot. Over the years I have also noticed that the drivers who manage to get the car into first gear in the

pits without any graunching are almost invariably the same drivers who don't hurt their gearboxes on the track.

By the way, it helps a lot to double pump the clutch when engaging first gear at rest. It helps even more to have someone give the car a push as you engage it. As one of my better drivers says, "Not graunching first is money in the bank". The bottom line of all this is that I simply do not know why some drivers can consistently shift without hurting the box and others cannot. Perhaps therein lies the art.

Pete Weismann, whom I consider to be the finest racing gearbox designer of all time - and who has worked with more outstanding drivers than anyone on earth - says that after more than 30 years in the racing gearbox business, he is convinced that the ability to shift properly is dependent on the person's innate sense of rhythm and that it is inborn - you either have it or you do not.

Pete goes a little further and says that good shifters are good dancers. I think that I go along with this one - although I also believe that anyone who is not a complete clutz can learn to shift adequately (I don't dance).

Ayrton Senna, whom I consider to have been the finest racing driver of his time, once said that when the gearbox and shifting mechanism is perfect, then shifting is "unconcentrational", i.e. he didn't have to think about it. When it was not perfect, he could deal with it, but shifting became "concentrational" - he had to think about it - and it slowed him down because part of his concentration was on shifting rather than on his next reference point, or the tactical situation, or whatever. This gets into the "ballistic" response of trained nerves and muscles in which the brain is out of the loop - more on this later.

The short life of the mechanical automatic gearbox in Formula One taught certain people a lot about the art of shifting. Patrick Head, certainly one of the finest engineers presently designing racing cars, has probably learned more that anyone else about shifting gears. He is said to feel that the force involved in shifting should not be a constant, but should be modulated during the shift either by the driver or by the software i.e. that a force vs distance plot would look like (FIGURE 23).

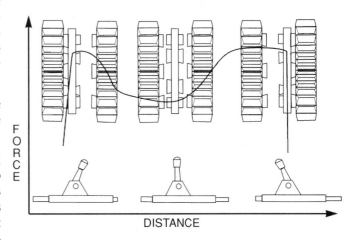

FIGURE 23

The idea is that the most force is required to disengage the gear against the dovetail of the engagement dogs. (Snatching the box out of gear just as the throttle is reduced and the dog ring is between the power on and power off sides of the engaged gear for a nanosecond or so is the ideal.) It can be consistently achieved. After the dogs are disengaged, the force should be reduced - the box will go into the next gear almost by itself. Continuing the disengagement force is not only not necessary, it will eventually either bend a shift fork or break something.

One thing is certain - the human brain/body combination is a wonderous device about which we understand very little. The accomplished racing driver shifts gears a lot faster than he can think about it. Along the way he modulates the forces involved - without realizing it. He also (usually, at least) feels when the thing either isn't going to go into gear or is going to go into the wrong gear and hesitates the shift. None of them can tell you how they do this - or, for that matter, how they sense and do a lot of things that we don't understand.

THE DOWNSHIFT

One of the very first things taught at any high performance driving school is the "heel and toe" technique of downshifting. Why it is still called heel and toe is beyond me - the term is left over from the days when the brake pedal was on the right hand side and the throttle was in the middle (even before my time). For the past thirty five years or so everyone has simply moved the shift lever into neutral while dipping the clutch, pivoted his ankle so as to "blip" the throttle with the side of the right foot while (hopefully) maintaining optimum brake modulation. While blipping, one moves the lever into the slot for the next lower gear and simultaneously releases the clutch.

That's all there is to it. While the downshift, like the upshift, should be heard but not felt, the technique is not difficult to master and is a source of great satisfaction to the purists among us. I should point out that the downshift situation is different from the upshift situation in that there is time to properly synch the engine revs. Further, there is a necessity to do so.

When you miss an upshift by a little bit, the dogs grind and you go into gear. When you miss it by a bunch, the box refuses to go into gear, you hurt the dogs a lot and you lose time. When you fail to synch the revs for a downshift, and it goes into gear, the rear tires will either drag or momentarily accelerate. If you really screw up a downshift the box won't go into gear and you approach the corner in neutral while frantically searching for the gear.

By definition, when you downshift a racing car, you are braking - usually hard. When you snatch the rear tires while braking hard, the car snaps into oversteer. This is not what you want in a braking area - especially while trail braking. Therefore you must blip the throttle for every downshift while the box is in neutral. Until you learn to downshift properly and consistently, there is no way that you can use your brakes to their maximum potential. So learn. You can learn on a street car.

The purpose of the engine is to accelerate the car. The purpose of the brakes is to decelerate the car. The purpose of downshifting is to select the proper gear for the forthcoming corner, and, sometimes, to stabilize the car - not to slow the car. The sequence of downshifting is brake and then downshift. If you are near maximum engine revs on a straight and downshift, you will over-rev the engine. No rev limiter can save you - the tires will drag the engine up to the rpm corresponding to the road speed in the gear you have just selected and that is that.

There are well known (and highly paid) drivers who habitually downshift before or simultaneously with braking as a matter of course. We call this act "the rod stretcher". FIGURE 24 is a slightly disguised (to protect the guilty) actual instrumentation plot of a well known driver's sins. These guys blow up a lot of engines. Their sins have always been audible to those of us who wander around the track. The advent of on board data recording has made their sins visible to those who remain in the pits.

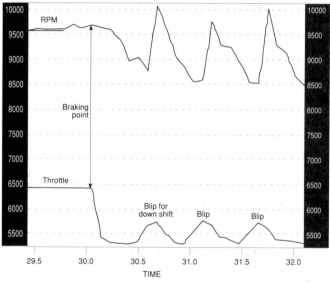

This driver has carefully kept RPM to the 9600 rev limit at the end of the fastest straight. But he exceeded 10,000 RPM on two of his down shifts.

FIGURE 24

At first I thought this exposure was a pity from my own selfish point of view. Not to worry, the guilty ones cannot be cured and they continue to blow up engines. There are times, many times, when you will want to use "engine braking" in the entry phase of certain corners. Depending upon the car's balance and the situation, engine braking can either slightly stabilize the rear of the car or slightly reduce understeer. This is fine - but make damned sure that you have slowed the car enough before you downshift. Because downshifting is intimately connected with braking, there was a discussion about downshifting in Chapter Four.

CLUTCH, DOUBLE CLUTCH AND NO CLUTCH

My first driving on public roads was in horse vans. This may or not have been good for the horses. It was very good for me. It taught me about lines, about looking and planning ahead and about smoothness (you do not even want to think about trying to explain why a very expensive show horse fell down in the van - especially not when you are 14 years old and don't have a license).

Trucks in those days did not have synchromesh. I also learned how to shift smooth and fast - with and without the clutch. Using the clutch required "double clutching". For an upshift you depressed the clutch, moved the shift lever into neutral, let the clutch out to allow the shaft speeds to match, depressed it again and moved the lever into the next gear. This sounds very slow. It is not. You had to be quick about it or the thing would slow down too much to accelerate in the next gear.

Downshifting was the same, but you blipped the engine before declutching the second time. Since a lot of effort was required to depress the clutch (and since we liked to show off), we often didn't use it, but waited for the revs to drop for the upshift, and just synched the downshifts.

Many authors (or maybe translators) who should know better recommend double clutching in the racing car - I'll be damned if I know why. I do not know of one racing driver who double clutches - either up or down. Some of the older vintage cars require it, but that's not what we are talking about here.

The technique of shifting a racing gearbox with the clutch is simple - for the upshift, you simultaneously back part way out of the throttle and depress the clutch. As you back off (as, not after, because you should catch it just as the driving torque comes off), move the shift lever smartly and positively into the slot for the next gear. The motion should be positive, precise and very fast - but not brutal. As (not after) you are moving the lever to the next gear, release the clutch - smartly - and simultaneously come back onto full throttle - also smartly.

The downshift procedure is similar. You are braking, so you are already off the throttle. While depressing the clutch, move the lever into neutral. As the box comes out of gear, blip the throttle enough to synch the revs (this is a feel sort of thing - don't even think about looking at the tach). At the same time move the lever into the appropriate slot and release the clutch.

In each case, really fast hand and foot movements are essential and timing is everything. There is no way to learn it except by practice. A driving instructor/racing school is not necessary. In fact, if you have taught yourself to shift properly before you go to school, the instructors will be able to devote that time to helping you with other areas and you will get more for your money.

NO CLUTCH

After you get good at shifting the non-synchro racing car you may notice that you are not depressing the clutch all the way. The truth of the matter is that most racing drivers don't - they just sort of jab at it with the left foot. It is therefore a relatively small step for the "skilled" driver to stop using the clutch at all. This allows left foot braking under all conditions. As I point out elsewhere, there are some significant advantages to left foot braking.

The way to learn clutchless shifting is to start with downshifts. Move the lever to neutral, blip the throttle a little too much and hold slight pressure against the lever - just enough so you can barely feel the dogs snicking against each other. As the engine revs drop into approximate synch, the gear will virtually engage itself. The same is true for the upshift - but without the blip. As the revs drop, the dogs will engage and pull the box into gear. Once you have mastered the downshift technique, start working on the upshifts and speeding up the shifts. You have to be real precise and real positive about things. The technique takes some learning and a lot of drivers never do learn it - of course, some drivers never learn to shift with the clutch. Clutchless shifting is a skill that every serious driver should learn - eventually you will lose clutch actuation during a race.

The question of clutch use is a matter of personal preference and confidence. My opinion is that if the driver is skilled enough and confident enough to learn how to do it well, he (or she) will have a performance advantage - at least in short races. The downside has to do with reliability - the clutch slips a minute amount on each engagement and softens the gear engagement procedure - acting as a sort of shock absorber for the whole drive train.

I do not recommend the clutchless technique in endurance races or in cars with synchromesh gearboxes. As a point of interest, to the best of my knowledge all the "automatic manual gearboxes" in Formula One were programmed to use the clutch for every shift (the program did it, the driver didn't). As a further point of interest, many of the engineers involved claim that the biggest single advantage of these gearboxes is that the driver keeps both hands on the wheel...

You can shift any street car without the clutch - except those units which feature "baulk ring" synchromesh. The process is a lot slower with synchromesh than with dog boxes, but the concept is the same. Because of the slowness, practicing clutchless shifting on street cars is a pretty useless exercise. You should, however, learn how to do it because sooner or later you will be racing a production derived car and lose clutch actuation.

THE SPEED OF THE SHIFT

Really fast upshifts, no matter how good the technique, hurt the engagement dogs. The faster you shift, the more you will wear the dogs and the greater your chance of missing a shift. There is an obvious trade off here.

When you are attacking, or defending hard, you must shift as quickly as you can. When you are in control of the situation, or waiting to attack or to defend - or engaged in an endurance race - it is time to treat the box with a little more kindness and consideration. With a face dog box, however, shifting too slow is just as bad as shifting too fast - maybe worse. The idea is to drop the dogs into their windows right now - not to allow them to ratchet against each other.

THE PENALTY BOX

There are three possible penalties for abusing the gearbox. The first is mechanical failure and retirement from the race. The second is the financial cost of replacing prematurely worn dog rings and gears. The third, and most benign, is being forced to hold the car in gear with your hand for a while because you have rounded off the dog rings. This is no fun at all and has a notable effect on lap time. So learn how to shift!

HELP

There are any number of "tricks" that the crew can perform to help the driver in his shifting. Anything that reduces the rotational inertia of the engine and drive train will also make shifting both easier and faster. But the first and foremost aid to good shifting is the correct assembly of the gearbox and shift linkage. I covered that in 'Prepare to Win' and 'Tune to Win' and nothing has changed.

It still takes a day to make a racing unit out of what you buy. Any slop anywhere in the linkage translates instantly into inconsistent shifting. Years ago when a driver had trouble shifting, we used to grind about 0.010" off the face of every other dog. We called it "help for the hamfisted". Hewland and X-Trac now offer "quick shift" dog rings with a lead-in bevel (see FIGURE 25). They help. Insist on them - and on proper preparation.

STANDARD   QUICK SHIFT

FIGURE 25

GEARING THE CAR

The second part of our discussion has to do with the selection of the optimum gears for the individual circuit. Because the internal combustion engine develops significant torque over a relatively narrow range of engine speed, all automobiles require some sort of multi-speed transmission. In the interest of maximizing power, racing cars feature relatively "peaky" engines and use five, six or seven speed gearboxes. We have literally dozens of alternate ratios to help us to efficiently "split the torque" and tailor the gearing requirements to specific circuits, engines, chassis and drivers.

The selection of optimum gear ratios is important, not only in terms of lap time but also in terms of driveability. There is no mystery involved and the selection is not particularly difficult. I am not going very far into gearing theory here - partly because it has been covered well by Paul Van Valkenburgh in his 'Race Car Engineering and Mechanics' and partly because you don't need to know very much about it.

The basic rules are very simple:

1) Determine and use the optimum rpm in top gear, the optimum maximum rpm in the intermediate gears and the optimum shift point.

2) Top gear is selected for the straight(s). The intermediate gears are selected for the corners and for most efficient acceleration.

3) It is better to have too few rpm at a corner apex than too many.

4) Always split the torque as many ways as practical - use the maximum practical number of gears on any given road racing circuit.

TOP GEAR

There is a theory which says that the car should be geared so that, at the end of the longest straight, it should just reach the rpm at which the engine develops its maximum power on the dyno. To my mind this theory is a bit simplistic.

In the first place, virtually every racing car utilizes some sort of "ram air" or "cold air" (or both) plenum chamber. These devices, properly designed, typically move the max power point a couple of hundred rpm up the curve from what we saw on the dyno. For most of us, this sort of thing is almost impossible to measure. The result can be estimated with the help of a manometer and a remote reading thermometer - and your engine builder.

Of more interest is the nature of the power curve. Most racing engines, no matter how "peaky" they may be, carry a lot of power past the peak. What we are interested in when we gear the car is the area under the curve in the operating range of the engine.

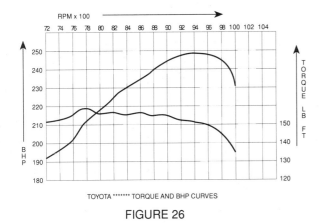

RPM x 100

TOYOTA ••••••• TORQUE AND BHP CURVES

FIGURE 26

To illustrate the idea, lets look at FIGURE 26, a typical dyno sheet for a competitive 1992 Toyota Formula Atlantic engine. Remember that we are, as always, looking for two things from our engine - minimum elapsed time and acceptable reliability.

Maximum corrected horsepower is 248.2bhp at 9200rpm. Assuming a 1000rpm drop from fourth to fifth, we will calculate the "area under the horsepower curve" for various maximum rpm in top gear. Shifting at peak horsepower and dropping 1000rpm we see (in top gear):

8200	225.1
8400	233.7
8600	236.8
8800	242.3
9000	244.2
9200	248.2

1428.2 total horsepower

Raising the max rpm to 9400 produces:

8400	233.7
8600	236.7
8800	242.3
9000	244.2
9200	248.2
9400	247.0

1452.2 total HP - a 1.7% improvement

9600 rpm results in:

8600	243.8
8800	242.3
9000	244.2
9200	248.2
9400	247.0
9600	243.8

1462.3 total HP - a 0.7% further improvement

Continuing the exercise to 9800 gives us:

8800	242.3
9000	244.2
9200	248.2
9400	247.0
9600	243.8
9800	223.0

1455.0 total HP - and a performance decrease

By carrying the rpm in top gear beyond the max power point, we pick up a significant amount of total power. There probably won't be any difference in top speed, but the difference in E.T. in top gear will be measurable. The downside is reduced reliability and loss of the ability to take advantage of a tow.

I tend to be pretty conservative in this department, usually opting to go about 200rpm over what I think is the installed max power point - but only with the co-operation and agreement of the engine builder.

THE SHIFT POINT

Exactly the same parameters apply to the selection of the optimum rpm at which we should shift gears. This points to a couple of basic truths:

1) For maximum performance you always have to shift past the peak of the horsepower curve.

2) Depending on the shape of the curve and the gear splits, you don't have to go very far over the peak.

3) There is a point after which more rpm equates to less performance, not more.

Some people who should know better - including various engine builders - seem not to understand the third point. There have been many cases where competent and knowledgeable engine builders recommended shift points that produced noise and wear, not performance. An experienced and sensitive driver should be able to feel the point at which acceleration begins to drop off.

So, we have established that the shift point is crucial - and that, while it is easy to determine the theoretical optimum, theory may be different from practice. So, how do we find out where the actual optimum is - with the engine installed in the car?

Finding the optimum shift point is a lot easier than finding the optimum rpm in top gear. This is fortunate as the optimum shift point is a lot more important on a road course than optimum top gear rpm. The hard way involves manometers, recording thermometers, slip rings on the driveshafts, etc. The easy way involves a stopwatch and a long straight.

Attach the stopwatch to your steering wheel (in a sedan you can just hang it around your neck). Approach a mark at the beginning of the straight at a given and repeatable speed in second gear, start the watch at the mark, accelerate through the gears using a constant shift point and stop the watch at a mark near the end of the straight - but before your braking point.

Start by using your engine builder's recommended shift point. Make a couple of runs - you should repeat to 0.10 second or so (if you don't, you are doing something wrong). Then try it using 300 rpm less. You may be surprised - especially with a showroom stock or production based car. Even with a pure racing car, you may be surprised. If the safe rpm limit is higher than the recommended shift point, try using more rpm rather than less.

The exercise doesn't take long and it need not interfere with practice time - you can do the comparison either during a test day or during practice for a race. Do not, however, try to compare shift points by reading rpm at the end of the straight - you are measuring elapsed time, not trap speed. I will have more to say on this subject later.

What you will learn from this little exercise, in addition to the optimum shift point, is how much it will cost you in lap time to back your shift points down a bit in order to conserve your engine when the situation permits. Those of you with a passion for calculation will doubtless figure out that, theoretically at least, the optimum shift point depends upon the gear split. Very true, but the difference is minimal and I, for one, am not about to tell my drivers to use different shift points for different shifts. And, yes, you could (and they did) program an automatic to do it.

GEARING FOR ACCELERATION

Because aerodynamic drag increases as the square of road speed, we have to gear our automobiles, street and race, so that the engine rpm drops will be less between the higher gears than between the lower gears. It is one thing to be a little short on available torque shifting from first to second at 70 miles per hour and quite another to be off the cam when shifting from fourth to fifth at 130mph. We can live with the first situation, but not with the second.

Given some basic information, it is pretty easy to gear a car for maximum acceleration from one given speed to another. The most scientific way is to use Bill Mitchell's 'Gear' program on a PC, with inputs of engine, chassis, aerodynamic and tire parameters along with a gear inventory allowing you to compare sets of ratios for optimum acceleration. Mitchell allows you to go further and enter an accurate track map, which, along with lateral tire capacity will allow you to compare alternate sets of gears in terms of lap time.

The easiest way is to select the lowest gear you are going to use on a given circuit to suit the slowest corner(s) and select the optimum top gear for the longest

straight. Mark these two gears on your gear chart. Select the intermediate gears so that a line drawn between the intersection of the vertical line from the shift point in the lowest gear you will use to the next gear, to the similar vertical line for the drop to top gear will be a straight line. You will be real close to optimum. FIGURE 27 illustrates the idea.

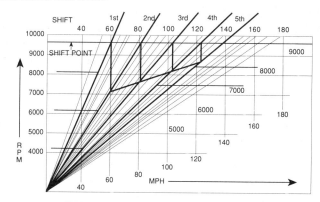

STRAIGHT LINE METHOD OF APPROXIMATING OPTIMUM GEARS FOR ACCELERATION - RPM DROPS DECREASE WITH INCREASING SPEED / HIGHER GEAR. PICKUP POINTS FOR UPSHIFTS FORM APPROXIMATE STRAIGHT LINE.

FIGURE 27

GEARING FOR THE CORNERS

Gearing for acceleration is all very well if you happen to be on a drag strip. Our race tracks have corners and the truth of the matter is that we can seldom, if ever, gear solely for maximum acceleration. We accelerate from corners, not christmas trees, and the length of our drag strip is dictated by the distance to the next braking area. We have to gear for the corners. At the point in the exit to each corner where you can give the car full throttle, your engine should be at or near its torque peak in whatever gear you are in.

With our Toyota Atlantic example engine, peak torque is at 7600rpm. Practical experience taught us that we wanted a minimum of 7800 at the full throttle point - and 8000 was better. Because of the relationship between road speed and drag, the faster the corner, the more important optimum exit gearing becomes.

STRETCHING A GEAR

Life being what it is, we fairly often run into the situation where we want to "stretch" a gear between corners. It goes like this. You come out of a slow corner at optimum rpm in first gear, shift up to second and reach your normal shift point to third fifty yards before the braking point for the next corner - which is also a second gear corner. Your current second gear is ideal for this corner and maybe some other corners on the circuit. If you install a taller second, you will be down on rpm exiting at least one second gear corner.

Shifting up to third for fifty yards and immediately back down to second would be upsetting, confusing and time consuming. What you want to do is to stretch second gear - i.e. take it above the normal shift point for a brief period. This needs to be discussed with your engine builder. Those of us who use relatively low shift points are often able to stretch gears as much as 600rpm with relative impunity. As an example, at the Trois Rivieres Atlantic race in 1992 (with the approval of Bertil Solensgog), our son Christopher stretched second gear 400 to 600rpm three times a lap when qualifying or when pressed. (He won and the engine was fine.)

Comfort yourself with the knowledge that the least harmful type of over-rev is the full throttle for a little bit kind. The most harmful is the over-rev in neutral followed closely by the closed throttle over-rev due to too early a downshift.

THE COMPROMISES

We can gear for acceleration or we can gear for corners. In either case we may have to either shift up and immediately back down or stretch a gear. So what do we do? As always, we compromise. When gearing for a corner, it is always better to have a gear that is a little bit too tall (too few rpm) than one that is too short (too many rpm).

There are several reasons for this:

1) The best that can be hoped for in shifting while still turning under full acceleration is to momentarily upset rear tire grip and lose a nanosecond. The worst that can happen is to miss the shift while you are depending on rear thrust to keep you going in the intended direction. Of course there is also the possibility of over-revving. Shifting while drifting can be done (and sometimes must be done) but it is always awkward.

2) Sometimes, particularly with powerful cars and slow corners, being right at the torque peak when you go to full throttle can prove to be an embarrassment of riches. Too much torque, applied too suddenly, can cause a snap to power on oversteer. It is true that you should be able to modulate the throttle to avoid this sort of thing (sideways is always slow) but it may be advantageous to use a taller gear - particularly if you have to stretch that gear elsewhere on the circuit.

3) This business is 98% mental. Being slightly undergeared gives you a tangible incentive to improve things by carrying more speed through the corner. If you are over geared, you cannot.

SPLITTING THE TORQUE

The reason that Indy Cars have six speed gearboxes and some Formula One cars have seven is not because those guys enjoy shifting. Whether we are talking about an open pit ore carrier or a Formula One car, the basic reason for the multi speed gearbox is to more efficiently use the available torque to accelerate the vehicle.

Racing is all about acceleration. It therefore makes sense to utilize the maximum practical number of gears for each circuit. The shorter the operating rpm band in each gear, the more area under the curve. It really is that simple.

Normally the extra shifts involved in using five gears instead of four or four instead of three are more than compensated for by the increased acceleration. Admittedly there are a lot of circuits where first cannot be used on the circuit simply because there are no corners slow enough to allow its use.

There are fewer circuits where second cannot be used for the same reason (Lime Rock without the chicane is the only one that springs instantly to mind). Of course, no one shifts on an oval except for changing fuel loads, yellow flags and fuel conservation. It has been tried, but without success. If it will ever work, it will work at Nazareth.

BEFORE YOU GET THERE

Practice time is precious. It is a shame to waste any of it by being way off on your gearing. It is also unnecessary. If you have never been to a given track, you can always ask someone who has - most racers share this sort of information. If it is a new track and no one has been there before, get a good track map, compare corner radii with known tracks to get apex speeds. Compare apex speeds and straight lengths with known tracks to get the top and intermediate gears. Or, better yet, use Bill Mitchell's 'Gear' program (compared to your analysis of known tracks) to do the whole thing.

It is always better to be geared too long (too few rpm) than too short. When I go to a new track, or even to a known one, I tend to gear about a tooth too long so that - in case we have more power, or a more slippery car, or better tires, or a better driver - we are not going to be geared too short in the first session. This does wonders for the driver's learning curve - and for the engine.

THE FREE LUNCH

For decades I have been listening to drivers say; "We're a a couple of seconds off, but as soon as we get the thing geared right, we'll be right there." Wrong!

If you are somewhere near close to the optimum gearing for a circuit, the most you are going to pick up in lap time is a couple of tenths. The time simply isn't there. What is there is a more driveable car in traffic and over the length of the race. A properly geared car makes your job easier and therefore, over the length of the race, you will be quicker. Proper gearing also makes things easier on the engine - always a point of interest.

SECTION THREE

LEARN TO WIN

7

"Only a fool learns exclusively from his own experience." Bismark.

TRAINING AIDS

It has been said that the real tragedy of life is that the human being is capable of learning only through experience. This may be so (I have seen no evidence to the contrary) but we can learn some things at least from two very different experiences - our own and someone else's. I submit that it is faster and cheaper to learn as much as possible from other peoples' experience. In this respect, at least, I agree with Bismark.

Since so much of this business is mental, and because there does exist a vast body of knowledge about how to do almost every aspect of it correctly, it is possible to accelerate your progress significantly - sometimes without the expense of driving a racing car. There are a lot of training aids available to the aspiring racing driver - you just have to have the wit to identify and use them.

READ TO WIN

It is unlikely that you will ever get to sit down and have a one on one discussion on the driving of the racing car with the likes of Jackie Stewart, Emerson Fittipaldi, Niki Lauda and Alain Prost. But you can sure as hell read what they have to say about it and, after you have a little experience of your own, you can differentiate between what the principal said and what the ghost writer (or translator) thought they meant. There is good stuff in the best of the books. I have listed my favorites in Chapter One and in the Appendix. Many are available at your library. Obtain them; read them and re-read them. Read them, not so much for the author's guidance on how to drive the racing car or how to conduct the race, but for the little tidbits of information that appear from time to time - and mostly to figure out how he got there. Read all of the technical articles in Racer, Race Tech and Racecar Engineering magazines.

HANGING OUT

Among the hardest things for any racing driver to do is to go to a race track when he is not racing. It is very frustrating. It is also very smart. You can learn a lot just by being associated with a team that is farther up the ladder than you are. If I were an aspiring young driver I would approach one of the leading teams in every series that raced near me and offer to polish wheels, go-fer, or whatever, on the weekends when I wasn't racing - just for the experience and the contacts.

If you are lucky enough to get on with a good team, you will learn the proper ways of going about things. When you get to the point where you are ready to move into a professional series, some of the people will have kept track of your progress, will know who you are and know that you are serious.

Perhaps the best example of this sort of thing is Alain Prost. After a meteoric career in Formula Three, Prost had no money and consequently nowhere to go. He attended every Formula One race that he could possibly afford to get to and made sure that the teams were aware of his existence and availability. McLaren eventually gave him a shot and the rest is history.

The Prost story would have been a lot different had he stayed home, writing letters and waiting for the phone to ring...

WATCHING

Any time that drivers as good or better than you are running, and you are not busy with your own preparation, you should be out there watching. You never know when you might learn something. When you are running a support race for a pro series you might be able to reverse the tables and talk one of the drivers or engineers that you met out there into watching you during one of your sessions - a bit of free of coaching. Most real racers are pretty good people and enthusiasts - they actually like helping young drivers who are serious (and who are not an immediate threat).

VISUALIZATION

The best training I have seen was in the US Navy. Military training uses a lot of repetition and lot of training aids. During flight training and in the driving of ships, the aspirant is strongly encouraged to spend all of his free time playing the mental "what if" game. The varieties are endless - from "what should I do if my M-16 jams?" through "what should I do if the engine quits right now?" to "what should I do if a tanker suddenly materializes out of the fog right ahead of me?"

You get to write your own scripts for the game and, if you are a serious person, you play the game for the rest of your life. The objects are several:

1) To get you thinking.

2) To ensure almost instinctive rapid and correct response to emergency situations.

3) To condition you to teach yourself and to keep your mind in gear.

It has been said that there are two things that no male can admit that he does not do well. Most of us spend too much time daydreaming about one of them and not enough time visualizing the other. If any male racing driver were to spend as much time effectively visualizing his driving life as he does (effectively?) visualizing his sex life, Michael Schumacher would have to move over. Visualization is the new sports buzzword for what athletes have been doing since the beginning of time - mentally running through the forthcoming exercise. It is daydreaming turned serious and carried several steps further.

For untold millennia primitive hunters have ritually pre-enacted the hunt. Prior to take off for every flight the Blue Angels visualize, together, the entire coming routine - they call it the "Zen flight". This is what olympic divers and gymnasts are doing just before they explode.

One of my favorite racing drivers, Price Cobb, can sit in a motel room chair and, with appropriate motions of hands and feet, (sound effects, also) come within a couple of tenths of his actual lap times. Price is not alone in this ability - most of the good ones do it.

Admittedly the scene looks a bit strange - a grown man sitting in a chair twisting his arms and kicking his legs to no discernible rhythm while accompanying himself with "vrooom, vrooom" noises. If a normal person were to walk in on the act, the looney bin collection squad would arrive pretty soon.

The medical term for visualization is "mental imaging". It is actually "seeing" reversed. In the process of human vision a stimulus in the outside world is transferred from the eye to the primary visual cortex in the brain and then on to higher brain centers until an object or an event is recognized by the observer. In mental imaging or visualization, the stimulus originates, voluntarily, in the higher centers and is passed down to the primary visual cortex where it is recognized. To the person doing the visualization, the experience can be absolutely real.

For the racing driver, the wonderful thing about visualization is that it requires neither a racing car nor a race track. All that it takes is a knowledge of both the car and the track, a willingness to try it and a belief in the validity of the exercise. Trust me, the validity is there.

The human mind is a wondrous thing - serious visualization is far better and more realistic than the most sophisticated video games. Every normal person has the basic ability to visualize - but you have to work at it in order to develop the technique to the point where it becomes a useful tool. To begin with, you should start with a circuit and a car that you know well. Visualization, at least for the racing driver, is a solitary exercise.

I'm not going to try to tell you how to visualize your racing - it's a self-taught sort of thing. As an example of how detailed and effective visualization can be, I have reproduced Price Cobb's course notes for Laguna Seca at the end of this chapter. These notes were generated, without warning, one morning at our breakfast table. The whole episode, including the writing, took about 30 minutes.

I think that every track that he has ever driven is equally inscribed on Price's personal RAM. I can still remember, in detail, tracks and laps that I haven't driven in thirty years. This is true of every front line professional driver - it has to be. The Senna stories in this regard are endless.

There are all sorts of ramifications to visualization. The late and much lamented Davey Allison watched videos of wind tunnel tests and, on the track, visualized air currents as colored smoke passing over the cars ahead of him. He used the visualization as sort of a road map for track position, drafting and slingshotting.

In order to visualize a race track, it is necessary to know the race track. Try to arrive at each race a day early. When you first get to the track, do several laps in a street car, on an ATV, on a bicycle or on foot. Do enough laps so that the track becomes imprinted on your brain and begins to "flow" for you. It helps if you can view the track from approximately the eye level that you will have in the race car. Then, in the transporter, the rent car or in your motel room, start visualizing. It will take a while to develop the technique. It will be worth it.

Videotaping the track cannot hurt (also from eye level) - then you can play it back in your motel room as an aid to visualization. Most successful drivers do a lot of this - just before each session. There is absolutely no sense mentally practicing something you didn't do very well. Once you have learned a track, use only good data - your very best laps.

THE RACING DRIVER AND THE COACH

A recent article in the sports section of the Los Angeles Times was headlined "Coach brings Jack Nicklaus's game back". It turned out that Mr. Nicklaus, arguably the greatest golfer in the history of the game and now on the senior tour, had been in a bit of a slump. He also had the good sense to ask a friend, who happened to be a teaching pro in California, to have a look. The teacher watched the Golden Bear for a while, corrected some aspect of his swing and Mr. Nicklaus gratefully returned to his winning ways.

Mr. Nicklaus apparently saw nothing particularly unusual in this experience and didn't mind its appearance in the press. Now Robert Trent Jones once said of the good Mr. Nicklaus; "I understand all that there is to know about the game of golf. I do not, however, understand anything at all about the game that Mr. Nicklaus plays." Nicklaus is sort of like Schumacher in racing. Can you imagine Michael asking Jackie Stewart to coach him out of a slump?

Pete Sampras, Boris Becker, Steffi Graff and Martina Navratilova don't step out of the hotel without their coaches. Joe Montana had several, and his every move was videotaped and studied. Most golf pros have personal coaches and all of them seek frequent analysis of their technique. The same is true of track and field athletes, boxers, skiers and bicycle racers. Football, baseball and soccer teams have as many coaches as players. Experienced fighter pilots attend top gun schools and are continuously coached by their superiors and peers. In fact, about the only athletes who do not use coaches are racing drivers and jockeys!

I offer no explanation for this phenomenon. I admit that ours is a business of giant egos, but the ego of the fighter pilot is every bit as large. In fact all individual sports demand large egos, and most team sports at least tolerate them. Besides, many racing drivers often ask the opinions of unqualified observers. It certainly isn't a question of lack of discipline. The self discipline of the successful racing driver is the strongest known to man. The question arises, would a coach have any realistic function in the world of professional motorsport? Hell yes, he would - even at the highest levels.

My personal theory of race car engineering is that my presence in the pits during a practice session or during a race is of minimal value. The engineer belongs out on the race track, watching cars. The chief mechanic can handle whatever is required in the pits - it's his job. If it is necessary for the engineer to communicate with the driver or the mechanical staff in the pits, that's what radios are for.

My job is to figure out how to make the car/driver package go faster and, in order to do a decent job, I need to add my input to that of the driver - which

means that I have to watch the car. I must admit, however, that as the cars get faster, as the suspension travels less and as my eyes get older, it is harder to see what is going on.

Anyway, I wander around race tracks a lot, on foot, on mountain bikes, four wheelers and rent cars. I seldom meet any of my peers out there. The ones that I do see are Alec Purdy, Jim Magee, Jack Roush, Kurt Roehrig, Bob Riley and Jan Zuidjidk. Howard Milliken cheats and sends his lady. At a recent Long Beach CART race, had I seen engineers from one highly regarded CART team out watching their cars, the result of the race might well have been different...

So what am I suggesting? I am simply saying that a wealthy or well sponsored young driver would certainly do well to hire a qualified coach - at least once in a while. Defining the term "qualified" is not, however, real easy and bad advice is liable to be worse than none.

Unfortunately, many successful drivers are not particularly good coaches or knowledgeable about vehicle dynamics and their interface with the driver, and many very successful mechanics, data scrapers and engineers are not particularly knowledgeable about driving. You don't have to be able to beat Pete Sampras at singles to effectively coach him - but, in order to get inside his head, you have to have played the game very well and at a high level. If you cannot get inside his head, no matter how much you understand about the physics and technicalities of tennis, you cannot coach effectively at that level.

It is the same in motor racing - every good coach that I have known has been at one time a good racing driver at a high level of the sport. Of course, that is not enough. He also has to be a thinker, a good communicator and be willing to sublimate his own ego to that of the driver. Unfortunately there aren't a lot of Rick Mears, Dick Simons, Ken Tyrrells, Eddie Jordans, Bob Earls, Tony Kesters, Peter Kuhns, Bob Lobenbergs, Richard Spenards or Carroll Smiths around. There never were and there never will be.

Some racers seem to think that a good on board data gathering system with a qualified data scraper is a viable alternative. It is not the same thing. The data system is an invaluable aid to a driver coach, not a substitute.

As an example, I recently witnessed an impasse between a young driver and a well known data scraper. The scraper was looking at overlays of steering angle, lateral and longitudinal g and throttle position. He was pointing out that, at the exit of one particular corner, the car was understeering strongly (albeit briefly) under full power. He maintained that the understeer was driver induced. It was.

The driver was attempting to explain that he had purposely induced the understeer at that particular point because the car was rapidly approaching a bumpy section of road and, if it weren't understeering when it got there, it would bounce into a strong enough oversteer to force him to take his foot out of it. The scraper had never been there, couldn't imagine such a thing and simply failed to compute. Impasse.

At any rate, one of the best investments that a young driver can make is to hire a qualified driver coach for the occasional day. Just make sure that the man is qualified to coach and that there will be neither a personality conflict nor a clash of egos.

RADAR GUNS

The ubiquitous radar gun, as it is normally used in racing, is not only useless, it is a distinct detriment to the progress of both car and driver. Nine times out of ten some genius sets up a radar gun at the end of the main straight and proceeds to announce who has the fastest and slowest trap speeds. This little bit of information is not only useless - it can be misleading.

I discourage my drivers from looking at or listening to straightaway radar speeds. Unless we happen to be at Bonneville, we are not interested in mph at the end of the straight. We are interested in how long it took us to get there, not how fast we are going when we do. We get paid for elapsed times (ET), not mphs.

"So what", you say, "is the difference?" The difference is that mph is largely a question of drag (in most current classes of racing, horsepower, in chunks large enough to influence top speed, is almost a given thing). Drag is profoundly influenced by download - the more download you put on a given car, the more drag will be induced (there is still no free lunch) and the slower will be the car's speed at the end of the straight.

The corollary is that the more download, the faster will be the car's exit speed from the corner preceding said straight. This may well make up for the increased drag and produce an almost equal top end with a better ET. In many cases, trimming the download to its minimum will result in a decrease in corner speed that will outweigh the increase in terminal velocity when it comes to lap time.

Another point to keep in mind is that download also contributes mightily to braking capability. Anyway, the place for radar guns, if there is one, is at the exit to the most critical corner on the race track and only there.

ON BOARD DATA COLLECTION

I admit that, in some ways, my attitudes toward racing may be a bit old fashioned - perhaps even reactionary. I view my role, and that of my peers, as one of the support staff. I believe that racing should be a contest between drivers, not between engineers.

I do not approve of many of the newer developments - particularly the electronic ones. I was very happy to see traction limiting, active ride and anti-lock braking effectively outlawed. I do not believe that telemetry should have a place in motor racing. I have serious reservations about ground effects, both tunnels and flat bottoms, and would loudly applaud effective and intelligent moves toward severely limiting the amounts of download generated by racing cars.

I do, however, firmly believe that onboard data gathering is good for the sport. I am a realist. I make my living as an engineer in motor racing and I really like winning. I really dislike losing. Therefore I use all of the tools at my disposal.

From the very beginning of on board data recording in motor racing, drivers have had two opinions of it - and two only. The intelligent drivers have recognized it for what it is - an invaluable aid to help them and their crews to more fully realize whatever talents and equipment God gave them. The less intelligent have opposed the practice stating that they would have nothing to do with a computer that was trying to replace them, that they didn't see how a computer could help them or that they couldn't be bothered to learn to use the thing.

My own position is that any racing driver who has realistic access to any level of data collection and who does not use it to the fullest practical extent is handicapping himself beyond anyone's ability to overcome. Senna himself, without the intelligent and prioritized interpretation of onboard data, would have finished behind lesser drivers - in lesser cars - who did have access to it. It's a bit like trying to fight a war without intelligence, doing root canals without x-rays - or bringing a knife to a gun fight. My opinion in this matter surprises no one who knows me.

The second part of my feelings, however, may well come as a surprise. Unless there is a person on the team whose primary job at the racetrack is the collection and filtering of data, we should not consider using much more than a simple engine rpm trace. Data scraping is only valuable so long as it does not interfere with preparation, priorities and common sense. If your operation is flat out just keeping ahead of the car - performing routine maintenance and carrying out the necessary changes between sessions - don't even think about data gathering without an expansion of personnel. Let the driver look at the tach!

If he is going to use the tach it should be analog, not digital.

The expansion, of course, can be as simple as renting the services on a part time basis of someone who is good at it. Another approach is for the driver himself to learn how to download the computer and to interpret the data. After all, most teams won't let the driver work on the car (rightly so - his mind is on other things). With a few channels of basic data, it isn't that hard to do - and it will pay large dividends.

There is a third aspect to my feelings about data gathering. When the driver disagrees with the computer, I tend to side with the driver. The driver is:

1) More sensitive than the computer.
2) More realistic than the computer.
3) More intelligent than the computer.
4) Able to prioritize.
5) Ultimately responsible for all of the decisions.

Data gathering is one thing. Data interpretation is another. Gathering all of the data in the world won't help anyone unless it is intelligently interpreted - and very quickly at that. This means that we normally only need to look at the fastest lap in any given run - unless, of course, the object of the exercise is to figure out why it was the fastest lap.

A page (or computer screen) of columns of numbers means little but mental discomfort to most of us. Most racers are not "number crunchers". Even the engineers in racing tend to be visually orientated people - at least we older (more mature???) engineers. We are more comfortable with graphs than with charts. The creators of the better data gathering and analysis software programs are aware of this and arrange things so that the data is presented as a series of x-y axis graphs.

In these graphs, y, the horizontal direction, is time (or distance) and x, the vertical dimension, is the data value. Normally each graph represents one lap. The better programs allow us to "zoom" or reduce the amount of race track shown in the graph so that we can examine the data in a given segment in more detail than is possible when the display represents an entire lap.

William C. Mitchell's software packages provide visual aids such as a track map giving graphic indication of lateral and longitudinal g, with steering angle, percentage of throttle and/or brake being used at any given time and a traction circle as windows on the computer screen. Mitchell's ideas are being widely copied - hard on Bill, but flattering...

THE OBJECTS OF THE EXERCISE

Data gathering serves three basic purposes:

1) To aid the driver/crew in maximizing the performance of the car.
2) To define the operating conditions of the engine, drive train (and sometimes the suspension) in order to improve reliability.
3) To aid the driver in improving his driving technique. (This can be a hard sell.)

This is not a book on data gathering or interpretation. Bill Mitchell, Walter Preston and I were working on that one - until Buddy Fey wrote it. Buddy's book 'Data Power' is good, damned good. Buy it.

WHAT DATA TO GATHER

There are a great many choices of data to be gathered - from a simple and inexpensive engine rpm trace to the umpteen channels of information that were telemetered to the McLaren/Honda pits and, on by satellite, to Tokyo. We are not going to consider the latter in this book. We will, however, briefly discuss what is available to the "average" racer - whoever he may be.

DATA IN ORDER OF PRIORITY

There are almost as many different ideas on the priorities of data-to-be-gathered as there are data gatherers. Here are mine - with reasons:

1) Engine rpm. If I can have only one channel of information, I want it to be engine rpm. From this we can determine gearing, wheelspin (if any), length of each braking time, driver's shift time and technique (up and down), corner apex speed, and off throttle time. We can also detect changes in any or all of the above from changes we make to the car - or to driving technique.

2) Miles per hour. Virtually every system that gives rpm will also give mph. It tells us instantly where the car is on the race track and helps to identify wheelspin, etc. Overlayed with a team mate's trace, the mph trace identifies very quickly where each driver is fast or slow. With the less expensive systems, mph is liable to have less RF interference than rpm and be a more readable trace.

3) Lateral acceleration (lateral g). This one tells us a lot about the performance of both the chassis and the driver. We sometimes try to use the lateral g trace as a relatively crude substitute for segment timing. Once an experienced driver has learned his (or her) way around a given race track, the points of beginning and end of lateral g build up will be pretty damned constant at each corner.

4) Steering angle. The steering angle trace tells us a lot about the understeer/oversteer balance of the car - and about the smoothness or lack thereof of the driver. Overlaid with lateral g, these areas become almost crystal clear.

5) Longitudinal acceleration (longitudinal g). This trace tells us how well the car/driver combination is braking and accelerating. Comparing the steepness of the acceleration curves before and after a change in chassis, download or gearing tells us what we accomplished. Overlaying or combining longitudinal g with lateral g gives us, in effect, the traction circle - so we can judge how effectively we are using the total tractive capacity of the tires. Mitchell's software actually integrates these factors and prints the traction circle as an on-screen window.

6) Throttle position. Part of this one is pretty obvious. Some drivers don't like it much. This is silly. A throttle position trace (as opposed to an on/off trace) can be a big help to the inexperienced (or to the experienced but bull headed or forgetful) driver. For example, it will show whether he is "rolling" in and out of the throttle on an oval, or upsetting the car with jerky throttle motions. It will show if he is inducing power oversteer coming off slow corners with a powerful car. It is a lot better if throttle position is shown as a percentage of full throttle rather than as a simple on/off signal. The other thing that throttle position does is improve the driver's self awareness. It is surprising how often a driver sincerely believes that he is flat out in a fast corner when the throttle trace shows a lift...

7) Exhaust gas temperature. This one lets us either tune our engine's fuel/air mixture strength to the optimum for the conditions of the day or check how well the engine management system is doing it for us.

8) Individual wheel speed. This one, at the rear wheels, gives us the only indication we are ever going to get about the behavior of the limited slip or self locking differential.

9) Suspension travel. Perhaps the most effective use of suspension travel data is in figuring out what to do with the shocks. As an example, with state of the art shocks, the transient load transfer is controlled by shock piston velocities in the 1 to 5 inches per second range while the vehicle behavior over bumps is controlled by shock forces in the 8 to 20 inches per second range. The external adjustments effect the 1 to 5 ips range while the higher speed forces can usually be changed only by re-valving. The first thing that the suspension movement trace gives us is the basic information

we need to tell us whether to adjust or to revalve. It also gives us a lot more. For instance, integrated suspension movement can give us roll angle, front and rear and pitch angle. Overlaying front and rear movement tells us whether or not we have our wheel frequencies in synch.

10) Ride height. Ride height is most accurately measured with lasers - which means that it is beyond the resources of all but the best funded teams. It is possible, however, to get a very good approximation of the dynamic ride heights, chassis rake and changes thereto from suspension movement - but you have to sample at a minimum 250 samples per second and you have to smooth the resultant trace. It would be pretty difficult to be really fast on the big ovals without it.

INTERPRETATION

Collecting data is one thing. Interpreting it is quite another. The best way to learn to interpret data is to be taught by an expert - Jeff Braun, Buddy Fey, Peter Kelly, Kelly Lowen, Tony Kester, Bill Mitchell or Kurt Roehrig, for example. The next best way is to spend 30 bucks and buy Buddy Fey's book. In fact, you should buy and study the book before taking lessons (or investing in a system). You could also look into spending a couple of weekends with a team that uses data well - trading go-fer services for learning curve. Whatever your method of introduction, you will be learning more about data interpretation as long as you stay in racing.

OVERLAYS

The real value of on board instrumentation comes when we start overlaying traces. The simplest example is overlaying traces from two different drivers - often to the benefit of each.

The most basic overlay is mph. This instantaneously tells us where each driver is fast or slow. Except for the slope of the deceleration and acceleration curves, mph doesn't tell us much about why one driver is faster or slower than another on a specific portion of the race track. Throttle position, rpm, steering angle, lateral and longitudinal g will tell the entire story. It is easy to end up with so many lines on the screen that nothing makes sense. A relatively inexpensive color monitor is a big help - as is a relatively inexpensive color printer.

THE NEXT BEST THING

The next best thing to on board data collection is, has been and always will be a detailed debriefing complete with annotated course map and comments. The procedure is described in Chapter 12.

THE LAST WORD

My last words to the driver on the subject of data scraping are; "Don't ever depend on it - especially for gearing information!" All data collection systems are electronic. Electronics (and electrons) hate racing cars. There is no such thing as a reliable electronic system in either race cars or aircraft. That simple fact explains why commercial and military aircraft (and civil aircraft flown by prudent people - at least under instrument conditions) have double and triple redundancy for crucial avionic systems.

We cannot afford the redundancy. Therefore our systems fail fairly frequently. The on board system in no way relieves the driver of the responsibility for reading the gauges - especially the tachometer. It is embarrassing to go into a qualifying session (or, worse yet, a race) with the wrong gears because you didn't look. It also severely reduces your chances of winning. The data gathering system is an aid to the driver's senses, not a substitute!

LEARNING - ON THE ROAD

Every driving book I have ever read (i.e. all of them) warns against the not uncommon practice of learning to drive fast by driving at racing speeds on public highways. The warning is valid. While I will defend our right to kill or maim ourselves by our own acts of idiocy (file this under improving the gene pool), driving at anything that resembles the traction limit on public highways is an act of total irresponsibility because of the very real danger to innocent (i.e. uninvolved) persons - and because of what it does to other peoples' (i.e. my) insurance rates.

Having said that, I must also point out that one of the the reasons that England produced star drivers in the Sixties was that there was only one motorway and lots of roundabouts and twisty rural roads. There are whole lot of things that the would be racing driver can prac-

tice and learn on the highway. Any wannabee driver who drives a road car with an automatic transmission is not serious about learning his craft. It is a lot cheaper to learn how to shift (up and down - with and without the clutch) on the highway than on the race track. The same goes for aiming points, transitions, smoothness and lines - as in corner - (but only on your side of the road). There are several definitions of "public highway". There were no race tracks where I grew up. I was no more (or less) responsible than any other kid, but I was less brave than most. There were lots of stretches of country roads, both paved and unpaved, that were neither blind nor bordered with ditches and/or trees. To my mind neither wire fences with wooden poles nor bushes counted. I used up a lot of bushes and some fence wire.

When we lived on Pensacola Beach, virtually no one else did - it was winter. There was exactly one road and no houses. The road had a some fast bends, a sharp esses and a bunch of second gear 90 degree corners. The terrain was level and you could see for miles. The road was bordered by relatively hard sand. Every day for months I put a couple of home made canvas sand mats in the MG TD and set out to learn how to do this thing. So long as one shot off the road straight - as opposed to sideways (backwards was OK), no serious harm could be done. I explored a lot of sand - but I also learned a lot. I also taught myself about smooth technique by slaloming between the dotted lines on that highway.

For decades international rallying has been dominated by Scandinavians. Recently we have seen a whole generation of Finnish race driving stars. Snow is just flat wonderful for learning car control. Dirt is just as good.

So don't piss and moan about no opportunity to learn/practice. Buy a cluncker with a stick - use cheap tires and the terrain God has given you and go learn. But please do it where it's safe - I or one of mine might be coming the other way.

PRICE COBB'S LAGUNA SECA (g.t.p.) COURSE NOTES

Turn 2 - In practice and when the tires and track are new/clean you can use a slightly different line. I begin the turn by braking extremely late into the turn, this can be done by using the lines/cones on the right side of the circuit delineating the new track from the old.

This is a classic trail brake corner. As the tires get miles on them, and the track becomes "greasy", (which is a given during the race) it becomes imperative to stay on the inside of the turn. (A long apex so to speak).

Turn 3 - I try to get over to the left side of the track as early as possible so that I can make this right hand turn with minimal braking as this turn is much faster than it appears at first. Quite often there is sand or debris on the surface making it more important yet to have kept the platform (chassis) as stable as is conceivable to keep maximum grip. Try to accelerate early and smoothly for a good shot through Turn 3.

Turn 4 - On new tires this turn is as fast as you are when you arrive, (flat out). However, as the tires age and the track becomes "greasy" it will be necessary to breathe the throttle to get a bit more weight on the front tires for a crisp turn in.

Occasionally there is debris on the circuit (sand), which causes the car to go wide on the exit. If you think that you might run part way off the surface, try not to lift off the throttle, since this will "open" a locker diff and make your car a bit unstable.

Turn 5 - Very tricky turn to do consistently well. Try to brake late but smooth. To carry any real speed through this turn, your turn in has got to be crisp and late to get the car over a bump with the least amount of chassis monkey motion. Later in the race this becomes critical as this turn becomes very greasy when combined with the bump.

Let's not forget that the exit in relative terms "falls off" and that you are now climbing a hill!

Turn 6 - It is imperative to get this corner right as it is the quickest and up hill to boot. Get the driver to work hard on getting his turn in correct. This is difficult in a fast car since the entry is blind until you crest a hill. The turn becomes visible and turn in should be initiated then at least if not just before the turn becomes visible.

Try hard to stay off the curb as this severely upsets the chassis for good cornering speed.

Turn 7 & 8 - Cork Screw. Work hard on making the car stop well on and off line into this turn since it is a great place to pass. The difficulty is that the car has just crested a hill and is trying to settle down while you brake!

If you have enough time, get the driver to practice positioning the car so that full power can be used before the car starts down the hill in the left hand part of the "screw". Use all of the exit of the cork screw so long as you can get back to the right half of the track. Even the middle of the road is probably good enough.

Turn 9 - This turn is a bit off camber and downhill to the left which tends to really chew up the right front.

Do all of your work to get this tire to live so that your car can be raced throughout the event.

Good exit speed here allows you to stay close to your enemy so that you will have a chance to set him up through turn 10 and lap him into 11.

Turn 10 - On new tires, this turn is absolutely flat. However, it is critical to use all of the road at the apron. To do this, it is generally a good idea to make the car ride the bumps well. Speed through here will give you a chance to pass your enemy into 11.

Turn 11 - Work hard on braking well into this turn as you will pass many cars here.

Try to make the transition from braking to throttle smoothly and quickly. Do this turn well and you will have a great shot up the hill into turn 1

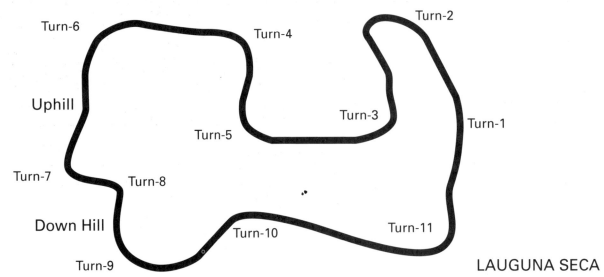

LAUGUNA SECA

Watkins Glen

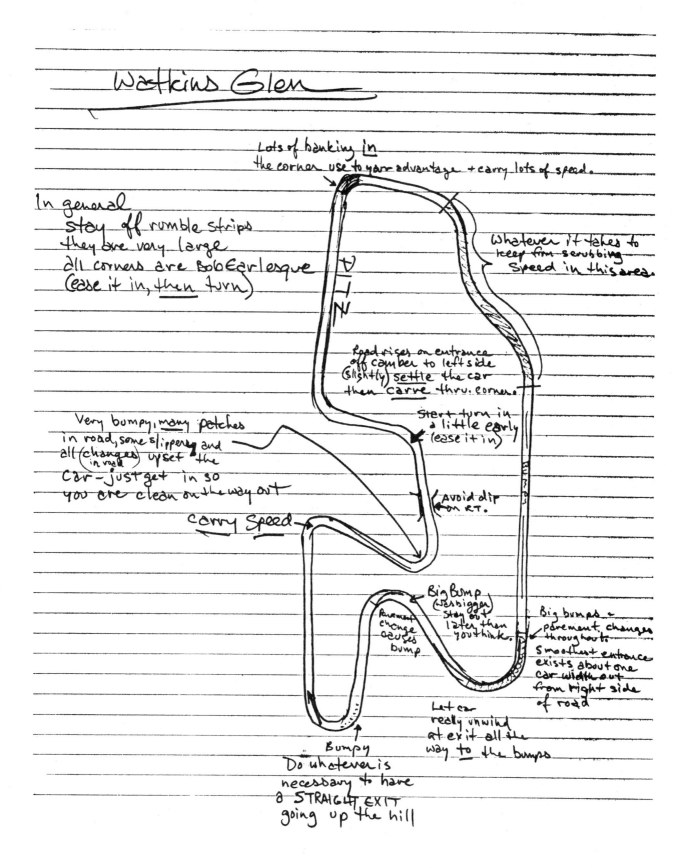

Lots of banking **in** the corner use to your advantage + carry lots of speed.

In general
stay off rumble strips
they are very large
all corners are Bob Earlesque
(ease it in, <u>then</u> turn)

Whatever it takes to keep from scrubbing speed in this area.

Road rises on entrance off camber to left side (slightly) <u>settle</u> the car then <u>carve</u> thru corner.

Start turn in a little early (ease it in)

Very bumpy, many patches in road, some slippery and all (changes in road) upset the car — just get in so you are clean on the way out

Avoid dip on RT.

carry speed

Big Bump (ver bigger) Stay out later than you think.

Pavement change caused bump

Big bumps + pavement changes throughout. Smoothest entrance exists about one car width out from right side of road

Let car really unwind at exit all the way <u>to</u> the bumps

Bumpy
Do whatever is necessary to have a STRAIGHT EXIT going up the hill

DRIFT LEFT, STRAIGHTEN FOR BRAKING, AIM LEFT OF "BEACH" SIGN, SLOW DRASTICALLY — T7 VERY SLOW AND GOOD EXIT IS ALL-IMPORTANT FOR STRAIGHT

OFF BRAKES, TURN IN BY 4TH WHITE LINE, BANKED TURN, APEX @ LAST YELLOW BUMPER

EASE ON POWER BEFORE APEX, APEX @ LAST YELLOW BUMPER, FULL POWER @ APEX

DRIFT LEFT ON T7 EXIT & STAY LEFT THRU T8

APPROACH 3-4' FROM LEFT, BRAKING

GRADUAL EASE TO LEFT OF T6

DRIFT RIGHT UP HILL, FULL THROTTLE

DOUBLE (DEEP) SET OF TIGER TEETH, STAY LEFT TILL END OF NEW (BACK SET) TEETH

EASE RIGHT BY T9

LEFT APEX 4 10 YARDS PAST TIGER TEETH, START LIFTING POWER, BEGIN BRAKING

TURN IN RIGHT @ FLAGGER STAND, STAY ON POWER THRU T4 (OFF CAMBER DOWNHILL), EXIT TO RIGHT OF SQUARE PATCH

RIGHT HAND APPROACH UNDER BRAKING, CROSS OVER TO LEFT

SET UP ON RIGHT FOR LEFT HAND BEND

APEX @ LAST YELLOW BUMPER, USE ONLY 2/3 OF EXIT TRACK

OFF BRAKES BEFORE 4TH WHITE LINE, TURN IN TO T3 @ LINE

SLIGHTLY OFF CAMBER, STAY RIGHT

START LEFT TURN IN TO T10 4 20 YARDS BEFORE ARMCO

SHOULD CARRY A CONSTANT ARC THRU T1 TO T2 APPROACH, WILL DRIFT LEFT OUT OF T1 AND ARC BACK TO RIGHT HAND T2 APPROACH

TO LEFT COMPLETELY @ 3RD WHITE LINE, LIGHTEN BRAKES OVER CREST 5' FROM LEFT @ 2ND WHITE LINE, ON BRAKES

TURN IN LEFT JUST PAST FLAGGER STAND, RIGHT OF CENTER @ 1ST WHITE LINE, START BRAKING

IGNORE 1ST WHITE LINE BEFORE DIP, APEX @ LAST YELLOW CURBS, STAY ON POWER UP HILL

ON LEFT @ 2ND WHITE LINE, START BRAKING

@ 3RD WHITE LINE, YELLOW PIT ENTRY STARTS — FINISH BRAKING

LATE APEX, ON POWER EARLY, STAY OFF BUMPERS BUT INSIDE WHITE LINE (RAIN COLLECTS @ APEX)

AFTER T12 EXIT, HEAD FOR T1 BLEACHERS

START/FINISH

Nissan BRIDGE

ON THE RIGHT UNDER BRIDGE, WHEELS INSIDE WHITE LINE, START APPLYING POWER, APEX @ BRIDGE

APPROACH STRADDLING OR TO LEFT OF YELLOW REENTRY LINE (WITH RAIN, LEAVE 3' ON LEFT, EASE BRAKING IN RUNNING WATER)

APEX @ END OF END SET OF BUMPERS

DRIFT LEFT ON EXIT, STAY RIGHT OF YELLOW PIT LANE LINE

WATCH OUT FOR RIPPLE BUMPS SEPARATING PIT ENTRY FROM TRACK — DESTROYS CARS!

CREST
UP
DOWN
UP
UP
DOWN
DIP
ARMCO
FLAT

6 7 8 9 10 5 4 3 2 1 11 2 12

ROAD ATLANTA
2.52 MI.

SECTION FOUR

ENVIRON-MENTS

8

"The idea is to approach each corner with the speed, confidence and dexterity of the Roadrunner - and without the destiny of Wiley E Coyote". Anon.

PERMANENT CIRCUITS

Racing circuits are conveniently divided into three pretty distinct categories - permanent road racing facilities, street circuits and ovals. Each presents its own set of demands - some similar and some not. We will discuss them separately, starting with permanent venues. Permanent road racing circuits offer challenges (and solutions) somewhat different from street circuits and ovals. The good circuits contain a variety of corners, including at least one really fast "separator of men from boys" and hopefully some linked corners or esses. Changes in elevation are always welcome.

Circuits such as Road Atlanta, Mid Ohio, Road America and Sears Point in this country and Brands Hatch, Imola, Monza, Spa Francorchamps (still part public road), Suzuka and Bathurst elsewhere are where road racing should take place. Of the flat circuits, the only ones that I have truly liked are the original Monza and the original Silverstone (really fast corners are what racing is all about). Of course, before single seaters and sports-prototypes got too fast for it, the original 14 mile Nurburgring mountain circuit was the only real racing track in the world. For touring cars, it still is.

The secret of success on permanent circuits is arriving at the best total set up compromise. Without electronic aids it is simply not possible to arrive at the optimum set up for fast and slow, banked and unbanked corners, long straights that demand minimum drag combined with slow and medium speed corners that demand maximum download, etc, etc, etc...

Maximum efficiency in slow corners demands relatively soft springs, while high speed corners demand a stable aero platform and relatively stiff springs to support the download. Arriving at the near optimum compromise requires study.

So study the track. Walk it, bike it, ATV it or rent car it looking, for the peculiarities. Learn the basic circuit before you drive it in a race car. While you are at it, find out where you can drop a wheel with no penalty and where dropping a wheel will cut a tire.

THE IMPORTANT CORNERS

From the driving point of view I do not believe in "give away" corners. To me, every corner on the race track is important - if only to make sure that you are positioned correctly and at the optimum speed for the next one. From the set up point of view, however, some corners are more important than others.

There is a popular theory that the most important corners on any road racing circuit are those that lead onto the longest straights. The theory is plausible and easily explained. It is also wrong.

Let's take Road Atlanta as an example (FIGURE 27). Turn Seven at Road Atlanta is a first or second gear cor-

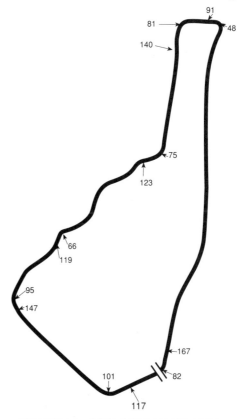

FIGURE 27 – MPH AT ROAD ATLANTA

ner with an apex speed (Trans Am car) of about 48mph. It leads onto one of the longest straights in the country. Most of the drivers who lose races at Road Atlanta believe that Turn Seven is the key to the race track and concentrate their set up efforts on a really good exit and power down from this corner.

The truth of the matter is that Turn Seven is the least important corner on the track. Turn One is the most important. Turn One is fast - 95mph in a Trans Am car, 120 in an Atlantic. The exit is steep up hill and it is followed by really fast esses. Every mile per hour you can carry through Turn One you also carry up the hill. Every mph you lose in Turn One will take forever to get back because of both the road speed and the hill.

What I am saying here is that the most important corners are always the fastest ones - simply because racing cars do not accelerate as fast from high speed as they do from low. It really is that simple. So the first thing to realize about Road Atlanta is that there is exactly one slow corner on the whole race track. There are seven fast corners and one medium speed corner. We know that a car which is at its optimum in slow corners will be sloppy and vague in fast corners, while a car that is good in fast corners will be perfectly driveable in slow corners - just a bit slow.

So why in hell would anyone concentrate their set up efforts at Road Atlanta on Turn Seven? Because they didn't analyze the requirements of the race track, that's why. Of all the ways to lose races this is one of the dumbest.

Certain TV commentators call certain permanent tracks "technical circuits". They do so without pointing out why these particular courses are "technical" and others are not. I am not certain what the term means (to me all race tracks are technical) but I am certain that some circuits incorporate features that require lines and solutions that are not immediately obvious.

Examples include tightening radius bends, adverse camber, corners that crest hills, corners which either begin or end on a hill, corners in which the road camber changes, and so forth. This sort of thing has been discussed and the technique(s) for dealing with each dissected in a dozen good books. I am not going to duplicate the efforts of my predecessors.

Actually, once the peculiarity has been discovered and defined, the solution should be evident - if not automatic. The basic rules are simple. Hills and banking on corner exits will catch you, allowing higher than normal entry speeds. Adverse camber and downhill stretches will throw you off. In a sequence of corners the most important ones are the first and the last. If there are only two in the sequence the more important one is the last.

To illustrate what I am talking about we will now discuss one of the more complex series of corners in this country. I will offer my idea of solutions to the problems offered.

Mid-Ohio is one of the country's best and most challenging race tracks. The complex of corners following the back straight is unique - and difficult. FIGURE 28 shows a flat plane projection with approximate maximum and minimum speeds - and gears - for an Indy Car written in. FIGURE 29 shows what it really looks like. The hill is steep and crest is in the middle of the left hander.

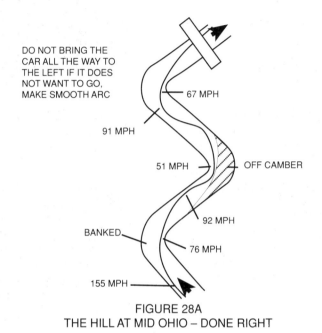

FIGURE 28A
THE HILL AT MID OHIO – DONE RIGHT

What FIGURE 29 does not show is that the shaded area of FIGURE 28A is off camber. What most drivers do is to follow a conventional line - shown in FIGURE 28B. The correct line is shown in FIGURE 28A. The reasons for this line are as follows:

1) The right hander at the end of the straight is significantly faster than the left hander at the top of the hill.

2) If you use all of the road at the exit of the right hander:

   a) You can carry more speed into and through the corner.

   b) You will carry more speed up the hill.

   c) You can brake less and later at the end of the straight - making it almost impossible for someone to pass you.

   d) If you must drive a defensive (inside) line at the end of the straight, you had better use all of the road coming out, because you must be on the inside going up the hill or - you will be passed.

4 – 4

Up hill.

Down hill.

FIGURE 29 – THE HILL AT MID-OHIO

3) If you use all of the road at the exit of the right hander, you will have great difficulty getting back to the right hand side of the road before the left hander. This doesn't matter because you don't want to be there anyway - because:

   a) The normal entry line to the left hander is off camber and the car won't turn out there.

   b) In this case being in the right place and pointed in the right direction (i.e. straight) when the car crests the hill takes precedence over corner entry.

   c) If you are on the inside going up the hill anyone who wants to pass you will have to do so on the outside. Let them try. (Watch a video of Unser Jr. versus Fittipaldi, 1993, or Villeneuve versus Rahal, 1995.)

4) If you hook up right and get a good shot down the hill you will have trouble getting all the way over to the left for the (faster) right hander at the

bottom. Don't worry about it - concentrate on getting the power down early. What you don't want to do is to get all the way over to the left so late that you have to turn abruptly and set up an oversteer pendulum which will prevent you from putting the power down.

It is tempting to fill this book with descriptions like this. There should be no need. If you let it, the track and the car will tell you what you need to know. If the track and the car won't talk to you, I can't help you.

Keep a detailed course notebook. Add to it every time that you visit each track, and refer to it before each visit. Include a really detailed course map. The good restaurants, welding shops, etc. are valid information. My race track logistics sheet is at the end of this chapter. It's not a bad idea.

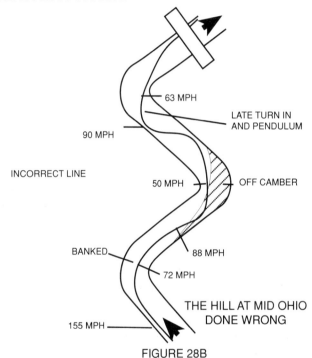

FIGURE 28B

SKIMMING THE SURFACE - DEALING WITH THE BUMPY RACE TRACK

People who build road racing tracks seldom have enough money to put down a good road surface. The typical road racing circuit in the USA has no proper foundation of crushed stone, gravel, etc. More likely a blacktop machine followed a bulldozer through the countryside and that was that. This sort of construction does not behave well with respect to winters, frost heaves and so forth.

Further, road contractors tend to understand vertical loads - as in heavy and as in truck - but they generally have no clue at all about horizontal loads - as in race tires, acceleration, braking and cornering. For these reasons our tracks tend to be very bumpy by European and Japanese standards. In fact the circuit that we consider the smoothest in North America, Circuit Gilles Villeneuve on the Isle Notre Dame in Montreal, is considered hopelessly bumpy by the Formula One Brigade.

The typical problems of our circuits are washboarded surfaces in the braking and corner exit zones and, in extreme cases, ruts in the corners themselves. The ruts tend to be repaired with concrete or epoxy, with all of the traction of wet glass. City street circuits which feel perfectly smooth at 40mph become a lot less so at 160.

Anyway, bumps on US road racing circuits are an inescapable fact of life. Historically there are two ways of dealing with bumps:

1) Stiffen the ride rates and shock damping so that the ride height can be kept low.

2) Soften the ride rates and optimize the damping so that the tires will stay on the track and then raise the car to keep the chassis off the ground.

Most of my regular readers probably expect me to advocate the soft and compliant approach. Wrong! It isn't that simple. A lot of what I feel should be done depends on the nature of the circuit and the type and location of the bumps.

I try to separate bumps first into critical and non critical. Critical bumps, to me, are those that upset the performance of the car in braking, cornering or acceleration. Non critical bumps are on the straights. My feeling is that we leave the car at its optimum stiffness and let the driver deal with the non critical bumps - often a minor adjustment in line helps a whole lot (also true in braking areas).

If all the corners are slow and ground effects (including flat bottoms) are not going to be very important (as on the emasculated track at Long Beach) then I feel the best approach is to soften and raise the car to gain tire compliance. We are not going to accelerate in any direction unless the tires are in contact with the track.

If the critical corners are fast and bumpy we have a problem - and we are going to have to compromise. Lime Rock is a case in point. Even though the majority of the corners are fast, I feel that the bumps are so severe that compliance takes priority over a stable aerodynamic platform - so we soften the car and raise it.

Actually, watching the stiff cars come through the downhill at Lime Rock, I contend that a compliant car offers an overall more stable aero platform than a stiff one which is bounding from high spot to high spot on the track. Besides, the compliant car is a lot less likely to break something. The "modern" shock absorber helps a lot in achieving compliance without ridiculous vertical travel. I will deal comprehensively with shocks in Chapter 18.

RACE TRACK LOGISTIC SHEET – updated _____

TRACK _____

TRACK OFFICE#: ( ) – _____ PERSON _____

TRACK MANAGER _____ RES#: ( ) –

SANCTIONING REGION#: ( ) – _____ PERSON _____

NEAREST
MACHINE SHOP _____

NEAREST
FAB SHOP/ HELIARC _____

NEAREST
RACE GAS _____

NEAREST
REAL AIRPORT _____

AIR FREIGHT NUMBERS:

AAL#: ( ) – _____ UAL#: ( ) –

TIGERS#: ( ) – _____ EMORY#: ( ) –

OTHER IMPORTANT/USEFUL
PEOPLE _____

MOTELS:

_____ ( ) – $____

_____ ( ) – $____

_____ ( ) – $____

_____ ( ) – $____

CHAMBER OF COMMERCE _____ ( ) –

BEST PADDOCK
LOCATION _____

BEST PIT LOCATION _____

OTHER
NOTES _____

_____

_____

HOSPITAL#: ( ) –

PARAMEDICS#: ( ) –

HELICOPTER AMBULANCE#: ( ) –

MAP TO HOSPITAL:

"If you try to go fast on an oval before your chassis is ready to go fast you will crash." –Bobby Rahal

"The Miles are tough race tracks." –Bobby Unser

OVAL TRACK HINTS

I do not claim to be expert at the art of oval track racing. I haven't done enough of it. However, it is a very real part of my professional life and it is almost bound to be a part of the road toward professional status for any journeyman racing driver in this country. It is great racing and we have to do it, so we had better learn to be good at it.

Racing on an oval is neither more difficult nor less difficult than racing on a road course. It is simply different - quite a lot different. The differences are more fundamental than the obvious one that on the oval we only turn left.

Because we only turn left, we can change the set up of the car to take advantage of this fact. On a road course, the car has to be set up so that it will, willingly, turn in both directions and at various speeds. It must also put the power down while turning in both directions at varying speeds and remain stable under heavy braking from varying speeds. None of this is true on the oval.

All of the corners are in the same direction and can (usually) be taken at about the same speed. This is not to say that all of the corners on a given oval will be identical - they won't - but at least those that we have to slow down for will usually be similar. We can take advantage of this fact to adjust our suspension to optimize cornering in these similar corners without having to compromise anywhere near as much as we do on road courses.

The other side of this coin is that since we don't have to compromise as much, we can approach perfection in the set up closer than we can in road racing - and we had better do so because any shortcomings in our chassis set up will be instantly obvious to our driver, our peers and our stopwatches. Regardless of what the fruitcup racers may claim at the bar, oval track racing ain't easy!

From the driver's point of view, three things stand out immediately. First, there is no place to hide - every mistake that you make will be glaringly obvious on the stopwatch and to the experienced naked eye. Second, the driver cannot make up for deficiencies in the chassis - either in design or in set up. On the average road racing circuit the driver can still carry a less than perfect car - at least to some extent. It simply cannot be done on an oval.

As Mr. Rahal pointed out, if you try to go faster than the chassis is ready to take you, you are going to find out about the third factor. Not only is there no place to hide - there is no place to go. When you make a big mistake you are not going into a run off area or down an escape road. You are going into the wall - and not at street course corner speeds. When you hit the wall on an oval, you usually hit it hard.

There are other characteristics that are not so evident. Chief among them are the twin facts that, to go really fast on an oval, you must be truly smooth and, to be successful at racing on the ovals, you must read the traffic and plan your passing moves laps ahead of yourself.

The road racing driver's natural tendency is to bring the car down to a "normal" apex in every corner. This is valid on 99% of all road circuit corners. It may not be so valid on ovals.

The road racing driver also has a natural tendency to apply opposite steering lock when he feels the rear of the car stepping out. When you do that on an oval, the rear tires instantly bite and, since the front tires are now pointed toward the wall, you hit the wall instantly. You cannot live with oversteer on an oval. Of course, excessive understeer will make you slow. The trick is the least amount of understeer that makes the car safe. It is not easy to find. When you lose it, spin it down to the inside. Things are softer there.

When the car is underpowered (or overtired) for the circuit in question, or if the banking is not constant, the car must be allowed to follow its natural arc - like the fall line on a ski slope or a roulette ball at the tables. Pulling the car down to an apex in these cases will merely cause the front tires to scrub, induce understeer and slow the car down. On any oval, the car must roll free through and off of the corners!

There is a factor of confidence on the ovals that is different from the road courses. On a road racing circuit the driver is acutely aware of how wide the road is at the exit of each corner. On the ovals, the perceptive (ie successful) driver will very soon become aware of how wide the entrance to each corner is. He will become aware of this simply because the way to learn how to go fast on short ovals is to drive the damned thing into the corner until you begin to lose control of it and then gather it all in before you hit the wall.

I am aware that this sounds crude and unimaginative - and so it is. But it is also effective. Until the driver realizes that there is an acre of black pavement before he is in the grey and two acres of grey before the wall, he will never develop the confidence to go truly fast on an oval. Watch Andretti when he gets surprised in traffic - the grey is driveable. Again, the unfortunate corollary to this blinding truth is that the driver who tries to go fast on a big oval before the car is set up to go fast is going to crash. Period. End of statement.

It is very difficult for the inexperienced driver to tell when the car is ready to go fast. For these two reasons it is not at all unusual for road racing drivers to crash a lot when they first go to the ovals. Like I just said, it ain't easy!

Another way of stating the same thing is that on a road racing circuit you concentrate on corner exit - using most of the chassis on the exit. On an oval track, you use most of the chassis going in - carrying more speed into the corner, taking an earlier apex and getting on the power later.

The learning process can be aided, and the crashes largely avoided, by a clear appreciation of the factors involved. There is an old saying at the Speedway to the effect that there are four key people on any team - the driver, the owner, the crew chief and the engineer - and that any one of them can be a rookie.

The biggest help for the rookie oval driver is an experienced and expert crew chief or race track engineer or teammate - preferably some combination of the three. Please note that "experienced" does not always equate to "expert".

SET UP

What we have to accomplish with our oval track set up is exactly what we have to accomplish with any racing car set up - we have to get the most cornering and accelerative power that the manufacturer built into our tires out of them. The differences are that we will be in the oval track corners longer than we will be in the average road racing corner and that we don't have to compromise the set up to let us turn the other way or at widely different speeds (low speed corner entry understeer does not exist on an oval - nor, in most cases, should corner exit wheelspin).

There are several possibilities here. For a start we can tilt the chassis - that is, raise the ride height on the right or outboard side of the car and lower the inboard so that the roll generated by cornering force will result in a level chassis in the corner. This is particularly important with cars that exploit any form of 'underwing'.

Then we can offset our static camber settings so that the tires will be at their optimum cornering camber angles in the turns. This means increasing the negative camber on the outside of the car and reducing it on the inside. With bias ply tires we will probably run static positive camber on the inside.

We can jack corner weight into the car in whatever direction will optimize the understeer/oversteer balance without worrying (much) about the adverse effects of uneven corner weights.

We can adjust the download for one range of cornering and straightaway speeds and we can offset the front wheel caster so that the car will naturally turn left.

We can also vary the rear toe in settings to get more grip with a car that only turns one way.

What we are trying to accomplish with all of this is a car with maximum grip in the corners, combined with minimum scrub. This last is super-critical because we will have quite enough trouble convincing our car that it wants to accelerate off the corners while pushing a big air load without adding understeer tire scrub to our problems.

Among the things that you don't need on the ovals is a "lively" race car. You will be a lot happier with slower steering compared to what is optimum for road courses. You will also be happier with a softer nose curve on the front shocks - to "slow the entry down" and make things more manageable. The rear shocks, on the other hand, should have a pretty steep nose angle to stabilize the rear of the car.

Cars with lots of tire - like Formula Atlantics - usually end up with front and rear wheel (not spring) rates pretty equal. Cars with limited rear tire widths (Indy Cars, Indy Lights) tend to run relatively more front wheel rate - 1.15:1 or so.

TIRES and DOWNLOAD

Tire temperature can be a major problem on ovals, especially if, as often happens in Formula Russell, Formula Ford and Formula Ford 2000, you are trying to race on road racing tires. In extreme cases the load transfers and the percentage of time that the car is actually cornering (the short straights don't give much cool off time) can result in blistered or chunked tires due to the actual physical degradation of the rubber. With any sort of luck (and sensitivity on the driver's part) the driver will either feel or see the blisters and stop before the tire blows. But a blistered tire can still ruin your whole day.

So how do we avoid overheating our tires on the ovals? First of all, we get the car balanced. A car that is understeering is going to scrub and overheat the outside front tire. The solution may be as simple as balancing the car to reduce the understeer and the scrub induced excessive temperature. The same is, of course, true of oversteer and blistered rear tires.

Before we go any further, we should note that, in my opinion at least, sliding induces a lot more tire temperature than download does. There are two valid approaches to the download versus drag equation on an oval. The first is to run minimal download and to concentrate on acceleration off the corners at the cost of corner entry speed and corner apex speed - in fact, at the sacrifice of cornering speed period. This won't work because you will be going slow through the corners. The second is to pile the download on to bring the corner speed up - even though the drag induced by the added download will slow the rate of acceleration off the corners. This won't work either.

The fast way is, as always, a compromise - just enough download. I generally lean towards download because download reduces tire scrub in flat out corners and so doesn't heat tires as much as sliding/squirming does. The reduced scrub will, of course, also make the car faster when it is loaded in the corner.

The danger here is that download can mask a multitude of chassis ills. So, as usual, I start out with less download than I think that I am going to use and, once the chassis is balanced, I add download until it slows the car down in terms of lap speed. Then I back it off just a little bit. Admittedly driver style and ability has more than a little to do with this decision.

Basically, to reduce tire temperature we can either reduce the amount of sliding that is going on or we can take dynamic load off the tire in question. We reduce the sliding by balancing the car, either with chassis adjustments or with download and we adjust the dynamic load with corner weight. This may sound a little contradictory - and, in one sense, it is.

HOW LOW?

How low do we run the car on an oval? In general, just as low as we can get it without destroying something by rubbing it against the asphalt or going to springs so hard that the car will "skate" instead of biting. There are a number of reasons for this.

The first is obvious - the most important factor in any car's cornering ability is the height of the vehicle's

TECHNICAL NOTES FOR THE OVALS

CASTER LEAD

The whole idea on the oval is to avoid scrub. The car must roll free in the corners. That means that the car has to be willing to turn in almost by itself - the act of turning it in will induce understeer which will in turn scrub the front tires and kill the momentum. The way to encourage the car to turn in by itself is to run caster lead. We all know that if the front caster on any car is uneven, the car will drift or pull or turn toward the wheel with the lesser amount of caster. So we either reduce the static caster (or trail) on the inside front wheel or increase it on the outside. How much is difficult to say but typically we are talking between 0.5 degree and 1.5 degrees less caster on the inside front wheel. Of course, the car must be re-bump steered. Caster lead does not sound like a big deal - but it is. It is, in fact, probably a bigger deal than tilting the car. It is essential.

CORNER WEIGHT

Everybody knows about corner weight - or "wedge". At least everybody thinks that they do. The theory is simplicity itself - add more inside weight to the end of the car that is misbehaving; this will increase the vertical load on the inside tire at the same lateral acceleration and reduce the syndrome - allowing more lateral g to be generated. Maybe! In actuality, the picture is not that simple.

Corner weight is not always what it seems to be. Because of kingpin inclinations and caster angle, dynamic corner weight is effected by steering angle. The relative corner weights that you read on the scales are indicative of what is actually happening in a straight line, but it all changes once you turn the steering wheel. With caster lead the effect is more pronounced. Try it on the scales! Anyway, it is all a question of balance - and it is not real easy to achieve, or even to recognize.

SPRINGS

Generally speaking, the ovals want moderately heavy springs and moderate bars. A stronger right front spring (i.e. stronger than the left front) will help prop up the outside front on corner entry. I believe - but cannot prove - that, when we are talking real horsepower, a stronger left rear will keep the pitch attitude more even on corner exit - but this is short strokes and without testing we will never get there.

As always, when you have achieved a good balance, either stiffen or soften the car by equal amounts of wheel rate and roll resistance (not spring rate and bar diameter) to find the optimum.

Continued...

center of gravity. The lower the center of gravity, the less lateral load transfer there will be for a given amount of cornering force and the faster the car will go around corners. This lowering of the c-of-g takes precedence over suspension geometry and everything else.

TECHNICAL NOTES FOR THE OVALS, cont.

PACKERS

Packers are hard - nylon or aluminum - spacers placed on the shock absorber piston rod to limit bump travel. They are very popular. I do not use packers on the ovals. I do not know of anyone who goes really fast who has not tried them and I do not know anyone who is going fast who uses them as the final limit for bump travel on an oval. They simply make things too critical. Most successful teams use closed cell foam bump rubbers with adjusting packers to keep the car off the race track at very high speeds.

TOE

Front toe is self centering so, to my mind at least, differential front toe-in will only effect Ackerman and I am not bright enough to figure out what, if any, the effect will be - except to offset the steering wheel. However, some fast people run toe-out on the left front and toe-in on the right front...

On the ovals we don't want a lot of toe. The turn radii are large and the steering angles are small. We cannot stand any understeer tire scrub. In my experience what toe there is at the front should be toe-in.

At the rear, the majority of the total toe-in should be on the right rear. The attitude of the car is then adjusted with left rear toe. Left rear toe-out will stick the back end (think about it)!

ACKERMAN ANGLE

Increased Ackerman (greater than classic) is a good thing for race tracks that feature slow and medium speed corners that offer virtually no steady state cornering. On the ovals the most that we should use is "classic" Ackerman and less may well be better. Increased steer angle on the inside front tire is just going to cause tire drag and understeer.

CAMBER

Camber must be offset so that the footprints of all four tires will be optimized in the corners. How much depends on the camber curves of the car. The static camber will always be greater than normal negative on the right side of the car and less than normal on the left. The amount depends on the tire characteristics, suspension geometry and race track. There are no magic numbers.

Again, I depend more on the appearance of the tire than pyrometer readings.

Continued...

On a paved oval we can usually run really low for two reasons. First, because the ovals are typically smoother than road courses and second, because we don't need anywhere near as much suspension travel. There is no low speed acceleration and, except for Indy Cars and Stock Cars, damned little, if any hard braking - no need to provide for pitch attitude changes. We can severely restrict roll because we will have enough download to largely negate the adverse lateral load transfer effects of stiff bars.

The second reason for running as low as possible is is not quite so obvious. With non ground effect cars, the lower the car is, the less air will pass under it. The less air that passes under the car, the less drag that air can produce by turbulence.

When running underpowered ground effect Super Vee cars on big ovals we couldn't run them very low simply because the whole secret to going fast was to minimize the aerodynamic drag induced by download. We didn't need much cornering power on the 2.5-milers: the cars could only go 165 or so, and the corners could be taken at that speed with very little download.

The way to make any ground effect car go fast in a straight line is to raise it, not lower it - break the ground effect to get rid of the induced drag. It also helps to raise (or to remove) the skirts. Fortunately the sanctioning bodies finally figured out that Super Vees on the big ovals was the SCCA's version of Russian Roulette. We don't have to play that game anymore.

PITCH

Strangely enough one of the big problems that fugitives from road racing have when they first come to the ovals is learning smooth. While we road racers tend to think that we have a patent on smooth, the truth of the matter is that we don't know the meaning of the word. If you want to see smooth, watch the experienced and expert Indy drivers on a 2.5 mile oval - or watch the very best of the Outlaws on clay.

Our drivers tend to do a bunch of things wrong on the ovals. They upset the car by right foot braking, they jab at the throttle and they don't use enough road at the entrance to the corners. With any form of underwing - either tunnels as in Indy Car and Atlantic or flat bottomed as in Indy Lights and FF2000 - the pitch attitude of the download producing parts is critical with relation to both total download and location of the aerodynamic center of pressure. With any car, the pitch attitude of the chassis determines the inclination of the roll axis.

On the ovals, even more than on the fast road racing circuits, we need a stable pitch attitude. So we roll out of and on to the throttle and, if we must brake, we brake with the left foot against partial engine power. And, if we seriously contemplate being fast, we will be smooth.

LEFT FOOT BRAKING

The main reason that I advocate left foot braking on ovals is simple: if you only need to slow down a little bit and you do it with the left foot against engine power with the right foot part way down, the pitch attitude of the car doesn't change much. Consequently, the car is not upset by the braking. This also works very well on some fast road racing corners.

The typical road racer's approach is to let off the gas and jam on the brakes - dropping the nose of the car significantly. When he has finished his braking he transfers his right foot from the middle pedal to the right hand one - instantly - and the nose comes up just as instantly. This gives us aerodynamic, load and camber changes just when we need them least - bad idea!

The proper way is to brake against part throttle so that the entire process is as smooth as whipped cream - even though it is hard on the discs, pads and brake fluid.

THE MILE MASTERS

I often hear that the chief characteristic of the "Mile Masters" - Andretti (Mario), Fittipaldi, Mears, Rahal, Unser (any) and, in past years, Sneva and Foyt - is that they are so good at setting their cars up, they can run anywhere on the track while the other cars are restricted to the relatively narrow "groove". And so they can!

The Masters can run any line that they choose, under any track condition - so long as they don't try to run as fast out of their groove as they run in it! In other words, the Masters change their line, and the speed at which they run it, according to the dictates of traffic.

Their anticipation of traffic has to be seen to be appreciated. It is seen best from the side of the hill at the Phoenix mile where you are high enough above the cars to begin to get an overall view. They plan their moves in traffic laps in advance and not only do they have no trouble with the traffic they are lapping, they also manage to time their passes so that the car behind will often be "scraped off" by the passing manoeuver.

Of course, every really good racing driver does exactly the same thing on road circuits - it just isn't as noticeable.

LAST WORDS ON OVALS

1) Until the driver has become expert, for lap time, listen to the stopwatch more than to the driver. It is very difficult for the inexperienced oval driver to evaluate changes. Of course, if the car is evil or unbalanced, listen to the driver.

   Segment times can be misleading because of the overriding importance of momentum and corner exit speed. The best way to evaluate what is going on is by interpretation of on board data and (when possible) overlaying traces with faster drivers. A simple engine rpm or mph trace is invaluable. If you don't have on board data, listen to the stopwatch.

2) Always start out with definite aero understeer. Take it out gradually as you get faster and more comfortable.

TECHNICAL NOTES FOR THE OVALS, cont.

TIRES

On the ovals cornering speed is very high, the car is in the corner longer than on road racing circuits and it is being pressed into the track surface by both the download and the banking. All of these forces combine to deform the sidewalls of the tires. This sidewall deformation upsets the cross-sectional shape of the footprint in a manner similar to that of an underinflated tire. This both reduces available traction and adds noticeably to scrub. Static tire pressure must therefore be considerably higher than on the typical road racing circuit - say 8 to 10 psi higher on the outside and 3 to 4 psi more inside. Start the race on tires with a few gentle and short heat cycles - they will stay with you longer.

TILT

I am unclear as to how much tilt is best. Basically, tilt makes the car scrub less in corners but slows down acceleration. The optimum amount for Atlantic cars on the miles is somewhere between 0.5 degree and 1.0 degree. Some very fast people only tilt the front and get their RF corner weight that way.

3) Don't turn the steering wheel any more than you absolutely have to - the effect is about the same as applying the brake.

4) When you lose it - and you will - don't put opposite lock on the car. Spin it down to the inside.

5) Don't allow the car to scrub in the corners. With underpowered cars it is sometimes necessary to turn pretty abruptly on the ovals in order to get the turning over with soon and get back to accelerating - or at least trying to.

6) When lapping people, don't expect them to get out of the way or to do anything predictable. Chances are that they are too busy trying to stay alive to look in their mirrors. Ongais always said that you have to make eye contact in his mirror before you can safely pass.

7) Anticipate the traffic and plan your moves well (laps!) in advance.

8) Remember that the track is wide in the first third of the corners.

10

"The toughest fights take place in the streets." Jack Dempsey

STREET FIGHTING

The future of our sport in the USA and Canada lies in the streets. There are several reasons for this and they all have to do with money. Real estate that is readily accessible to large crowds is just too valuable to build new racetracks on - or, for that matter, to keep some of the existing tracks alive.

While circuits like Mid-Ohio, Elkhart Lake, Road Atlanta and Willow Springs are secure at least for the foreseeable future, Riverside is a giant Mall, Bridge-hampton is sand dunes and all of the old airport circuits are gone. On the other hand, the cost of creating a circuit within the confines of city streets, while not exactly petty cash, is not excessive and a number of cities have discovered that a once-a-year major street race brings in a lot of revenue and establishes a certain image.

It all started with Trois Rivieres - but no one noticed until Chris Pook made Long Beach a happening. It spread to Toronto, Vancouver, Des Moines, Detroit, Miami, and, despite abortive efforts at Tacoma, Columbus, Spokane, St Petersburg and San Antonio, several other cities are apparently eager to join the fun. I, for one, am looking forward to a genuine revival. Just maybe, racing could become a major sport in the USA. Anyway, it behooves each of us to study the special demands and circumstances required by racing in the streets.

Strictly speaking, there is no such thing as a typical street course. Detroit is fast. Toronto is medium speed. Trois Rivieres is slow. Long Beach is flat with slow corners and long straights. Des Moines has a lot of elevation changes. Some are bumpy; others are smooth. All of them are lined on both sides with unyielding concrete.

If there is a typical street circuit corner, though, it is what I call a "boulevard stop sign" corner, one you approach at relatively high speed, brake hard, turn 90 degrees and rocket down another straight toward a corner very similar to the one that you just left. The corners are very likely to feature at least one bump (usually in the braking area) and at least one surface change.

For the most part street racing is stop and go racing. It resembles road racing in that there are a variety of corners, and it resembles oval track racing in that the walls have no mercy - there is a definite, finite and immediate penalty for every driving error. The walls won't move; there are no run off areas and damned few escape roads.

Street circuits have other standard characteristics - the roads are crowned, there is little grip to the road surface, the cars tend to overheat and there are very few places to go when an accident takes place in front of you. The crown is purposely placed on the roads for drainage and it means that many corner entries and exits are off camber. There isn't much grip, firstly because the road surface is always dusty at the opening of practice and there is no rubber down. These conditions are self curing as the weekend wears on.

The big thing to remember here is that, at least during the first session, you must never - not ever - move off line to let a faster car through. Until the track has "come in", the line on which there is some grip will be exactly one car wide and you depart from it, at any speed, at your peril. I have lost a couple of cars in the first session at street circuits through experienced and capable drivers being uncharacteristically polite.

What doesn't change very much, however, is the fact that the road surface has been polished by millions of miles of street traffic and has very little if any "tooth" to it. I pointed out in 'Tune to Win' that a lot of the traction generated between the tire and the road is due to mechanical gripping between the rubber and surface irregularities of the road. A polished surface inhibits this adhesion to a marked degree.

Even though rubber will be laid down as the weekend progresses, the level of grip will never approach that of a purpose built race track. Therefore, to work well on a street circuit, the car must be relatively softly sprung. This will mean, of course, that even with state of the art shocks, you will have to run it somewhat higher than normal.

So be it - even with a ground effect car. The cornering speed on most street circuits will be so low that the tunnels (or inclined flat bottom) won't be generating much download in the corners anyway. Where the trade off point lies depends on the individual car, engine and circuit. If the circuit is bumpy, then the car will have to have a reasonable amount of rear droop travel - previous comments about ride height apply.

From the driving point of view, the fastest street fighter is always going to be the one who brakes deepest into the corners - with control. From the car set up point of view, the two basic requirements are the ability to point into slow corners well and the ability to put the power down early and completely with a minimum of fuss and wheelspin. Strangely enough these three factors are not at all mutually contradictory.

Racing in the streets requires even more discipline and more foresight from the driver than racing on permanent circuits. When you hang a rear wheel an inch off the outside of the exit of Turn 14 at Road America you raise a little dust. When you hang a rear wheel half an inch off the outside of the exit of any turn on a street course you imbed it in the wall.

At the same time, the driver must be super aggressive - with the race track in order to go fast and with traffic in order to get by. It is tough racing and this is no place for a car with a knife edge set up. The successful street racing car will be forgiving.

On the typical street course we used to wind up with relatively soft front springs so that the car would turn in, a big front bar to keep it from falling over after it turned in and to transfer load back onto the inside rear wheel on acceleration, a relatively soft (if any) rear bar to minimize the lateral load transfer onto the outside wheel, and a fair amount of rear spring to keep the car from falling over.

Anti squat should be reduced to a minimum (remember, you have to squat to go) and the rear shocks should be soft in bump - especially at high piston velocities. If the road surface is bumpy, you can't run a lot of rear rebound either, or the car will "jack down" and bounce its way into oversteer.

These days we are using low piston velocity bump control in the shocks, rather than big front bars and big rear springs. Typically the front wheel rate is stiffer than the rear (remember that the driver feels and reacts to the stiff end of the car) and we run light front bars, if any.

We often wind up with all the rear wing you can get short of stalling. As always, the front wings are adjusted to balance the rear. There are exceptions to this - at Long Beach we run very little wing while at Vancouver we run very little with Atlantic cars and a fair bit with Indy Lights and Indy Cars.

Engine overheating is another question entirely. The problem here is that the engine is doing a lot of very hard first and second gear work at low air stream velocities - in traffic - while the car is running around in a concrete canyon with relatively stagnant air which tends to get overheated from the cars.

If the car is not marginal in the cooling department to start with, there may not be a problem. If it is, there will be. What we do then is forget all about the niceties of cooling duct design (because we simply no longer care about cooling drag), open up both the inlet and exit ducts for the water and oil heat exchangers and, in extreme cases, go to thicker water cores and larger oil coolers. These last items can be hung right out in the airstream if necessary. Cut and hack become the order of the day. Hoping that the problem will go away simply will not work (it never does).

A higher pressure radiator cap will merely raise the boiling point of the coolant - not reduce the temperature. Substituting plain everyday water with a little soluble oil and/or aluminum anti corrosion compound for the ever popular anti-freeze will lower the water temperature a little bit. Anti freeze prevents freezing - which is not a problem in any of the racing that I do - and prevents corrosion, but its thermal transfer properties are inferior to those of water. Red Line's 'Water Wetter' actually works by increasing the surface tension of the water and so reducing the temperature.

Substituting a good synthetic engine oil for the popular racing oils will drop the oil temperature about five degrees. Along that line, if the engine oil temperature runs higher than the water, it is possible to drag the water temperature down by cooling the oil further. Anyway, the time to fix a street course overheating problem is before you get to the track. If your car's cooling system is marginal at road courses, fix it before you go to the street fights.

Everything I have said about cooling in the streets is equally true of cooling at altitude - the first Denver CART race was just plain funny. With the exception of one team, the most experienced racers in the country were completely caught out by the fact that, although a turbocharged engine with the same plenum pressure as it had at sea level will produce almost the same power as it did at sea level, the air at 5000 feet will not do the same amount of cooling per cubic foot. Big embarrassment. Dumb!

You may find that some crew chiefs are reluctant to change the basic car set up for street courses. This is because some racers simply do not understand the basics of vehicle dynamics - and a few are not interested in learning. This is the time for a frank discussion of the authority structure of the team and/or a restructuring of same.

Punctured tires are a fact of life during the early sessions on most street courses. The reason has to do with the spring steel bristles that are shed in their thousands by the street sweepers. Not all of them get picked up when the course is prepared (why they don't use a big magnet I do not know). These mini spears are usually found right up against the walls. Most of them can be avoided by staying a foot or two off the wall during the early sessions - something you should be doing anyway until you have learned both the circuit and your car very well indeed.

FINAL WORDS

I have very little patience with those people (usually TV commentators and unsuccessful drivers) who keep harping on the intimidating nature and proximity of street circuit walls. The walls are there for everyone. The people who merely drive racing cars may be intimidated by walls. Real racing drivers are aware of walls but have some sort of strange affinity for them - they truly enjoy the challenge of drifting right up to the wall under full power. It is not a coincidence that the best drivers win consistently in the streets - even in less than competitive cars.

11

"Racing in the wet is not more dangerous than racing in the dry, it is just more difficult." Denis Jenkinson

RACING IN THE RAIN

Most drivers in this country seem to regard racing in the wet as some sort of aberration that is best avoided - and certainly never practiced. On the other hand, drivers in Europe (and especially in the UK) regard racing in the rain as normal. This tells us two things - it rains less in the US than it does in Europe - and the overseas drivers are better at racing in it than we are.

There is nothing we can do about the disparity in climate (nor would I want to). But it is a fact of life that not-quite-good-enough-to-make-it-in-Europe drivers are coming over here in droves, armed and ready to take what few paying seats there are away from our home-spun heroes. Our heroes had damned well better learn to race in the wet.

It's not actually that bad. In fact the major problem is not lack of traction but lack of visibility. The lack of vision is due to two separate and unrelated factors: spray from the car ahead and fogging of the visor/goggles/windshield.

In the case of the closed car, if the team is not capable of arranging a supply of warm air to the inside of the windscreen and effective wipers, then you shouldn't be driving for it. It simply isn't that hard to do - and it will rain. Even if it takes a plug-in blower motor, defrosting should be available in every closed road racing car.

The matter of the visor/goggles is less simple. In my day, although I normally wore a "bubble shield". In the wet I wore surplus flight goggles with ventilation holes moulded into the frames - no problem. The advent of the closed face helmet put paid to the use of goggles by any intelligent racing driver. (Yes, that includes sedan and closed car drivers - in my opinion, those NASCAR and IMSA drivers who wear open faced helmets are crazy).

The primary cause of visor fog is the humid breath of the wearer. The newer helmets have flow-through ventilation and this, combined with preventing said exhalations from reaching the visor, is the most effective method to prevent fogging.

This means sealing the nose/mouth (breathing) area of the helmet from the visor cavity. Again - not that difficult. What we are talking about here is a custom fitted helmet with cheek and nose pads. Get with Simpson on this one. Anyone who wears any other manufacturer's helmet, in my opinion, needs his or her brains tested. Simpson also has the best of the "fog free" visors.

Having sealed the visor from your hot and steamy breath, Simpson's new "stick on" anti-fog layer is the best of a long line of solutions. It works. Congratulations Bill! Rain-X on the outside of the visor is also a good idea.

There are several other tricks. One of the more popular ones used to be the drilling of ventilation holes in the top and bottom of the visor. The problem with this was that, unless you had a very effective wind deflector in front of your head, the ventilation holes would let in water as well as air. You were then faced with the problem of water on the inside of your visor - not good! Today, with flow-through helmets, the holes are superfluous.

There is, however, a lesson here. If water is hitting your visor in the wet then air is hitting your helmet in the dry and, whether you realize it or not, your head is being buffeted and you are causing yourself unnecessary fatigue. Build an effective deflector. A slot in the cowl through which you push a carved on old visor is the best way that I know of to do this. Stop beating yourself on the head - it will pay off wet or dry.

SPRAY

There is no real solution to the problem of visibility in the spray of the car(s) ahead. It would help somewhat if the sanctioning bodies would insist on real rain lights - as in aircraft marker lights, or at least light emitting diodes. They do not and the mandated rain lights are so puny as to be useless. Putting a real one on your own car is not illegal and just might save you from getting hit.

The best way to avoid spray is to be out in front (if you are the only one who can see, it is fairly easy to break free of the pack). Other than that, you just try to avoid as much of it as you can and hope for the best. Remember that the driver kicking up the spray can see even less of you than you can of him. Not fun!

WATERPROOFING THE CAR

The time to waterproof the sensitive parts of the car is when the car is being built - not just before the grid. One of the proprietary dielectric silicones should cover every electrical connection. If the engine air intake is forward facing, a rain shield should be fabricated before it is needed.

VEHICLE DYNAMICS IN THE WET

Things are different in the wet - several things. Obviously, even with rain tires, there is less grip. But there is less loss of tractive capacity in some directions than in others. For instance, the car will stop astonishingly well in the wet - but acceleration is severely limited.

Actually, acceleration is only limited by your ability to sense the wheelspin limit and modulate the engine output to match. However, this is something that you are probably not used to having to do and, unless the throttle response is perfect, the car is not going to help you in your efforts to control wheelspin.

The lateral capacity of the tire is diminished more than the longitudinal capacity. This means that, regardless of how much download we throw at the car, we are not going to approach the cornering force that we achieve in the dry. Therefore there will not be as much roll - and we won't need as much roll resistance. This is good because we want as much load on the inside rear tire as we can get. All of this means that, if we are certain that it is going to be wet, we can back off on both springs and bars.

SHOCKS IN THE WET

When it rains, lots of things happen at once. The single most notable thing is that the driver cannot see. Shocks cannot help this. The next most notable thing is that the co-efficient of friction between the tires (even the best of rain tires) and the road is dramatically reduced. The immediate result is that the reduced g-forces will generate less load transfer - both lateral and longitudinal.

Equally important, when a tire breaks traction in the wet - either through wheelspin or a lateral skid - it will take longer to return to traction. This means that we must soften the suspension to increase the compliance between the rubber and the road - especially on corner

exits. In the world of shock absorbers (detailed in Chapter 18), this means as much low speed bleed as we can get.

However, the car will be going virtually as fast on the straight portions of the track (where the major bumps tend to lurk) as in the dry. Unless we are certain that the rain will continue and have time to change the springs, we will still need significant forces in high piston speed bump and in rebound to deal with the upsets. It is no fun at all to drive a street car with worn out shocks down a bumpy, wet and puddled road. What we have here is a conflict of interest!

The conventional (and correct) solution is to significantly reduce the shock forces in high piston speed bump and slightly reduce the rebound and low speed bump control and let the driver deal with the result. If you have been so foresighted and fortunate as to do real wet weather testing, and have the funds, you should have a set of rain springs, shocks and bars ready to go on the car.

TESTING IN THE WET

The only way for a driver to learn how to drive fast and safely in the wet and the only way that a team is going to learn how to set up the car for the wet is to test in the wet. This seems pretty obvious. But many teams refuse to test in the wet - stating that it is too dangerous and that they cannot afford to crash the car. Unclear on the concept!

If you don't trust your driver to test in the wet, when there are no other cars around to help him go off or for him to hit, then how in hell can you trust him to race in the wet - with an untested car?

BRAKING IN THE WET

Since the car has less longitudinal grip, it has less forward load transfer under braking. Therefore you need to move the brake ratio to the rear - again, how much must be determined by test. Don't even think about trail braking in the wet. The car will stop, it will turn and it will accelerate, but the only way that it will combine lateral and longitudinal accelerations is that it will slow down (barely) while spinning.

THROTTLE MODULATION

One of the major problems in rain driving is throttle modulation. Most drivers prefer a short or quick throttle in the dry - even with the super cars, there isn't a lot of throttle modulation going on - the tires are so good and the download so great that, in many corners, it's pretty much on or off.

Not so in the wet - the typical short throttle is very liable to produce wheelspin and embarrassment. The solution is pretty simple. Two positions for the throttle cable - either at the pedal end or at the throttle end. With electronic engine management it is usually preferable to do the two position bit at the pedal to avoid upsetting the throttle position sensor.

WET LINES

The idea in the wet is to drive where the best traction is. The traction will not be found on the "normal" line, which is relatively polished from traffic and covered in rubber (slippery when wet) and, possibly, oil. Nor will it be found on any part of the track that is painted - including the curbs and rumble strips at the exits of corners.

Instead of braking and turning in from the extreme edge of the road, it is often better to approach the corner a car width to the inside, cross the normal line and exit on the outside. This is not a hard and fast rule - you should always be looking for the part of the track with the most traction.

The one thing you can be certain of is that when there is both standing water (puddles) and wet but not submerged pavement, the grip will not be in the standing water. Yet we see experienced drivers with perfectly good eyesight trying to brake or accelerate in a river when there is wet but above-water pavement a few feet to one side. Some people just don't think!

SECTION FIVE

ON TRACK

12

"In Formula Three, most of what we call testing is actually driver training."
– Glenn Waters

TESTING

Every major racing team regards testing - those long hours at a deserted race track far from the crowds and excitement of race day - as crucial to its success. Talk to any team whose achievements didn't match their expectations and you are likely to hear the plaintive cry, "We never got to test".

Testing has been going on as long as motor racing has. But things have changed a lot in the past few decades. Until the middle Sixties, chassis development was limited at best. Aerodynamic development was virtually unknown, limited to "streamlining". The drivers were expected to adapt to and drive around handling problems. I well remember Cooper going to Goodwood for the initial test of its 1960 Formula One car. The team had Jack Brabham and two front and two rear anti roll bars. Brabham won the World Championship that year.

Testing was mainly component testing or endurance testing - does the new or redesigned widget work and, if it does, is it reliable enough to race? That sort of testing still goes on, of course, but it is mainly for the works teams.

Except when the widget breaks, component testing tends to be pretty boring for all concerned - which is one reason that the big works teams employ test drivers (the race drivers want to play golf rather than thunder around endlessly waiting for something to break). The other reason, of course, is that the teams and sponsors don't want to risk the stars in unproven equipment...

From the driver's point of view, component testing and endurance testing are pretty straightforward and often not particularly challenging. He does what he is told to do, drives the car consistently as hard as he is instructed to, listens or feels for what he is told to listen or feel for, answers the questions honestly and, at least in the early phases of his career, feels very lucky indeed.

If you should be so fortunate as to land a testing contract, you get to drive some really neat cars, spend time with some really smart people and get paid for it. You will probably have a lot of time to interact with the people because the whole team will spend a lot of time either changing parts or waiting for new parts to

get there. Use this time wisely. Learn. Impress the team with your professionalism. Let your enthusiasm show. Testing contracts can lead to racing contracts. As examples I give you David Coulthard, Adrian Fernandez, Damon Hill, Mike Groff, Johnny O'Connell and Paul Tracy.

The kind of testing that concerns us in this chapter is development testing - making the combination of car and driver work better and go faster. Every racing organization, at every level, does this sort of testing to some extent.

Just as wind tunnel testing is liable to degenerate into "mindless blowing of air", so a lot of so called race track testing turns out to be just "driving around". Driving around is valuable - but only for seat time and, even then, purposeless seat time is of limited benefit, simply because it does tend to be mindless.

Testing is expensive. While the crew may be on salary, track rent, worn out tires, engines, gears, brakes, etc, are a long way from being cheap. We tend to think of time as being free - it is not. Time spent doing something non-productive could have been spent doing something productive.

In order to get your money's worth from a test, there must be a reasonably detailed plan. The plan should be written. It should include:

1) The reason(s) for the test.

2) The priorities involved in the test.

3) The procedure(s) to be followed,

    if...
    then...

4) The parts needed for the test.

5) The people needed for the test. Bring enough people to be able to change the parts/configuration quickly, if possible without the driver working on the car.

Two very basic test schedules are appended to this chapter.

EARLY DAYS

At the very beginning of your career, your testing must consist of "seat time". Until you are comfortable in the environment and relaxed enough at your personal limits to be able to concentrate on what the car is actually doing, you will do very little meaningful vehicle development testing. For this reason alone it is essential that your training wheels be well sorted out and well balanced - no one is going to learn how to relax and go fast in an ill handling race car.

This does not mean that for your first day on a race track you want the set up that won the class championship last season - you almost certainly do not. It has been said that all racing drivers draw the line that defines the outer limits of tire adhesion. Some draw it with a roller. Others draw it with paint brushes of various sizes. The great ones draw it with a drafting pencil. It is likely that last season's champion uses a somewhat finer brush than a novice driver is going to be comfortable with - and a car that is fast but too nervous for you to be relaxed in is just as bad a learning tool as an ill handling car.

That is one of the reasons that I advocate the school series as the initial training ground. If you decide to bypass the schools, ask someone knowledgeable (the manufacturer, for instance - or a good rent-a-racer with experience of the same car) for a good basic start out set up.

At this stage you should not drive at a comfortable level - you won't learn anything. When doing driver training (or when practicing for a race) you should drive at a level where you are not quite comfortable - not scared, but not comfortable. To improve, you must stretch the envelope. It's a fine line.

Once you have reached the relaxed-enough-at-speed level - and realized that your racer can be improved - it is time to start testing. Every chance that you get.

In the beginning you will be learning as a driver more than you will be improving the car. Before you go to the track, review your notes and write down - in detail - what you feel that the car was doing wrong the last time that you drove it (and what it was doing right). Sit down, analyze your notes and try to figure out both why it was doing whatever it was and what, within the limits of your resources, you can do to try and improve it. Prioritize your ideas; write your plan down; assemble the parts you will need; go to the race track and start testing.

Always begin by base lining the car the way that it was the last time at that track (or with a known good set up). Get the tires hot and get yourself up to speed before you make any changes at all. When you are up to consistent speed with the baseline set up (you don't need a personal best here, let alone a lap record) come in, do

a detailed debrief (self debrief if necessary) and a track map (I'll explain this concept later).

Now make your first scheduled change and repeat the process. Stay out no longer than it takes you to analyze the effect(s) of the change. Make only one change at a time and, at this stage on your learning curve, make no small changes.

There are several important considerations for you, the driver, to remember and to concentrate on:

1) Always analyze all of the effects of each change - good and bad. Always put your analysis in writing (or on tape to be transcribed later) before going out again.

2) You must be completely honest and objective about the whole exercise. There is nothing more frustrating than the driver who suggests a change and then drives the car harder to prove the merit of his suggestion - except maybe the engineer who refuses in the face of hard evidence to admit that his pet idea didn't work.

3) Be sensitive to the state of your tires. When they start to go off, either change them or quit testing. You can use greasy tires for driver development - to learn how to deal with understeer or oversteer, for example - but you cannot do vehicle development on them.

4) Be sensitive to the state of the race track and of the day - changing race tracks and changing days continue to lead the most experienced teams astray. The very best of the UK Formula Three teams are masters of adjusting the car for the day.

5) In testing, subjective "feel" is every bit as important as lap time.

6) Don't be afraid to change things. The only way that you, as a driver, are going to learn the effects of changing anything on the car is to change it and see what it feels like. There is nothing sacred about car set up. Just because the factory recommends 3/4 degree of negative camber or 3 degrees of castor doesn't mean that it's right. The fact of the matter is that most race cars are released for sale with very little testing.

7) Keep your level of driving consistent - and hard. There is no sense at all in trying to develop a car at 80% of your personal limit. It will be a different beast at 98%. Don't adapt your driving to the car. This is, of course, the opposite of what you have to do during a race - then you must adapt to the car. It's a conflict and partially explains why many excellent racing drivers are poor test drivers. The best way to avoid adapting is to not give yourself the chance - do only a few laps after each change, just enough to feel the difference. Of course, that means you have to be ready to drive the car, hard, immediately. It's good practice.

8) Write a formal test report (typed). A couple of simplified samples are appended to this chapter.

WHAT TO TRY

As usual, deciding what to do is as difficult as doing it. (The only real decision we ever have to make in life is what to do next.) The first order of business is to get the car balanced with the base line set up. In order to do this, you are almost certainly going to have to separate the low speed balance from the high speed balance - even if the car does not feature download generating appendages.

The if - then table at the end of chapter 17 may be of help, at least in the beginning. These suggestions are indicative of trends - none of them are cast in stone. I strongly suggest that you start with the relatively low speed end of things - it's easier to feel things at 60mph than it is at 120.

Once you are pretty well satisfied with the general balance of the car, (don't hold out for perfection here - time is more important than perfection) try stiffening the ride by about 10% in wheel rate (see Tune to Win Chapter Six for an explanation of wheel rate vs spring rate). Keep the front to rear couple as close to the same as practical (front to rear couple = front wheel rate/front wheel rate + rear wheel rate).

This should make the car quicker to respond to your inputs - more responsive. It may also, of course, make the car slide rather than stick - but that is what we are trying to find out. Since it will probably not be possible to keep the front to rear ride ratio exact, any difference in the understeer/oversteer balance may have to be trimmed out with the bars.

If the shocks are adjustable, next try adding more rebound force to each end to compensate for the increase in spring rate. If you and the stopwatch like the results, stiffen the bars (again in equal steps of resistance, front and rear) and try that.

Continue the exercise until it makes the car either uncomfortable or slower - then back it off a step. If you don't like the first stage of stiffening, soften the car by the same amount and try that.

You will find that a relatively soft car is better in slow corners and a relatively stiff car is better in fast corners - no surprise. A soft car is better over bumps and a stiff car is better when the circuit is smooth. The characteristics of the individual circuit will determine the best compromise.

Don't be afraid to try things. Change the cambers, the toes, and the shock settings, and feel the effect of each change on stability, braking, corner entry, midphase and exit. Change the rake of the car. Change the brake balance. If the car has wings, vary the total download and the download balance.

All of this is time consuming, but it is the only way that you can build your knowledge base and your sensitivity. It will all pay dividends later.

For a lot of this sort of thing you are looking for feel as much as lap time. You don't need optimum tires, or even a crisp and race ready engine. You are building experience, not breaking lap records. Be honest, objective and consistent. Write it down. Make your own if-then list. Think. Analyze. Learn.

All of this is for when you are effectively working alone - developing your personal experience base and your own skills with the race car. The next subject is for if and when you get to the stage where you are working with an experienced and competent team. Again, always remember that experience and competence are not synonymous. Experience is valuable only if we learn from it. Many people and many race teams do not.

THE DRIVER'S ROLE IN TESTING FROM THE ENGINEER'S POINT OF VIEW

The engineer requires four things from the test driver:

1) Speed.
2) Consistency.
3) Honesty.
4) Physical and mental endurance.

Regardless of how much on board data gathering equipment is involved and regardless of how much of it is working or how quickly the results can be downloaded, graphed, printed, compared and analyzed, the driver remains the principal data gathering system. He should also be the most reliable.

LEVELS

We talk of the level of driving effort in "tenths". Driving all out - at the very edge of your personal performance envelope - is referred to as "driving at ten-tenths". What we don't talk about is that the ten-tenths that Senna uses for a qualifying lap is a different thing from the ten-tenths that leaves a Formula One driver drained at the end of a 200 mile Grand Prix. What we are actually talking about is the level of intensity of our total personal output.

The level of this intensity - physical, emotional and mental - is time dependent. It is actually a level of concentration. We drive at one level when qualifying. This level is definitely not comfortable and cannot be sustained. We drive at another, sustainable, level when racing - with a bit held in reserve for when we need it, either to attack or to defend.

This racing level should be barely sustainable for the length of the event and should be right on the edge of being almost comfortable - with occasional (and usually unintentional) forays over the edge of the comfort zone. This is the level at which you should drive - most of the time - while testing. Of course, eventually you will drive the car right on the edge - to continue the development of both car and driver, and to have some fun.

Just as it takes a distance runner a while to learn to recognize his efficient sustainable pace, so it will take time and effort for you to recognize the maximum level of intensity that you can keep up for any given time - and to enter into that level at will. When testing, it is important to realize when you become too tired to efficiently continue - and to stop when you get there.

Continuing to drive after you have exceeded your ability to concentrate is not testing and is not macho. It is dumb. You will be able to tell when you have reached the point because you will start to make little mistakes. Stop and explain the situation to the crew - the pros will have noticed your condition before you did. They may not appreciate your lack of fitness, but they will understand and will appreciate your honesty.

Make sure that they realize that you have misjudged both the physical requirements and your own conditioning - and that you will not let this happen again. Relax, drink some water, lie down for a while. You may have another half hour of good time left in you. If you haven't, work on your conditioning.

An experienced driver should be able to do about 200 miles of meaningful testing per day - and almost endless hours of endurance testing. Those guys don't spend all those hours in physical training because they enjoy it. Nobody enjoys it! It is part of the price of admission to a rather exclusive and privileged club. Besides, it beats working! It helps to drink enormous quantities of water and to really relax while the crew is making changes - it's all a matter of discipline.

THE RIGHTS OF THE DRIVER

In order for the driver to do his job properly he must know and understand what is going on during any test. While the driver is mainly a mile producer and information gatherer during endurance testing, in any sort of development testing he should be a key element in the decision making process. Since his neck and his career are on the line, he should have the final say on things like chassis and aero balance. Many engineers consider drivers to be development dolts. In order to earn his say, the driver has to prove his right to one - leading the objectivity parade is a good way to start.

THE DRIVER DEBRIEFING

Driver debriefing has been going on as long as motor racing has. The exercise did not make the magazines until Formula One teams obtained motorhomes. Once this happened, the drivers soon realized that they had a plausible excuse to escape the journalists after each ses-

sion. With a, "Sorry, I have to debrief", they disappear into the privacy of the motorhome. The reality of the situation is that debrief is exactly what they are going to do in there - and it is going to take at least an hour.

The availability of concrete information from on board data gathering and telemetry systems has not downgraded the role of the driver in the development of the racing car, in the tuning of the car to the circuit, or in debriefing - in fact it has enhanced his role. The aircraft industry has access to a lot more electronic aids than we do - they could probably fly their experimental aircraft by remote control - but they still use highly skilled and experienced test pilots and they debrief the hell out of them.

Every fighter pilot, even Blue Angels, is debriefed after every mission. Charts of numbers and lines on a computer monitor are wonderful aids - but only the input of the pilot/driver can convert the squiggles into meaningful information that will help sort out the machine. And only the driver can prioritize the changes to be made.

Every driver should be debriefed after every session in the car - and the information should be put on paper. Each of us has only so much storage room in our brain. It is a lot of room, but it is finite. The more of it we use up trying to remember non-pertinent details, the less room there is for new stuff - or for creativity. Besides, retrieval of brain-stored information is both time consuming and somewhat less than perfect.

If the information is not written - legibly - confusion is inevitable and soon. It will go something like this: "Look, Fred, last session you said that that car was really good coming off turn five - we haven't changed anything and now you say it has way too much power-on understeer coming off the same turn?"

"That isn't what I said!"
"Yes it is!"
Etc, etc, etc, - downward spiral. Paper is cheap!

The minimum number of people required to conduct an effective debriefing is exactly one - you, the driver. The maximum number is no more than five - the driver, the engineer, the crew chief, the data scraper and, if required, the engine man. In the beginning of your career you will almost always have to do it alone. Don't let that deter you and don't let your priorities allow you to skip the debriefing. If you are doing your own work, you may not have time between sessions but do it at the end of the day.

A "fill in the blanks" debrief sheet helps a lot. One is appended to the end of this chapter.

One of the natural laws of motor racing states that there is never enough time between sessions. It is very important to get the crew moving right away rather than waiting for the debriefing session to end. If there is a major problem it is important to get the crew started on it - even before it is defined - and certainly before the actual debriefing starts.

Does the engine need to be changed? Will the gears be changed, the diff adjusted, springs changed, shocks re-valved? Is there a major vibration, a slipping or non-releasing clutch, brakes pulling one way or the other? Things like that take time. If there is nothing major wrong, the crew should get started on the standard post session check list - fuel, fluid levels, nut and bolt check, corner weights, etc. There is no reason for the crew to ever sit around waiting for the results of the debrief.

The key to effective debriefing is the track map. It does not need to be a detailed course map with track widths, elevations and corner radii - a tracing will do nicely. The gears and the basic car set up are recorded on it before each session. The driver then goes around the track in his mind. First he does gears and engine rpm. From the driver we need the rpm in whatever gear at the end of each straight and at the exit of each corner. A guess at the rpm at the point in the corner where the driver picks up the throttle is a big help.

With a gear chart and the procedures described earlier it should now be a pretty simple matter to determine what, if any, changes you want to make to the gearing. This is step one for two reasons - first, it gets the driver's mind moving and second, a gear change is liable to be the most time consuming act performed between sessions. It allows us to hand the mechanic(s) a sheet of paper with the new gears written on it so that they can get started.

I find a debrief form, similar to that at the end of this chapter, helpful - especially after the first session. It is absolutely amazing what drivers will adapt to in a racing car. Unless someone asks about pedal position or the amount of force required to shift or what-have-you, they are very liable not to mention it. It isn't that they forget - they just shut what they consider to be trivia out of their minds. Remember Senna's remarks on shifting?

The real meat of the exercise is to optimize the performance of the car/driver combination on the race track. This means in the corners. Every corner on the track should be broken down into four phases - the initial response to turn in, the corner entry or off-throttle phase, the neutral throttle (if any) or throttle pick up phase and the full throttle corner exit phase. The behavior of the car should be described, in detail, for each phase of each corner on the race track. The driver should do all of this, by himself, before anyone else joins the exercise.

Now we have a course map that looks like FIGURE 30. And now is the time for the team brains trust to get together and try to figure things out. This is not a book on vehicle dynamics and I am not going to try to tell you how to do this. Just don't lose track of the basics:

1) Corner entry is more important than corner exit if only because what happens during corner entry determines what will happen on corner exit - and when it will happen.

2) All really fast race cars exhibit some degree of corner entry understeer. This not only makes for stable corner entry, it provides the excess rear tire capacity needed to allow early and hard power application.

3) At road speeds below 80mph, cornering characteristics are mainly influenced by the mechanical set up of the car. At speeds of 120mph and above, the major influence is aerodynamic. Don't confuse the two and try to fix a mechanical problem with aero changes or vice versa.

The in-between speed range is liable to be confusing - but, if the mechanical balance is good at low speed and the aero balance is good at high speed, the medium speed corners should also be good. I don't like to make mechanical and aero changes at the same time and I feel it is best to work on the critical corners first.

4) Oversteer slides and wheelspin may make you feel like Juan Manuel Fangio (who did damned little of either). They also will advertise your lack of grasp of the essentials of the game to those who know what they are looking at. Also, they will make you slow.

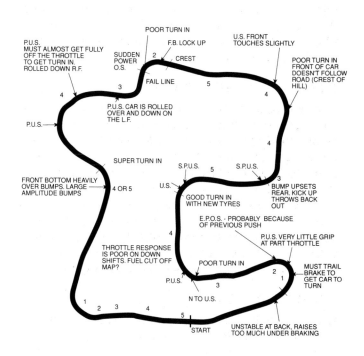

FIGURE30

You, the driver, should keep a copy of the track map and the notes from each debriefing. While everyone else is working on the car, you should make your own composite map, complete with driver notes - similar to the map shown in our discussion of visualization. This will serve as an aid to your visualization exercise and as a permanent record that you can refer to the next time you come to the circuit.

DRIVER'S DEBRIEF SHEET

CIRCUIT _____

SESSION# _____

DATE _____ TIME _____

COCKPIT:

PEDAL POSIT _____ LEFT FT REST_____

HEEL PLATE _____ WHEELPOSIT _____

SHIFTER POSIT _____ HAND CLEAR _____

SEAT/KNEE SUPPORT _____ HARNESS _____

MIRRORS _____

COMMENTS _____
_____
_____

BRAKES:

PEDAL FEEL _____ FORCE REQ'D _____

FT TO R RATIO _____ VIBRATION _____

PULL _____ FADE _____ BOIL _____

STABILITY-SMOOTH _____

STABILITY-ROUGH _____

COMMENTS _____
_____
_____

TIRES:

BALANCE _____

COMMENTS _____
_____

TRANS AND FINAL DRIVE:

RATIOS:

I _____ II _____ III _____ IV _____ V _____

UPSHIFT _____ DOWNSHIFT _____

JUMP OUT _____

FORCE REQ'D _____

CLUTCH _____

COMMENTS _____
_____
_____
_____

ENGINE:

OP _____ OT _____ WT _____ FP _____

LAMBDA _____ THROTTLE RESP: TIP IN _____

UPSHIFT _____ DOWNSHIFT _____

FEEL _____
_____

COMMENTS _____
_____

CHASSIS:

ST LINE STABILITY _____

OVER BUMPS _____

SLOW - MEDIUM - FAST

INITIAL TURN IN _____

CORNER

ENTRY _____

TRANSITION _____
_____

CORNER

EXIT _____

RIDE QUALITY _____

WHEELSPIN _____

BOTTOMING UNDER

BRAKES _____

BOTTOMING AT

HIGH SPEED _____

BOTTOMING OVER

BUMPS _____

COMMENTS _____
_____
_____
_____
_____
_____

FILL IN THE TRACK MAP ON THE NEXT PAGE.

_____
_____
_____
_____

TEST SCHEDULE, SOME CIRCUIT, SOME CAR, SOME DAY

DAY ONE

TODAY WE WILL BREAK IN THE CROWN WHEEL & PINION AND BED THE DISCS.

AFTER THE FIRST FOUR OR FIVE LAPS STOP AND LET US CHECK THE CAR FOR LEAKS, WHEEL TIGHTNESS AND HUB BEARING TIGHTNESS. IF AT ANY TIME YOU FEEL, HEAR, SENSE OR SMELL SOMETHING WRONG, STOP AND TELL US ABOUT IT.

CW&P: THE OBJECT IS TO WEAR DOWN THE HIGH SPOTS ON BOTH GEARS SO AS TO ACHIEVE OPTIMUM MESH - WITHOUT CREATING A LOT OF HEAT. THE STANDARD METHOD OF SEVERAL LAPS AT CONSTANT THROTTLE SETTING AND LOAD MERELY TURNS ALL OF THE HIGH SPOTS GLOWING RED AND CREATES LOCAL SPOTS OF VERY HARD METAL WHICH LATER BECOME PITS - LEADING TO PREMATURE AND EXPENSIVE FAILURE OF THE PINION.

THE PROPER PROCEDURE IS TO BEGIN AT ABOUT ONE THIRD TO HALF THROTTLE IN THE NORMAL GEARS, PUT A LOAD INTO THE GEARS FOR FIVE OR SIX SECONDS AND LET THE CAR COAST (IN GEAR) FOR A LIKE PERIOD. THIS PUTS HEAT INTO THE HIGH SPOTS AND THEN LETS IT DISSIPATE. THE PROCEDURE IS REPEATED AT INCREASING THROTTLE, LOAD AND TIME IN GEAR UNTIL ABOUT 20 TO 25 MILES HAS BEEN DONE. AFTER ABOUT 10-15 MILES THE PINION IS INSPECTED.

AFTER 20/25 YOU SHOULD BE GOING HARD AND THE PROCEDURE IS COMPLETE.

BRAKE DISCS: THE OBJECT IS NOT DISSIMILAR TO THE GEAR SET. THE PROBLEM IS THAT YOU HAVE TO WAIT UNTIL THE INITIAL RING AND PINION BEDDING IS DONE BEFORE USING THE BRAKES HARD ENOUGH TO BED THE DISCS. AGAIN THE OBJECT IS TO PUT HEAT INTO THE DISCS (AND PADS) GRADUALLY - NOT TO WEAR DOWN HIGH SPOTS BUT TO AVOID THERMAL SHOCK WHEN THE DISCS ARE NEW. YOU CAN DO GRADUAL STOPS AFTER FIVE LAPS OF GEAR BREAK IN AND MODERATE STOPS AFTER ABOUT 10/15 MILES. DON'T DO HARD STOPS UNTIL 20 MILES OR SO. THEN DO ONE HARD STOP FROM TOP SPEED AND LET THE DISCS (AND PADS) COOL FOR A FEW LAPS BY HARDLY USING THEM BEFORE BRINGING THE CAR IN.

AT THIS POINT WE WILL THOROUGHLY CHECK THE CAR FOR TIGHTNESS, ETC. (INCLUDING THE PINION BEARING NUT, SHIFT FORKS, ENGINE A-FRAME BOLTS,

ETC.) WE WILL ALSO SET THE BRAKE RATIO (IMPOSSIBLE TO DO WITH NEW DISCS AND PADS).

YOU SHOULD NOW HAVE A GOOD PRELIMINARY FEEL FOR YOUR FIT IN THE COCKPIT, PEDAL POSITION, HEEL REST POSITION, ETC. AND WE WILL ADJUST AS NECESSARY. YOU CANNOT GET THE MOST OUT OF THE CAR UNLESS YOU AND THE CONTROLS ARE PROPERLY POSITIONED AND YOUR BODY IS PROPERLY SUPPORTED AND BRACED - SO DON'T FEEL THAT YOU ARE NIT PICKING WHEN YOU ASK FOR ADJUSTMENTS, NOW OR AT ANY TIME DURING THE SEASON. IT WILL TAKE A WHILE TO GET IT RIGHT.

NOW START DRIVING THE CAR AS FAST AND HARD AS YOU FEEL COMFORTABLE WITH. THE CAR SHOULD BE PRETTY WELL BALANCED TO START WITH. IF NOT, WE WILL CHANGE IT NOW. IF ALL HAS GONE WELL, YOU GET TO SPEND THE REST OF THE DAY GETTING USED TO THE GOOD THINGS IN LIFE AGAIN. WE WILL ADJUST THE CAR AS NECESSARY. DO TEN TO 15 LAPS AT A TIME SO THAT YOU GET A RHYTHM GOING. IF THE TRACK STARTS RUSHING AT YOU OR IF YOU STOP MAKING PROGRESS, BRING IT IN. WE'LL TALK AND YOU CAN THINK ABOUT IT FOR A WHILE.

AGAIN IF ALL GOES WELL, TOWARDS THE END OF THE DAY START DRIVING AT THE LEVEL WHERE YOU ARE NOT QUITE COMFORTABLE - START STRETCHING YOUR ENVELOPE. AS YOU GET GOING FASTER, THE PERCEIVED CAR BALANCE WILL CHANGE AND WE WILL ADJUST IT AS NECESSARY.

DAY TWO

WE WILL START THE DAY BY BEDDING A SET OF PADS - THE PADS YOU WILL BE RACING ON ALL SEASON. PLEASE READ AND ADHERE TO THE "BURNISHING NEW PADS" INSTRUCTION SHEET THAT COMES WITH THE PADS.

ONCE AGAIN, AFTER THE PADS ARE BEDDED, I WANT YOU TO DRIVE AT THE LEVEL WHERE YOU ARE NOT QUITE COMFORTABLE. DON'T WORRY ABOUT SPINNING - BUT DON'T TAKE CHANCES WHERE THERE IS SOMETHING TO HIT.

ONCE THE PADS ARE FULLY BEDDED WE WILL DO BRAKING DISTANCE PRACTICE FROM HIGH SPEED TO FULL STOP. YOU WILL HAVE JUNK TIRES SO DON'T WORRY ABOUT FLAT SPOTS. CONCENTRATE ON STOPPING THE CAR FROM VERY HIGH SPEED IN THE MINIMUM DISTANCE - UNDER FULL CONTROL. THIS MEANS DEVELOPING FULL BRAKING FORCE AT HIGH SPEED AND HIGH DOWNLOAD VALUES AS QUICKLY AS POSSIBLE WITHOUT "BOUNCING" THE TIRES AND THEN MODULATING AS THE DOWNLOAD DIMINISHES WITH DIMINISHING SPEED.

IF THERE IS A SUITABLE SEQUENCE ON THE TRACK WE WILL DO BRAKING TO CORNER ENTRY NEXT - CONCENTRATING ON THE MINIMUM BRAKING DISTANCE THAT WILL ALLOW YOU TO ENTER THE CORNER UNDER CONTROL (I.E. WITH-

OUT FLAMING FRONT TIRES) SO THAT YOU CAN GET THE POWER DOWN EARLY - AND KEEP IT DOWN.

IF THERE IS NO SUCH SEQUENCE WE WILL RUN A "SHOCK SCAN" TO FAMILIARIZE EACH OF US WITH THE EFFECTS OF SHOCK ADJUSTMENTS. THE EXERCISE STARTS AT THE BEGINNING AND GOES THROUGH THE PROCESS OF ADJUSTING SHOCKS TO SUIT A PARTICULAR CAR AND CIRCUIT. THE IDEA IS TO ADJUST THE BUMP (COMPRESSION) FORCES TO SUIT THE BUMPS IN THE CRITICAL AREAS OF THE TRACK - CORNER EXITS, CORNERS AND BRAKING AREAS. WE BASICALLY IGNORE BUMPS ON STRAIGHTS UNLESS THE CAR BOTTOMS. WE WILL START OUT WITH VERY LITTLE REBOUND ADJUSTMENT AND ADD BUMP FORCE TO MINIMIZE THE UPSETS. ONCE THE CAR IS HAPPY (OR RELATIVELY SO) OVER THE CRITICAL BUMPS WE WILL ADD REBOUND, ONE SWEEP AT A TIME TO TIGHTEN UP THE CAR - I.E, TO STABILIZE THE PLATFORM AND GET RID OF THE CADILLAC RIDE SYNDROME.

ONCE WE HAVE ACHIEVED SOMETHING CLOSE TO OPTIMUM SETTINGS WE WILL OVER AND UNDER DAMP THE CAR - AGAIN TO GET THE FEEL OF WRONG SETTINGS.

NEXT WE WILL STIFFEN THE CAR WITH SPRINGS - KEEPING THE RIDE RATE PERCENTAGE AT A BALANCE - JUST TO TEACH US ALL WHAT HAPPENS. IF THIS MAKES THINGS WORSE, WE WILL SOFTEN THE CAR THE SAME WAY - AGAIN FOR EDUCATION WHICH WILL TRANSFER LATER.

BY NOW WE SHOULD HAVE SOME IDEA OF WHERE THE CAR WANTS TO BE AT SOMETRACK - AND WE WILL LET YOU PLAY FOR THE REST OF THE DAY.

REMEMBER, IF YOU WANT SOMETHING CHANGED, EVEN IF IT SEEMS MINOR - OR IF YOU JUST WANT TO SEE WHAT HAPPENS, YOU HAVE ONLY TO ASK. THERE ARE SIX PEOPLE HERE WHOSE ONLY PURPOSE IN LIFE (TODAY) IS TO HELP YOU.

DAY THREE:

CAR #1

1) WARM UP CAR AND DRIVER, ESTABLISH VEHICLE MECHANICAL AND AERO BALANCE AND BASE LINE LAP TIME. RECORD BASE LINE DATA

2) INSTALL TEST REAR WING # 1 (UPPER ELEMENTS ONLY). RE-ESTABLISH AERO BALANCE, BASELINE AND RECORD.

3) INSTALL TEST REAR WING # 1 AS UPPER ELEMENT OF STOCK BI-PLANE. RE-ESTABLISH AERO BALANCE; BASELINE AND RECORD.

4) INSTALL STOCK BI-PLANE REAR WING WITH SINGLE ELEMENT UPPER RE-ESTABLISH AERO BALANCE; BASELINE AND RECORD.

5) INSTALL STOCK BI-PLANE REAR WING WITH DUAL ELEMENT UPPER RE-ESTABLISH AERO BALANCE; BASELINE AND RECORD.

6) WITH BEST REAR WING SET UP INSTALL RAISED NOSE AND WINGS. RE-ESTABLISH AERO BASELINE AND RECORD.

7) WITH BEST OVERALL AERO SET UP, INCREASE DOWNLOAD UNTIL IT SLOWS CAR.

8) AT SOME POINT, SCRUB PADS (& TIRES) FOR NEXT RACE.

CAR # 2:

1) WARM UP CAR AND DRIVER, ESTABLISH VEHICLE MECHANICAL AND AERO BALANCE AND BASE LINE LAP TIME. RECORD BASE LINE DATA.

2) INCREASE ROLL RESISTANCE WITH BARS BY EQUAL INCREMENTS FRONT AND REAR UNTIL IT MAKES CAR SLOWER. RECORD.

3) REPEAT (2) WITH RIDE RATE BY SPRINGS. RECORD.

4) WITH BEST SET UP, RUN A SHOCK SIGNATURE. RECORD.

5) AT SOME POINT BED PADS (AND TIRES?) FOR NEXT RACE.

ENGINEERING AND DEVELOPMENT REPORT

REPORT No.   CSCI 92-11
DATE.   8/16/92
TRACK.   TROIS RIVIERES, QUEBEC

PURPOSE

PLAYERS TROIS RIVIERES FORMULA ATLANTIC RACE

VEHICLE(S)   SWIFT DB4
DRIVER(S)   CHRISTOPHER SMITH
PERSONNEL   CARROLL SMITH
WILLI OPPLIGER
JOHN MORGAN
WALTER AND JUDY PRESTON
APRIL MARVIN

INTRODUCTION AND VEHICLE PREPARATION

ENGINE #91-01 WAS REBUILT AND INSTALLED WITH BURNS EXHAUST AND JENNINGS CARB INLET HORNS. REFORMULATED DAECO 118 RACE GAS WAS USED. REAR WING CONFIGURATION WAS SWIFT BIPLANE LOWER ELEMENT RAISED 1.0". WITH CONNELLY DUAL PLANE UPPPER ELEMENT. LARGEST OUTBOARD TABS WERE FITTED TO OEM 10.25" FRONT WINGS. FRONT WING SUPPORT CABLE WAS FITTED. PENSKE TRIPLE ADJUSTABLE SHOCKS WERE FITTED

PRACTICE. FRIDAY AM 8/14/92

WITH THE INITIAL SET UP THE CAR WAS REASONABLY WELL BALANCED BUT TENDED TOWARD INITIAL UNDERSTEER AND DID NOT PUT THE POWER DOWN AS WELL AS CHRISTOPHER FELT IT SHOULD HAVE. CHRISTOPHER WAS FASTEST BY 0.1.

QUALIFYING. FRIDAY PM 8/14/92

THE CAR HAD A BAD INITIAL UNDERSTEER FOLLOWED BY A SNAP TO POWER ON OVERSTEER. CHRISTOPHER FELT STRONGLY THAT SOMETHING WAS BROKEN AND STOPPED SEVERAL TIMES. REALIZING THAT THE GRID MIGHT WELL BE SET IN THIS SESSION, HE PREVAILED AND QUALIFIED SECOND TO STUART CROW IN THE NEW RALT. AFTER THE SESSION IT WAS DISCOVERED THAT THE RIGHT REAR SHOCK ABSORBER HAD DEPRESSURIZED.

QUALIFYING. SATURDAY AM 8/15/92

BECAUSE THE CAUSE OF THE LACK OF PRESSURIZATION HAD NOT BEEN DETERMINED THE ORIGINAL PENSKE SHOCKS 2 WAY ADJUSTABLE WERE INSTALLED. SEALER HAD BEEN SPREAD ON THE TRACK OVERNIGHT MAKING IT IMPOSSIBLY SLIPPERY. THE TRACK WAS SEVERAL SECONDS SLOWER THAN IT HAD BEEN FRIDAY. THE CAR WAS BASICALLY IMPOSSIBLE AND CHRISTOPHER, REALIZING THAT TIMES WOULD BE SLOW, DID MINIMAL LAPS.

PRACTICE. SATURDAY PM

THE CAR WAS SOFTENED (700 REAR SPRINGS, 650 FRONT WITH 1 TURN OF PRELOAD.) SHOCK ABSORBER BUMP FORCES WERE REDUCED. THE TRACK HAD HOWEVER "COME BACK" AND THE CAR WAS TOO SOFT. AGAIN MINIMAL LAPS WERE COMPLETED.

WARM UP. SUNDAY AM

ORIGINAL SPRINGS WERE RE-FITTED, BUMP FORCES WERE REDUCED TO ALMOST ZERO ADJUSTMENT AND THE FRONT RIDE HEIGHT WAS RAISED. CAR WAS "PRETTY GOOD" BUT TURN IN WAS SLIGHTLY TOO SUDDEN.

RACE

SMALLER FRONT WING OUTBOARD TABS WERE FITTED. FRONT RIDE HEIGHT WAS DROPPED 1/8". AFTER THE WARM UP LAPS REAR RIDE HEIGHT WAS DROPPED 1/2 TURN.

CHRISTOPHER GOT AN OUTSTANDING START AND LED INTO TURN ONE. HE LED EVERY LAP - INITIALLY FROM CROW WHO WAS PUSHING BUT NOT THREATENING UNTIL HE RETIRED WITH A BROKEN 1/2 SHAFT ON LAP 10. FROM LAP 27 UNTIL HIS RETIREMENT WITH A BLOWN ENGINE ON LAP 40, JACQUES VILLENEUVE SENIOR AND CHRISTOPHER RACED HARD. VILLENEUVE CLOSED TO WITHIN 0.2 SECONDS BUT WAS UNABLE TO MAKE A MOVE BECAUSE CHRISTOPHER WAS CARRYING MORE SPEED INTO THE CORNERS WHILE VILLENEUVE WAS WASTING TIME SLIDING. AFTER VILLENEUVE'S RETIREMENT, CHISTOPHER CRUISED HOME - WINNING BY 22 SECONDS FROM EMPRINGHAM AND VILLENEUVE JR.

CONCLUSIONS AND RECOMMENDATIONS

WILLI AND CHRISTOPHER DID A VERY GOOD JOB OF ANALYZING THE TRACK CONDITIONS AND THE CAR'S REACTION TO THEM. THE CAR WAS NOT GOOD UNTIL THE RACE, BUT IT WAS AS GOOD AS IT HAD TO BE DURING THE RACE. IT TURNED IN WELL AND PUT POWER DOWN REASONABLY WELL. THERE WAS SOME MID PHASE UNDERSTEER BUT THAT MAY WELL HAVE BEEN THE PRICE OF PUTTING THE POWER DOWN. BRAKING WAS VERY GOOD.

THE 2 DEGREE SHOCK ABSORBER PISTONS PRODUCED BETTER COMPLIANCE OVER THE BUMPS THAN THE STANDARD PISTONS. DATA RECORDING SHOWED NO DISADVANTAGES. IF CHRISTOPHER AGREES, THEY SHOULD BE THE STANDARD ROAD COURSE CONFIGURATION.

IT SEEMS THAT, ON SLOW CORNERS, A RELATIVELY SOFT REAR ANTI-ROLL BAR AND RELATIVELY STIFF REAR SPRINGS GIVE THE CAR BETTER ABILITY TO PUT THE POWER DOWN - PROBABLY BECAUSE OF REDUCED CAMBER CHANGE AND LESS LOAD TRANSFER TO THE OUTSIDE TIRE.

REDUCING THE SHOCK ADJUSTABLE ABSORBER BUMP FORCES TO MINIMUM ADJUSTMENT SEEMS TO HAVE HELPED TIRE COMPLIANCE ON THIS SMOOTH CIRCUIT.

REDUCING FRONT REBOUND FORCE SEEMS TO HAVE IMPROVED THE CAR'S ABILITY TO PUT THE POWER DOWN.

THE REAR WING CONFIGURATION WAS EXCELLENT - PROVIDING VERY GOOD LOW AND MEDIUM SPEED DOWNLOAD WITH MINIMAL DRAG.

OVERLAYING OUR DATA WITH EMPRINGHAM'S SHOWED THAT WE HAD A CONCLUSIVE ENGINE ADVANTAGE - PROBABLY DUE TO OUR FUEL AND EXHAUST SYSTEMS. IVEY'S TRIAL OF OUR EXHAUST SHOWED A NOTABLE IMPROVEMENT IN LOW END RESPONSE AND POWER.

AS THE RADIOS HAVE NOT BEEN RELIABLE, WE WILL HAVE TO IMPROVE OUR PIT BOARD SIGNALLING. ALTHOUGH IT HAD NO BEARING ON THE OUTCOME CHRISTOPHER SHOULD HAVE BEEN WARNED THAT VILLENEUVE WAS GAINING ON HIM EARLIER THAN HE WAS. WE WILL ALSO HAVE TO DECIDE ON A DEFINITIVE SIGNAL FROM CHRISTOPHER FOR LOSS OF RADIO CONTACT.

BEFORE EACH SESSION CHRISTOPHER AND WILLI SHOULD DISCUSS WHAT CHANGES TO MAKE TO THE CAR IN THE EVENT OF THE FOLLOWING CHASSIS OR SUSPENSION PROBLEMS.

INITIAL (TURN IN) UNDERSTEER

MID PHASE UNDERSTEER

POWER ON UNDERSTEER

POWER ON OVERSTEER - SMOOTH TRACK

POWER ON OVERSTEER - BUMPY TRACK

THE DISCUSSION SHOULD RESULT IN A WRITTEN "IF-THEN" LIST TO BE KEPT IN THE PITS DURING THE SESSION SO THAT CHANGES CAN BE MADE WITHOUT TIME CONSUMING DISCUSSIONS.

DRIVER REPORTED THAT THE FEEL OF THE CAR WITH THE TWO DEGREE SHOCK PISTONS WAS SIGNIFICANTLY BETTER - ESPECIALLY WHEN BRAKING OVER THE BUMPS INTO TURN 1. DATA SHOWS 1.9 BRAKING G VS 1.6 G AT THIS POINT.

DATA ALSO REVEALED THAT THE ABILITY OF THE CAR TO PUT THE POWER DOWN FROM SLOW CORNERS WAS IMPROVED WITH THE 2 DEGREE PISTONS - PEAK LONGITUDINAL G WAS INCREASED BY 0.07 TO 0.1 G.

13

"80% of success at motor racing is knowing how to go motor racing properly."
– Steve Millen.

PRACTICE TIME

A lot of psyche games are involved in successful racing - at every level. It has to do with the establishment of a pecking order. I'm not talking about the childish stuff - turning mirrors to the sky on the grid or asking; "which one of you ——s is going to finish second today?" People who are really good at anything don't strut - they don't have to. The best way to establish yourself at the head of the pecking order is by consistent professionalism, backed by consistent speed.

For the racing driver, professionalism starts with being ready. Nothing pisses a crew off much more than, after they have taken the time and trouble to get the car ready on time, to find that they are losing track time because the driver isn't ready. Pretty soon their attitude becomes; "If he doesn't care enough to get himself ready, why should I bust my butt?"

It's all downhill from there. The driver whose crew won't go the extra mile for him simply is not going to get anywhere in this business. When the driver arrives at the race track ready to go to work - that is, early, confident, and with his gear organized and clean. When he has taken the time and the trouble to get himself fitted to the car before it arrives at the track. Then his crew (and his car owner) will be impressed.

When the driver makes sure that his car is at the head of the line for practice and that he is in it and ready to go several minutes before he has to be, then his crew and car owner will be further impressed - and the opposition may even notice.

When that same driver is instantly quick - because he took the time to study a course map and drive/ride/walk the course dozens of times the day before practice began and then drove hundreds of laps in his mind - then the crew will be happy and the opposition will be impressed. The driver will have moved toward the front of the pecking order - in his own eyes as well as the eyes of his peers.

Professionalism means being ready when you get to the race track, always being quick and going on about your business with your crew. Professionalism means being ready before the car is, always giving 100% and inspiring the crew to match your own performance. It means never screaming and shouting and never complaining or upbraiding anyone in public (in public means with more than two people present - the upbraider and the upbraidee).

Professionalism means saying thank you - a lot - to the individual crew members, both in private and in public. It also means never criticizing a crew member directly - that's what the crew chief is for. Talk to your crew chief calmly and forcefully when you are displeased with any aspect of the crew's performance. Believe me, the word will trickle down.

Professionalism also means comprehensive debriefing after every session - whether testing or racing. If the crew chief/engineer/team manager is not capable of conducting the debriefing, then you will have to do it - and you will have to make damned sure that the crew chief is present and understands what is going on and the reason behind any changes you want to make. If you are so fortunate as to have a car owner, it is a good idea to have him (or her) sit in on these sessions - they not only like to know how their money is being spent, they enjoy being a part of the operation.

PRACTICE & THE DRIVER

If testing belongs to the engineering staff, however small and inexperienced they may be, then the practice sessions for the actual race belong to the driver. The purpose of practice on the race weekend is for the driver to learn his way around the race track and for the driver and the crew to optimize the performance of the car (as developed during testing) and the driver on that particular circuit. Practice time on race weekends is precious - and there is never enough of it. Don't waste any of it. This is no time to be experimenting.

The first rule is to be ready when you arrive at the race track. I have never understood the people who arrive at the track and immediately start working on the car. The race track is a silly place to prepare a car - do that at home and arrive with a car that is ready to be teched, warmed up, have the practice tires put on it and go out onto the race track. You won't look stupid and you will get better results.

Being ready when you get there means an equipment check list for the transporter. Leaving stuff behind is as inexcusable as it is common.

LEARNING THE TRACK

Practice is for learning the track and for setting up the car. You have to learn the track quickly. Learning race tracks, like learning anything else, is a developed skill - you have to learn how to do it. You will not learn the track quickly by rushing around at warp speed, locking brakes and sliding through corners.

The big problem for beginning drivers is learning how to go really fast without making mistakes. Throwing the car, sliding the car, locking wheels - all that kid stuff - leads to mistakes. The key to speed is discipline, precision and smoothness. The system that I think works best is to drive the first few laps on a track that is new to you at a moderate pace, following what you perceive to be the line and taking each corner in the gear that you think will be the racing gear, but at moderate (not slow) speed.

Drive what you think will be the racing line at all times and drive in the gear that you think will be the right gear for the part of the track that you are on. Concentrate on remembering what the track looks like past the point where you can see it. Soon the track will begin to "flow" for you - you will be driving a race track, rather than a series of strange and unconnected corners, and you will begin to develop a rhythm. Once the track flows, you can start working on speed.

Work on the fast corners first - almost invariably they are the most important (and the most difficult). Typically the beginning driver tries to go too fast in the slow corners and is himself slow in the fast corners. Realistic evaluation, experience and maturity will cure the condition.

Look for and use the helpful natural features of the track - camber, uphill exits, etc. Look for and don't get caught out by harmful features - off camber sections, decreasing radius corners, sharp drop offs at the edge of the track, avoidable bumps, etc. Remember that you need landmarks (aiming points) and that your turn in point and turn in speed for each corner is actually determined by your braking point.

As you gain experience, your learning curve will steepen simply because you will have done more of it and driven through more corners (there are a limited number of basic corner configurations). It will never become easy - if at some point you think that it has, you simply aren't maximizing your potential.

In the early stages of your career, unless the car is evil, there isn't a lot of sense in stopping to make set up changes until you have learned the track and are pretty close to the potential of car and driver. On the other hand, there isn't a lot to be gained by driving around in a car that needs adjusting.

TO STAY OUT OR TO COME IN

At every level of racing, during every practice and qualifying session, virtually every driver is faced with the same dilemma - whether to stay out on the race track zooming around in a car that is considerably less than perfect or to come in and have the fault(s) attended to.

The question is more complex than it appears. The human learning curve being what it is, the more thinking laps that the driver does, the faster he will get (unthinking laps don't count). On the other hand, you can only go so fast in a car that is trying to kill you. On still a third hand, it won't do much good to stop if:

1) There is not enough time to make changes.

2) The driver has not learned the track.

3) The driver has not defined the deficiencies in his mind.

- or if -

4) There is insufficient expertise or equipment available to make intelligent changes. In this case it is best to either stay out there and learn to deal with what you have or to seek either another form of employment or a different support staff.

There are a couple of concrete rules here:

1) If the engine is missing, running on less than the requisite number of cylinders, detonating or otherwise trying to self destruct, bring the car in and fix it.

2) If the car is actually dangerous, bring it in.

3) Make a real effort to define what is wrong. "It won't stop," is about as helpful as, "The engine misses". Let's have some detail here!

Does it miss at high rpm only or does it miss coming off corners at relatively low rpm? Does it miss at the same point on the race track each lap? What is the fuel pressure at the point when the missing begins? Does it feel like electrical or fuel?

It is unlikely that your crew (if any) can hear the miss. It is unproductive and embarrassing - as well as time consuming and potentially harmful - to be sent back out to define the problem more closely.

4) No matter how far off the gearing may be, you are not going to correct it during a session. Stay out but don't overrev the engine - if the correct gear for

a corner is too short, use the next taller gear. If top gear is too short, back off on the straight. Don't be stupid.

5) Always have an "if - then" list, written, in the pit. Sample entries: "If the engine misfires at high rpm only, check battery voltage first. Bypass master switch second."

There are also a couple of usually valid generalities:

1) During the first session on a new track, if the car is driveable and not self destructive, stay out and learn the race track.

2) During a qualifying session, if you are prevented from going faster by a quickly corrected car problem, come in early and attend to it. You will be faster and more comfortable both during the session and during the race.

Juan Manuel Fangio, the five time World Champion, once told Denny Hulme and me that he had never driven a perfect lap. I will guarantee that you haven't. When you think that you have maxxed out, realize that there is more to come. Don't stay out "measuring yourself against the competition" or trying to go 1/10th faster. Come in, think about things, make an adjustment, go back out and go faster.

The secret to success in practice and qualifying is to be able to drive and think at the same time. To do so takes effort, intelligence and experience. You do not have to be Gary Anderson, John Barnard, Rory Byrne, Patrick Head or Adrian Reynard. You do need to be able to divide each corner into at least three phases in your mind and to both visualize and describe what the car is doing in each phase.

Early in your career you will not be able to do this - you will be too busy trying to save your life. You should, however, work at it very hard. We engineers have a lot of information at our hands these days. Without a sensitive and honest driver who can answer our detailed questions, we are still lost.

"I don't know" is an honest and acceptable answer. So is, "I forgot to look". So is, "If I look at the tach at that point on the race track you are going to need a new car." We can accept all these answers.

We can even accept a guess or a "gut feeling" - as long as it is identified as such. In fact, we often ask for a gut feeling. What we cannot accept is a lie - it will only hurt the effort. In addition, we will eventually figure out that you are lying (we have our ways) and that will be the end of the good part of the relationship. Also remember that we engineers talk to each other - a lot - about you.

So, if you know the race track and the car isn't right - and there is time to do something effective about it - bring it in and fix it. The improvement to the car will result in a better time and, perhaps more important, give you a better car to race with.

Don't kid yourself about this - the car will not fix itself and your crew, no matter how skilled and dedicated they may be, can't fix it if you don't stop. Have a definite plan or description in mind when you stop and remember that they cannot read your lips through a full face helmet.

QUALIFYING - THE FACTS

The easiest time to win a motor race is during qualifying. The next easiest time is at the start. The number of racing drivers who downgrade the importance of qualifying and the start never fails to amaze me. Statements like; "I don't care where I qualify," or, "I don't mind if I lose a couple of positions at the start, it doesn't make any difference in a 100 mile race," are rubbish.

The bottom line is very simple. When another driver leads you off the grid or out of the first corner, you will have to pass him before the race is over. Otherwise he will beat you. It really is that simple.

"So what?" you say, "I'll wait until things settle down and then pick them off one at a time." More rubbish!

Not in any truly competitive class of motor racing you won't. If you are not in a truly competitive class of racing at this stage in your career, you are wasting both time and money. Beating up on middle aged Doctors and Lawyers in Sports 2000 is not going to advance your career.

The most difficult aspect of racing is not simply going fast - or even going fast consistently - or in lasting the distance. The single most difficult thing to do in racing is to get by someone who is as fast (or even almost as fast) as you are. It can take laps to get by an uncooperative (or unconscious) driver who is seconds slower than you are.

Unless the object of your attentions is leading the motor race, when you do get by him you are then faced with the necessity of making up the time that you lost while the two of you were tripping over each other. This may be impossible. The easy way to finish ahead of someone is to start ahead of him - and stay there. The only way to start ahead of him is to outqualify him.

In almost all forms of racing grid position is determined by qualifying speed. In order to start at the front, you have to qualify at the front. It therefore behooves every driver to learn how to qualify well.

CRAZY TIME - BUT NOT FOR US

The final ten minutes of the last qualifying session are liable to be crazy time. Not because ride heights have been lowered to the sparking point and the cars are circulating

with a couple of gallons of fuel on board. It will be crazy because most of the drivers' adrenaline level has risen and they are liable to be over-revving, banging off curbs (and each other) and generally conducting themselves like idiots in search of that last half of a tenth. Natural - and human - but dumb!

Instead of a time to go berserk, qualifying should be a time for discipline and planned programs. There are actually three tasks to be accomplished during the time allotted to practice and qualifying. The driver must learn (or relearn) the track; the car set up must be optimized for the race, and the car must be qualified.

Even ignoring qualifying tires (and fuel), the optimum set up for a fast qualifying lap may well differ in some details from the optimum race set up. The differences may be several and subtle - but they are all foreseeable.

Fuel weighs six pounds per gallon. Even for a 100 kilometer race, the car will be faster with just a couple of gallons of fuel on board. You may be able to run the car a bit lower, or get away with shorter gears, or more ignition advance, or a leaner mixture, or a little less understeer for a couple of laps. These are all things to find out about in testing - not just before qualifying. But,

above all, the disciplined driver can concentrate harder for a couple of laps than he can for the race distance - and that is where the qualifying lap comes from.

We set the car up for qualifying, you sets yourself up for one or two perfect laps and then you just have to go out there and do it. There is no sense staying out lap after lap trying for that one good one - if nothing else happens, the tires will go off. You just have to pick your time and go do it.

I have been fortunate in working with a sizeable number of drivers who could do it any time that I asked them to. Sometimes, when you have the fastest combination of car and driver present on the day, it pays to set your time early when the track isn't crowded and people aren't quite so crazy. That way you cannot get caught out by an oiled track, a session cut short, or what have you. You can then sit back until the last ten minutes and not wear things out.

With ten minutes to go, though, I send the driver out to do it again or to circulate at a modest pace - with both driver and crew looking for a clear lap. They are a lot easier to find when you are not pressed. When you get one, take advantage of it - just in case someone else's adrenaline beats your previous effort.

Before qualifying take a real good look at the location of the timing stand/lights relative to the race track itself. On a one lap basis you may be able to gain a tenth or so just by using the track's geography to your advantage. The most obvious cases that I have known were the old Road America and the original Vallelunga circuit near Rome.

The timing point at Road America used to be at the apex of Turn 14. On their hot lap the smart drivers used to enter Turn 14 way too fast to get through it - the run off area was flat and harmless. The line at Vallelunga was at the start/finish - but, in the days before download, you had to get on the brakes before the line if you wanted to get through Turn One fast. On the qualifying lap you just went in too deep and then saved your life by braking across Turn One and blowing the exit.

In both these cases, a little bit of time could be gained at the end of the qualifying lap. It is more common to be able to do so at the beginning - or, rather, before the actual beginning of the lap. Remember we talked earlier about the first third of the corner being where the genius driver shines? That is true in terms of total lap time, but there are lots of corners where, if you are purposely slow and off line in the entrance, you can get on the power earlier and come out slightly faster than you would on an optimum total corner. If one of these corners happens to precede the timing lights, you can gain a little bit at the beginning of your hot lap.

QUALIFYING TIRES

Whether you have qualifying rubber or just a fresh set of race tires to qualify on, they are not going to develop optimum stick for more than a few laps. The qualifying tires are usually junk after no more than two laps. The race tires won't go off much, but they will definitely lose their edge. This means that you don't have much time to get your hot lap in - and slow traffic can ruin your best effort.

Senna was reputed to be able to watch the monitor, visualize where every car was on the race track and pick his time to qualify. Senna was able to do a lot of things that mere mortals do not understand.

There really is no solution to this slow traffic problem - you just have to pick a spot when it looks like you can get a clear lap and go for it. Unfortunately, slow traffic is very liable to be unaware traffic.

When you are in the middle of the only perfect lap you have ever done and come up on Joe Slow - in the wrong place - you will be sorely tempted to go for it. Unless you are absolutely and completely certain that Joe knows you are there, and you know Joe, don't do it. Joe will do something so stupid that it had never entered your mind. He will collect you - damn near every time. Accept the loss of the lap, pass him safely and try again.

Another technique that has never worked is to slow down and let the slow traffic get way ahead of you. No one has ever let them get far enough ahead to do even one fast lap before they are in the way again. The best way to get away from a clump of slower cars is to either pass them or come safely through the pits.

QUALIFYING DOWNLOAD

There are circumstances when you want a lot of download to qualify and less to race. An example is Road America. Here, on one track, are combined the three longest straights in North America - but there are also twelve corners, most of them fast. Believe it or not, the fast way around (on a one lap basis) is with a fair bit of download so that you can carry speed through the fast corners. But you cannot race that way simply because an equal car with less download will get by you on the straights and, by being ahead of you, will prevent you from using your download in the braking areas and corners. Like I said, a lot of this game is mental and it takes a lot of thinking about things to succeed.

HOW LONG

Human nature being what it is, I often find it necessary to restrict young drivers to a specific amount of time or number of laps to qualify - this is especially true when you have to race on the same tires you qualify on. My reasoning is that, if they can't get it done in five laps, it is highly unlikely that they can do it in 50. They hate me for it. Every time that I break down and give them the "just a couple more laps" that they beg for, all they do is wear out the tires. I don't break down much these days. When an experienced professional driver asks for more laps I give them without question - these guys know what they are doing.

THE IMPORTANCE OF BEING FIRST

None of the above should be interpreted as as downgrading on my part the importance of qualifying - I believe in it as much as anyone and more strongly than most. Within reason I will do whatever it takes to put the car on pole.

The pole is important for several reasons. In some series it carries a championship point, sometimes even a considerable sum of money. It does wonders for the state of mind of driver, crew, car owner and sponsors. It assures you of the Sunday morning headline - regardless of what happens in the race. Most of all, perhaps, it establishes the pecking order. I agree, to a large extent, with Senna's famous statement: "Qualifying tells you about the drivers; there is luck involved in the race."

14

"He fears his fate too much, or his deserves are small,
he who will not put it to the test, to win or lose it all." (traditional)

THE RACE

It has been said that the racing driver should know the race track as well has he or she knows their lover's body. I know that, thirty years after I last drove a race car in anger, I can close my eyes and visualize, in detail, every race track that I knew well.

It is important that the track you think you know so intimately is the actual track you are going to race on - as opposed to the one that you qualified on yesterday, or a couple of hours ago. They may not be exactly the same. That is, of course, one of the reasons why it is so easy to get caught out by changes in track conditions - we expect "normal conditions".

It is especially easy to get caught out on the first lap of a race. It is always several hours since you have driven the track at speed - sometimes not since the day before. Equally often there have been other races between your last session and the race. In this case we can be certain that the track has changed. There will be more rubber down than there was. There may be "marbles", or oil sweep here and there. There may be oil spots. Braking markers, or even barriers, may have been moved. The only chance that you will have to figure all of this out will be during the pace lap(s).

In those countries where motor racing is a major sport, what we call the pre-race pace lap(s) or parade lap(s) are referred to as "reconnaissance" lap(s). To my mind this is a better term. It is crucial for a driver to know, in detail, the exact condition of the race track that he is about to race on - especially during the first lap. It's rather like a pilot getting a weather report before take off.

This sort of thing is particularly important in the early stages of a driver's career - when other people are very likely to have raced on the track (and made a mess of it) since he last saw it. For example, after a 200 mile CART race, that part of the track you have mentally reserved for a demon out braking shot may well be covered with marbles. Unless you notice this on the pace lap, your demon move may well bring you to grief.

There are many possible variations on this theme. They range from oil spots to marbles to sand to moved barriers (or braking markers) to oil sweep. If you don't see them and take note of them before the race starts, you will have no one to blame but yourself when either you fall foul of one of them or the observant opposition runs away on the first lap.

We know that the driver who is able to pull out a sizeable lead on the first lap has a big advantage - both physical and psychological. Watch Schumacher or Tracy - or tapes of Prost or Senna or Mansell! There are several aspects to working out an early lead. One of them, of course, is being on the pole, or at least the front row, to start with. Another is getting a really good start - whether standing or rolling. Both take practice, thought and concentration.

Still another aspect is learning to drive the footprints of the tires - rather than the geography of the race track. This is especially true when the tires are cold and the adrenaline is up. The driver whose excuse is that he was caught out by cold tires is really saying that his receptors were not completely open - he wasn't listening to what the car and the tires were trying to tell him. The same goes for the driver who ran over sand or dirt, got his tires dirty and went off at the next corner. The same corner, sure, but the next corner - come on. Drivers can (and do) fool TV commentators with excuses like this. They cannot fool their employers with the same line. Actually, they cannot fool the retired driver type TV commentator - it's just that ex-drivers are (usually) too loyal to the breed to expose them.

However, the pole sitting driver who gets a demon start, drives the footprints perfectly and didn't notice the marbles on the exit of Turn Four is very liable to find himself watching the rest of the race from somewhere just downstream from those same marbles.

According to the people who worked with him, Jackie Stewart (and there has been no one more canny) could tell you more about the immediate condition of the race track after a single pace lap than the other drivers could after a 200 mile Grand Prix. I suspect that the same was true of Senna and Prost - both masters of the demon first lap.

So use the pace lap(s) for something constructive. As we saw earlier, squirming all over the place in a (ineffective) effort to heat your tires won't do you any good at all. God has given you the reconnaissance laps to study the track. Use them.

THE START

Having discussed the psychological aspects of the pole, we should also consider the psychological aspects of the start. Coming out of the first corner, the drivers behind you are fully aware of whom they will have to pass in order to win the race. They are also aware that, during the early laps, the leader is running on a clean track while the rest of the pack is scrambling in traffic and losing time. The leader can concentrate on going fast while the followers have to devote a reasonable portion of their attention to traffic. The pressure is always on the follower - and pressure leads to mistakes.

TO STAND OR TO ROLL

In almost a century of motor racing we have come up with exactly two methods of starting the race - both bad. Most of the world uses the standing start. In this country we have the rolling start - the standing start being used only in Toyota Atlantic. There is considerable disagreement over which method is better - and less dangerous.

I personally think that, except for the ovals, the rolling start lacks a few things and is probably no safer (you have the same accident in turn one as with the standing start but the cars are going a lot faster) and the spectacle is a lot less. Admittedly it is easier to stall the car, burn out the clutch, break a halfshaft, etc. on a standing start - so the rolling start makes it less likely (although not impossible) that the track will be littered with stalled, bogged or sideways motor cars at the actual start.

THE ROLLING START

The procedure is simple. After some number (hopefully pre-decided and announced) of pace laps, the cars line up two abreast in qualifying order and come down to the starter at a speed decided by the pole sitter. If the cars are properly lined up and no one is too obviously trying a Texas start, the starter waves the green flag and the race is on. No passing is allowed until the green flies and often no passing is allowed before the start line. Straightforward enough? Not necessarily!

It is easier to gain an advantage on a rolling start than on a standing one. Indy Car and NASCAR understand what I am about to say. If I cause some cases of cardiac arrest in certain other organizations, so be it. We are not talking about a gentleman's sport here. If you want a gentleman's sport, go play croquet.

Anyway, the rules state (normally) that there can be no passing prior to the start/finish line. Since the officials (except for CART and NASCAR) are normally both blind and excited out of their minds, it can pay to have someone video taping the start to protect your interests.

The frequency with which drivers are caught in the wrong gear during rolling starts is equalled only by the number who are caught sound asleep. It is enough to make one wonder about the mental acuity of some of our heroes! Anytime you are coming down toward a starter be prepared, mentally and physically, for a start.

No matter how many pace laps have been promised, no matter what you think the pace car (if any) has or has not done, no matter how ragged the line up seems from where you sit, no matter how many drivers' arms may be extended skyward - be ready. Otherwise you will eventually be caught asleep. When this happens your position, your ego, your self respect, your reputation and your relationship with your crew and your car owner will suffer.

Unless you are on the pole, you don't get to choose the road speed at which the race will start. You do, however, get to choose what gear you will be in and, within limits, what rpm your engine will be at. You had better be in whatever gear puts you near your engine's torque peak. This will do two good things - it will assure you of maximum acceleration and it will keep you from having to throw a shift immediately after the start.

If the road speed chosen by the polesitter leaves you between gears (clever him!), take the numerically higher ratio and throw an early shift. Revving to almost redline with the clutch in and banging the clutch out at the start will give you a jump from flywheel inertia - if you do it right and if the drive line and engine will take it.

If you come down to the starter with your engine all loaded up, when you plant your foot nothing will happen until the engine has coughed all the badness out of its innards - and you deserve whatever happens to you.

The mind game at the rolling start takes place in the first row - the rest are pretty much a captive audience.

The starter/ chief steward will always tell the front row exactly the same thing: "We want a safe, slow and fair start". The only way that he will get a slow start is if the pole sitter feels he has a measurable acceleration advantage. Since the pole sitter, by definition, cannot jump the start, he is going to do his best to start early - either by faking the second place driver out of his Nomex undies or by hanging him up against the wall in the last corner before the start line and then departing.

In the first instance, there will be a certain amount of jockeying back and forth, getting on and off the throttle (maybe even braking) going on. The object being to do a phony start, then back off to force the outside car to pass. He then has to back off to avoid a penalty. The pole sitter goes as the outside car backs off.

Watch Price Cobb or Christopher Smith when they are on the pole for a graphic lesson on how to do this even to very experienced drivers. From mid pack, let your conscience (and your fear of getting caught) be your guide. Why they don't video tape starts is beyond me....

Last word on the subject. If there are races on the schedule before yours, watch each start. Race starters, like the rest of us, are creatures of habit and are very liable to wave their green flag when the pack is at a pretty consistent distance from the starter's stand.

THE STANDING START

Spectators like standing starts - they are spectacular! I like standing starts because I think that anything that adds to the skills demanded of drivers is a good thing. Until their drivers learn to do them consistently well, car owners and mechanics are not liable to like standing starts because they don't like replacing the parts that get broken during the learning process.

Race starters should like standing starts simply because it makes their job easy. We used to have considerable difficulty with the starter - some misunderstood their place in the great scheme of things and tried to outtrick the drivers, causing all sorts of havoc. The advent of electronically controlled starting lights has almost completely solved the official type problems.

Again the procedure is simple and straightforward. After two reconnaissance laps, the cars line up in staggered grid positions, do one parade lap and are lined up again. When the last car is in position a marshal signals the starter from the back of the grid. The starter then initiates the electronic start procedure.

A red light comes on and four to seven (randomly selected) seconds later the green light comes on automatically. The race is on.

Supposedly any car that moves out of its marked box before the green will be penalized either with a stop-and-go or a 30 second penalty (the choice is the crews' - not the officials'). Since the appointed start judges are liable to be both incompetent and prejudiced, it is well to video tape the start. As I said, why the officials don't is beyond me.

No one in his right mind would take the stop and go unless they have to stop anyway. Opt for the 30 second penalty, assemble your witnesses, your video and your lawyer and do battle at once. Don't wait for the end of the race - especially if your driver is innocent or another is flagrantly guilty and uncaught.

You cannot play any games on a standing start. There is absolutely no sense in planning your "moves" ahead of time because no one has any idea what is going to happen. You merely have to concentrate on doing it right; deflate your senses; open your receptors and go for it when it happens.

If you are on the pole, you get to choose which side of the track you start on. (The same is true of the rolling start.) Don't automatically assume that you want the inside. Go look at the race track. The inside pole slot may be in a ditch - as at Long Beach. Or it may be bumpy. Or the first corner may be so close and so fast that you want the outside for the first corner to get the inside for the second...

The starting technique depends largely on the characteristics of your car. For example, in Formula Three, with no horsepower, lots of torque and not much tire, one holds the engine well over its peak power rpm (because of the intake restrictors, the engines are safe a couple of thousand rpm over what they will pull in any gear), sidesteps the clutch and takes advantage of the inertia of crankshaft, flywheel and clutch.

With Atlantic cars, one holds about 9500rpm and does a duck walk with the clutch and the right foot. There is no way to describe how to "get the car up on the tire" by balancing engine and clutch in about a nanosecond. You will recognize it when you do it right. Once you have felt it, you should be able to repeat it.

The proper amount of wheelspin results in a rocket start. Few current Atlantic drivers do this consistently well. If it starts to bog (big tires and not a lot of torque), dip the clutch. In this case a carbon/carbon clutch helps a lot. For too much wheelspin (unlikely in an Atlantic car) back out of the throttle just a little bit.

The only way to learn how to do a standing start is to practice. Those car owners and crews who refuse to do so are in the same category as those who refuse to let the driver practice in the rain - losers. If you don't trust the driver in the wet, why in hell should you trust him in the dry? If you are afraid to wear out or break parts practicing starts, why are you racing? You sure as hell aren't racing to win!

The carbon/carbon clutch, while expensive in initial cost pays for itself very quickly in the standing start business. When practicing starts, give the clutch, particularly a sintered clutch, plenty of time to cool down between starts. Hot clutches wear fast and the plates warp. This not only costs money, warped plates creep on the grid and can get you disqualified. The best clutches are Tilton's.

With some clutches there is a very real danger of creeping on the grid with the revs up and the clutch in. What happens is that a combination of heat from minor slippage between the driven and driving plates, combined with centrifugal force from the high revs acting on the diaphragm spring, starts to engage the clutch and the car begins to creep. Proper pivot ring geometry - as in AP and Tilton clutches - and a limited amount of time at high revs helps a lot. The four to seven second rule is a good one.

WHEN TO START

With the light controlled standing start there really is no choice. It's like drag racing - you wait for the green. Otherwise you run a very strong risk of being penalized. With the rolling start, especially in club racing, there are some options - especially if the rules do not prohibit passing prior to start/finish. Even if they do, lagging back and getting a real running start has a lot to recommend it - especially if you are not on the pole. Unlike swimming and track, there is usually (except in CART) no immediate penalty for a jumped rolling start - if the starter lets the pack go, those who may have committed minor transgressions have gotten away with them. Especially those not at the front of the pack.

THE RESTART

In the US, most professional races will have at least one restart. Restarts take place in single file. Hopefully the pace car will turn off its lights at the start of the last yellow flag lap and dive decisively for the pits at the first opportunity. It is then up to the starter and the lead car (who should be leading the race. There is no conceivable excuse for the pace car not to pick up the race leader.

Most sanctioning bodies forbid passing on a restart before the start/finish. The advantage on a restart lies with the race leader - who gets to depart whenever he feels like it and at whatever speed he chooses. This is as it should be - after all, he is leading the race and the chances are that the pace car penalized him more than anyone else. It is also his privilege to throw a fake at the second place car just before he departs.

It is up to the rest of the drivers not to be caught asleep and to attempt to arrange their own start so that they arrive at the start/finish going faster than the car(s) in front of them. It helps a lot to keep your tires warm during yellow flag laps. If they cool down you will be in trouble during the restart lap from both lack of temperature and lack of air pressure. Bleeder valves are invaluable in this regard - they cannot, of course, add pressure but the fact that your starting pressure will be 3 to 4 psi higher than it would be without them is crucial.

TURN ONE

Regardless of the type of start, the majority of racing accidents happen at turn one on the first lap. If you do not win the start and are not leading the charge, when you arrive at turn one you will find yourself in very close company indeed - surrounded by maniacs, all of whom have cold tires, some of whom have cold brakes, few of whom have any idea where to shut down for the corner from a start rather than from a flying lap. (You, of course, took the trouble to find this out in practice.) Further, most of them are convinced that they can win the race in this corner.

There is absolutely no sense trying to make a detailed plan - this is one of those situations where you have to take it as it comes and take your best shot every time you get a chance. My own idea has always been to be really aggressive (being conservative will only get you hit), gain as many positions as possible at the actual start, take whatever opportunities present themselves during the charge to turn one and then to concentrate on surviving turn one.

The best way to do this is to do whatever it takes to get an inside line at something less than the limit of adhesion - that way you will (almost) always have somewhere to go. Mind you, there is no sense leaving a lot of adhesion or a lot of room for your friend on the outside - just make damned sure that no one behind you thinks that there is any room at all inside of your car. In most cases, by the time you get to turn two the pack will have strung out a bit and you can get on with the serious business of racing.

LAP ONE

There are a great many otherwise excellent drivers who are constitutionally unable to go all out on the first lap - cold tires, and unknown track conditions being the usually stated reasons. Anyone who charges out onto a race track that another race has just coated with oil and rubber and tries to equal his qualifying time on cold tires has a short future.

One has to leave a certain margin at the exit of every corner and that margin should be a bit greater on the first lap. But the driver who is not racing when the green flag falls, like the driver who cannot feel the footprints of his tires and must drive geographically, is never going to be an Indy Car or Formula One winner.

Likewise, of course, the driver who tries to go from the middle of the pack to the front on the first lap is not going to make it. Further, he is very liable to take someone else with him - perhaps several someones, none of whom will appreciate his efforts. I believe that each of us is born with certain inalienable rights, including the right to put our own necks into unreasonable jeopardy any time that we choose to do so. I further, and equally firmly, believe that no one is born with or acquires the right to place another driver's neck in the chop position unreasonably.

If you have qualified badly, or made a nonsense of the start, or have spun and are coming back through the pack, accept what is past and do your damnedest to make up for it during the race - but temper your determination with a touch of sanity and judgement. If someone else insists on being insane, help him on his way if you can do so without major risk to yourself. Otherwise let him go - he will probably screw things up sooner or later anyway and you can get by him safely. The start of a motor race should be viewed as a time of opportunity - not a time of insanity.

PACE

In the short races at the beginning of your career there is no such thing as pacing either yourself or your car. In long races you have to conserve both - and it doesn't matter whether you are talking about the 24 hours of Nelson Ledges in a showroom stock car, the 24 hours of Le Mans in a prototype ,or the Indianapolis 500.

TACTICS

To my mind, tactics - in the sense of the word as used by the TV commentators and most journalists - simply do not exist in events of less than 500 miles duration. The tactical situation is very simple. If you are leading and in control of the race, you work out a big enough lead so that you do not have to take chances in traffic - say ten seconds.

In this country there is no sense driving your car hard enough to build up a bigger lead (unless you can get a lap on the field on an oval) because of the almost inevitable yellow flag and attendant pace car. If you are not leading, or if you are leading with opponents snapping at your heels, drive as fast and as hard as you can without making mistakes.

LEADING

One of the more difficult things for the driver to learn is how to lead a race. The number of drivers who fall off the road the first time that they find themselves leading a race is very close to the total number of drivers who have ever led a race. The solution is simple - discipline.

Concentrate on driving the car, not on the fact that you are leading. While you must be aware of what is going on behind you, you must also realize that the only way that someone in an equal car is going to get by you is for you to make a mistake - either in driving or in tactics (like leaving a door open).

If your head is on straight, the pressure is all on the driver who must get past - there is no such thing as pressure from behind. When you are so fortunate as to have a reasonable lead, watch your pit board and run to the second place car. Hopefully your crew will notify you if someone is climbing through the pack fast enough to displace the second place car and catch you - but keep an eye on your mirrors just in case.

PASSING

The most difficult thing to do in motor racing is to pass another well driven car with equal performance. Hell, it's often difficult to pass cars that are being lapped. Unless the other driver makes a mistake, competitive passing in road racing is almost always done (or at least set up) under the brakes.

It takes a determined and positive move. Unless the move is both well planned and well executed, the inexperienced (or unthinking) driver who makes a demon pass under the brakes may well end up being repassed half way down the next straight.

Referring to FIGURE 31, the passing driver will inevitably find himself way too far on the inside to take a "normal" line. Even though he adjusts his apex point to compensate, his apex speed, and therefore his corner exit speed, must be lower than normal. If the passed

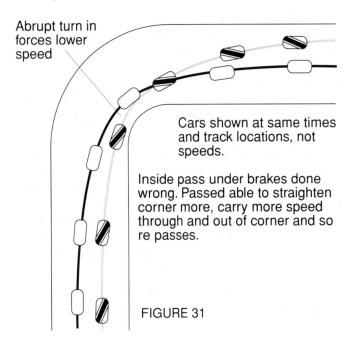

Abrupt turn in forces lower speed

Cars shown at same times and track locations, not speeds.

Inside pass under brakes done wrong. Passed able to straighten corner more, carry more speed through and out of corner and so re passes.

FIGURE 31

driver uses his head and does things just right, he can take a later than usual apex, get on the power early (even from a lower apex speed), exit the corner faster and drive by the demon braker on the straight.

The solution, illustrated by FIGURE 32, unsporting as it may seem, is to plant yourself directly in front of the car you have just passed. This slows him down to your speed - or less - and very effectively prevents the repass. You might not be able to get all the way in front but as long as you have an "overlap", if you use all of the race track, he has to give way - or go off. See Fittipaldi vs Unser, Mid-Ohio 1993 or, for that matter Fittipaldi vs Unser, Indianapolis 1989.

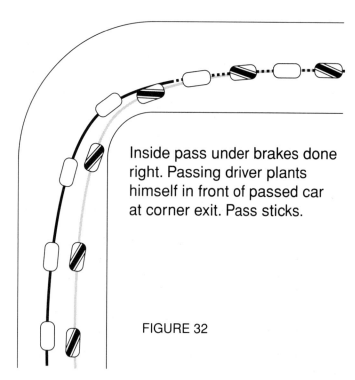

Inside pass under brakes done right. Passing driver plants himself in front of passed car at corner exit. Pass sticks.

FIGURE 32

CORNER EXIT PASSING

We often see two cars circulating together, separated in places by inches, lap after lap while the driver behind tries desperately to get by. The driver in front, wide awake, is driving a legitimate defensive line when he has to. Every time that the driver behind lunges in an unsuccessful attempt to pass under the brakes he loses a couple of car lengths (at best) and it takes him a few laps to catch back up and try again.

In many cases, there is a better way. Two cars are seldom truly equal all the way around the race track. If you study the situation carefully you will probably find someplace on the track where your corner exit is better than his - or someplace where you can make your corner exit better than his.

Drop back just a little bit, drive that corner perfectly, judge your distance so that you come out of the corner almost on his tail but going faster than he is. You can then get a tow and slingshot by him on the straight. He, of course (and the spectators and television commentators) will attribute your pass to superior power. In fact, most of the straightaway passes between equal and almost equal cars are the result of superior corner exit speed - it just doesn't show up until midway down the straight.

HEAD GAMES

We have previously discussed the mechanics of passing. We have not discussed the psychology of passing. I have mentioned that it is almost impossible to pass a well driven equal car unless the driver makes a mistake. This makes the psychology of passing very simple indeed - hound the guy until he makes a mistake, either by braking too late and sliding wide, by losing control or by leaving a door open, then force your way past.

This means making a lot of feints, even in places and situations when you have no intent of actually trying to pass. It also means concentrating on your own car, the race track and the situation, rather than on the rear tires of the car you are trying to pass. When you concentrate on the other car, your opponent is actually driving your car - think about it.

It also means being ready to pass anytime that the lead driver makes a mistake (see Mansell at Surfer's Paradise, 1993). Finally (for now) it means being very decisive - once you have committed yourself to the pass, go through with it. When considering this last statement always remember the first law of racing; "The guy on the outside loses."

This law is not immutable - but it comes pretty damned close. If you have managed to get even (or even almost even) and inside of another car at the entrance to a corner - and you appear to be determined (it helps to have a reputation) - the other guy is probably not going to turn into you and cause an accident which will inevitably involve him. On the other hand, if you are on the outside and he is skilled, determined and aware, he may view your presence as an opportunity.

LAPPING

Lapping slow cars is dodgy at best. Quote Mr. Mansell after his championship winning performance at Nazareth, "When you follow eight cars down the back straight I defy anybody to second or third guess what the fourth or fifth guy in line is going to do."

Exactly why certain drivers being lapped are consistently unaware of the presence of the fast car(s) and/or unable to figure out what to do has been beyond my understanding for forty years. The good part of this is that it is always the same drivers who get in the way and do it all wrong every time, so you eventually learn to recognize them - even if the stewards do not.

It seems to me that if the television commentators can figure out who the chronic offenders are, (David Hobbs' comment about "xxxxxx xxxxxxxxxxx, the blind Frenchman" remains my all time favorite Hobbsism) the officials should eventually be able to figure it out and do something about it. However, the unconscious driver being lapped will remain a very real hazard for the foreseeable future and it is up to you to deal with him. Some drivers are very good at bobbing and weaving their way through lapped traffic - Unser and Fittipaldi, for instance. Some are not - Tracy, for instance. Those who are seem pretty much follow a pattern:

1) When possible, plan your pass well in advance and adjust your speed so that you pass the guy in the safest and most advantageous part of the race track. The idea is for you not to lose momentum and, when possible, to make the pass at such a time and in such a location that the driver behind you gets held up. This requires forethought and planning on your part.

2) While your presence can be announced, if necessary, with gentle taps in sedan racing, the technique does not often work with open wheeled cars. With the chronic offenders, it helps to make eye contact in his mirror.

3) It is always true that the guy on the outside loses. It is especially true when the guy on the inside doesn't know that you are there. In the case of the blind driver being lapped, you can also lose on the inside.

4) Never be directly behind a car that you are lapping when you are approaching a braking zone or a corner. The reason that you are lapping him is that he is slower than you are - a lot slower. He may well be going to brake earlier than you can conceive that he would and enter the corner at a slower speed than you would believe possible.

5) Make no indecisive moves. Once you have decided to go - GO.

The traffic masters are like good broken field runners in football or good fighter pilots - they have highly developed senses of situational awareness. They see traffic patterns developing ahead of them and sense where the safe holes will be when they get there. Some of this is inborn but some of it is developed.

My next suggestion may sound ridiculous - but it works. One way to practice this sort of thing is to purposely walk fast in pedestrian traffic consciously looking for the developing pattern of holes in the traffic ahead of you. It may get you some unfriendly comments, but you will learn. It also works on the freeway, but may result in unplanned conversations with uniformed public servants.

I'M KILLING HIM IN THE CORNERS...

...But he's walking away from me down the straight.

If I had $10 for every time that I have heard that song, Christopher would be in Formula One today. For some reason that escapes me many drivers (and all spectators and most commentators) are unable to understand the difference between time and distance on the race track.

It is very simple. Sixty miles per hour translates to 88 feet per second. Two absolutely equal cars, one half second apart, travelling 180 miles per hour at the end of a straight will be separated by 132 feet, about eight car lengths. When they finish braking for a 60 mph corner, they will still be separated by half a second - but the linear separation will be 43 feet, about two and a half car lengths.

To the uninitiated (ignorant?), it will appear that the following car has outbraked the unholy bejesus out of the leader. As they exit the corner and accelerate the time difference will stay the same, while the linear rubber band stretches and it appears that the lead car has a significant power advantage. It is astounding how many experienced racers flat refuse to understand this phenomenon. Don't be one of them.

Of course, if your car owner, sponsor or the press wants to believe that you are down on power...

William C. Mitchell's data logging software has a window that shows a car exactly one second ahead of your car. It gets smaller on the straights and bigger in the braking areas. It is very instructional.

BEING PASSED

No matter how good you get at this game, you are occasionally going to be passed. When you have been outsmarted, outmaneuvered and/or outdriven, don't make the situation into an accident. Don't make it easy for him but, when he has you, give it to him - and then try to get it back.

IN DEFENSE

Weaving down the straight to prevent being passed is indefensible and stupid (except maybe on the last lap). If all chief stewards were of the calibre of Wally Dallenbach, ("one weave may be OK, two gets you a black flag stop and go") it wouldn't happen. As Price Cobb said at Macau some years ago; "If these Formula Three idiots would spend as much time racing as they do blocking each other, Senna might not get away from them".

The defensive line, on the other hand, is a perfectly legitimate portion of the race track. When battling for position, he who leaves the door open for his worthy opponent to pull a demon braking manoeuver down the inside is either asleep or stupid.

Of course, the defensive line is a two-edged sword. When you are not using the whole road at the entrance to a corner, you will have to brake early, apex early, carry less speed through the corner and exit slower. This may well create an envelope of opportunity for the following driver - if he has faked you into protecting yourself on the inside when there was no need to. In this case he can hang back, get a better exit and kill you on the exit - particularly if the next corner happens to be in the opposite direction.

BEING LAPPED

Every driver occasionally finds himself in the position of being lapped. You may be driving a GT car in a WSC race or something may have gone wrong with your car - whatever. Don't be an idiot, let the faster car by. But do it right. Acknowledge his presence and wave him by when practical. Don't surprise him with kindness - stay on the normal racing line.

Be very aware that there may be another fast car (or cars) directly behind the first car, so don't tuck into his slipstream unless you are absolutely certain that he is alone. If you are fighting for position while being lapped, try to prevent the car behind you from rocketing by you with the lapping car.

PASSING IN PRACTICE

There is justification for a passing accident when going for the win at the end of a race - witness Fittipaldi vs Unser, Indianapolis 1989. The driver who is willing to settle for second in a competitive car will seldom be first. There is no justification for a passing accident during practice - or even during qualifying. The possible gain is simply not worth the risk.

LAST WORDS

My last words on the subject of lapped cars is a quote from the late Peter Gregg who, immediately after losing the 12 Hours of Sebring by getting involved with a slow car in the closing laps of the race, said; "When there is an incident between a fast car and a slower car, by definition it is the fault of the faster driver." For a lesson in professionalism and class I suggest we compare this statement to what we normally see and hear on TV interviews. We have to be honest with ourselves.

THE PIT STOP

If the race will last longer than either your fuel or your tires, you will get to make a scheduled pit stop. If the race lasts longer than four hours, you get to hand your car over to your co-driver - an act that will fill you with mixed emotions.

Television has made the public aware of the importance of pit stops. Tactics and strategy have been at least partially explained to the public and the pit crews are no longer completely unsung. To date no one has even mentioned the importance of the driver's role in the pit stop. It is critical.

First and foremost the driver has to bring the car in at a speed that is fast enough not to lose time and slow enough to both be safe and not earn a penalty for excessive speed in the pit lane. Exactly why it is that drivers seem unable to equate what the tach says with the pit speed limit is beyond me - especially when the Pi dash has a speedo function.

The driver must identify his own pit and stop the car precisely on a predetermined spot, again without losing time - all this in a crowded pit lane full of both people and cars, not all of whom are fully predictable. The pit lane can also be wet in spots. It is best if he does this without screeching tires, let alone locking them. The stop itself must be firm and decisive - none of this stopping short and rolling into place.

If the rules require the engine to be shut off for refuelling, then he should shut it off, clean, before he stops - the fuelers are going to plug in the instant he stops. If tires are going to be changed, it is vital that he obey the "brakes on" and "brakes off" signs - or at least get his foot off the brakes the instant the car goes up on the jacks. If he is going to get out of the car, he must do so quickly - and the same goes for the driver getting in.

Under most long distance rules, the drivers do not count as men over the wall if they are just helping each other in and out. The number of times I have seen a good stop ruined by a couple of fumble-fingered drivers trying to buckle one of them into the car is about the same as the number of teams that don't plan and practice driver changes.

Successful long distance teams practice pit stops like Jackie Joyner Kersey practiced for the Olympics. The exiting driver must loosen the shoulder straps before the car stops. The physical act of strapping the new driver in must be practiced - or else it will be fumbled.

The atmosphere during a stop is not conducive to good communication. If the radios are working, during the stop is no time for the drivers to discuss anything. If the radios have failed, make it brief - very. The incoming driver does not need to be told that it is hot and uncomfortable in the cockpit - he knows that. He does need to know about any aberrations that the car (or the track) may have developed since last he saw them.

In order to be both brief and effective, your little speech, like your excuses, should be rehearsed before you stop. Don't worry about telling the team manager anything that he doesn't need to know before the car leaves. There is plenty of time for that after it has gone.

If, on the other hand, there is something wrong with the car that needs to be attended to during the stop and which no one but you knows about, tell the pre-designated person-in-charge-of-the-pit-stop just as soon as you can - and then carry on about your business. It is not your job to choreograph the ballet - or to get in the way of the dancers. Transmit your message, get the other driver in and get out of the way.

RADIO DISCIPLINE

All of this transmission of information is made a lot easier and more convenient if the team happens to have radios - particularly if the radios happen to be functioning effectively. Exactly why it is that we can talk to people on the moon and at the bottom of the ocean but not to drivers who are a few hundreds of yards away is beyond me.

There is an art to the effective use of radios. Ever since intrepid airmen first installed radios in their birds, radio discipline has been a big problem. It seems that there is an inborn human tendency is to babble into a microphone at every given chance - you may never have had a chance to listen to a military air control net, but it is not a lot different from your every day CB channel.

There are two things to remember. Speak slowly and distinctly so that the poor devil on the other end has some hope of understanding what you are saying. Don't talk for the sake of talking. Assuming that the poor devil on the other end is professionally qualified to talk to you, he is very liable to be busy with fuel or tire calculations, trying to keep an official, your car owner or a wandering journalist happy while you are busy babbling.

God knows we have enough trouble counting to ten without distractions. Besides, while the poor devil would probably be interested in the fantastic pair of 42DDs at Turn Ten, he will never get to see them for himself and, further, your babbling will destroy forever any illusions he may have had about your single minded concentration on the job at hand.

THE UNSCHEDULED PIT STOP

Every so often something goes wrong during a race and the driver gets to make an unscheduled pit stop. If the malady is terminal, that's it, the day is over. If the malady is repairable, the pit stop itself may well determine how much money - and how many points - you get to take home at the end of the day. Again the radio makes things easy - the driver briefs the crew on the situation and the pit stop is similar to a scheduled event.

Without a radio, a chinese fire drill is a real possibility. Don't worry about the fact that it is unlikely that you will be able to give the crew any warning - on most tracks they will see you slow. There should be prearranged very simple hand signals while you are in pit lane - even for something as obvious as a flat tire; they may not be able to see which one. Use arm and hand signals, not fingers - no one on earth can count fingers extended in a moving race car.

When you do stop, the crew will immediately start to take care of anything that has been reported on the radio or is obvious. The person in charge will appear at your side. If you don't have radio contact, the only way that he will be able to hear is to stick his ear in front of your mouth - so raise your visor. You are wearing a full face helmet and a head sock - he cannot read your lips! Explain the problem and then do as you are told by the person in charge.

LEAVING THE PIT

As a driver you cannot see when the pit crew has finished. You also cannot see, very well, what is going on in the pit lane behind you. You are therefore in no position to determine when you should leave. It is vital that one person who is in a position to see everything and who is capable of making rational decisions be designated to send the driver out - with a very specific signal.

If your organization has not so designated a person and his signal, insist that they do so. Never trust a pit marshal to send you out - they are often not qualified by either experience or temperament to make the decision. The sender outer should be standing directly in front of the car so that you cannot leave until he tells you to - at least not without running over him.

The sender outer will also tell you when to start your engine. If you start it before he tells you, to you may very well find yourself disqualified. If you leave before he tells you to, you may find yourself with an open filler cap, a jack under the car, a loose wheel, an injured mechanic or a collision. None of this will contribute to your success or to your popularity. When the designated man tells you to go, GO! He may be playing it pretty close with a car behind you on pit lane, so get out of there.

The same holds true for the situation when the car coming down off the air jacks is the signal to go. Do so without stalling the car, without abusing the clutch or halfshafts, without losing control in dirt, liquid or just due to wheelspin. You are racing and the clock is running, so get out of the working pit lane and into the traffic lane as quickly as feasible and accelerate to whatever speed is allowed (or that you think you can get away with).

Remember that any car parked and not up on the jacks can pull out ahead of you at any time. At the end of the pit lane you may well find an official with a flag who will either wave you out or hold you until he thinks it is safe. In either case obey him. No matter how vigorously he waves you out, check your mirrors before pulling out into the traffic lanes.

Before you leave the pit, pump the brakes up - even if the pads haven't been changed. Remember when you get to the first corner that you have at least some of the following: cold tires, cold new tires, new pads, boiled brake pads, a full fuel load and/or a changed set up.

At Daytona remember that the first corner is in the pit lane - better men than you have hit it!

The first lap after a pit stop is similar to the first lap of a race - you have to drive it at the limit of your (cold) tires but not beyond that limit.

THE BLACK FLAG PIT STOP

A driver is given the black flag when he has committed a rule infraction serious enough for the chief steward to decide to call him in for a disciplinary discussion/time penalty - or when his car is observed to be in an unsafe condition. In the case of an infraction the regulations state that the crew chief must be notified of the infraction and the intent to black flag before the flag is shown.

In the case of an unsafe car, there may not be time for the notification. In either case, there are two possible approved procedures; the car stops at a predesignated "black flag" station and is met by a steward - or it stops in its own pit and is met by a steward. Which procedure will be followed should either be printed in the supplemental regulations or announced at the drivers' meeting. If it is not, ask.

I have given a great deal of thought to the best course of action to be taken in a black flag situation and I have come to some very definite conclusions. The decision to black flag a driver is usually an arbitrary one on the part of the stewards - and, in SCCA and IMSA, they are very often wrong. Except in matters of safety the stewards are required to notify the team prior to black flagging the driver.

In professional racing, if they are wrong, a calm and reasoning team manager stands a chance of either correcting their thinking on the spot or of talking them into deferring the decision and assessing a time penal-

ty at the end of the race if the decision stands. This will do no good what-so-ever if the car has already stopped. If there is something dangerously wrong with the car, the driver has a much better chance of feeling or seeing it than the officials do. The crew has a better chance of seeing and assessing it than corner workers do.

Except for CART, my instructions to my drivers - during the race - are to ignore the black flag until I call them in - and then calmly deny having seen the thing. Radios make this difficult for more than a lap or two. If it is a rule infraction, they aren't going to penalize you any more for not seeing the flag for a couple of laps while your team manager states his case. I must add that the display of the meatball with your number alongside it is a good time to take stock of your automobile. I must also add that in the UK or in any major league FIA or CART race, you had damned well better obey the black flag pretty quickly.

I have never seen a race won because a driver stopped for a black flag. I have seen several lost because the driver stopped for an unwarranted black flag. I have seen a few won because he didn't; "What flag, my visor was really dirty and the sun must have been in my eyes." The best one was Peter Revson winning a Can Am race at Laguna, collecting $15,000 for the win and paying a $500 fine for not seeing the flag. Sometimes we have to be pretty firm with officialdom.

On the other hand, when you own crew calls you in, come in. It has to be pretty damned serious for them to call you in, the decision is not taken lightly - and what they are trying to do is save your life. Again the radio helps - although it may well suffer from intermittent failure during an infraction discussion between the stewards and the team manager.

When you do stop, take your lumps and concentrate on getting back into the race. It will do no good to argue and less to lose control.

THE FLAT TIRE PIT STOP

Racing tires are forever going flat, usually because they have run over some hard and sharp object - either on or off the racing surface. When a tire goes soft you will feel it - probably before you see the change in shape or color (assuming open wheels). You then get to make a decision based on your position in the race, the number of laps remaining and whether you think you can nurse it home faster than you can stop and change it. The decision is yours alone - but remember, the leak will not stop.

Because of the sidewall construction, it is more difficult to detect a leak in a radial tire than a bias ply. It is much more feasible to nurse a blistered tire than a soft one (lighter braking, less abrupt turn in, less abuse of that end of the car).

When a tire does lose air, the natural tendency is to rush into the pits and change it. This is one of those situations when you need all of the discipline you can muster. If you continue at speed the tire will disintegrate. With a full bodied car, at best the disintegration will demolish the bodywork. With an open wheeled car the tire may well wrap itself around the suspension - making for a really long pit stop. Take your lumps and crawl back to the pits so that the car will arrive there in one piece, and you can get back into the race.

THE CHINESE FIRE DRILL

Despite everyone's best intentions, every so often a pit stop will turn into a chinese fire drill. In the case of an oversight, like an air hose or a tire in front of the car, all the driver has to do is point. Screaming and shouting will be contra-productive. If it is major, it is up to the person-in-charge to sort it out - an out of control driver will only make things worse. Besides, if you just sit there, a textbook picture of control and discipline, you will add to your reputation and image.

WHEN THE CAR BREAKS

When the car breaks terminally, don't try to drive it back to the pits unless you are certain that you can do so without causing further damage - it is expensive. Park it in a carefully chosen place of safety. If there is no place of safety and it won't move, wait for the dust to clear, wait for a break in traffic, get out of the car and out of the vicinity - fast!

In any case, stay with the car until a member of your own crew gets there to take charge. Don't let the safety crew hurt it. Even though they may be trained and competent, the safety of the car, in which you make your living, is your responsibility until your crew gets there. The corporate staff will appreciate your efforts. Very rarely, we have to be firm with safety crews.

HOW TO CRASH

Sooner or later you are going to lose control of the car. I'm talking about total loss of control here - not the catching of an inadvertent slide. You will then have an incident. Whether or not you have an accident is up to you and to the Gods of Chance. Your task is to evaluate the situation, make the right decision and follow it by the right action(s).

The basic rule is this. When you realize that all is lost, lock up the brakes and keep them locked until the car has slowed enough and is pointed in the right direction for you to regain control or until the car has stopped - whichever comes first.

Regaining control is a relative term - just enough control to pick which tree you are going to hit can be very important. Remember that you have no directional

control with the tires locked up. Depending on speed, sometimes it works to point the front wheels in the direction you want to go and release the brakes just before you hit - sometimes.

It is important to push the clutch in and keep the engine revs up while spinning or while the brakes are locked. Otherwise, even if you survive the exercise with the car in one piece you will be faced with a dead engine. Hot racing engines are not easy to restart.

If you are going to hit, it is always best to go in backwards - let the wings, the gearbox and all that stuff absorb the impact while you are supported by the seat. Side impacts against flat objects are next best and frontal impacts are the worst, so spin the thing if you can. If you can't, try to go in sideways.

Unfortunately there is no way to tell or to teach a driver how to recognize the point when there is no longer any chance of regaining control. Prost says that this recognition is instinctive. I feel that it is intuitive - instinct tempered by experience.

At any rate, once all is lost, slow the thing as much as you can before you hit. Remember that once the brakes are locked, if you are in the entry phase of the corner, the car will go at a tangent to its original direction. If you are in the exit phase (i.e. past the apex and have power on) it will probably spin to the inside.

One of the reasons it is a good idea to walk the circuit before driving it is that walking with your eyes open will let you identify the spots (if any) where you can get off the circuit with relative safety. There is no sense looking for them at the instant a bunch of cars piles up in front of you.

It is probably a good idea to at least try to retract your feet just before you hit (although the chance of their staying retracted in a severe impact is doesn't even exist) - and to let go of the wheel to save your wrists and thumbs. Just before you hit is not a good time to wish that you had properly tightened your belts or that you were wearing arm restraints.

After the impact, don't do anything (except hit the fire extinguisher if you even think there might be a fire) until your vision clears and you are oriented. Unless it is on fire or under water, don't release your harness until you have oriented yourself and are pretty damned sure that the wreck is not about to be hit by another car.

If the thing is upside down, use your best judgement. If your brain is clear, your body seems to be functional and it looks safe, I wouldn't wait for the corner workers/safety crew - unless the marshals are British or Australian or it is a CART race. If that is not the case, get out and get yourself to a place of safety. There is nothing you can do to help or to protect your car - get the hell out of there.

Do not cross the track until you are certain that it is safe to do so - and that you have a place to go to.

If your helmet has hit anything at all it needs at least a check up by the manufacturer and a new liner. They are not reusable. If your helmet has hit something, so has your head. Even if your helmet has not hit anything, your brain may well have decelerated, hard, against your skull. Get checked by a real doctor. The same goes for any sort of back discomfort. Don't be a hero.

After any crash it is essential for you to determine what caused it. If it was a mechanical failure, you want to make damned sure that it doesn't happen again. If it was a mistake on your part, ditto. If you got caught up in someone else's accident, there may have been something more you could have done to avoid it. Even if the accident was totally someone else's fault, you need to be certain of that, too - if for no other reason than to avoid that driver in the future.

Normally I have little time for shrinks. Sometimes, however, they make sense. One of their pronouncements regarding flying accidents is that a full investigation of the accident and discovery of its causes helps the pilot to regain his confidence - even when the accident was entirely his fault. I buy that one - the only thing that really frightens us is the unknown.

If you don't know why it happened it can nag at you - consciously or subconsciously. Once you have figured out, in detail, why you ended up on your head, you say to yourself; "Right, well we won't do that again!" and carry on.

SECTION SIX

AT THE OFFICE

15

"If you drive these things long enough, sooner or later one of them is going to bite you." – Paul Hawkins"

If you have a ten dollar head, wear a ten dollar helmet." – Frank Matich

SAFETY AND COCKPIT CONTROLS

Before you step into your office you will dress in an appropriate hat and suit. Nomex is wonderful stuff. So is Proban. Several manufacturers make adequate fire suits. My favorite helmets and suits are made by Simpson. Adequate fire suits are of one piece and of three layer or the equivalent construction. Test after test has proven that there is no such thing as an adequate fire suit unless Nomex or Proban underwear is worn under it. Most drivers still will not wear the underwear unless forced to do so. If you think that a three layer suit and underwear is hot, try a fire.

THE SEAT

Many people who drive racing cars have no idea what it is to sit in a really good racing car seat. This is a pity - it is not possible to drive consistent really fast laps in the modern racing car without one. The reasons are simple indeed:

1) When you have to brace your body against g-forces to keep from flopping around in the cockpit your sensory receptors are not fully operational.

2) Those receptors that are open are confused by the motions of your torso, head and inner ear.

3) A portion of your already inadequate powers of concentration is being wasted keeping your body in place.

4) Finally, some delicacy of control has inevitably been lost - for one, you are hanging onto the steering wheel.

The seat and the safety harness should hold the driver's torso, pelvis and thighs virtually immobilized. In order for this to happen, a custom fitted seat is required - there is no choice.

I reckon that the best production seat for single seat cars is the one designed by David Bruns for the Swift family of cars. Although David is a medium size (and maximum talent) person, the seat fits just about everyone in the world pretty well - but not well enough. What is required is a two part seat. The driver's thighs should fit snugly into two channels, while his pelvis, torso and shoulders must be supported by the seat itself. This usually means a foamed-in-place seat.

In a single seat car - at least least one with a "monocoque" chassis - the chassis itself forms the required rigid support for the seat. In sedans and some sports cars, a rigid seat shell must be provided for both support and safety. There is no such thing as an adequately rigid single skin fiberglass or aluminum seat shell. My personal feeling is that the best seat shells are made from Nomex or paper cored honeycomb with glass, Kevlar or Kevlar and carbon skins.

The best standard sedan seats are the units copied from the one that Paul Van Valkenburgh designed for Mark Donahue more than two decades ago. Illustrated by FIGURE 33, they are now marketed by several houses. While they lack rigidity, the concept and shape are right and rigidizing one should be pretty feasible.

FIGURE 33

FIGURE 34

The very best custom sedan seats are those designed and manufactured by sports medicine specialist Broc Walker and marketed under the TRAC-TEC name. Illustrated by FIGURE 34, they are the very best available - and can be custom fitted to the individual driver.

No purchased seat is going to fit the individual driver properly. It cannot. The solutions are two - a custom seat by a professional (major race teams and rich kids only need apply) or a homemade custom job. Racers have been making two part foam seats since about a week after two part foam appeared on the market (see sidebar).

Don't be discouraged if it takes several tries to get your seat just right. What feels good in the shop may not feel so good on the track. Experienced professional drivers often make four or five seats before they are satisfied. The same is true of pedal, shift lever and steering wheel adjustments. Keep at it, the final results will be worth it.

We don't have to worry about retaining the seat in a single seat race car. It is moulded into the monocoque. In the case of a tube frame single seater, I advocate skinning the inside of the cockpit with thin sheet aluminum - just to properly brace the seat. In the case of the sedan race car it is absolutely critical to securely attach the seat to major structure. Every year racing drivers are killed when the seat comes loose in a violent accident. Don't let it happen to you.

In many cars, the driver's head is necessarily located in close proximity to unyielding hard objects - like the roll over structure. While most sanctioning bodies at least pay lip service to the necessity for an impact absorbing head rest and steering wheel pads (the common foam rubber on fiberglass is just plain dumb), none of them have yet had anything to say about the hard edge of the current single seater high cockpit surrounds

or roll over bar forward braces. None of them, to my knowledge, have anything to say about side support/protection for the driver's head. Sauber is to be commended in this respect. CART at least insists on high cockpit sides.

Hopefully you will never get to be astonished at how far your neck can stretch in a severe impact - or, for that matter, your shoulder harness. Foam rubber is a truly poor impact absorption material. Ensolite isn't bad. Styrofoam is better. Bicycle handlebar foam tubing is useless on roll bars and braces. Use the right stuff; custom designed roll bar padding - give your helmet every bit of help that you can. Along those lines I will repeat my previous statement that, in my opinion, helmets are made by Simpson Safety Systems. The shoulder harness, to be effective, should be 3" wide.

One of the things that race cars do - a lot - is crash. When you are involved in a crash, there are certain factors that determine whether and how seriously you are going to be hurt:

1) Your skill and foresight in minimizing the severity and type of the impact aided and abetted by sheer dumb luck.

2) The energy absorbing qualities of the structure around you and the bits that break off.

3) The strength of the "survival capsule" in which you are sitting.

4) The quality of your personal safety gear - particularly your helmet.

5) The strength and placement of your safety harness.

When you are headed for the wall it is too late to think about any of this - except item (1). The SCCA's GCR tells you all that you need to know about the proper placement of the harness. Far too often the proper placement and attachment of the safety harness is ignored by car manufacturers. I have seen (and corrected) race cars from outstanding manufacturers with woefully inadequate and poorly located harness mounts - some with the heads of the mounting bolts sticking through the floor where they routinely got ground off and the shoulder harness securely mounted to thin sheet aluminum. The SCCA never noticed these - nor the roll over structures that tear off when an upside down car contacts the earth at speed. All that the SCCA requires is a sheet of paper signed by someone stating that the roll over structure meets the GCR requirements. Some do and some don't. So look - and think - and make it right.

THE DEAD PEDAL

Every racing car should have a "dead pedal" or left foot rest. The device not only serves to keep the driver's foot off the clutch when he is not using it, it also serves as an effective body brace and enhances the driver's ability to "feel" the car.

While the modern formula car footbox is pretty narrow, there is always room for a left foot rest - it doesn't have to be very wide. It must, however, be adjustable. The correct position is just rearward of the clutch pedal so that the driver cannot inadvertently rest his foot on the clutch pedal. If necessary, the width of the clutch pedal can be safely reduced to make room for the left foot rest.

THE HEEL REST

There should also be an adjustable heel rest plate extending across all three pedals. This ensures consistent placement of the feet and also serves as a body brace.

STEERING WHEEL POSITION

There are a couple of theories on the correct positioning of the racing car steering wheel. Three things are certain:

1) It is a bad idea to have the wheel so low that your hand hits you thighs at any point in the travel.

2) The straight armed position made famous by one S. Moss may look elegant (which is why he did it) but delicacy of control requires the arms to be slightly bent at the elbow. You should sit close enough to the wheel so that your arms will be slightly bent at the elbow throughout the range of travel.

3) The steering wheel must be far enough from both the dash and the shift lever so that your hand cannot contact either. The same is true of the cockpit surround.

With pure racing cars the steering is so quick that one full turn is all that is required from lock to lock and there is virtually never a reason to change the position of your hands on the wheel. With racing sedans and some of their derivatives needing two to three turns from lock to lock, this is not true. Particularly in slow corners, it is a good idea to "pre-position" your hands so that, in the corner, you will have adequate steering lock available without removing your hands from the wheel.

In other words, your hands should be at an approximate "ten to two" position while the car is cornering. This means either moving your hands to the anticipated position in the corner before turning in or sliding the wheel through one hand during turn in, gripping it in the proper position with the other hand when the lock is on and then moving the original hand to its proper position on the wheel. The technique is

MAKING A SEAT

The process of making a custom seat from two part foam is disarmingly simple - which means, of course, that it is easily screwed up. The first step is to purchase the two part foam - either from a large plastics house or a boat shop. You want the two pound per cubic foot density. While you are there buy some one quart unwaxed paper mixing cups - they are really good for fiberglass, too. To do the mixing, bend a coat hanger or a piece of 1/8" welding rod into a paddle frame and chuck it into a drill motor.

Buy a box of full size super heavy duty garbage bags. Before even thinking about foaming the seat, protect the tub with taped in place bags. If you do everything right there will be no spillage - but if any foam escapes it is a real bitch to clean off and garbage bags are cheap.

Assuming that he can see out of the car, the driver should always sit with his butt on the floor. Driver weight is a significant portion of total vehicle weight and the easiest way to lower the center of gravity is to lower the driver. Besides, he will get significantly better feel with his butt on the floor. If he cannot sit on the floor (as in sedan), then the seat shell must be really rigidly attached to major structure - both for driver feel and for safety.

The first real step is to prop the driver (in his driving shoes) into a close approximation of your best guess at final position, stuff pillows and foam in place to keep him there and adjust the pedals. Attempts to create a custom seat with the driver out of position are doomed to failure from the beginning.

Make the seat back (pelvis/torso) first. With the driver in a driving suit (preferably old and sacrificeable), tape the closed end of a super heavy duty garbage bag just forward of where his butt will be. Position the driver on top of the bag, smooth out the wrinkles as best you can, mix up a suitable batch of part A & B foam (remembering that it will expand to eight times its mixed volume), lift the driver and pour the mixture into the open mouth of the bag.

When it starts to expand, the driver sits back down and positions himself properly. He should press against the left foot rest and thrust his pelvis back into the seating area with his back slightly arched and his torso at his preferred angle - and hold that position until the foam sets up. The seat should extend forward to partially encapsule the rib cage area for lateral support - the driver has to insert himself sideways into a proper seat. The seat back should extend above the shoulders.

When the foam has set, the garbage bag is peeled off and modifications are made with knives, sanding blocks and shur-form files. The finished seat is then covered with a fabric material - stretchable Nomex is best but any wool or cotton is okay. (Spray glue works fine.)

When the pelvis/torso part of the seat is done, the same procedure is followed for the thigh support. The thighs should be supported in separate channels (with a ridge between them) almost up to the knee joint. The forward edge of these channels must have a generous radius to prevent restriction to blood circulation. The knees should be very close together (this forces proper foot work on the pedals).

The same procedure is followed to custom fit a fiberglass or aluminum seat shell.

HEAD RESTRAINTS

A major, and completely unaddressed, driver safety problem is neck extension on impact. Review the video of Paul Tracy's big accident at the Indianapolis Motor Speedway on May 3, 1994. Watch his head hit the steering wheel, twice, and then think.

If the safety harness is properly designed, installed and tightened, the driver's torso is effectively constrained by it. The shoulder straps will stretch slightly in a massive impact, but not more than a few inches. The drivers neck and head, on the other hand, are not restrained at all - and the head is necessarily encased in a relatively heavy helmet. The human neck is very flexible - it has to be.

Paul's accident (which did not result in serious injury) proves several things:

1) *Shoulder straps must be properly positioned and as tight as the crew can make them - there is no way that the driver can properly tighten them. Attachment points either too high or too low will result in preventable torso movement.*

2) *The human neck stretches like a slinky when subjected to heavy impact.*

3) *Paul is in really good shape.*

4) *The steering wheel is not a proper head stop. We must develop some form of effective head restraint - both lateral and longitudinal.*

The path, if not the answer, has been staring us in the face for some years now. Jim Downing and his brother-in-law have investigated the problem intelligently and their HANS (Head And Neck Support) device offers an effective if not ideal solution. In its current form it is a bit bulky and it may or may not restrict swivelling too much - but it will damned well keep the driver's head where it belongs in any survivable accident.

I am certain that, if funds were made available, Jim's device could be very quickly optimized (the FIA, FOCA and CART have the funds and access to the engineering expertise). I was greatly encouraged to read that after the Imola accidents both Williams and McLaren contacted Jim about his device. I was further encouraged to read that Kyle Petty is wearing one. I am discouraged that the FIA, FOCA, CART and even NASCAR have not mandated it.

easily learned by practicing on a street car. If you have to turn the wheel several revolutions (as in show room stock car in a hairpin) you will have to do the old hand over hand procedure - but make sure that your hands are properly positioned once you are in the corner.

INSTRUMENTS

No driver looks at his instruments very often - nor should he. I believe in warning lights - bright warning lights. I also believe in a shift light - or shift light sequence. I will point out, however, that even if you have warning lights and a shift light, it is still a good idea to make sure that you can see and read your instruments (and operate all of the switches, anti roll bar and brake bias adjusters) from the driving position.

I realize that all of this sounds obvious and simplistic. Maybe it is - but none of it costs any money and all of it will contribute significantly to your success.

PEDAL POSITION

Just as the arms should remain bent at the elbow while steering, so the legs should be bent at the knee in the driving position. I have always thought that correct pedal positions should be pretty obvious. Not so! I am continually amazed at the number of experienced drivers who do not understand the importance of correct pedal position.

To begin with, the brake pedal, under normal racing foot pressure, should be inclined slightly rearward at the top. If it is vertical, or over vertical, then increased pedal pressure will result in decreased mechanical advantage - making modulation almost impossible. To allow efficient and natural "heel and toe" downshifts, the throttle pedal should be almost even with or very slightly forward of the brake pedal under normal racing pressure. This is true even for left foot brakers - part way through a race you may be forced to start right foot braking.

THROTTLE CONTROL

We have seen that any time a tire is visibly spinning, the car is not accelerating as hard as it could be. At relatively low road speed and high torque values there are only two ways to control wheelspin - a sensitive and educated right foot or an electronic traction control.

There is little or no throttle control required to drive a Formula Ford 1600 in the dry. There are those who say that with current tires and download, throttle control is not necessary in any car in the dry. If this were true, one wonders why the Formula One brigade spent so much money on electronic traction control.

A particularly graphic example of the need for throttle control was presented at the 1992 Mid Ohio Indy Car race when the two Penskes driven by Mssrs. Fittipaldi and Tracy were fitted with electronic traction control (now, wisely, outlawed by CART). Standing at the top of the hill turn - where every fast car gets some wheelspin as it unloads under full power - Mr. Tracy's car sounded like it had a serious and continuous high speed ignition miss for as much as a full second. Mr. Fittipaldi's car - with a faster trap speed - had the occasional barely audible stutter.

Mr. Fittipaldi was modulating his throttle with his right foot as he had through three World and one CART Championships and God knows how many Formula One and Indy Car wins. Mr. Tracy was merely planting his right foot. Mr. Fittipaldi, as always, was a joy to watch. Mr. Tracy would have been very exciting to watch had he not had the traction control. Penske's traction control functioned by randomly cutting spark, so it gave rise to some pretty serious engine and drive train vibrations: guess who was hurting his car and who was not.

There is a lot to be said for discipline and technique - especially when it is combined with skill and experience.

When we get to race cars that have serious power to weight ratios, the effectiveness of throttle modulation is one of the major differences between the Prosts, Sennas, Schumachers, Unsers and the rest. It is not just a question of wheelspin, it also has a major effect on vehicle balance and is the most effective driver-influenced method of avoiding sudden corner exit oversteer. It is a learned skill and the younger you learn it the better off you will be - and the better you will be in the wet.

In order to effectively modulate the throttle, the engine must have really good throttle response. If it hesitates, stumbles or burbles no one can effectively modulate the throttle. In this case you are probably better off to mash the thing and live with the attendant oversteer and wheelspin. However, there is no reason why you should have to put up with poor throttle response. Notwithstanding the fact that racing carburetors were designed with about 1 lateral g in mind, your engine builder/tuner should be able to give you excellent throttle response with any system.

Some engine builders simply do not realize the importance of throttle response. (It doesn't show up on the dyno.) Insist on it. If your man cannot or will not give it to you, either hire someone else or learn to do it yourself. Needless to say any car utilizing electronic engine management should have near perfect throttle response. If it does not, have it fixed.

CHEATING

At some point in every racer's life he has to make his peace with cheating. I do not approve of cheating - at all. Of course, like every other successful racer, I differentiate between taking advantage of loopholes in the regulations, stretching the grey areas and outright cheating. In any given racing series, I will not start the cheating. If someone else starts it, I will appeal to them and to the officials to stop it. If my efforts do not succeed, then I'll show them how it is done - and I learned from the best. If I ever retire I'll write 'Cheat to Win' and get rich.

There are racing series (mainly sedans and "spec" series) where stretching the rules is the accepted norm - it becomes a game between the tech inspectors and the crew chiefs. Everyone expects it and there is no disgrace to getting caught. NASCAR comes immediately to mind - although the appointment of Gary Nelson as Chief of Tech seems to have gone a long way towards stopping that contra productive little game. Australia did the same thing some years ago when they named Harry Firth Chief Tech Inspector after he had run General Motors' race team for decades. Now IMSA has found Don Schneiders. Clever moves, those. It's called "To Catch a Thief..."

Anyway, it is my firm conviction that cheating in any form is bad for racing and that it is the responsibility of both the competitors and the officials to make sure that it does not happen. CART does an excellent job. SCCA does a truly miserable job. CART and NASCAR enforce the published rules with qualified people and back the people up. The SCCA typically, at least in so called "Pro Racing", does none of the above. IMSA's rules and the enforcement seemed whimsical at best until Schneiders changed all that. Good job, Don.

There is simply no way on God's green earth that any sanctioning body can hire someone qualified to outsmart, as a group, the smartest and most experienced engineers and crew chiefs in the business. Therefore, racing regulations should be written by the competitors, preferably the designers and builders. An entrants group should define the purpose of the rules and the chassis designers should then write the chassis, aero and safety rules. The engine builders should write the engine rules.

Without a fully qualified and equipped tech inspection group, with autonomy, restrictive rules or a "spec" series - even "spec engines" - are an open invitation to cheat. Even with such a tech group, restrictive rules, designed by well meaning but unqualified people to decrease the cost of racing, invariably increase it. It is therefore incumbent upon racers to keep each other honest - this can only happen if the sanctioning body is willing to take immediate, firm and impartial action when it is required.

Continued...

Anyway, there are certain minor items that I do not consider to be cheating - and which I would never give any thought at all to not doing. These include using ballast where it is not allowed, adding a little fuel capacity for safety's sake, building in a fully structural cage and subtly altering the geometry of a production based car. It is all a question of degree and, within limits, the racer does what he has to do. The old saying, "You are cheating. I know you are cheating because I'm cheating and you're beating me," is pretty true in showroom stock and its derivatives.

I seldom tell the driver what is going on in the rule bending business - in fact, I tell as few people as possible. The driver has no need to know and, should the stretch be detected, he should not be held culpable - the crew chief and the entrant should. Unfortunately, that's not the way it works. The driver is necessarily held responsible for rule infractions in the preparation of his car. Keep this in mind when temptation comes your way.

FLY BY WIRE

There is a tendency in Formula One to do away with the mechanical connection between the throttle pedal and the throttle. I think this is a really bad idea. Electronics should always have benign failure modes. If something goes wrong inside the management unit, so long as the driver can shut the throttle, the result is unlikely to be a disaster to anything but the engine.

We have seen some pretty spectacular happenings when something went awry in the active ride systems. These incidents pale to insignificance when compared to the results of an electronic malfunction jamming the throttle open. If the combined resources of the entire aerospace industry and the U.S. Air Force cannot keep the B-2 from occasionally burrowing into a cliff while under terrain following radar control (or the Airbus from falling out of the sky when the fly by wire computer disagrees with the pilot), I don't want to know about electronic throttle control in my race car.

THE REV LIMITER

The electronic rev limiter is a marvellous device. It saves engines by preventing on-throttle over-revs. As I have pointed out previously, it does not save the early downshift over-rev.

The rev limiter is not a shift indicator. Regardless of the type of limiter, hitting it slows the car. In the case of the "hard" limiter, hitting it slows the car a lot - sometimes you lose 500rpm before the engine returns to full song. So place the tach where you can see it - and analog tachs are a lot better shift indicators than digital ones.

If you are having trouble in this department, have a shift light (or lights) installed. Personally I like the yellow-yellow-yellow-red lights used by Williams.

COCKPIT ADJUSTERS

Time is the racer's most precious commodity. We never have enough of it. Anything that wastes time or even needlessly consumes time is contra-productive and expensive. This is particularly true of practice or testing time. Stopping the car to make minor adjustments is time consuming. Allowing the driver to make minor adjustments, without stopping, is very productive - especially if he remembers what he did and what effect it had. (This is what radios are for.)

So, if the driver is intelligent, it is a serious advantage to have as many cockpit adjustable features as practical. Brake bias is a must. Rear anti-roll bar (if one is fitted) is damned near a must. If the driver is both sensitive and rational I feel that he should also have control of the front anti-roll bar (but only if the wiggly ends of the blades are linked together a la Swift - FIGURE 36) - and shock absorber bump (low piston speed)

FIGURE 36

would be real nice. If the driver is not intelligent or if he is an inveterate tinkerer, cockpit adjustments will only lead to increased confusion.

Except for the brake bias, the driver adjustable features are as much analysis tools as they are fix it tools. There are two purposes to the idea:

1) To give the driver a way to adjust the handling and response of the car within narrow limits - sort of like the trim tabs on an airplane.

2) To assist in the analysis of the behavior of the car by observing the effect of small adjustments to the total roll stiffness and/or roll couple distribution. We can do this either to define the cause of a fault or to determine a way to go. For instance, if the car is faster with both anti-roll bars in the full stiff position, we would think seriously about going to either the next larger bars or stiffer springs - and so it goes.

For the race itself, the objective is to start with a balanced car and with the adjustable elements in their middle positions - allowing the driver to adjust in either direction (oversteer or understeer), as the race progresses and the car, the tires and/or the race track deteriorates. Inevitably at least one of them will. Except on Sprint Cars, it is illegal to utilize cockpit adjustment of wings. As I read the rules, this is illegal only during the actual race and official qualifying. The next time I run a team, the front wing angle of attack will be cockpit adjustable for testing.

Quick answers are what we are looking for. McLaren's Indy Cars at one time utilized hydraulically controlled cockpit adjustable wedge. They used motorcycle master cylinders and hydraulic spring perches. Clever!

If I were running an oval track car, and if it were legal, my driver would be able to jack a little bit of corner weight around - and to quickly and positively return to datum. For testing, it might be worth thinking about driver controllable rake. If the front and rear motion ratios are the same (as they always should be and seldom are) driver controlled tilt is a possibility.

REACTION TO THE INEVITABLE

I am writing this immediately after the period in which Formula One lost Ratzenberger and Senna and damned near lost Wendlinger. In the same black half year NASCAR'S Winston Cup, the safest major series on earth, lost Neil Bonnet and Rodney Orr and damned near lost Ernie Ervan.

It is interesting to compare the reactions of the participants, journalists and fans of the two series. Senna's death resulted in worldwide hysteria and knee jerk reactions from the Italian government, the CSAI, the FIA and the worldwide popular press. The only reported voices of reason were from Michael Schumacher ("We must learn from this,") Niki Lauda, and, perhaps surprisingly, FIA President Max Mosley - who took immediate, controversial and effective action to improve circuit and vehicle safety.

Mr. Mosley stated that, if he held to the Concorde agreement, nothing would ever happen, that he was being paid to govern and that he was damned well going to do so. His initial edicts were not exactly universally acclaimed by the engineers involved so he listened to them and modified the rules in the light of their recommendations. Bravo Max!

In NASCAR the losses were mourned, but everyone, including the press, realized that the possibility of death is always present in motor racing, that no one is more aware of this fact than the drivers and that, to the drivers, the rewards outweigh the risks. Period. End of story.

As an ex-driver, a long time racer and the father of a current driver, I agree with the NASCAR attitude. But I also feel, very strongly, that not enough attention is being paid to either circuit safety or driver protection in most racing series - worldwide. So here I go climbing on my soapbox again. Bear with me.

DRIVER PROTECTION

Not very long ago, the most common injury to open wheel and sports car drivers was extreme trauma to the lower extremities caused by the collapse (or removal) of the forward portion of the chassis on frontal impact. CART has done a very good job of addressing that problem with its "safety capsule" chassis specifications and testing requirements - although they have yet to insist on moving the driver's feet behind the front wheel center.

FOCA and the FIA lag behind in a few areas but are catching up. I feel honor bound to point out that TV commentators' statements to the effect that the FIA mandated increased legroom around the "knee" bulkhead allows the driver to pull his feet back before he hits is nothing less than uninformed and non-thinking idiocy. Give a thought to trying to hold your legs and feet back in any frontal impact of more than 3 g. It simply cannot be done.

For that matter, even though the forces involved in a roll over are a lot less than those generated in frontal impacts and your arms and hands weigh a lot less than your legs and feet, you cannot hold your arms and hands in place during a roll over and arm restraints should therefore be mandatory in all racing - not just Sprint Cars and Midgets.

The current major cause of serious injury is the intrusion of hard objects into the cockpit - objects such as wheels, control arms and wings. Partial solutions are pretty obvious - raise and strengthen the structural cockpit sides, as CART has done and the FIA is doing. The (to me) obvious next step is a properly designed and executed full cage - who cares what it looks like - besides, no one complains about the aesthetics of Midgets and Sprint Cars any more. When the front wheel hits the wall, all too often the control arms tear loose from their mounting points and become spears. The usual damage is to the feet and legs but when all of the stars line up wrong, the damage is fatal - as in the case of Senna. There is very little excuse for this . The solution is largely a matter of thinking about the possibilities and being willing to sacrifice a (very) few pounds of sprung mass in the name of driver safety.

In most designs the forward mounting points of the front control arms are outside the driver's safety capsule and, assuming that the front bulkhead is of adequate strength, the forward legs should not present a significant danger. The problem centers around the mounting of the rearward legs of the front control arms - typically on the "knee" bulkhead.

The solution(s) do not require structural genius - just forethought. With the raised noses of current Formula One cars, the mounting points for the front lower control arms are typically outside the cockpit and the provision of sufficient anti-intrusion armor is pretty simple.

David Bruns, one of the brightest of designers, takes a different approach to upper arms. David pinches the inboard end of his upper control arms to form a natural "kink point" at the least loaded portion of this least loaded control arm. On impact the arm folds rather than penetrating. Of course this allows the wheel, tire, upright and brake assembly to move rearward and upward rather smartly, but a realistic cage would go a long way towards solving that problem.

Along these lines, it has been pretty well proven in CART that carbon skinned aluminum honeycomb tubs do not do an adequate job of preventing wheel intrusion - witness Brian Herta's accident at Toronto. The inclusion of a sheet aluminum stiffener would help a lot. This and the commonality of engine mounting dimensions are the only good ideas I saw in the Tony George/IRL/USAC initial proposed chassis regulations.

Continued...

REACTION TO THE INEVITABLE, cont.

However it is done, containment of the spears and cannonballs is a feasible exercise in design and fabrication that needs to be addressed right now. It should not require complete redesigns of existing structure - add ons should be effective, if slightly heavy. A proper cage and effective anti-intrusion provisions would keep the hard bits where they belong - outside. Proper head, neck and arm restraints would keep the soft bits where they belong - inside.

I reckon it is a very good thing that the Formula One Drivers' Association has been reformed. I hope that, under the leadership of Lauda and Berger, they will insist on being heard and listened to. However, drivers tend to be pretty non-technical and they also tend to be pretty blase about safety. Remember how long it took to get them to wear a helmet - or to use a safety harness. Or count the percentage who, even today, don't wear Nomex underwear or select their helmets on the basis of who offers them the most money.

The effective input should come from the engineers who design the cars. I suggest that if the sanctioning bodies were to lock the heads of each of the design teams (including engines and tires) in a meeting room equipped with lots of paper, a single rest room and a water cooler and inform them that they were living on McDonalds until they had all signed the regulations that they were about to write, we would end up very quickly with some simple, effective, equitable and safe regulations. Of course, at some point we, like the flying contingent, have to accept the fact that some accidents are simply not survivable.

CIRCUIT SAFETY

First we either removed the trees or separated them from the race track with Armco barrier. Then we replaced the Armco with concrete. Then we made gravel pits - although not enough of them. All of these were major steps forward. But somewhere along the line some of us seem to have lost track of how the system is supposed to work.

It may seem painfully obvious that there should never be a concrete wall at right angles to any conceivable racing car trajectory. Yet the FIA circuit safety committee and Senna himself approved the Tamburello corner where he died. It seems painfully obvious that a patch of concrete prior to a wall will not slow a car in the same way as a gravel trap - yet what the television audience thought was a gravel trap that Senna sped across on his way to the wall was indeed concrete.

It seems painfully obvious that, in order to be effective, a gravel trap must be both ridged and long enough to do its job - yet at North America's "best" facility, Mid-Ohio, the Keyhole and Turn Five traps are too short to be effective.

The areas which require gravel traps would seem to be painfully obvious. Yet A.J. Foyt had to suffer crushed feet before an effective gravel trap was erected at Road America's Turn One. The list could go on. And on.

HOW TO SLOW THEM DOWN

I do not agree with the popular opinion that the cars have become too fast for the drivers. Racing cars are not meant to be easy to drive at the limit of tire adhesion and the difference between the good drivers and the great drivers is and always will be the ability to balance the car at the absolute limit of tire adhesion.

I do, however, agree that the cars have become too fast for the circuits and that we have to slow them down. There are some fundamental faults in the current proposals to regulating a reduction in speed - particularly the proposal to increase the weight of the current cars.

While increasing the minimum weight of new designs will allow the use of stronger structure without a performance penalty, increasing the mass of existing cars simply means that they will hit harder. How you keep the designers from using ballast in the most advantageous locations instead of using the added weight for its intended purpose, I do not know.

The engineers who design the cars, engines and tires are a lot smarter and more experienced than the people who write (and enforce) the regulations. Every time that the sanctioning bodies come up with regulations to slow the cars down the engineers immediately design the new restrictions into obsolescence. So far as the chassis and aero end of things goes, my locked room proposal was perfectly serious. So far as the engine regulations go, Keith Duckworth, the best of them all, had the solution a decade and a half ago. "Make each engine use a fuel flow valve which limits the pounds per hour of fuel into the engine to a specific maximum and make the engine designers design around that." For sure we would wind up with some very fuel efficient engines - and it would take nothing away from the show.

PIT STOPS

To me, the biggest mystery of modern times is why we haven't had a Formula One pit disaster of epic proportions. Who in hell cares whether it takes six seconds or 16 seconds to change tires. At least they figured out (after Imola) that entry and exit chicanes and an enforced speed limit are absolute necessities and that no one should be allowed in the pit lane itself until the car is about to stop. The NASCAR rule of no one over the wall until the car does stop would be better yet. The thought of a pressurized gasoline fire in a pit lane that looks like an ant hill is beyond my imagination - as is the mentality that accepts the possibility (Hockenheim was just a minor preview).

16

"First rate people associate with and hire first rate people. Second rate people associate with and hire third rate people." – Roy Kiesling

DON'T BURN THE HANDS THAT SUPPORT YOU

Every time you manage to climb one more level of the stepped pyramid that is motor racing's mountain, you will be faced with two problems - climbing the next step and not slipping back down. This will be true even if you should achieve what you now envisage as the ultimate step and end up where Michael Schumacher, Al Unser Jr. and Jeff Gordon are as I write. (Someone eventually must, it may as well be you.)

It may seem the ultimate position to you but Schumacher, Unser and Gordon know that there is more to come - there always is. And there are more people trying to knock them out of their seats than there are people trying to do the same to Saddam Hussein.

No one gets beyond the first couple of steps on their own. You climb the pyramid with the help and support of your crews, your sponsors and your friends. The higher you get, the more financial and technical support you need. It is also true that the higher you climb the more you must offer in return for support. It never gets easy. It will therefore pay you to cultivate long term relationships within the business - if for no other reason than to avoid a reputation as a one way SOB with a very short memory.

The first relationship we are going to discuss is that between you, the driver, and them, the hard working, dedicated and ever cheerful support staff - your crew. Regardless of their number, pay scale or level of experience and/or expertise, there are several factors to be considered.

1) The ratio of man hours spent working on the racing car to man hours spent driving it is literally hundreds to one. Regardless of your personal levels of skill, daring, determination and experience, your racing results will be directly proportional to the skill and dedication of your crew.

2) It is quite common for "the crew" to think of the driver as a spoiled, over privileged, over sexed, underbrained and undermannered brat - regardless of

age. In the lower classes of racing, at least, it is often difficult to disagree. In professional racing, for the most part, I like to think that this perception is largely mistaken.

Part of the attitude has to do with the crew's perception of relative positions on just about any scale you can think of. Part of it has to do with the crew's misunderstanding of just what it is that the professional racing driver does and just how hard it is to do it properly. And part of it has to do with a lack of appreciation of what it took for the driver to get where he is and the prices that he pays to stay there.

3) From the very beginnings of the sport, one of the features common to the relationships between the really successful racing drivers and their crews is that the crews of the star drivers have always been willing to walk on burning coals to get "their driver" another tenth of a second. This has been true even when the crew has been perfectly aware of the foibles and personal shortcomings of the driver (and aware they will be - no man is a hero to his butler or to his mechanic). For confirmation read Alf Francis' and Ermano Cuoghi's books and consider the nature of the relationships between the authors (two of the most successful racing mechanics in history) and their drivers, respectively Stirling Moss and Niki Lauda.

4) The only person who can create this working relationship is the driver. The car/team owner cannot do it. Neither the team manager nor the engineer can do it. In fact, just as the mechanics, these individuals will be victims of the successful driver's seduction.

THE "EASY TO WORK WITH" MYTH

The development of the required relationship has little to do with the driver being "easy to work with". Successful racing drivers are very demanding people. They have to be. None of them have ever been "easy" to work with - challenging to work with, rewarding to work with and even fun to work with, certainly. But easy, never. Some, in fact, have been just plain difficult - Foyt, Matich, Surtees, and G. Hill come to mind. It doesn't matter how difficult or demanding the driver is, so long as he is:

1) At least equally demanding of himself.

2) Willing to drive all of the race car that the crew can give him - every time.

3) Properly appreciative of the crew's efforts - in public and in private. This also means strict conformance to the old military rule of; "Praise in public, censure in private".

4) Unfailingly honest in his private and public evaluation of his performance - i.e. never blaming the car or crew for lack of success.

ATTITUDE (again)

One thing is certain, unless your crew is convinced that you want to win the motor race more than you want anything else on earth on that particular day, your chances of winning it are slim. It is not enough that you know that - they have to know it as well. I am not advocating a juvenile "rah rah", "pep talk" sort of attitude here. I am talking about walking tall and exuding confidence. It also helps to smile, be cheerful and act as if you truly enjoy driving racing cars. This sort of attitude is catching.

I am not advocating that the driver spend every working hour with the crew - even on race weekends. Far from it. The driver who is always underfoot is very liable to become more of a nuisance than an inspiration. Peter Revson used to say that the driver should show up in the workshop once in a while because the crew needs occasional comic relief. What we need here is quality time with the crew.

You actually have two objectives in nurturing this relationship - improving your performance in the car you are driving now and establishing a reputation within the industry of being a driver who is "good to work with". Every driver who has been around for even a little while has developed a reputation of some sort among the crews. A good one can further your career. A bad one will hurt you. In fact this intra mural reputation will do your career at least as much good as a media generated reputation.

RULES OF CONDUCT

This is not a "How to Make Friends and Influence People" book. I will, however, point out a few of the basic rules of conduct:

1) Always be dressed and ready in time to be first in line to practice or qualify.

2) Be on time for driver's meetings, etc. Don't make the officials go to the crew and have somebody chase you. Be on time and ready for testing. Early is better.

3) At the track, the crew should always know where you have gone and when you are coming back.

4) Do not use crew transport (four wheelers, three wheelers, motor scooters, rent cars, etc.) to move your butt around the paddock. Buy a scooter or a bicycle - or walk.

5) Dress properly - i.e. neatly.

6) Speak properly - with a minimum of profanity. Bad mouth no one.

7) Never leave any sort of a mess in the transporter - this most especially pertains to driving gear.

8) Introduce your lady friend(s), family, friends, sponsor(s), and prospective sponsor(s) to the crew - individually and by name. And then make damned sure that they stay out of the way. Make especially certain that they never park themselves in the door of the transporter.

9) When you want the car changed, especially if it might look like a niggling change, explain why. Explain it to the crew chief, not to the poor devil who is going to have to actually do the work. That is the crew chief's prerogative.

10) Along that line, always respect the chain of command within the team. You make your requests to the engineer or to the chief, not to the helper(s).

11) Do nice things for the crew:

a) When possible drive them around the race track in a rent car and tell them a bit about the place and the race car.

b) Hand out photos of their car and their driver (you) with them (individually if at all possible).

c) Always say good morning. By name, individually. The same goes for thank you and good night. "Is there anything I can do/get for you before I leave?", is a nice line.

d) An occasional dinner for the lads is called for. So are gifts at the end of a successful season - (or even, to a lesser extent, an unsuccessful one).

Derek Warwick, although he never won a Grand Prix, was gainfully employed for ten years or so in Formula One - with respectable teams. He said; "show up early and stay around after to encourage mechanics and be present with the sponsors - do the whole job!"

LEADERSHIP

The development of the successful relationship here has a lot to do with leadership and with charisma. It has been said that leaders are born, not made. This is wrong. Find and read the book entitled "Naval Leadership". Leadership has to do with honesty, precept and example. It can be learned. Charisma, on the other hand, if it cannot be learned, can at least be enhanced. If all this sounds pretty cold blooded, it is meant to. This is a cold blooded business.

LONG TERM RELATIONSHIPS
- AND ONE NIGHT STANDS

In the "old days" (when, according to the current generation of racing drivers, everything was different - and better - than now) it was not uncommon for the star drivers to have a personal mechanic (now called race engineer) who went with them from team to team.

Through the years there have been many instances of magic driver/engineer combinations: Fangio/Sivoggi, Moss/Francis, Clark/Chapman, Brabham the elder/Tauranac/Billingsly, Piquet/Murray, Lauda/Cuogi, Andretti the elder, first with Brawner, then Magee, then two Chapmans and then Cicale (remarkable that, but so is Andretti the elder), Foyt/Bignotti, Petty/Inman, Steve Kinser/Karl Kinser. Those are just a few.

Not a bad idea. Good working relationships are too hard to establish and nurture to give up just because of a change of employment. Substitute the job title Race Track Engineer for Mechanic and it should work very well today. Mssrs. Rahal and Prescott come to mind.

What I am saying here is that, all other things being equal, the driver with the most inspired crew will win. There is only one source of inspiration for the crew. You had better learn how to do it. Because you will frequently be working with different crews for short periods, you had also better learn how to establish that relationship very quickly.

War story time.

WAR STORY

Many years ago I was contracted on a one shot basis to run James Hunt as a teammate to Gilles Villeneuve in Atlantic cars at Trois Rivieres. In those days visiting Formula One drivers were a regular feature at Trois Rivieres. I was there because the team felt that Hunt would be a very difficult driver to work with and did not wish to dilute Gilles' effort by spreading responsibilities too thin.

I took the job because I wanted to go to Trois Rivieres, because I could use the money and because I figured that Tyler Alexander had almost certainly taken off whatever rough edges Mr. Hunt might have had - and because after the flock of drivers I had worked with, there was no way that James Hunt could be a serious problem.

There was to be one day of testing at Ste Jovite. When we were introduced, Mr. Hunt stated that he saw two alternative ways in which we could approach the task. We could fool around trying to suit the car to his driving style, or we could set the car up just like Gilles' and he would learn to drive it. He suggested that as he had not driven a similar car in several years and that Gilles had won all the races that year, the second plan of action might well be the wisest. I found nothing to object to in this line of reasoning and we proceeded.

Testing and practice went very well indeed and an epic battle was shaping up between Gilles and James. The field was split into odd and even numbers for qualifying. Gilles' session was dry. James' was damp. Each was quickest in his session but James was sixth or seventh overall.

Being staunch Villeneuve supporters (and no fools) the Quebecois officials gridded the cars in absolute order of qualifying times. Mr. Hunt said; "Right, we're not going to win this one. By the time I get past the cars ahead of me Gilles will be gone. We will, however, finish second.

"I'll get by everyone except Brambilla pretty quickly. He'll hold me up as he always does. I'll do what I can to get by until about five or six laps from the finish and then, if I have to, I'll boot him off. Have a nose ready in case I need it."

And that is exactly what happened. As luck would have it, he didn't need the nose.

During the entire exercise James conducted himself as a complete professional. He explained what the car was doing and what he thought might improve it - and deferred to legitimate experience when we disagreed (seldom). He unfailingly called each crew member by name. He came by the garage each night to see how things were going and lend encouragement.

James left immediately after the race to go to Japan and win the World Championship but his brother came by with an autographed color 8"x10" print of James, the car and each individual crew member. I was (and remain) impressed. He even found out that Saturday was our son, Christopher's, birthday. He brought a piece of cake by the garage for him and gave him excellent advice. "Don't ever let them call you Chris", he said, "If I were Jim Hunt, you would never have heard of me."

As I write this, Christopher has just won the Atlantic race at Trois Rivieres. Gilles' son Jacques finished third and was on the podium with Christopher. Despite his best efforts, the press calls Christopher, "Chris". Pity!

End of war story.

RESPECT AND FRIENDSHIP

I should point out that what we are talking about in this relationship bit is respect and that this respect does not necessarily include friendship. Friendship, in this case, is the frosting on the cake - nice, but not necessary. One of the most successful driver/engineer relationships of my career was with a driver that I neither liked nor respected as a human being. The feeling was mutual.

Each of us had entered into a one year agreement before the personal incompatibility and the personality faults that caused it were apparent to either of us - or the agreement would not have been made. I respected his skills and talents as a driver. He respected mine as an engineer and manager. This mutual respect and our individual desire to win united us into a formidable team. We won 23 of 25 races in a very tough series.

My sanity was saved by my relationships with my family (of whom I saw damned little), the second driver, the members of the best racing team I have ever put together and the factory liaison men and engineers who supported the effort - all of whom are still friends after fifteen years. The driver's sanity may not have been salvageable to begin with.

RESPONSIBILITIES AND BAD APPLES

So far, I have been talking about the driver's relationship with the crew as if it were a one way street with all of the responsibility for the relationship resting on the driver. This is not the case - the driver simply has more to gain or lose from the establishment of a good relationship and so it is up to him to protect his interests.

At the same time, when a personality clash erupts, or when the driver loses faith in one of the support staff (or vice versa) it is time for the staff member to go away. We are not talking about a marriage here. There is no reason - and no time - to try to save the relationship. The old saying about one rotten apple in the barrel applies. Be real firm - have the man replaced and carry on. I do not allow any member of my crews to bad mouth our drivers - even in private.

SENDING THE CREW TO SCHOOL

What I am about to say in ending this section is going to make me very popular with my friends Mssrs. Barber, Bessmer, Bondurant and Coutre. It might even plant an idea in one of their fertile minds - in which case I want a royalty. It is even going to make me popular with the better racing mechanics, engineers and team managers of the world. This is good. At the same time it is going to make my name even more unpopular than it is now with the lower ranks (speaking of both attitude and ability) of these same people. I don't mind.

What I have to say is that every person who fills a position on a racing team other than that of unthinking parts changer should go through a real race driving school (not an SCCA exercise in ego and ignorance). Further, the better driving schools might think about tailoring a course specifically for the racing mechanic/engineer/manager.

Whether we are talking about Formula One or SCCA Improved Touring, the first basic problem in "setting the race car up" for any given circuit is one of communication between driver and crew. The other basic problems, human ignorance and bloody mindedness, come after communication is established.

One of the more popular scenarios in this theatre features the driver trying to explain to an experienced and capable chief mechanic that the car, which was lovely testing (or racing) at track "A" is now an undriveable pig at track "B". The chief, who has never driven a racing car and has no real idea "what it's like out there" gets all confused and defensive.

The reason often is that the tracks involved have completely different characteristics - one, for example might feature mainly long, fast "sweeping" corners while the other might be a "stop and go" street course. Nothing in the chief's background or experience has prepared him to realize that a racing car - any racing car - will behave differently in very slow corners than it will in fast corners and that the "setup", which is at best a compromise, must be changed to suit the nature of the critical corners on the individual race track.

Another version has to do with pedal positions. The mechanic - who has never missed a downshift going into a fast corner because he couldn't blip the throttle - is very liable to consider "endless messing about with the silly pedals" contra-productive at best. The same holds true of shift linkage, dead pedals, throttle springs, etc. The list goes on and on with new items added daily.

I submit that a good school course is the fastest and most cost effective way to bridge this all-too-common communications gap - especially if it were explained to the race driver instructors what the purpose of attendance really was. If the instructor(s) are not experienced and successful racing drivers, pick another school.

THE CARE AND FEEDING OF THE RACING SPONSOR

One of the very first things that the aspiring racing driver must learn is that he will have to operate on other people's money. It doesn't matter if your name is Rockefeller, no one has enough personal wealth to support an Indy Car, GTP, Winston Cup or Formula One habit. If you are not aiming for a seat in one of the above, why in hell are you reading this book?

I have already pointed out that you are going to have to find sponsorship - probably very early in your career. That's the good news. The bad news is that, once you find it, you will have to fight to keep it - everybody in the world will be trying to take it away from you.

I recently had lunch with an executive who has been responsible in the past for some pretty meaningful corporate sponsorship of motor racing. The talk, as it will, turned to drivers. I was astonished to hear him state that the driver who had done the best job for him was Jan Lammers.

The selection of Lammers as his favorite didn't particularly surprise me - the little man is a fine racing driver. The reasons, however, did. He liked Lammers because Jan always wore the corporate clothing, mixed well with the clients and was invariably where he was supposed to be when he was supposed to be there. Again, I wasn't surprised that Lammers did all these things - I was astonished that every driver at that level didn't. After some investigation, I still am.

I also recently spent time with a team sponsored for a single event by a large cigarette company. The team members wore the team gear - always. The drivers did - most of the time. Those of the team members who smoked, and both drivers, smoked opposing brands of cigarettes - in public. Dumb! If you don't like the sponsor's product, at least look like you have some loyalty. You can always put your own cigarettes in the sponsor's package.

Every sponsor expects a return on his (or her) investment. There are many types of returns. You had damned well better ensure that your sponsor(s) are getting every type of return that they want - and that the whole world knows it. Racing results are the most obvious return - but they may not be the most important.

Even a superficial comparison of the results of any professional racing series and the list of long term sponsors will reveal that many drivers and/or teams who have not managed a significant result in years manage to obtain and retain big time corporate sponsorship. On the other hand, we can all make a long list of supremely talented winning young drivers whose careers came to a halt due to lack of support. We can also list drivers with little or no discernible talent or results who have managed long and lucrative careers through long term sponsorship.

There is a lesson to be learned here. I learned it far too late. There are two basic types of sponsors - enthusiasts and business people. While there is such a thing as an enthusiast-type sponsor with no real business interest in racing, there is no such thing as a business-type sponsor who is not also an enthusiast. The potential legitimate payoffs from racing sponsorship, at least in the USA (except for NASCAR), are simply not significant enough for anyone to sponsor a racing driver or team from a pure investment standpoint.

While an advertising/PR campaign focused around a motor racing involvement may be an effective way to spend advertising dollars, you will have hell finding an ad man who will agree. The portion of a corporate advertising budget that goes directly to a racing team is not "billable". No part of that money sticks to the agency. So, typically, the first people in line to take your hard earned sponsorship away from you are not the other drivers/teams (they are, however, definitely in the queue), but the Madison Avenue types who work for your sponsor.

Right behind them will be the corporate accountants. There is an old adage that goes; "Money men are like cats - they may appear domesticated, but they are never tame." Corporate accountants look upon our whole world and everyone in it as frivolous, irresponsible, counter productive and silly. They may, of course, be right - but, for the most part, they are dull.

I digress - again. I'm good at it. So, other than by winning races, how do you keep a sponsor happy? By finding out what they really want and making damned sure that they get it - and by protecting your back at all times. It's that simple - and that difficult!

Step one in keeping the sponsor(s) happy is to make sure that they are not hassled. Attending races is a form of relaxation for sponsors and their friends/associates. It is your responsibility to ensure that they enjoy the experience. Start by making sure that their accommodations, rent cars, event passes, etc. are actually arranged and that there will be no snags. Meet them at the airport and take them to the motel and to registration if you can.

Make equally sure that the car, crew, transporter and equipment are spotless, that sponsor identification is prominent, that the crew knows the important people by name and that they (the sponsors) know what's going on at all times. A bored or disgruntled sponsor is well on his/her way to being an ex-sponsor.

Along these lines, it is crucial to make sure that your sponsors are not hassled by the ever present race track Gestapo. Informing the sanctioning body officials that they will be there, and explaining to those officials the importance of sponsorship (to the sanctioning body, not to the entrant) helps a lot. You have to be careful here because the sanctioning body may well attempt to talk your sponsor into sponsoring their series. Frank and separate discussions with all parties may forestall this unpleasantness.

The Gestapo members that you have to worry about are not race officials but the gate people, bleacher attendants, parking lot people, etc. - the little Hitlers on their day off from the supermarket. Do whatever you have to do to obtain the proper person and car passes (this means buy them - both the sanctioning bodies and the track owners are far too shortsighted to figure out that hospitality to sponsors is in their long term interest). Then explain to your people, in detail, where the passes allow them to go - and where to park.

Give them a map showing the track, the entrance gate, their parking place and your paddock. If you have to give up your own parking pass to get them next to the transporter the walk won't hurt you. Go to dinner with them if you can. If you cannot, make sure that they know where the good restaurants are - and be aware that if you don't go to dinner with them, someone else may.

If there is a spare (and qualified) team person available to shepherd the sponsors when you are busy, great. This can be a girlfriend, wife, parent or friend of virtually any member of the crew - but they must be qualified to do the job with respect both to information and social skills. If such a person is not available, then you will have to do it. Part of this job is making very damned sure that your sponsor is not scammed by your rivals while at the same time avoiding rampant paranoia on your own part - and making sure that your sponsors do not feel isolated. Not a simple task.

Your job for the sponsor does not end when you leave the track. Your job is to both promote his products and to increase his enjoyment of motor racing. His racing involvement is a very real part of his business or his social life - or both. This means bringing your car - and yourself - to his place of business from time to time to meet the troops and press the flesh. It means going to trade shows if his company uses them. It means being available and articulate any time that he wants to show off his racing driver to employees, associates, clients or friends. It means visiting branches or associate firms when you are in their area and entertaining associates at the track. It means writing thank you letters, news letters and sending video tapes. Basically it means paying your way.

When things are going well at the track, explain what is happening and why. When things are going badly, don't make excuses and don't whine. Above all resist the temptation to point out that more money would cure the problem(s). Which leads, more or less gracefully into Smith's Ten Commandments of sponsor relations:

1) Always wear clean sponsor identification at any racing related event - and make sure that your crew does as well. Do not allow any competitive products within sight, sound or smell - ever.

2) Make sure that the track announcer and the TV commentator (if any) mention your sponsor's name(s) every time they mention you or your car. They will seldom do this without being asked. Ask!

3) Make sure that your sponsor gets onto the victory podium every time that you do.

4) Never ask (or hint, which would be worse) for more money than you originally agreed on.

5) Never make excuses for your performance.

6) Pick up your fair share of the bar bills and dinner tabs.

7) Learn all that you can about your sponsor's business and show your interest. Ask if there is any way that you can help.

8) Never miss an opportunity to play golf (or whatever their game may be) with your sponsors.

9) Provide your sponsor(s) with photos, video tapes, newspaper clippings, etc of your successes - or even of your not so successful efforts, so long as the sponsor identification is prominent.

10) Never fool with (or give the appearance of fooling with) the sponsor's women.

THE PRESS

As I write this, motor racing is at the end of one of its cyclical golden ages. This one was brought about by television coverage. It is slowly going down the toilet with cigarette advertising and the Japanese and European economies. It has already outlasted ours.

Racing will survive but things are going to get tougher and rides are going to be even harder to find. In every racing country but ours, (including such industrial giants as Mexico and Finland) the popular press covers racing in depth. Even here, what I fondly refer to as the "lunatic fringe" press has a certain amount of influence on decisions made by racing teams and corporate sponsors.

What all of this means to you is that your image as perceived by the media and your relationships with the representatives of the media will have a profound effect upon your career. Cultivate them. Talk to them. If they don't know that the reason you crashed while leading is that the wishbone broke, they will only report that you crashed while leading. Listen to them. The very best of them understand this business in depth and can give trenchant advice - but only if asked.

Do not, however, be a toady. Do your job. Go out of your way to help them to do theirs. Treat them like human beings. You can trust almost all of the regulars. If you ask them not to print or repeat something, they will not. You cannot, however, trust any of the "visiting" journalists from the non-racing media. Be very careful in answering their questions. It is unlikely that they would deliberately mis-quote you but they are very liable to be apprentice Mike Wallaces in search of sensation.

You can't reasonably ask to proof a newspaper story and there is no way to retract what you might say in a live TV or radio interview - so be careful. It is reasonable to ask to proof a magazine feature article - and you should.

More or less along these lines, (and because it does not fit anywhere else) I will add that if you are ever going to amount to anything in this business, you will have to become a competent public speaker. If you are like most of us, the very thought terrifies you. It need not. Public speaking is, like everything else, a learned skill. Don't try to learn it yourself. Join a branch of Toastmasters or take a night school or Carnegie course.

Otherwise you are going to embarrass yourself the first time you are called upon to speak anywhere but on the podium - and needlessly waste an opportunity. As a point of interest, Marlboro (and some of the Professional football teams) have a series of formal courses that their drivers and players are required to take in order to learn how to effectively interact with the media and the public. Think about it.

OFFICIALS

I sometimes feel about race officials the way I feel about police - I do not understand why anybody would do it, but I am damned glad that somebody does. The sanctioning body's officials have a job to do. It is not an easy job. There is no valid reason for any of us to make their job harder. The officials can make your life easy or they can make it difficult. You want them on your side. If they respect your abilities and your attitude it is even conceivable that they might be able to help your career.

From time to time each of us feels that an official decision - almost always one that affects us directly and personally - is wrong. Ranting, raving and profanely questioning the abilities and/or ancestry of the official(s) in question is guaranteed to cast whatever decision we are debating in stone. A calm and reasoned discussion just might work. Even if it doesn't, the rational and courteous approach will enhance your reputation and might help the next time.

Don't be a doormat. When you feel that the officials are wrong, you should discuss it with them - privately, calmly and reasonably. Before discussing anything having to do with the regulations, read them and be very sure of your ground. When they make a difficult call right, they should be complemented. The further you get in the sport, the more competent the officials become (for one thing, at the top levels they get paid).

At the regional and even the National SCCA level you can run into some real little Hitlers. By the time you get to CART or Winston Cup you will be find some pretty damn impressive people. In between you will find in between officials, often unqualified and inexperienced, but almost always trying hard and sincere enthusiasts. Work with them rather than against them.

THE FANS

The bottom line that allows a fortunate few of us to make a good living at motor racing is written by the fans who pay admission to watch our show and/or purchase the sponsor's products. The millions of dollars that make motor racing possible come in ten bucks at a time - at the gate, at the parts store and at the supermarket. When the fans stop paying, we stop racing.

The admission-paying fan feels that his paddock pass entitles him to an autograph and at least a smile and a friendly word from his favorite driver(s). He is dead right. When you first reach the level where someone actually asks for your autograph, the chances are that you will cheerfully sign them all day and all night - but it gets old quickly.

Like it or not, the fact that the fans are paying your salary (or you hope that someday they will be) makes you beholden to them. It is one more responsibility that you should not duck.

The second side of this coin is that a large part of the reason that any corporation sponsors any aspect of motor racing is the hope that their involvement will convince these same fans to purchase their product. Part of your job is to sell that product. Part of that job is the personal aspect - pressing the flesh.

NASCAR understands this very well (they understand all aspects of racing very well). Richard Petty's career stretched for almost a decade after he stopped being a competitive racing driver. The Outlaws seem to understand it. While SCCA and IMSA would have no idea what I am talking about and CART isn't a lot better, there are individuals within those august bodies who know on which side of the bread to find the butter.

I have seen Mario Andretti still signing autographs in the dusk. Dick Simon runs a fan friendly operation and keeps going year after year with no real race results. Dominic Dobson is a genius. The Archer brothers are really good at it.

War Story, horror department. A couple of years ago a friend of mine, who happened also to be an acquaintance of an "up and coming" Indy Car driver managed to interest a corporation in the possibility of associate sponsorship on the driver's car. The amount of money was both reasonable and needed. An appointment was made to meet with the driver and discuss the arrangements - at a race.

On the appointed day my friend, having purchased tickets and paddock passes for all concerned, presented himself and the prospects at the team motorhome. The prospective sponsors, excited and enthused by their initial exposure, were ready. The driver, in civvies, his day over emerged from the motor home. "Hi" he said, walked on by and disappeared. Embarrassed friend, unimpressed sponsors and no deal. Dumb!

War Story, happy ending department. At the 1993 Toyota Atlantic double header at Laguna Seca, Mark Dismore, in Bill Fickling's Swift, won the Saturday race. A spectator, who also happened to be in marketing, was so impressed that he looked Mark and Bill up after the race and arranged significant sponsorship for the Sunday event.

Yes, there are miracles great and small in this business but they only happen to people who treat other people well. If you sit by the telephone and wait for the miracle, you will grow old. If you are too busy for the fans, the miracle will not happen to you.

THE IMPORTANCE OF A NAME

I have recounted the story of James Hunt telling Christopher to "never let them call you Chris". What he meant is that everything you do must be calculated to make people remember you. This includes your name, your uniform, your helmet color scheme, the way you put your name on the car and your general bearing and demeanor.

Speaking of names on cars, when you put your name on the car, put in on large enough so that it can be read from trackside. You never know who might be watching.

ATTITUDE - LAST TIME

There is only one thing sure about your ability to win any given motor race. If you are not absolutely certain that you can win it, you won't. It helps if everyone else present on the day is also aware that you can win it - and that you intend to.

Turning one's mirrors skyward on the grid is kid stuff and sheer lunacy. Braggadocio and posturing is silly. Quiet but visible confidence is what we are looking for here. To point out what I am talking about, we are going to end this section with one last war story.

Some years ago, on the eve of a Naval Air Station dinner dance, a Squadron Commander addressed his pilots thus: "Gentlemen, you are Naval Aviators. When you walk across that dance floor tonight, I expect to hear your balls clank."

SECTION SEVEN

ADVANCED DRIVE TO WIN

17

"The more things change, the more they remain the same." – Denis Jenkinson

THE OLD RULES CHANGE

Mike Costin started it. I continued the line. Paul Van Valkenburgh and Len Terry added to it. All of us put into writing what were basic truths at the time we wrote them:

1) Run the car as soft as you can get away with in ride and control the roll with anti roll bars.

2) Soften the end of the car that is not working - either with springs or with bars.

3) Keep anti-squat and anti-dive to a minimum.

4) Use lots of camber change to keep the outside tire upright.

Costin's book was published in 1964. Terry's came out in 1973. Mine started in 1975. 95% of what we said is still valid - even the points on which we disagree. But technologies are, by definition, expanding fields of knowledge. As any technology advances, we must learn to take advantage of the improvements in both knowledge and components.

GROUND EFFECT AND THE OLD RULES

The quantum leaps in aerodynamic download that have taken place since 1978 have forced changes in tire and suspension design which require us to change our thinking with regard to tuning the chassis.

THE PITFALLS OF DOWNLOAD

Thirty years ago racing cars were lucky to reach 1.2-g lateral or braking force. Today 3.6-g, while uncomfortable, is not uncommon. Lap times have fallen commensurately. While advances in tire technology (and size), suspension design and engine performance are responsible for much of the gain, the major portion is due to the enormous increases in aerodynamic download.

Enough has been written about the generation, effects and efficient use of download that I am not at all tempted to add to that body of written knowledge. I will, however, contribute a few words of caution - for download can be a mixed blessing.

Balanced aerodynamic download increases cornering force, braking force and driver confidence. It is easy to say that if a little download is good, more is always better. However it is not possible to generate download - by spoilers, by wings, by ground effect tunnels or by inclined and assisted flat bottoms - without inducing aerodynamic drag. So increasing download also increases drag.

Things being what they are, even the most efficient racing car in the world increases drag by a minimum of one pound for every eight to ten pounds of download - and five or six is more common. The drag increase reduces top speed and, all other things being equal, increases elapsed time between corner exit and braking point (it slightly improves braking - very slightly).

Of course, the increased download improves corner exit speed and moves the braking point down the track closer to the next corner. As always, the download versus drag trade off is a compromise. The trick lies in determining the optimum amount of download for a given car on a particular circuit - and sometimes under particular circumstances. As an example, in 1994 there were only two Grand Prix circuits (Monaco and Hungary) where Formula One cars used all the download they could get.

We all know that download (and drag) increase as the square of road speed. What we may lose track of is that some download generators are more appropriate to low speed than high - and vice versa. A Formula One car at Monaco looks like a 747 on take off - flaps and tiers and Gurneys all over the place; "To hell with the drag, we've got thrust and we need lift!"

In the case of the 747 the length of the runway is limited, engine power is not and the object is to get the thing into the air. Formula One cars have lots of power, at Monaco the corners are more important than the short straights and so corner apex and exit speed take precedence over maximum speed. Further, the road speed in the corners is relatively low so high lift, high drag wing appendages are the order of the day.

At Indianapolis or Michigan on the other hand, Indy Car wings look more like an F 104. Corner speeds are in the 220mph range so a small single element wing with a laminar profile will generate tons of download and do so much more efficiently than a multi-plane wing (they pull the flaps and slats up on the 747 in order to even get to cruising speed). Of course, the underbodies are also liable to be different as well, but that is beyond our scope. The same thing, to a much lesser extent, is true of the Formula One cars at Hockenheim or Monza.

What is within our scope is the simple fact that what generates download at low road speeds - Gurney flaps and other forms of spoiler in particular - also generate insane amounts of drag at high road speeds. There have been few more astute observers of the science of making race cars go fast than Danny Ongais. Among his few but wise sayings is; "Take the wing off the thing and get the chassis working."

Ongais is right. The best way to arrive at the optimum download for any given circuit is to start with a known amount of balanced download that is at least 10% less than you think that you are going to end up with. Get the chassis and driver working and then add download until it makes the car slower.

When the critical corners on a given circuit are slow - as at Trois Rivieres - the car needs a lot of Gurney flap to achieve download. But tall Gurneys generate insane amounts of high speed drag so, if the corners are slow but the straights are long, the Gurneys must be relatively small. Further, large Gurneys kill the acceleration off fast corners. The same is true of spoilers on cars that don't allow wings.

What I am trying to point out here is that even experienced drivers fall into the trap of running too much comforting download. The only way that I know of to avoid the trap is to start your weekend with significantly less download than you think you will ultimately need.

The other trap-to-be-avoided is the common slavish copying of what the competition is doing with respect to download. It is, of course, always necessary to be aware of what the opposition is doing - but the best you can hope for when copying set ups is to be a consistent one step behind. Of course, if the guy who is usually the same speed as you, or slower, is suddenly faster than you with significantly different download, you had better try it.

Here are the rules:

1) If all of the corner speeds are similar (and high), then a single element wing will be more efficient than a multi element wing - providing that the rules allow enough wing area to generate the required download.

2) Normally, in clean air, front download increases with increasing road speed at a greater rate than rear download. This is because the front wings run in clear air and in ground effect while the rear wing is in neither.

   a) When overtaking in fast corners, Rule Two is very liable to be reversed. The front wings are accustomed to clean air and so are more affected by the turbulent wakes of other cars than the rears which are always in dirty air. This is arranged by a benevolent deity. While sudden traffic-induced aero understeer in fast corners can step up your heart rate, it beats the hell out of sudden oversteer.

   b) When being overtaken - particularly in sedans - the car moving into your draft is very liable to remove your rear download, especially if it is generated by a spoiler. Watch NASCAR on TV and see last sentence of Rule Two (a) above.

3) Ground effect tunnels (at least good ones) are more efficient than wings - at least at higher road speeds. A good tunnel can have a lift to drag ratio of 10:1 - 12:1 whereas multi element wings tend to run in the 5:1 - 6:1 range.

4) Contrary to popular opinion, a stalled wing still produces lift (or, in our case, download). The reason that stalled airplanes fall out of the sky is that the available power is not sufficient to overcome the vastly increased drag from the stalled wing. This means that it is sometimes viable to stall the front wings in order to match the maximum rear download available on circuits with very short straights and slow corners. It helps a lot if all of the corners are about the same speed.

This is not a simple business.

In fact, there is another side to the download versus drag story. There are circumstances when you want a lot of download to qualify and less to race. It goes like this. If a given race track has long straights combined with a lot of close together or linked medium speed corners - where passing will be very difficult - while you may be faster in qualifying with a lot of download, the first time you come to that long straight, those clever devils who trimmed their cars out after qualifying may stream right on by you. Everything in racing is a compromise and every compromise has to be reasoned out. Like I said, it is a mental business at the top.

RAKE AND STUFF

For years we have known that increasing the rake angle of any racing car will decrease corner entry understeer - often at the cost of putting the power down on exit.

Usually what is actually happening is that raising the rear ride height raises the rear roll center while lowering the front lowers the front roll center - resulting in a relatively higher rear roll center. This increases the swing axle jacking forces at the rear and/or decreases them at the front. The result is decreased rear lateral capacity, especially under the brakes, and decreased corner entry understeer - better balance. Naturally we pay for it in decreased overall grip and (probably) some loss of traction coming off the corner.

Is it worth it? In most cases, yes - balance is more important than grip. Sure, we would be better off to run the ideal roll axis inclination and cure the understeer some other way - but rake is quick and easy and time is often short. And yes, it works the other way - reducing rake will usually help put the power down (and hurt the turn in) for the same reason.

Ground effect aerodynamics complicates this picture more than somewhat - whether we are talking about tunnels or flat bottoms. Now we have an ideal mechanical roll axis inclination and an aerodynamic rake axis that will produce the maximum lift over drag ratio. It is real nice if the two happen to coincide. They can, but only in well designed and well developed cars.

It gets more complicated than this. On most race tracks the straights are significantly faster than the fastest corner(s). The aerodynamic rake angle that produces the most efficient lift over drag will also induce a lot of drag. Lift induces drag and that is all there is to it.

Reducing rake reduces both lift and drag - as does raising ride height. The late and unlamented active ride systems raised the front ride height in proportion to road speed and significantly reduced aero drag. It is possible to at least partially achieve the same results with passive suspension. It takes a sophisticated data logging system and good interpretation.

The idea is to run the most efficient aerorake for the fastest corner(s) on the circuit and let the rear wing forces reduce the rear ride height at speed - rear wing forces will always be greater than front wing forces. Of course, this requires rear wheel rates softer than front - but the driver feels and responds to the stiffer end of the car and so, if you want to drive the car properly, the front wheel rates will be stiffer than the rear anyway.

CURE WITH STIFF OR CURE WITH SOFT

Along these lines, when I was young the technical end of life was a lot more simple than it is now. When a car either understeered or oversteered, we usually softened the misbehaving end and that pretty much fixed things. This is one of the areas where some of the fundamental cause and result relationships have changed somewhat since I wrote that particular section of 'Tune to Win'.

What has happened is that the enormous amounts of download generated by ground effects have made aerodynamic considerations of overwhelming importance on both "tunnel" cars and flat bottomed cars. As both the amount of download generated at a given speed and the location of the aerodynamic center of pressure are functions of ride height and pitch angle, suspension movement has been severely reduced - on flat bottomed cars it has almost become a thing of the past.

These days download often demands zero droop and virtually zero roll suspension systems. With these and the tires that they have spawned, the old "soften the end that isn't working" concept has changed almost completely - at least on ground effect cars. For instance, back when we allowed relatively large suspension movements, we designed in a lot more camber compensation (negative camber generated in bump travel to keep the outside tire more upright in roll). Since we now severely limit the amount of suspension travel and of roll, we don't need as much camber change.

We now concentrate our geometric efforts on roll center envelopes and on keeping the tires upright under braking and accelerating loads. With this sort of geometry, if the car squats or rolls on power application, the outside rear tire may well change camber enough to upset its footprint enough to cause sudden power on oversteer from too soft a suspension rate. Ground effect has forced us to adjust our thinking and our priorities.

Since the driver feels - and reacts to - the stiffer end of the car, most good drivers set the car up with the front ride and roll resistance wheel rates stiffer than the rear. This gives good solid feel in the critical second phase of the corner and helps put the power down on corner exit.

Conversely, the driver who slides the car a lot - Gilles Villeneuve or Keke Rosberg style - will usually set the car up with the rear stiffer than the front. Not a good way to go. While Keke did win the World Championship, he won damned few Formula One races. Gilles was probably the most exciting and charismatic driver of the "modern" era - but likewise he won few Formula One races. Sliding reminds me of Shakespeare's line: "full of sound and fury, signifying nothing."

TO RARB OR NOT TO RARB

On road courses, I like to stiffen the rear of the car with spring rather than bar. Anti roll bars reduce roll angles - but they also transfer load from the inside to the outside tire in a corner. Exactly what we don't want. Most current Formula One and Indy Cars run with no rear bar at all. I don't think that I would go that far - especially with a monoshock front suspension. A quickly changed and relatively weak Rear Anti Roll Bar makes a very convenient trim tab at small cost in load transfer.

TIGHTEN THE CAR

We often hear the expression, "we've got to tighten this baby down," or, "we've got to loosen the thing up." You can tighten it down either by adding download to the car or rebound control to the shocks. In the first case you pay your penalty in aerodynamic drag while in the second the car may jack itself down over surface irregularities. In each case the idea is to add more until it makes the car slow - either through reduced acceleration due to download induced drag or by lack of compliance from the jacking down.

In NASCAR parlance, to loosen means to take away understeer and to tighten means to add understeer.

SNAP

At every level of skill and experience, the most common complaint of the racing driver is; "It pushes like crazy on corner entry then snaps to oversteer the instant I get on the throttle. Only a driver of my experience, skill and daring could have brought this thing back to the pits in one piece. Fix it!"

We shall assume a certain level of objectivity on the part of all concerned - that the driver is not abusing the car by, for instance, entering the corners with the front tires on fire, that the car is properly aligned and corner weighted, etc, and that the crew is willing to listen. In that case, nine times out of ten in this day and age (the mid Nineties), entry understeer followed by throttle connected snap to exit oversteer is one of two things: a "fall over" problem or loose anti roll bars.

What usually happens is that the car is set up with too little front suspension roll stiffness relative to the rear. When the driver turns the steering wheel, it feels as if the car turns in instantly, but then the front "washes out" leaving the driver to deal with a lot of "Phase Two" understeer. When he jumps on the throttle the relatively strong rear roll stiffness causes oversteer.

What has actually happened in this case is that the car didn't really turn in - the initial lateral load transfer in response to the steering input caused it to "fall over" onto the (relatively) unsupported outside front wheel and it felt like it turned in sharply. This did bad things to both load transfers and tire cambers so the understeer reported for duty. When the driver applied the power, the rearward load transfer straightened the front up, the front tires bit while the relatively strong roll stiffness slid the car into power on oversteer.

This can be a very confusing situation for all concerned. The problem is liable to be more pronounced in slower corners. The road to salvation leads through the realization that the problem can exist and a thorough and detailed debriefing to an increase in front roll stiff-

ness. Whether the solution lies in more spring or more bar is a subject for experimentation during testing - and the results should be noted in the ever growing "if-then" book.

If there is an excuse for getting caught out (the first time) by the fall over syndrome, there is none for the loose anti roll bar bit. Yet it is not at all uncommon for very competent teams to spend days chasing their tails trying to define and cure the cause - while overlooking the obvious.

The whole idea of the anti roll bar is to restrain roll immediately when a lateral force is developed. It is meant to be either a linear or a raising rate device. If any part of the anti roll bar linkage has any appreciable amount of slop (looseness), upon corner entry the vehicle will roll some amount before the bar restrains it. Further, the sprung mass of the vehicle will accelerate onto the bar with a big thud. All of this leads to a vague and imprecise car - which may get real sudden when the roll catches up with the bar.

"It doesn't want to turn in, but once it has turned, it's better," is one quote. Another is; "It falls over on itself going in and then it washes out."

Conversely, when the driver gets on the power and the car unwinds, there is a corresponding dead period before the rear anti roll bar catches the car - and when it does, the car snaps to oversteer. This situation may also lead to the driver "hurtling" the car at the corner in an effort to overcome the understeer. This technique, while spectacular - and easy - invariably results in excessive amounts of wheelspinning oversteer on corner exit. It is much appreciated by the unknowledgeable fan. It is less appreciated by the knowledgeable car owner/team manager. It is slow. So pay attention to your anti roll bar linkage and improve the quality of your life.

We are talking about very small increments of slop here. Bottoming any part of the suspension or coming hard onto unprogressive bump rubbers will do the same thing. One of the easiest consulting jobs I ever did was determining that a very consistent snap oversteer problem on a new car was caused by a trailing arm contacting the tube frame when the car squatted under power. Easy money doesn't come my way very often!

SKIDS

The skid plates that protect the underbody of virtually every racing car in the world are meant to just touch the track under the most severe bottoming conditions experienced at that track. Dragging the skids down the straight slows the car noticeably. Don't do it.

ANTI DIVE AND ANTI SQUAT

Anti-dive and/or anti-squat (see Tune to Win Chapter Three) in the suspension system tends to do good things on high speed smooth corners and bad things on bumpy circuits and/or slow corners. Since anti is basically lifting one's self by one's bootstraps, it tends to stiffen the suspension in reaction to longitudinal load transfer. This is real good when the major concern is pitch attitude, front camber under the brakes or rear camber on acceleration.

When we are talking about rough roads, however, anti stiffens the suspension just when we need suspension compliance in bumpy braking areas or corner exits. For the typical slow and rough circuit take most of it out and run the car 1/8" higher - it will pay off in both lap time and danceability in traffic.

Our English cousins seem to have a problem with this - Silverstone is not located in the USA. However, in the case of high horsepower cars with soft springs and sophisticated shocks (lots of low piston speed control and divergent medium and high speed control), a lot of rear anti-squat is required to keep the platform stable under acceleration. This is not a simple business...

WHEEL TRAMP

Many years ago, in the days of solid front axles and kingpins, front wheel "shimmy" and "tramp" were fairly common and very unpleasant. The advent of the independent front suspension led to the development of the wide based upright or "steering knuckle" with upper and lower ball joints rather than the kingpin. Shimmy and tramp pretty much went away. The arrival of the "zero droop" and preloaded suspension has brought with it the possibility of front wheel tramp under the brakes. It is still exceedingly unpleasant. The cause can be a loose or worn lower ball joint, loose or worn shock absorber bearings or insufficient shock absorber droop forces at small damper piston displacements. The quick fix is to reduce the preload and increase the spring rate so as to end up with the same wheel rate.

THE HANDLING CLINIC REVISITED

Checklist of Causes and Effects

SECTION ONE: EFFECT LISTED FIRST, THEN POSSIBLE CAUSES

INSTABILITY

Straight line instability -- general

Rear wheel toe-out - either static due to incorrect (or backwards) setting or dynamic due to bump steer and/or deflection steer.

Vast lack of rear downforce or overwhelming amount of front downforce.

Wild amount of front toe-in or toe-out.

Loose or broken chassis, suspension member or suspension link mounting point.

Straight line instability under hard acceleration

Malfunctioning limited slip differential.

Insufficient rear toe-in.

Deflection steer from rear chassis/ suspension member or mounting point.

Straight line instability -- car darts over bumps (especially single wheel bumps)

Excessive Ackerman steering geometry.

Excessive front toe-in or toe-out.

Uneven front castor/ trail setting.

Uneven front shock forces, incorrectly adjusted bump rubbers/ packers.

Front anti-roll bar miles too stiff.

Insufficient rear wheel droop travel.

Instability under the brakes -- front end wanders

Too much front brake bias.

Excessive front damper rebound force.

Instability under the brakes -- car wants to spin

Excessive rear brake bias.

Unbalanced ride/ roll resistance - too much at the rear.

Insufficient rear droop travel.

Excessive rear damper rebound force.

Insufficient rear negative camber (usually in combination with one or more of the above).

RESPONSE

Car feels generally heavy and unresponsive

Tire pressures too low.

Excessive aerodynamic download (note: if car feels sluggish on acceleration at high speed, the culprit is often a rear wing Gurney lip that is too high).

Car feels sloppy, is slow to take a set in corners, rolls a lot, doesn't want to change direction

Insufficient damper forces.

Car too soft in ride and/ or roll.

Insufficient tire pressure.

Car responds too quickly -- has little feel -- slides at slightest provocation

Car too stiff for inexperienced driver.

Excessive ride or roll resistance.

Excessive tire pressure.

Excessive rear toe-in.

Excessive damper forces.

Insufficient downforce.

UNDERSTEER

Corner entry understeer -- car won't point in and gets progressively worse

Excessive front tire pressure.

Insufficient front track width (compared to rear).

Excessive front roll stiffness.

Front roll centre too high or too low.

Insufficient front damper bump force.

Insufficient front downforce.

Excessive dynamic positive camber on laden (outside) front tire.

Braking too hard and too late.

Insufficient front roll resistance -- car may be falling over onto outside front tire due to insufficient front track width or diagonal load transfer under trail braking. Understeer can often be cured by increasing front roll resistance even though doing so will increase the amount of lateral load transfer.

Corner entry understeer -- car initially points in then washes out

Excessive front toe-in or toe-out.

Insufficient front wheel travel in droop (non droop limited cars only).

Insufficient front damper bump resistance.

Incorrectly adjusted packers (car rolls onto the packers).

Non-linear load transfer due to the spring/ bar geometry, to roll centre migration or to incorrect roll axis inclination.

Corner entry understeer -- car points in and then darts

Incorrectly adjusted packers (see above).

Insufficient front wheel travel.

Nose being sucked down due to ground effect.

Excessive Ackerman steering geometry.

Corner exit understeer -- slow corners

Big trouble! Often a function of excessive corner entry and mid-phase understeer followed by throttle application while maintaining the understeer steering lock. This causes the driving thrust on the inside rear tire to accentuate the understeer. The first step must be to cure the corner entry understeer.

Can also be caused by 'unloading' the front tires due to rearward load transfer on acceleration. Increasing the rear ride rate or anti-squat and/ or reducing the front damper low piston speed rebound force usually helps.

OVERSTEER

Corner entry oversteer

Severe rearward ride rate/ roll resistance imbalance.

Diabolical lack of rear downforce.

Severely limited rear wheel droop travel.

Broken or non-functioning outside rear damper or front anti roll bar.

(A slight feeling of rear tippy-toe type hunting on corner entry can be due to excessive rear toe-in or to excessive rear damper rebound force.)

Corner exit oversteer -- gets progressively worse from the

time that power is applied

Worn out limited slip differential.

Insufficient rear spring, bar or shock (low piston speed bump control) allowing car to "fall over" onto outside rear tire.

Excessive rear roll stiffness.

Excessive rear negative camber.

Too little rear toe-in.

Insufficient rear download.

Note: If car feels as if it is sliding through the corner rather than rolling freely, reduce the rear toe-in and see what happens.

Corner exit oversteer -- sudden -- car takes its normal corner exit set then breaks loose

Insufficient rear suspension travel (lifting the inside tire due to droop limitation or bottoming the outside wheel due to bump limitation).

Dead rear damper.

Incorrectly adjusted packers.

Sudden change in outside rear tire camber.

Too much throttle applied after driver's confidence level has been boosted by car taking a set.

Does not put the power down on the exit of smooth-surface corners

Excessive low piston speed bump force on rear damper.

Excessive rear tire pressure.

Excessive rear roll resistance (probably from bar rather than springs).

Tires gone.

Excessive rear dynamic negative camber -- either from download or from camber change on squat.

Does not put the power down on the exit of bumpy corners

Any or all of the above.

Excessive rear low piston speed damper force.

Excessive rear rebound force force jacking the car down and losing compliance.

Insufficient rear droop travel.

Understeer in, snap to oversteer on power application

The most common complaint of all! Too little front roll resistance -- falls over on turn-in then snaps.

(A) Front anti roll bar plus front spring or (quick indication) front bump setting. Stiffening front anti roll bar will transfer load back onto inside rear tire on corner exit.

(B) If (A) cures understeer but the car still snaps, it is almost certainly falling over at the rear on longitudinal/ diagonal transfer. Can add rear anti roll bar or rear

spring. Rear anti roll bar will transfer load away from inside rear tire. Spring will not. Spring will decrease traction over exit bumps, bar will not.

(C) Check for proper inflated shape of front tires.

(D) Loose anti roll bar linkage/ blade sockets can have same effect.

SECTION TWO: CAUSE LISTED FIRST, THEN POSSIBLE EFFECTS

RIDE AND ROLL RATE

Too much spring -- overall

Harsh and choppy ride.

Car will not put power down on corner exit, excessive wheelspin.

Much unprovoked sliding.

Too much spring -- front

Initial understeer, though car may point into corners well.

Front end breaks loose over bumps in corners.

Front tires lock over bumps.

Too much spring -- rear

Oversteer immediately upon application of power exiting corners.

Excessive wheelspin.

Too little spring -- overall
Car contacts race track a lot.

Floating ride with excessive vertical chassis movement.

Sloppy response.

Car is slow to take its set; may take more than one.

Too little spring -- front

Chassis grounds under brakes.

Excessive roll on corner entry.

Initial understeer -- car doesn't point in (although it may well feel as if it points in as it falls over onto the outside front tire).

Too little spring -- rear

Excessive acceleration squat and accompanying rear negative camber.

Car falls over on outside rear tire as power is applied, causing power oversteer.

Too much anti roll bar -- overall

Car will be very sudden in turning response and will have little feel.

Will tend to slide or skate rather than taking a set.

May dart over one wheel or diagonal bumps.

Too much anti roll bar -- front

Initial corner entry understeer which usually becomes progressively worse as the driver tries to tighten the corner radius.

Too much anti roll bar -- rear

Corner exit oversteer. Car won't put power down but goes directly to oversteer, with or without wheelspin.

Excessive sliding coming out of corners.

Too little anti roll bar -- overall

Car may be slow in response, generally sloppy.

Car is reluctant to change direction in esses or chicane.

SHOCK ABSORBER FORCES

Too much shock -- overall

A very sudden car with harsh ride qualities, much sliding and wheel patter.

Car will not absorb road surface irregularities but crashes over them.

Too much rebound force

Wheels do not return quickly to road surface after displacement; inside wheel in a corner may be pulled off the road by the damper.

Car may "jack down" over bumps or in long corners causing loss of tire compliance.

Too much bump force

Harsh reaction to road surface irregularities.

Car slides rather than sticking.

Too much low piston speed bump force

Car's reaction to lateral and longitudinal load transfer too harsh.

Too much high piston speed bump force

Car's reaction to minor road surface irregularities too harsh - tires hop over "chatter bumps" in braking areas and at corner exit.

Car's reaction to major bumps can be violent.

Too little shock -- overall

Car floats a lot in ride and oscillates after bumps.

Car dives and squats a lot.

Car rolls quickly and may tend to "fall over" onto the outside front tire during corner entry and onto the outside rear during corner exit.

Car is generally sloppy and unresponsive.

Too little rebound force - overall

Car floats - oscillates after bumps - the 'Cadillac ride syndrome'.

Too little bump force - overall

Initial turn reaction soft and sloppy.

Excessive and quick roll, dive and squat.

Too little high piston speed bump force

Suspension may bottom over the largest bumps on the track, resulting in momentary loss of tire compliance and excessive instantaneous loads on suspension and chassis.

Too little low piston speed bump force

Car is generally imprecise and sloppy in response to lateral and longitudinal load transfers and driver steering inputs.

Dead shock on one corner

Surprisingly difficult for the driver to identify and/or to isolate

At the rear, power oversteer in one direction only.

At the front, initial understeer in one direction only.

WHEEL ALIGNMENT

Front toe-in -- too much

Car darts over bumps, under the brakes and during corner entry.

Car won't point into corners or, if extreme, may point in very quickly then wash out.

Front toe-out -- too much

Car wanders under the brakes and may be somewhat unstable in a straight line, especially in response to one wheel or diagonal bumps and wind gusts.

May point into corners and then refuse to take a set.
Rear toe-in -- too much

Rear feels light and unstable on corner entry.

Car slides through corner rather than rolling freely.

Rear toe-in -- too little

Power-on oversteer during corner exit.

Rear toe-out -- any

Power oversteer during corner exit or in a straight line.

Straight line instability.

Front wheel castor -- too much

Excessive physical steering effort accompanied by too much self-return action and transmittal of road shocks to driver's hands.

Front wheel caster -- too little

Car too sensitive too steering.

Too little steering feel and feedback.

Front wheel caster -- uneven

Steering effort harder in one direction than in the other.

Car pulls toward wheel with less caster.

Camber -- too much negative

Inside of tire excessively hot or wearing too rapidly. At the front this will show up as reduced braking capability and at the rear as reduced acceleration capability. Depending upon the track and the geographic location of the tire measuring point, inside tire temperature should be 10-25 degrees Fahrenheit hotter than outside.

Camber -- too much positive

Outside of tire will be hot and wearing. This should never be and is almost always caused at the rear by running too much static positive camber in an effort to pre-

vent excessive negative under the influence of the wing at high speed. Will cause corner exit oversteer and reduced tractive capacity. If extreme, may cause corner entrance instability. At the front it is usually caused by excessive chassis roll or by insufficient roll camber compensation in the suspension linkage and will cause understeer after the car has pointed into the corner.

Bump steer, front -- too much toe-in in bump

Car darts over bumps and understeers on corner entry.

Bump steer, front -- too much toe-out in bump

Car wanders under the brakes and may dart over one wheel bumps or in response to wind gusts.

Understeer after initial turn in.

Bump steer, rear -- too much toe-in in bump
Roll understeer on corner entry.

Tippy-toe rear wheel instability on corner entry.

Darting on application of power on corner exit.

Bump steer, rear -- any toe-out in bump

Same as static toe-out but lesser effect.

SUSPENSION GEOMETRY

Rear roll centre too low -- or front too high

Roll axis too far out of par-

allel with mass centroid axis leading to non-linear generation of chassis roll and lateral load transfer; the tendency will be toward too much load transfer at the rear, which will cause oversteer.

Front roll centre too low -- or rear too high

Opposite of above, tending toward corner entry understeer and three wheeled motoring on corner exit.

Front track too narrow in relation to rear

Car tends to trip over its front feet during slow and medium speed corner entry, evidenced by lots of understeer. Crutch is to increase front ride and roll resistance and to raise front roll centre.

TIRES

Too much tire pressure

Harsh ride; excessive wheel patter, sliding and wheelspin.

High temperature reading at centre of tire.

Too little tire pressure

Soft and mushy response.

High tire temperatures, with dip at centre of tread.

Reduced footprint area and reduced traction.

Front tires "going off"

Gradually increasing understeer.

Rear tires "going off"

Gradually increasing oversteer.

Inside rear tire of larger diameter than outside (reverse stagger)

Drags inside rear, which reduces corner entry understeer.

Increases corner exit oversteer.

OTHER FACTORS

Limited slip differential wearing out

Initial symptoms are decreased power-on understeer or increased power-on oversteer and inner wheelspin. The car might be easier and more pleasant to drive but it will be slow. When wear becomes extreme, stability under hard acceleration will diminish and things will not be pleasant at all.

18

"You have to keep the tires on the ground. That is what the shocks are for."
– Jan Zuidjidjk

THE RACING
SHOCK ABSORBER

When I wrote the shock absorber chapter of "Tune To Win", it was 1978 and not much had happened in the world of the racing shock absorber since Koni brought out the double adjustable in 1965. What I had to say was valid and was about as much as anyone except Jan Zuidjidjk could have said at the time. Hank Richten had retired; Ken Anderson was probably still in high school; Kurt Roehrig was building engines at McLaren; Jeff Ryan was in high school; Jeff Braun, Tom Janesek and Mike Diefenbach were in grammar school; Tim Neff was surfing the Sydney beaches; Howard Milliken was not doing shocks.

In 1984, when I added a page on shocks in 'Engineer to Win' the only aspect that had really changed much was that the "gas shock" with its twin advantages of increased piston area and reduced aeration had begun to replace the hydraulic shock absorber. Bilstein was the only supplier and its shocks, while excellent, were not externally adjustable.

It is now 1995 and there has been a quiet revolution. The revolution started on MotoCross tracks and didn't really reach our world until a couple of unrelated events occurred almost simultaneously:

1) Rick Mears, at the urging of his off road racing brother, Roger, tried a set of Fox double adjustable gas shocks on his Penske Indy Car.

2) The over riding requirement for constant ride height and pitch attitude brought about by ground effect forced chassis designers to severely limit suspension travel.

Rick liked the Fox shocks. Ken Anderson at Fox got interested in circuit racing. Roger Penske recognized one more commercial opportunity, hired Ken away from Fox and started Penske Racing Shocks. This gave Ken an unprecedented opportunity to do serious development. It has spread from there - with Ken as the mentor of a generation of young shock engineers.

The last few years have seen more progress in the world of shock absorbers than the previous half century. There is still no need for a driver to be a shock engineer. It is, however, essential for the driver to know how the shocks can influence the behavior of the car under various conditions and to be able to report if not to analyze that behavior.

THE PROBLEM

Every automobile, road going or racing, uses some form of suspension spring(s) in order to prevent the vertical loads imposed on the wheels by road surface irregularities and/or dynamic load transfers from being transmitted to the chassis and/or its occupants. Under the loads imposed by accelerations to either the sprung or unsprung masses, the springs compress and allow the wheels (unsprung mass) to move in relation to the chassis (sprung mass).

When a spring is compressed under load, the force that caused the compression is stored within the spring as potential energy. When the load is removed the stored energy is released. The spring then extends with a force proportional to the original load.

In the case of an automobile (running without suspension droop limiting) this force will always be sufficient to carry the wheel past its ride height position and into droop - thus forcing the chassis to rise above its ride height position.

The spring (and the chassis) will then oscillate at the natural frequency of the unsprung mass - carrying the sprung mass with it - until the internal friction of the spring and the suspension pivots dissipates the stored energy. The greater the upset, the greater the magnitude of the oscillations and the longer they will last.

If these oscillations were not damped, every time that one or more wheels were displaced vertically, the vehicle would proceed down the road like four pogo sticks in loose formation until the energy stored in the springs was finally dissipated as heat. As we see daily on the public highways, this oscillatory nonsense is detrimental to the suspension geometry, the stability of the platform (both aerodynamic and mechanical), the compliance of the tires with the road and the comfort (both physical and mental) of the occupants. It cannot be tolerated in any high performance vehicle.

THE SOLUTION

The automotive shock absorber was developed to control (or dampen) the release of the energy stored in the suspension springs. It does so by converting the released kinetic energy, which is difficult to get rid of, into thermal energy (heat) which is relatively easily dissipated into the airstream - assuming that the designer(s) have made provision for the shocks to be exposed to said airstream. Normally this conversion is accomplished by a hydraulic damper consisting of a piston moving in an oil filled cylinder.

The piston is attached to either the sprung or the unsprung mass by means of a suitable piston rod, and the cylinder is attached to the other mass. Both the end of the piston rod and the end of the cylinder (shock body) are provided with suitable pivots - normally spherical bearings - so as to allow the suspension to swing freely. The piston contains metering orifices which are controlled by valves - allowing restricted passage of the fluid.

When relative motion occurs between the sprung and unsprung masses, the piston is forced through the oil in the cylinder - resisting the motion. By metering the flow through the valves and orifices the rate of movement can be altered and controlled. On the extension (or rebound) stroke, part of the energy stored in the compressed spring can be damped before it is transmitted into the sprung mass. On the compression (or bump) stroke, the rate of spring compression and therefore of wheel movement can be controlled.

Very basically, the compression stroke controls the motion of the unsprung mass and the extension stroke controls the motion of the sprung mass.

The hydraulic shock absorber is inherently velocity sensitive. The faster the piston moves through the oil (or the more vertical wheel acceleration that takes place), the greater will be the force of resistance. This is due to one of the fundamental laws of fluid dynamics - a fluid's resistance to flow through any given orifice increases as the square function of fluid velocity (just like drag - same law).

The law is immutable, but the resistance and the effects can be modified by spring loaded valves and/or

progressive orifice locations to obtain virtually any desired "damping characteristic". The characteristic of any given shock is the term used to describe the relationship between piston velocity and resultant force.

As shown by FIGURE 37, this characteristic can have one of three forms. It can be linear - in which case damping resistance will increase at the same rate as piston velocity. It can be digressive - in which case resistance will increase at a lesser rate than piston velocity. Or it can be progressive - in which case the damping resistance will increase at a greater rate than piston velocity. To my knowledge, progressive valving is not used in circuit racing.

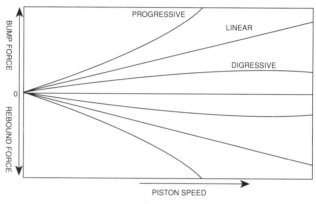

LINEAR, PROGRESSIVE AND DIGRESSIVE DAMPING

FIGURE 37

By careful design the three basic characteristics can be combined to give compound characteristics - the curve can be progressive for a portion of the velocity range and then change to linear or digressive. The characteristics of the curve on either stroke are controlled and modified by varying the size, number, configuration and complexity of the metering orifices and valves.

Springs are inherently displacement sensitive devices. Shocks are inherently velocity sensitive. With clever design and development the two can be made to complement each other to the benefit of overall vehicle performance.

The conventional shock absorber piston is manufactured with a series of axial holes (FIGURE 38). The holes (or metering orifices) are sealed by stacked disc valves. The number, thickness, stacking order and diameter of the discs determines the amount of hydraulic force required to open the valves and allow fluid to pass (FIGURE 39). The greater the piston velocity the greater the hydraulic force. The greater the force, the wider the opening and the greater the fluid flow. The greater the fluid flow, the less the resistance. Sounds simple, doesn't it!

Since we usually need more rebound resistance than bump (at least on street cars) the passages on the bump

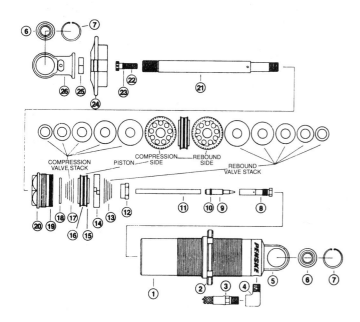

COMPONENTS OF A DOUBLE-ADJUSTABLE DAMPER
MADE BY PENSKE SHOCKS.
FIGURE 38

side of the piston typically have more effective area than those on the rebound side. The forces and the characteristics of the unit can be varied by the number and size of orifices, the number, thickness, diameter and stacking order of the discs and by the angle of the piston faces.

Often the piston will also have one or more "bypass" or "bleed" passages separate from the valve con-

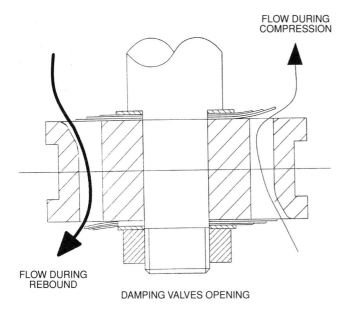

FLOW DURING
COMPRESSION

FLOW DURING
REBOUND

DAMPING VALVES OPENING

FIGURE 39

trolled metering orifices. So long as there is sufficient bleed capacity to deal with the forces involved, the valves remain closed. The bypass circuit therefore determines at what point the valve stack will begin to open. This means that, to adjust the damping forces at high piston velocities, the disc valves must be changed or adjusted while, to adjust the low piston speed forces, the bypass orifices must be changed or adjusted.

The disc valves are usually adjusted (as opposed to changed) by varying their preload while the bleed orifices are normally adjusted by means of a needle valve. Of course either of these adjustments will also change the point at which the stack begins to open... Maybe this isn't such a simple deal after all.

FUNCTION

Shock absorbers are misnamed. They do not absorb road shocks - the springs do that. The automotive "shock absorber" has three basic and inter-related functions:

1) To rapidly dampen the energy stored in the suspension springs as they compress in response to vertical accelerations of either the sprung or unsprung masses. The damping both reduces the oscillations of the vehicle chassis and, by reducing the dynamic wheel and tire fluctuations, helps to maintain consistent tire contact with the road surface.

2) To temporarily increase the effective rate of the suspension springs during compression - thus allowing softer springs to be used. These are the only shock functions of primary interest to the designers of our passenger cars who do a lot of talking (and often much less engineering) about the "critical damping rate".

3) To modify the transient effects of load transfer - lateral, longitudinal and diagonal - on both the sprung and unsprung masses - during corner entry and exit. This function is of primary interest to the designers of circuit racing cars who are not much interested in the critical damping rate - although they are vitally interested in the possibility of reducing spring rates (the lower the spring rate, the more the mechanical grip).

This multiplicity of function allows the shocks to effect the transient oversteer/understeer balance of the car during corner entry and exit as well as to stabilize the vehicle's behavior and to limit the vertical motion of the unsprung mass in reaction to road surface irregularities. It should be noted that the shock absorber affects only the "transients". It has no effect during steady state running or in cornering when there is no suspension movement - a rare situation indeed in motor racing.

TYPES OF SHOCK ABSORBER

Hydraulic shock absorbers fall into two broad categories - double tube and mono tube. These terms are seldom used. The terms in common use are "hydraulic" for double tube shocks and "gas" for mono tube shocks. When a shock is compressed, a portion of the piston rod enters the hydraulic chamber, displacing some of the oil. Provision must be made for this displaced oil to flow to some sort of reservoir - otherwise the shock will be hydraulically locked and the suspension will not move at all.

In the double tube shock (FIGURE 40) the piston and oil are contained in the inner tube (cylinder) while the outer cylinder serves as a reservoir for the oil displaced by the piston rod during the compression stroke. This outer cylinder contains both oil and air. Under severe operating conditions, the oil and air can emulsify at the interface. A similar thing can result from cavitation of oil passing through small orifices at high velocity. In extreme cases it is also possible for the fluid to actually boil in the cylinder.

Any of these conditions will produce aerated fluid of reduced viscosity. The result is shock absorber "fade" - similar to the spongy brake pedal that results when brake fluid boils in a caliper. Despite the use of advanced silicon based fluids, before the advent of the single tube racing shock absorber, shock absorber fade was not uncommon in racing. Efforts to substitute nitrogen for air in the reservoir and to contain the "gas" in the reservoir in a sort of condom proved effective only in advertising.

While relatively new to racing, the mono tube shock (FIGURE 40) has been in passenger car use for several decades. The patent, issued to DeCarbon in France in the 1950s, has been in the public domain for a long time. The basic shock consists of two chambers arranged in series within a single cylinder. The actual damping mechanism is purely hydraulic and is identical in function to that of the double tube shock - oil is metered through suitable orifices and valves in a piston which is forced to move through an oil filled cylinder.

Instead of a concentric reservoir cylinder, the displaced oil flows into a chamber downstream from the piston. The bottom of this chamber is formed by a second, floating, piston. On the other side of the floating piston is a separate chamber containing nitrogen under pressure. As oil is displaced the floating piston is forced downward against the nitrogen pressure.

Because of the requirement for the floating piston and the nitrogen chamber, the single tube shock absorber is necessarily longer than the double tube. This can be a disadvantage when the packaging envelope is tight. For this reason, and to increase the volume of both oil and nitrogen, many mono tube shocks are configured with the floating piston located in a remote reservoir. The mono tube shock is a more complex device that the double tube. It is also a better shock absorber.

It is better for three reasons:

1) The damping fluid is never in contact with air (or nitrogen) and so cannot emulsify.

2) The possibility of cavitation and of boiling is greatly reduced by the fact that the damping fluid is always under pressure (typically 75 to 350 psi).

3) Within the same package dimensions, the area of the metering piston is greatly increased, producing an intrinsically more sensitive shock and allowing more precise control over the characteristics of the shock.

This last feature is particularly important with the limited suspension travel of the modern racing car. The typical double tube racing shock does little or no damping for the first 4 or 5 mm of piston travel. When the total piston travel is liable to be in the neighborhood of 8 to 20mm this is simply not good enough. Current single tube racing shocks begin effective damping at less than 1mm of travel. They are, in fact, so sensitive that very high quality spherical bearings with no axial freeplay and minimum friction must be employed as pivots in order to gain full benefit from the most effective of the shocks.

Along these lines, cleverer designers are arranging their wheel to spring/shock travel ratios to increase the amount of spring/shock travel per increment of wheel

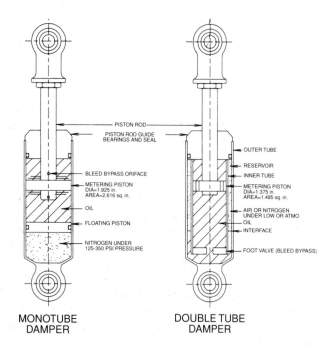

MONOTUBE DAMPER   DOUBLE TUBE DAMPER

MONO AND DOUBLE TUBE DAMPERS

FIGURE 40

travel to make the shocks more effective (and to allow the use of lighter weight springs). The really clever ones are making the front and rear motion ratios the same.

OPERATION

Worldwide, virtually all serious competition vehicles currently use single tube "gas" shock absorbers. The major manufacturers are, in alphabetical order, Bilstein, Dynamic, Fox, H-K, JRZ, Koni, Ohlins, Penske, Quantum and WP. Some of the Japanese technology is advanced, but, except for Howard Milliken and H-K, not yet marketed.

Functionally all of these shocks are similar. Through clever and complex metering devices (and through quality control) some are more advanced than others. Except for Bilstein, they all offer external adjustments to the amount of damping force exerted during both the compression and extension strokes.

Bilstein has always claimed that its shocks are "self adjusting" and so have not needed any in service adjustments. What they have actually meant (advertising is wonderful and the Germans are the masters of it) is that their shocks are velocity sensitive - as is every other hydraulic shock absorber. In fact they now offer an externally adjustable shock for NASCAR. It will be interesting to see how its wordsmiths rationalize this one.

THE EFFECT OF CHANGING NITROEN PRESSURE

The pressure of the nitrogen in the gas chamber is transmitted to the hydraulic fluid in the working chamber as "nose pressure" and delays the start of cavitation. The higher the pressure, the further the beginning of cavitation is delayed. The situation is analogous to that of the pressure cap on the coolant water system - a 15 psi pressure cap will raise the boiling point further than a 7 psi cap.

Unfortunately, the nose pressure created by the nitrogen must be overcome before the piston begins to move on the compression stroke. For this reason the most efficient nitrogen pressure will almost always be the lowest pressure that will prevent cavitation of the oil. Depending on a multitude of factors - the basic design of the shock, track characteristics, suspension travel, spring rate and the proximity of heat radiating or generating devices like exhaust systems, oil tanks and turbochargers - this static pressure will vary from 75 psi. to 350 psi.

An increase in chamber pressure has two separate effects:

1) It increases the static pressure or "nose force" in the hydraulic chamber by the amount of increase in nitrogen pressure. This increase, while it will reduce the point at which cavitation begins, also reduces

the "sensitivity" of the shock - more force is required to initiate piston movement.

2) It slightly increases the initial spring rate of the shock. Only the piston rod actually displaces oil in the shock body (the oil flows through the piston). A typical piston rod diameter is 0.620" - giving an area of 0.302 square inches. Therefore each 100 psi increase in nitrogen pressure will effectively increase the initial resistance to movement of the shock absorber by 30lb.

The effect is similar to that of preload in a suspension spring in that the resultant increase in initial resistance does not represent a true increase in the operating spring rate of the shock/spring unit, nor in the operating ride rate of the vehicle.

Mechanical springs are basically linear, or close to linear, devices - i.e. an increase in spring rate will effect the ride rate of the vehicle through the range of suspension travel. Increasing the nose pressure on a monotube shock, however, effects only the amount of force necessary to begin suspension movement.

This becomes more clear if we reverse the process. For example, a linear mechanical spring with a rate of 100lb per inch will compress 1 inch when subjected to a load of 100lb. In order to compress the spring further the load must be increased - a 50lb increase in load will compress the spring a further 0.5" - etc. On the other hand, if a monotube shock is pressurized to the point where the extension force is 100lb, a load of 100lb will be required to begin compression and a load of 101lb will slowly compress the shock completely.

For this reason, and because of the adverse effect on shock sensitivity, increasing the nitrogen pressure is a poor way of tuning a chassis. Those of us who have tried to save time in practice by attempting to use nitrogen pressure to determine whether or not a spring change would be beneficial have invariably become confused. It should, however, be noted that an increase in nitrogen pressure will indeed raise the ride height of the car slightly.

I should also point out that there is a divergence of opinion about the relationship between nitrogen pressure, cavitation and shock "sensitivity". Some engineers feel that any rational increase in gas pressure can be "balanced out" by readjusting the ride height at the spring perch. From the balance of forces point of view this is valid - but droop limiting and/or spring preload ruins the theory. At any rate, the people that I listen to agree that the optimum chamber pressure is the minimum required to prevent cavitation. In fact, a very slight amount of cavitation can be beneficial when more sensitivity is required - as in "chatter bumps" at the exits of slow corners.

Finally, changing the nitrogen pressure does not affect either the characteristic or the magnitude of the damping forces generated by the shock absorber. Damping forces are determined solely by the hydraulic section of the shock and are regulated internally at the piston/valve face. The oil on either side of the metering piston is at the same pressure. Therefore, changes in nitrogen pressure have no effect on the damping forces produced by the shock.

THE REAL WORLD

The necessity to be able to quickly adjust the shocks to optimize performance at different circuits has been obvious for decades. In fact, the pre-historic friction shocks were adjustable by changing the preload on the friction discs. When I was a young racing driver we had Armstrong shocks with adjustable rebound. Whether we knew how to do anything intelligent with them is open for discussion - but we did have them.

Externally adjustable shocks either change the preload on the valve stack or modify the effective area of a metering orifice. Changing the preload on the shim stack explains why, until very recently, we were unable to effectively separate low piston speed forces from high piston speed forces from outside the shock and why any adjustment to bump also affected rebound to some extent and vice-versa.

While the external adjustments effect the magnitude of the damping forces, the range of external adjustment is limited and very few external adjustments affect the actual characteristic curves of the shock. Racing suspension development has reached the point where it is a significant advantage to be able to change not only the damping forces, but also the characteristics of the shocks to suit different circuits.

As an example, shocks with completely different characteristics are required between tracks featuring smooth fast corners and those featuring slow bumpy corners - or between banked tracks and flat tracks. For many years it was common for major racing teams to keep several sets of shock absorbers on hand with different valving. This allowed quick and efficient tailoring of the both the magnitude of the damping forces and the characteristic of the shocks to the individual race track. Sprint and Midget teams still do this.

Another alternative is for the shock manufacturer to supply a service van at each event and revalve everyone's shocks. This is, however, time consuming and, in view of the limited practice time available, is not a satisfactory solution.

There are two other alternatives - field revalvable shocks and shocks with a range of adjustment great enough to cover any sane operating requirements.

Penske and Quantum provide field revalvable and re-pistonable units. Koni recently introduced its 2812 single tube damper which features replaceable pre-assembled and flow tested valving cartridges.

The range of adjustment of all of the "state of the art" shocks is steadily increasing. Currently, if we know the type of track we are going to and are basically familiar with the car, it may not be necessary to revalve at the track. It is, however, nice to have the option - and it is necessary to revalve for different types of race tracks. It would be really nice to have two sets per car so that they could be changed during a session.

One of the problems facing the race engineer is that the rate of lateral and longitudinal load transfer and therefore the transient oversteer/understeer balance of the car is affected by the forces and characteristics of the shock absorbers at "low" piston velocities - say 1 to 4 inches per second - while the car's behavior over bumps is affected by the shock's force characteristics at relatively high piston velocities - say 8 to 20 inches per second.

As we said earlier, until very recently it was not possible to separate the two - any adjustment affected the entire range of piston velocities. Further, the compression and extension adjustments were not really independent of each other. Any adjustment to compression had a noticeable effect on rebound and vice-versa. These two factors limited what we could do with the shocks. As always, we compromised - usually settling for the best behavior we could obtain over the bumps (if they were critical - and ignoring them if they were not) and using the shocks for transients.

The procedure described in 'Engineer to Win' (pages 205 & 206) and now called a "shock scan" is still the best way I know of to optimize shock adjustment. To this day - regardless of the sophistication of on board data gathering and the experience of the team and its drivers - many major racing teams do a "shock signature" or "shock scan" at fairly frequent intervals (and every time that they become confused). This exercise consists of running through a planned series of adjustments and noting the results - both objectively and subjectively.

The trouble is that the scan is time consuming and therefore beyond the means of smaller teams - especially those running the "many dollars per mile" cars who need it most. Pity! As a point of interest, the major teams also carry a shock dyno in the transporter and employ a shock absorber specialist technician. The dyno can give two graphs. The most useful one is the force vs velocity curve of FIGURE 37.

The original graph is the force vs displacement curve or "egg" illustrated by FIGURE 41 which mainly tells us that the shock has been correctly assembled. The usual scenario is that the race track engineer tells the

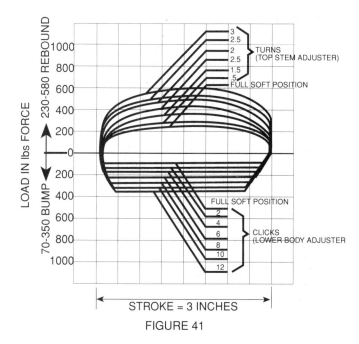

FIGURE 41

shock technician what forces and characteristic curve he wants and the technician selects the piston/valve stack that he thinks will give the desired result. The dyno is used to verify that result.

STATE OF THE ART

Quantum and Penske now make and market shocks in which, within limits, the low piston speed bump control can be adjusted independently of the high speed. Rebound is adjusted separately. Quadruple adjustables exist but, to the best of my knowledge, Penske no longer uses them and now only Quantum is exploiting them. The current shocks of these manufacturers allow bump adjustment with virtually no noticeable effect on rebound and vice versa.

The design of the Quantum and Penske racing shocks allow the individual race team to revalve (and re-piston) their shocks quickly and efficiently - changing either the magnitude or characteristics of the damping forces, or both. In order for the shock to be revalved, the nitrogen must be discharged and recharged. The nitrogen chambers are fitted with a standard tire valve and a charging tool is supplied.

BASIC THEORY AND PRACTICE

In an oversimplified view, the behavior of the racing car in response to major upsets (i.e. bumps) is largely controlled by the high piston speed bump forces in the shock. The car's reaction to the extension force of the springs compressed by a big bump is controlled by the high piston speed rebound. The car's transient response to load transfer, on the other hand, is largely affected by both the bump and rebound forces of the shock - but only at low piston velocities.

The car's ability to "put the power down" out of corners, its behavior over the crests of hills and out of washboarded slow corners is affected by both low and high piston velocity bump (but mainly by high speed bump) - depending on road speed and surface irregularities. One way of looking at things is that if the chassis is moving within the wheels, we are talking about low piston velocities and if the wheels are transmitting force to the chassis, we are talking about high piston velocities.

This means that, if we are really clever, we can use lots of low speed bump force to support the car and reduce the spring rates, thus increasing mechanical grip. At the same time, by reducing the bypass orifice to zero or near zero and playing with the stack of disc valves we can arrive at a digressive curve at high piston speeds and arrange for the valve stack to "blow off" at some value of piston velocity, thus allowing the suspension to "soak up" the forces transmitted when, for example, the driver clouts a kerb.

The right combination is not easy to find and varies from track to track - which is why the top teams carry a shock technician and a shock dyno.

The basic function of the racing shock absorber is to minimize the variations in vertical force at the tire contact patch - in other words, to be kind to the tires.

As we have noted, the driver "feels", reacts to and steers the stiffer end of the car. Again very basically, we will always (if there is such a word in racing) have more bump force on the front of the car and more rebound on the rear. The increased bump at the front will give the driver more feel, will slow down the nose dive under braking and make the turn in more positive. The reduced bump at the rear will allow the rear to settle and "comply" on corner exit. The increased rebound at the rear will keep the platform stable while the reduced (slightly) rebound at the front will keep things sensitive and give the driver feel.

Until recently we were more likely to effect the vehicle's behavior in corners with rebound adjustments than with bump. Conversely, we will modify the behavior over hills and hummocks and putting the power down with bump. We will keep the platform (both aero and mechanical) stable with rebound and with low speed bump.

There are a few basic rules. On smooth circuits with fast corners - as in Elkhart Lake or Mid Ohio - you need very little high piston speed bump control (no bumps). As the corners get slower, they will usually get bumpy and more high piston speed bump control will be needed simply because there will be bumps.

Conversely, fast smooth corners call for more rebound control - to keep the platform stable. Bumpy corners cannot stand so much lest the car jack itself down - or the wheel be unable to return fast enough to maintain compliance.

With cars lacking download we cannot stand too much rear rebound control in slow corners because, without the air speed produced download, we are liable to lift the inside rear tire and see our traction go up in smoke. Like too much download, too much overall rebound can make the car feel very secure to the inexperienced driver - but the car will be tied down "too tight to dance" and will be relatively slow.

When the circuits get bumpy, don't fall into the trap of insisting on a low ride height and stiff springs to keep the car off the ground. Go down on springs, up on ride height and run a fair amount of rebound and not much bump - let the wheels comply to the race track. It will do you no good to run low and only hit the high spots on the race track - you will hit them far too hard and, besides, your tires will not be on the track very much. Traction is everything in this business and if the tires are not in contact with the track surface, there can be no traction - forward, rearward or sideways.

The other trap to be avoided is the prevalent belief that shocks are important only on bumpy circuits. The second shock function - control of load transfers and stabilization of the platform - is equally important on smooth circuits.

BASIC PROCEDURE FOR ADJUSTING SHOCKS FOR A GIVEN CIRCUIT

The idea is to set the bump forces to suit the bumps in the critical areas - corners, corner exits and braking zones. Add bump control to minimize the upsets until the car becomes harsh and loses tire compliance and traction. Do this with the rebound adjustment near minimum. Then add rebound force, one increment at a time to "tighten up the car" and stabilize the platform - i.e. to reduce the rate of roll generation (make the car more positive) and to reduce the "Cadillac float syndrome".

Getting the base line shock settings will take some time and is for test days, not race weekends. Rebound and low piston speed bump control is so effective on the "state of the art" shocks that many teams are running without anti roll bars (which transfer load in the wrong direction) and are controlling roll with spring placement, low speed bump and rebound.

With triple adjustables, with the rebound set at guess #1, start with the low speed bump 1 increment off soft and set the high speed bump for the critical rough portions of the track. Then adjust the low speed bump

for load transfer. Basically, if the chassis is moving within the wheels, adjust the low speed bump. If the upset is being transferred to the chassis from the wheels, adjust the high speed bump.

In general, the rebound adjustment seems to respond better toward the high end of the adjustment so it is advantageous to keep the shim stack such that you are always in the upper half of the adjustment range.

Lastly, don't allow yourself to be misled by driver discomfort over bumps that don't matter. Bumps that don't matter are those that don't cause the tires to break traction or the car to bottom hard. You can effectively cure bottoming over single bumps on the straight with shock bump forces.

Dealing with multiple bumps or bumps on the critical portions of the track - i.e. braking areas, corners and corner exits require changes to either ride height or springs. If the car is uncomfortable (but not terrifying) over some bumps on the straight, either miss them by changing the line or ignore them. Concentrate on the adjustments that are going to pay off in terms of lap time.

Earlier I stated that we basically use the bump control to adjust the behavior of the car over bumps and the rebound control to adjust the load transfer characteristics (i.e. the handling or balance) of the car. This, as you might suspect, is an over simplification.

The corner entry behavior of any car can be profoundly influenced by the low piston speed bump control of the front shocks - stiffer giving a more positive turn in. Of course, the instant that the load has been transferred, the piston ceases to move and this effect goes away. Increasing the front low speed bump resistance, unlike increasing ride rate or roll resistance, will only effect the initial turn in - i.e. the period of time while the load is being transferred from the inside front tire to the outside. It often works fine on street courses. If the low and high speed bump adjustments are effectively independent, the increased low speed bump will not affect the car's behavior in reaction to upsets - even if the corner happens to be bumpy. the other hand, corner exit understeer (power on understeer or PUS) can often be reduced by increasing the front rebound forces - thus preventing the front tires from "unloading" as power is applied. The downside here is heavy steering and the possibility of "jacking down" over bumps.

Current thinking (1994), profoundly influenced by what was learned during the unlamented active ride period in Formula One, is that the low speed bump forces should be very strongly progressive with a sharp break point at the transition to high piston speed and a digressive high speed bump curve. The idea is to control load transfers with low piston speed shock forces and let the suspension move and soak up the impacts at high piston speeds - as in chatter bumps and curves. No one is using anywhere near as much rebound as we used to - the shocks are almost 50/50 and the bump/rebound curves are almost mirror images of each other. The force vs velocity curves look something like FIGURE 41. Current practice is minimum (or no) bleed, dished pistons and a non-progressive stack - the idea being to make the stack work at low speeds rather than the bleed because the stack is controllable. The dished piston is similar to rational preload in a suspension spring - deforming the valve discs allows them to hold a predetermined force until they blow off.

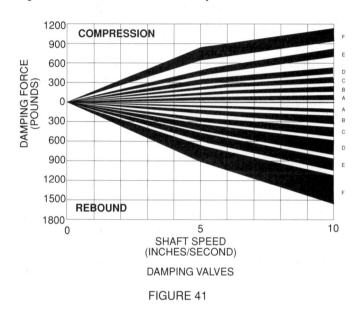

FIGURE 41

Once they overcome the preload, the valve stack is soft. The set up is digressive by nature. This will hold the platform firm but will break preload at a given piston speed and allow the suspension to become supple. So by preloading the the stack we can control harshness over bumps and curbs while retaining a stable platform on the smooth bits.

HILLS

When cars crest hills, whether or not they are turning, the rear wheels tend to unload and spin - sometimes they come off the ground and spin a lot. We have already seen that wheelspin - any wheelspin - is a bad thing. Assuming that there is sufficient rear droop travel, decreasing the rear rebound forces will often dramatically reduce wheelspin under these conditions. If the rear is droop limited (and/or pre-loaded), increasing the rebound control may help.

BUMP RUBBERS AND PACKERS

"Bump rubbers", properly used, can be a big help - particularly on bumpy race tracks. The idea is that they serve as auxiliary springs used only to keep the car from bottoming on the big bumps without having to go to heavier than optimum suspension springs. Do not use rubber. The closed cell polyurethane foams now used have the interesting property of low hysteresis (i.e. they do not return the total amount of energy used in compression) and therefore do not rebound as strongly as as a spring (the excess energy is used up in internal friction and given off as heat).

Properly shaped and adjusted, they are so progressive that the driver cannot feel the contact between the shock body and the bump rubber. Improperly shaped (cylindrical vs conical) the bump rubber effectively becomes a packer and one end of the car or the other will dart in an unpredictable fashion when contact is made. The adjustment of the bump rubbers is critical - for instance we do not want to roll onto them and suddenly increase the wheel rate at corner entry. To my mind packers are only used to adjust the height of bump rubbers.

There is a place for non-progressive bump rubbers. With download cars, when the straights are significantly faster than the corners the aero download at very high speed will compress the springs enough to drag the car on the race track. There are only three ways to prevent this - higher ride height, stiffer springs or packers.

With ground effect cars we obviously do not want to raise the right height any more than we absolutely have to. Neither do we want to run stiffer springs than necessary - that will cost us mechanical grip. Cylindrical foam bump stops, carefully adjusted for height with thin nylon packers can be useful under these conditions - just be certain that the car will not "thump" onto them in the fast corners (it's OK if they are already on them when they get to the corner).

THE FUTURE

Until the sanctioning bodies (rightly) outlawed electronic aids in general and "active" and "reactive" suspension in particular, "semi-active" shocks (or suspension units) with real electronic controls were very close to being marketed at what would have been, for racing, realistic price levels.

They would not have done everything that the active units do. They would also not have cost millions of dollars or required truly extensive development programs by the individual teams. In their most basic form they would have offered cockpit adjustable low piston speed bleed - both bump and rebound - with an option of semi active damping. The semi active units would have sensed road speed, spring compression, and accelerations. Shock forces would have been adjusted electronically to maintain a more level platform.

Another option would have been simple track mapping to change the forces according to the characteristics of the individual section of track being negotiated - softer overall wheel rates and higher ride heights for slow corners, for instance. These advanced units would have used microprocessor controls based on computer simulations of the race track - modified by real time track testing - to provide instantaneous "near optimum" resistance, force and damping levels. This is not star wars, it would have been (and may have been) available in 1994. As you would expect, I am sincerely grateful that this sort of thing has been outlawed by all of the sanctioning bodies. However, electronic feedback loops and controls are not absolutely necessary for "semi active" shock force and ride height control - it can only be a matter of time until hydraulic flow control valves are built into the units. Look for considerably more advanced racing shock absorbers to become available to a very few teams in the immediate future.

There is a lot of lap time in shock absorbers - but it takes a lot of thought, a lot of testing and a lot of work to find it. While I do not believe that shocks can be truly optimized for any given circuit without on board data gathering - and knowledgeable interpretation of the gathered data - intelligent driver debriefing combined with experienced eyes watching the car on the race track will get you 90% of the way.

The day of the shock absorber as we have known it is done (as is the day of the coil spring). The day of the pneumatic/hydraulic suspension unit is just beginning. To see the future, watch 1994 tapes of Stefan Johannson's 1993 Penske Indy Car as compared to any other car on the track. No darting, smooth as silk, incredible tire compliance. The car used Ken Anderson's first generation pneumatic suspension units (air springs) with his Quantum dampers. Rumor has it that a major Indy team recently did a real back to back at Mid-Ohio and found a repeatable 1.0 second advantage.

As I said, the day of the coil spring suspension is over. Very soon we will see pneumatic/oil suspension systems which will allow instant in-pit changes to wheel rates, rate curves and damping. Again, all of this came about because of what people learned during the active ride period.

19

"Diffs aren't important any more; we have so much download that they don't matter."
– Formula One designer who has never won a race.

THE RACING DIFFERENTIAL

Like the interest in torsional rigidity, emphasis on the importance of the differential in racing has been cyclical. There have been periods when designers and teams felt that the diff was crucial and there have been periods when they felt that it was unimportant. It seems to me that, like torsional rigidity, the characteristics and performance of the differential in the racing car are always of critical importance.

BASICS

Let's begin by examining the function of the diff - why do we need the damned thing at all?

We need some sort of differential because the automobile (as opposed to the motorcycle) is a dual track vehicle with a finite (and considerable) distance between the wheels on the left side and those on the right. When an automobile (racing or road going) deviates from a straight line to go around a corner, the wheels on the outside of the turn must travel a greater linear distance than those on the inside and must therefore turn at a faster rotational speed. The wider the vehicle's track and the shorter the corner radius, the greater will the differential in wheel speed.

On a non-driven axle this makes no difference. The wheels on opposite sides of the vehicle are not connected to each other. The rotational speed of each wheel is therefore independent from that of its axle mate. With a driven axle, however, each wheel must be connected to the power source. In any turn, therefore, if no provision is made for "differential action", the inner wheel, although it is covering a lesser linear distance, must rotate at the same speed as the outer.

Since lateral load transfer ensures that the outer wheel will be more heavily loaded, it will revolve at the rate dictated by its linear path and the inner will literally be dragged along in a combination of rotation and drag. This "dragging" of the inside tire on a driven axle is not acceptable from the points of view of comfort, control, tire wear and drive line reliability.

Accordingly, automobiles have historically been fitted with differentials which allow the driven wheels to rotate at differing speeds. In every differential that I know of the driving torque follows the same path, as is illustrated by FIGURE 42.

Engine torque is transmitted through the clutch and the gear train to a pinion gear. The pinion drives a ring gear which is bolted to the differential housing. The housing transmits the torque to the differential unit which is fitted with "side gears" (sometimes termed "end gears"). The side gears are splined to axles or half shafts which drive the wheels.

The torque path is: engine, clutch, gear train, pinion, ring gear, differential housing, differential, side gears, axles, wheels, tires. The gear train and the ring and pinion set multiply the torque.

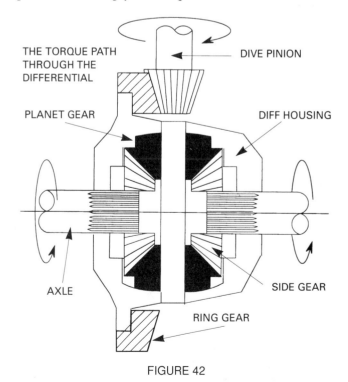

THE TORQUE PATH THROUGH THE DIFFERENTIAL

DIVE PINION

PLANET GEAR

DIFF HOUSING

AXLE

SIDE GEAR

RING GEAR

FIGURE 42

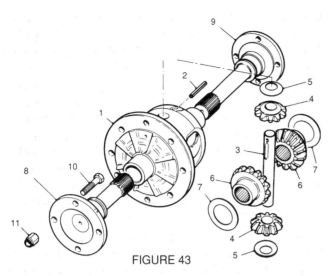

FIGURE 43

EXPLODED VIEW OF A CONVENTIONAL HEWLAND OPEN DIFFERENTIAL.
1: HOUSING. 2: SELOC PIN. 3: CROSS SHAFT. 4: STAR WHEEL.
5: DISHED WASHER. 6: GEAR WHEEL. 7: FLAT WASHER. 8: DRIVESHAFT.
9: DRIVE SHAFT. 10: DRIVE SHAFT BOLT. 11: NYLOC NUT.

Most passenger cars are fitted with "open" differentials - illustrated by FIGURE 43. These devices are "force balancers" that direct equal amounts of torque to each drive axle while allowing them to rotate at different speeds.

In the open differential, schematically illustrated by FIGURE 44, an axle or half shaft is splined to each bevel "side gear". The side gears are supported by and free to turn in the differential case. A "differential pinion shaft" is located in the housing between the two side gears and perpendicular to them. In this configuration, when the differential housing is turned it will revolve around the side gears. The differential pinion shaft will revolve with the case but the side gears and the axles will not turn and the vehicle will not move.

In FIGURE 45, we have added two differential pinion bevel gears - mounted on (and free to turn on) the differential pinion shaft. The pinions are in mesh with the side gears. Now, as the differential housing revolves, the differential pinion shaft and pinions move with it.

OPEN DIFFERENTIAL CASE, PINION SHAFT, SIDE GEARS AND AXLES

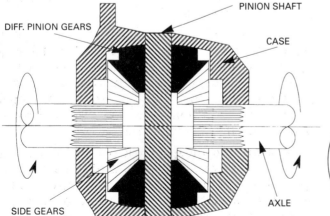

FIGURE 44

DIFFERENTIAL PINION GEARS MOUNTED
ON SHAFT AND DRIVING SIDE GEARS

FIGURE 45

FIGURE 46

OPEN DIFFERENTIAL IN STRAIGHT LINE RUNNING BELOW TRACTION
LIMIT. DIFFERENTIAL PINION SHAFT AND GEARS ROTATE AS A UNIT.
PINIONS PULL BOTH END GEARS BUT DO NOT TURN ON PINION SHAFT.
NO RELATIVE MOTION BETWEEN PINION GEAR TEETH AND END GEAR
TEETH. AXLE SPEEDS EQUAL.

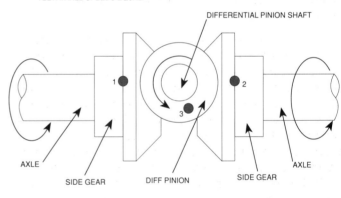

FIGURE 47

OPEN DIFFERENTIAL IN TURN CONDITION. BOTH END GEARS MOVE
FORWARD, BUT GEAR 2 (ON OUTSIDE OF TURN) REVOLVES FASTER
THAN GEAR 1. PINION GEAR TURNS ON PINION SHAFT, ROTATING IN
MESH WITH BOTH END GEARS. DOT ON END GEAR 2 HAS MOVED
FORWARD - AHEAD OF PINION GEAR - WHILE DOT ON INBOARD GEAR
LAGS BEHIND.

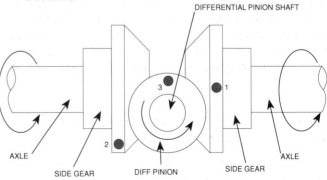

Since the pinion gears are meshed with the side gears, they drive the side gears, axles and wheels with them.

In straight line running (up to the limit of tire adhesion) as illustrated by FIGURE 46, the differential pinions and the side gears move with the housing. There is no relative motion between the teeth of the pinions and those of the side gears. The marks numbered 1, 2 and 3 revolve together.

When the car enters a turn - FIGURE 47 - the pinions continue to revolve with the housing. Since the outside tire must turn faster than its mate on the inside of the turn, the outboard side gear rotates faster than the inboard. The differential pinions, in addition to pulling on the side gears, now begin to rotate on their shaft. This rotation allows the pinions to compensate for the difference in rotational speed of the side gears - while continuing to drive both side gears. This differential action is self adjusting to any variation in axle speed - but only until one wheel begins to slip.

When one wheel begins to slip or to spin, the housing will continue to rotate the pinions but, instead of driving both side gears, the pinions will take the path of least resistance, rotate on their shaft and "walk" around the axle connected to the wheel with the most traction. All of the torque will be directed toward the spinning wheel.

Under "normal" conditions the open differential is a perfectly satisfactory device, delivering uninterrupted power to each driven wheel and providing smooth differential action when needed. However, when the available torque exceeds the tractive capacity of the driven tires, either through a decrease in the frictional characteristics of the road surface, through lateral load transfer or through an excess of torque (or any combination thereof), all of the power will be delivered to the tire with the least amount of grip. This leads to wheelspin and reduction of both traction and control.

With the road going passenger car this is normally a concern only under conditions of severely reduced traction - sand, rain, snow or ice. The power to weight ratio of the racing car, however, combined with the extreme lateral load transfer achieved under racing conditions, makes inside wheelspin almost a given when exiting slow and medium speed corners. Having said that, I must also state that under certain conditions, the open diff can work very well on racing cars. More on this later.

A LITTLE BIT OF HISTORY - OR MORE THAN A COMMON LANGUAGE SEPARATES US

In the early years of the twentieth century every town in the United States boasted a dirt oval track used for the plebian sport of harness horse racing. They are still visible from the air. It was only natural that the infant sport of auto racing would evolve around these readily available and almost indestructible facilities. Our paved ovals are the direct descendants of these dirt tracks.

On the typical oval track the corners have very similar radii and degrees of banking. By using rear tires of different diameters ("stagger") the problems of inside tire drag in corners can be eliminated and the cars can be given a natural tendency to turn left. A differential is therefore not needed. American oval track cars evolved around the solid differential or "spool". The spool is light, inexpensive and reliable. It is also a bit hard on axles and axle joints of every type.

In Europe horse racing took place on grass surfaced tracks (rightly so, turf is much less damaging to the horses' legs). The thought of noisy smoking automobiles churning up the carefully nurtured racing surface was inconceivable to those who governed the sport of kings.

Racing on the eastern side of the Atlantic began on the public roads and progressed to the artificial road circuits used today.

Tire stagger does not work when the corners are taken in both directions and/or at widely varying speeds. The "spool" or "locked" rear end is usually a most unsatisfactory device for road racing - basically because the dragging inside wheel causes extreme corner entry understeer. The solution is to unload the inside rear tire on corner entry - by restricting droop travel, by an extreme rear anti roll bar, by a lot of shock absorber droop force or by some combination of the three.

The trouble with all of these is that each of them leads to difficulties both in putting the power to the road properly at the exit of slow corners and during the transition from two wheel to one wheel drive and back again. The higher the power to weight ratio, the greater the problem (which is why spools have been used successfully in Formula Three cars on selected circuits - no power and lots of grip).

Yes, Porsche did use a spool in the 917 and in many versions of the 962 - in the sole interest of reliability. No driver ever preferred the spool and in every back-to-back test, limited slips were faster. Used with tire stagger, the spool causes a significant amount of straight line tire drag - which must be a bad thing in terms of both acceleration and top speed.

Proponents of the spool hold out a final advantage - in the case of survivable one wheel drive line failure the spool brings the car back to the pits for repairs. This is stated to be of great interest in long distance races - and so it is. The fatal flaw in the argument is that this ability is not unique to the spool. Any of the lockers provide one wheel drive and most of the limited slips, driven gently, will also bring you home.

Along those lines, the last disadvantage of the spool is that, should a drive shaft or drive shaft joint fail under power, the car will turn in the direction away from the failure at unbelievable speed and with inconceivable violence. There is no recovery.

THE NEED

What is needed, then, is a differential capable of limiting unladen wheel tire spin (or slip as the boffins term it) under high torque loads but which will allow differential wheel speed in corner entry and low torque applications. There are several such devices available. Generically they are usually termed "limited slip differentials" although, to quote Pete Weismann; "They are limited and they slip."

The term is less than all encompassing. Functionally these diffs can be divided into three distinct groups: limited slips, torque sensing differentials and self locking differentials. As the terms suggest, limited slips limit wheelspin to varying degrees; lockers lock the drive axles together under acceleration and torque sensors bias the amount of torque delivered to each drive axle according to how much traction is instantaneously available at each tire.

All of the limited slips and torque sensors function by delivering the majority (or all) of the input torque to the wheel with the most traction. The ratio between the maximum amount of torque that a given differential can deliver to the tire with the most traction and the amount of torque that can be accepted by the unloaded tire is termed the "bias ratio" and is expressed as a ratio with respect to unity.

A differential with a maximum bias ratio of 4:1 can, therefore, deliver four times more torque to the tire with the most traction than can be supported by the tire with the least traction. Lockers, like spools, lock the driven wheels together and have a bias ratio of infinity. As a point of interest, the open differential also has torque biasing capability, but it is very low - typically around 1.5:1.

The optimum bias ratio is a factor of available torque, suspension design, tire characteristics, corner radius and just about anything else that one can think of. Typically, with the limited slips, higher bias ratios lead to increased understeer. For this reason, it is as well if limited slips are field adjustable. With torque sensors there is no need for field adjustability and with lockers there is no possibility.

THE CAM AND PAWL LIMITED SLIP

I believe that the late Dr. Ferdinand Porsche was the first to arrive at a practical solution to the wheelspin problem by fitting his landmark 1934 Auto Union Grand Prix car with a ZF cam and pawl "limited slip" differential. This unit biases the torque toward the tire with the most traction.

The current generation of this device, illustrated by FIGURE 48, consists of concentric inner and outer cams. The inner cam is splined to the left side drive axle while the outer floats in the housing and is splined to the right side drive axle. A series of pawls or, in the US, "chicklets" is captured between the cams and located by a "cage". The cage is integral with the housing and consequently with the ring gear. The cage drives both the inner and outer cams through the pawls.

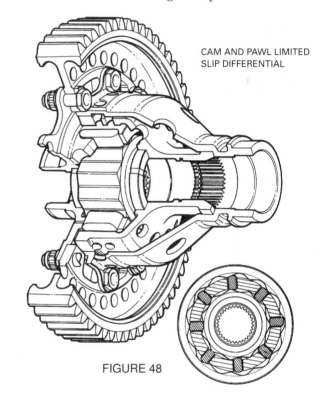

CAM AND PAWL LIMITED SLIP DIFFERENTIAL

FIGURE 48

Under normal straight line conditions the inner and outer cams rotate at the same speed, the pawls wedge between the inner and outer cams and the diff is inactive. In turn conditions under low torque the pawls slip between the cams and allow differential action - the effect is the same as an open diff. Under heavy torque loads, lateral load transfer or in conditions of reduced traction, when one wheel starts to overspeed, the cam splined to that axle increases speed - partially wedging the pawls between the inner and outer cams and limiting the amount of slip that can take place.

The pawls actually "ratchet" between the cams - allowing some slip. The amount of allowed slip can be varied by the design of the cams - but only within narrow limits. The best that can be hoped for is a bias ratio of about 3:1 - a 75% lock - when everything is new. Note that the device acts to limit slip only after the slip has begun.

The cam and pawl has a lot of things going for it. It is light and it has a low moment of rotational inertia. Its on and off characteristics are progressive and benign, making it easy to drive. It causes no instability or tire drag understeer on the over-run or corner entry - making "trail braking" stable. Its locking action is very "soft" or progressive. There are no surprises lurking within the cam and pawl. For this reason it is the chosen diff of a number of Formula One teams who cannot afford to do much testing.

There are also disadvantages. 75% lock up is the maximum. The rear of the car may tend to feel a little unstable under heavy torque loads - especially on a bumpy track. The major disadvantage, however, lies in the suicidal nature of the device.

Its mechanical design ensures that the cam and pawl is inherently self destructive. When the thing is working, the hardened steel pawls ratchet between the hardened steel cams, ensuring a high rate of wear and a constantly decreasing amount of limiting. The more the parts wear, the more inside wheelspin develops and the more the parts wear. It is the automotive equivalent of the graveyard spiral. In the wet the wear rate approaches infinity.

Some of the proprietary dry film lubricating processes (Neo Seal among them) and the better molybdenum disulfide additive greases prolong life somewhat, but parts replacement is constant and expensive. Frequent dis-assembly, cleaning and repacking the moly is a must - the grease tends to centrifuge out.

The decreasing efficiency is a bit difficult for the inexperienced driver to detect and one may well find oneself wondering where the lap time has gone. If the peaks of the inner cam are worn more than .010" or .015" you can bet that performance has deteriorated. The parts are not easy to make. We sometimes run into brand new inner cams that are tapered in side elevation - with attendant unfortunate performance and accelerated wear.

THE "CLUTCH PACK" LIMITED SLIP DIFFERENTIAL

Clutch packs or "plate diffs" have been around for a long time. As shown in FIGURE 49, they are basically an open diff with a series of friction discs splined alternately to the diff housing and to each side gear.

The early street versions of the clutch pack wear fairly unsatisfactory in that if they had enough locking action to do any good they tended to be pretty fierce in action and to wear quickly. They also sent all of the torque to the tire with the least grip. Those clutch packs that feature either cone clutches or springs are still unsatisfactory. In the past few years, however, thanks to a lot of work by Mike Endean at Xtrac and by Hewland,

CLUTCH PACK LIMITED SLIP DIFFERENTIAL

FIGURE 49

the Salisbury limited slip and its close cousin, the Hewland Powr Flow, have become the most common of all racing units.

Although the mechanical design details differ between Xtrac and Hewland, functionally the two units are identical. Engine torque is transferred through the pinion to the ring gear which is bolted to the differential housing. "Ramps" or "cams" are splined to the I.D. of the housing. Torque is transmitted from the housing to the "ramps" to the differential pinion shafts (Xtrac) or trunnions (Hewland) and thus to the pinions. The beveled pinions and side gears are thrust apart as soon as any torque develops (i.e. as soon as the car moves). The more the torque, the greater the spreading force.

Since the ramps are in angular contact with the bevel gears, the spreading force is transferred as a function of ramp angle. The spreading load from the bevel gears through the ramps presses the friction discs together resisting the overspeeding of either axle - or limiting slip.

The torque path, illustrated by FIGURE 50, is pinion, ring gear, differential housing, ramp body (radial drive), pinion gear, side gears, ramp cam (spreading load), clutch discs, axle shaft. As the limiting action is a direct function of the spreading force exerted by the bevel

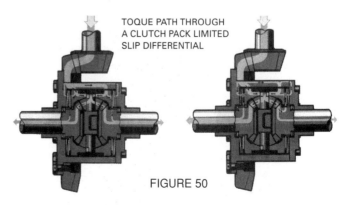

TOQUE PATH THROUGH
A CLUTCH PACK LIMITED
SLIP DIFFERENTIAL

FIGURE 50

gears and thus of engine torque, when properly set up the unit functions progressively and smoothly.

The bias ratio or amount of lock up is dependent upon four major variables:

1) Driving torque.
2) The "order of stacking" or number of "active" clutches employed. Typically, as shown by FIGURE D-10 we get our choice between one and six active clutches. As you would suspect, more active clutches give more lock up.
3) The material used in the friction discs.
4) The angle of the ramps. This angle determines how much of the driving torque is directed axially against the friction discs.

As is also illustrated by FIGURE 50, of the available ramps the 30 degree variation transmits the most spreading load or clamping force to the friction discs and the 90 degree ramp transmits the least. Since we want minimum lock up under braking, especially trail braking, typically we use an 80 or 85 degree ramp on the coast side ramp with a 45 degree ramp on the power or drive side.

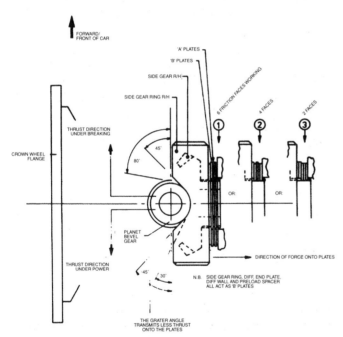

TUNING THE HEWLAND POWERFLOW CLUTCH PACK (VIEWED FROM ABOVE), BY MEANS OF RAMP ANGLES AND NUMBER OF ACTIVE CLUTCHES. THE LEAST SPREADING LOAD IS TRANSMITTED BY THE 90deg RAMP, THE GREATEST BY THE 30deg VARIATION.

FIGURE 51

The original 90 degree coast ramps tended to chip and have largely been replaced by 85 degree units. For faster corners with more download some teams use 60/30 ramps. I have never been happy with 45/45 (too much corner entry and mid-phase understeer), but I know some very successful people who are - in the UK.

I don't know anyone who likes them in slow corners or on bumpy courses. Personally, I cannot conceive of using any ramp of less than 80 degrees on the coast side.

Currently many successful teams are using 80/80 ramps with little or no preload, depending on the spreading forces of the bevel gears to limit the slip. This is a very benign set up if there are no really slow hairpins (or not much available torque).

By juggling ramp angles, preload and the number of active clutches, the bias ratio can be changed from that of an open diff to that of a spool - remembering always that more lock up permits less differentiation and therefore causes more trailing throttle understeer.

The most common misconception with these units is that the amount of preload on the clutch plates is a primary determining factor of the amount of lock up. It can be, but things are a lot better if it is not. The spreading force of the bevel gears is an order of magnitude greater than any conceivable preload.

To my mind, minimum preload should be used only to ensure that the diff's transitional characteristics from power off to power on remain consistent and that the unit will limit slip when one wheel is completely unloaded. One of the problems with the clutch packs - especially on road cars and with sedans - is that, when a driving tire is completely unloaded, the diff functions on preload only - the ramps don't come into it. This probably explains why those racing cars that use rear droop limiting and/or spring preload run lots of preload in the diff.

The preload is adjusted by shimming the friction discs. I have had better results measuring preload with a depth micrometer or with a feeler gauge than with a torque wrench. Having said this, however, I must admit that I usually run no preload at all - I find that the galling of the friction plates is considerably reduced and that the unit is more consistent without it. I run either 45/85 or 80/80 ramps depending on the car and the track and I am real fussy about what oil I use (currently Neo's "Jaguar" 75/90 gear oil).

THE INTER MOTION POWER LOCK DIFFERENTIAL

My major objection to the clutch pack or plate limited slip differential has always been what I perceive as a lack of consistency - especially in the transitional period from over-run to power on. Percentage of lock up and the time required to achieve it are functions of ramp angle and preload. Preload is a function of temperature and plate wear. Effective ramp angle produced spreading force is a variable function of trunnion point load against ramps, of bevel gear wear - etc, etc, etc...

Wear of any or all of the components is liable to change the operating characteristics of the diff during the race - or during the practice period. When the car's power down performance changes one is never quite sure whether one is chasing chassis, tires or diff. While the Salisbury/Powr Flow units are the most adjustable of the limited slips, in order to change any of the variables it is necessary to remove the unit from the car which delays testing and simply cannot be done during a practice or qualifying session.

The clever devils at Inter Motion have figured out a couple of things. First they determined, as I have, that there was no operating condition in road racing where any differential characteristic other than completely open would be advantageous under braking or over-run conditions and so they stopped even considering any coast ramp other then 90 degrees. This simplified the exercise considerably.

They then considered the power down end of things and theorized that, at least under the typical UK and Continental environment of fast corners and smooth road surfaces, a conveniently adjustable preload would be the most practical solution to the efficient optimization of differential characteristics for prevailing operating parameters and weather conditions. They have done so by making the number of planetary bevel gear pairs variable (one pair or two), by mounting then in a carrier and by very cleverly making the preload quickly and precisely adjustable (within limits) from outside the housing.

Testing indicates that "hook up" is, for practical purposes, independent of the power side ramp angle (at least under UK and Continental operating conditions). This means that meaningful changes can be effected during a practice or qualifying session and, therefore, that the optimum overall setup should be able to be more closely approximated than with other diffs. In addition, changes can be made on the grid in the event of rain or even of extreme temperature change.

In prototype form this diff has been around for a while. As a well kept secret it has achieved notable success in several series. It is now commercially available in several sizes.

THE EMCO LIMITED SLIP DIFFERENTIAL

As I have pointed out, in the plate or clutch pack limited slip differential, the clamping action on the friction plates is the result of the spreading force exerted on the side gears by the spyders or planet gears and the major purpose of the ramps or cams is to regulate how much of this spreading force is apportioned to the acceleration and deceleration (over-run) parts of the equation. I also stated that one of the major difficulties with the units is a lack of consistency in operation - largely caused by wear of the ramp faces, spyder and side gears.

FIGURE 52 – EMCO LIMITED SLIP DIFFERENTIAL

Emco Gears, the respected Chicago based gear manufacturer, designed the Emco Gear.94 differential to rectify these problems (FIGURE 52). The problems of wear and stress related failure are addressed through the use of the latest aerospace design, materials and manufacturing processes. The ramp wear problem is done away with by the simple expedient of deleting the ramps completely.

The Gear.94 differential utilizes the spreading force of the spyder and side gears to clamp the friction plates directly - without going through ramps.

The unit is assembled without preload, in fact the stack specification is .005/.007 loose. Under braking the reverse load transmitted through the drive shafts generates a light spreading force which forces the end caps outward, taking up the clearance and generating a light drag on the clutch stack which stabilizes the rear of the car. This drag is light enough to allow the unit to differentiate and thus allow the car to turn in freely.

On the over-run and under neutral throttle conditions the unit is an open differential - there is no differential-caused understeer at the apex of slow corners or during the transition from power off to power on.

As soon as significant power is applied the spreading force of the spyder and side gears applies a clamping force on the friction plates which is proportional to the amount of torque being applied and the unit becomes a very effective limited slip differential. Under full power the unit is locked. The degree of lock up is adjusted by varying the number of active clutches.

Less complicated and lighter than the other clutch packs, the Emco Gear.94 differential was extensively tested in Indy Cars and registered its first win (Jacques Villeneuve) at Road America in 1994. The unit is currently available to fit Indy Cars, Indy Lights and Formula Atlantic Cars. I hope to test this unit in the near future, hopefully against an Xtrac viscous coupling unit.

RELIABILITY OF THE PLATE DIFF

The only reliability problem normally experienced with plate diffs occurs when the differential pinion gears wear and move inwards - reducing the bearing area of the ramps. This inevitably leads to fractured ramps and unpleasantness - see FIGURE 53. The solution is to keep an eye on things and to replace the bevel gears before it happens. Genius is not required.

FIGURE 53 – FRACTURE CLUTCH PACK RAMP

The friction discs do wear and the preload should be checked and re-adjusted as necessary. Gas nitriding the discs cuts the wear by an order of magnitude. The plates can also gall - usually due to excessive preload. Gas nitriding helps this condition as well. Carbon/carbon friction discs have not, to my knowledge, been tried, probably because of the frangible nature of the material and the necessarily small size and area of the splines.

Embarrassment occurs when the ramps are installed backwards. Don't laugh, it has happened to the best and most experienced of teams. Me, I refer to FIGURE 51 every time the diff goes together.

These units have the advantages of availability, adjustability, moderate mass and a low moment of rotating inertia. The trade offs between ramp angles and number of active clutches makes it possible to tailor the diff to suit most circuits pretty well - although some diff caused corner entry understeer will always be present. The big trick is getting the device to behave properly when changing direction quickly - as in chicanes or short esses. My initial information indicates that the Emco unit has no troubles in this department.

HYDRAULIC CONTROL

It is also possible to use hydraulic control to exert the clamping force. Nissan Technologies raced a hydraulic diff in IMSA GTP for several seasons and there are several hydraulic diffs in use in Europe, with electronic control. No one is willing to say very much about them.

THE GERODISC

The Gerodisc limited slip (FIGURE 54) from ASHA Corporation, Santa Barbara, California is a speed sensitive differential utilizing a gerotor oil pump to load a clutch pack.

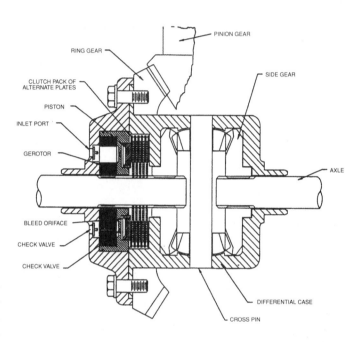

CROSS SECTION THROUGH THE GERODISC
FIGURE 54

The pump is included in the diff housing with the rotor driven by one axle and the stator integral with the case. It is therefore activated by differential wheel speed. So long as wheel speed is identical, no pressure is generated. When one wheel overspeeds pressure is generated by the pump and, through suitable circuitry, exerts clamping force on the plates. The amount of clamping force is proportional to the overspeed.

The input volume of the pump is controlled by fixed inlet ports and the outlet pressure is controlled by variable discharge orifices. One way check valves are incorporated on both sides of the pump. The hydraulic pressure developed by the pump activates a piston which compresses a conventional clutch pack.

Since the pump speed is directly proportional to differential wheel speed, so is the bias ratio. Engagement should be smooth. The characteristics of the device can be tailored to expected operating conditions by varying either the clutch pack or the pump output. Remote hydraulic control could be adapted.

The unit should be compatible with ABS and traction control and appears to be suited to front wheel drive, rear wheel drive and all wheel drive. Its major advantages would appear to be smoothness and automatic variation of bias ratio. At the time of writing the unit has had a very successful debut in Indy Cars.

THE VISCOUS DIFF

The viscous coupling type of limited slip differential is virtually unknown in the United States. This is a pity as the viscous diff may very well be the wave of the future. Illustrated by FIGURE 55, the output shafts and the diff case are splined to alternate perforated discs - in the same manner as the clutch plates in a plate diff. The unit is filled with a silicon based viscous fluid which resists shearing in some magical fashion. When one wheel tries to markedly overspeed, the resistance of the fluid to shearing inhibits the relative motion between the alternate discs and so limits the slip.

VISCOUS DIFF

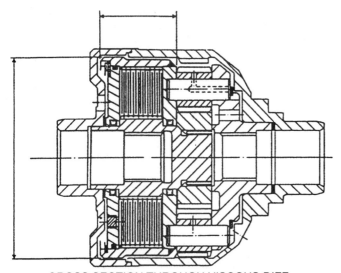

CROSS SECTION THROUGH VISCOUS DIFF

FIGURE 55

Understanding nothing of chemistry, I think of the viscous coupling as chains of molecules holding hands through the holes in the plates. Like us, the molecules get stronger with exercise. The amount of lockup and the characteristic shape of the torque biasing curve can be varied by the number of plates, the number and configuration of holes, the amount of fluid (density of pack) and by altering the characteristics of the fluid.

On our side of the water, at least, there is a popular misconception that the fluid's resistance to shear increases with heat build up. This is simply not true. The resistance increases with shearing effort - like I said, molecular magic. There is a further misconception that the units are temperature sensitive. Wrong again. Within the design operating range (roughly 70 degrees C. to 150 degrees C.) the viscous coupling is remarkably stable.

Temperature does, however, play an important part in a condition termed the "hump mode". Like any differential, the viscous will generate a lot of heat when there is a prolonged period of speed difference between the driven wheels. This heat causes thermal expansion of the viscous fluid - which pushes the metal plates together. The resulting metal to metal contact allows the transfer of significantly higher torques than can occur in the viscous mode and results in improved traction under such extreme conditions. The time of slip until the onset of the hump mode can be controlled in manufacture by varying the volume of the viscous fluid within the coupling (density of pack).

Viscous diffs are manufactured by the million by GKN Axles - for passenger vehicle use. FF Developments manufactures both road going and racing units. While the best known racing application of the FF Developments diff is in Super Touring cars, Xtrac has its own version which has been successful in both Formula One (Tyrrell) and CART (Penske).

The viscous diff is equally suited to front wheel drive, rear wheel drive and four wheel drive. It offers some important advantages over its mechanical cousins. It is light and has a low moment of rotational inertia.

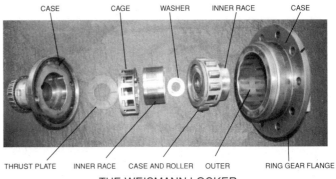

CASE   CAGE   WASHER   INNER RACE   CASE

THRUST PLATE   INNER RACE   CASE AND ROLLER   OUTER   RING GEAR FLANGE

THE WEISMANN LOCKER

FIGURE 56

Properly designed for the application it is more consistent than the clutch packs. It is the most tunable of all the diffs (although not in the field). It may well be the racing diff of the future.

THE TORQUE SENSING DIFFS

Limited slip diffs are differential wheel speed sensitive. In other words, one tire has to lose traction before the unit begins to function. Torque sensing differentials direct increased torque to the tire with the most traction before the other tire exceeds its traction limit and starts to spin. They actually split the available torque between the drive axles in proportion to the amount of traction instantaneously available to each. The theoretical advantages are obvious.

THE WEISMANN LOCKER

In the Sixties and Seventies virtually every winning race car in the world, Formula One, Formula Two, Indy Cars, Can Am, Formula 5000, Trans Am and Manufacturers' Cup used the Weismann Locker - a true torque sensing locking differential. Even though they have been out of production for a decade, a few remain and a few teams still use them. I would if I could but the Weismann family appears to have no intention of making them again. However, because I believe in the unit, because marrying a Weismann to a Viscous Coupling would result in the ideal diff and because a well known Formula One designer has recently shown interest, I will describe the Weismann Locker - just in case...

Illustrated by Figure 56, the Weismann essentially consists of two one-way sprague clutches, each of which consists of an inner cam, an outer cam, a series of cylindrical rollers and a roller cage. The individual inner cams are each splined to a drive axle. The profiled outer cam is a unit with the diff carrier and the ring gear. The rollers are captured between the cams and located by cages. The cages are lightly preloaded to the inner cams by a spring captured in the inner end of each cage.

The cages themselves are each keyed to a strong "C" spring located between the inner cams so that they cannot rotate independently of each other. The inner cams are preloaded against paper clutch plates located between the outboard ends of the inner cams and the housing. This allows the inner cams to rotate with respect to the housing/outer cam without galling parts. The preload is effected by a central belleville washer.

Under trailing throttle (over-run) conditions, there is not enough torque to force the rollers up onto the outer cam. Under differential wheel speeds they roll on the surface of the inner cams and the diff is, for all practical purposes, open. When engine torque is applied any attempt by one wheel to overspeed forces the rollers, hard, against the ramps of the outer cam. This wedges the rollers like crazy against the inner cams and the unit is locked - no slip at all. So the Weismann is open on the over-run and locked under power - the ideal combination.

Since the Weismann locks 100% there is a significant performance advantage lurking there - especially for cars featuring high power to weight ratios and limited download. In order to take full advantage of all that the unit has to offer, one basic rule has to be applied. Never apply power in a corner while there is any understeer lock on the car.

If you break this rule, the thrust from the inside rear wheel will drive you into the wall - right now. This means that the driver must be aggressive with the car on corner entry. Because the car will use the full potential of both rear tires for acceleration, the chassis can be set up with less corner entry and mid-phase understeer than would normally be the case - we don't need as much excess rear tyre capacity. This sounds complex and might seem a lot for the driver to remember but in practice it all happens pretty automatically.

The disadvantages of the Weismann, other than availability, are its weight (in between the cam & pawl and the Salisbury) and its sensitivity to lubricants. Like any one way clutch, the Weismann functions by friction. The current generation of gear lubes typically contain heavy doses of friction modifiers which can cause the rollers to skid on the inner cams - we used to call it "popping". The sensation is exceedingly unpleasant for the driver.

Any amount at all of Molybdenum disulfide or like compounds will render the Weismann diff completely inoperative. The trick used to be a straight mineral-based 75W90 gear oil with 10% of Lubrizol Corporation's "Anglomal 99" added. Shell blended it for years under the numbers SL7923 in the US and SL6909 in the UK. As near as I can tell SWEPCO 101 is the same stuff. It smells like long dead fish. Gears and Weismann diffs love it. I have no idea how the unit would react to a synthetic oil - and neither does Pete Weismann. I suspect not very well.

Under normal conditions the Weismann offers no real advantage to the car/driver combination that is not traction limited at some point on the circuit. However, there are a couple of conditions under which the Weismann is pure magic. The first is when we drop one driven wheel off the track. Since any wheelspin will be on both wheels there is no loss of directional control and, so long as the driver keeps his foot in it, there will not be a control problem. The other magic moments are in the wet, for the same reasons.

THE TORSEN

Like the Weismann, the Torsen ("TORque SENsing) diff has been around for a long time. Unlike the Weismann, for the first several decades of its life, it was unsuccessful - the concept and design were ahead of the manufacturing capability of the inventor. Mike Hewland (on whom blessings be) once told me that, "Gleason wrote the book on gears in the 1920s, all we have learned since then is metallurgy."

The Torsen, designed by Mr. Gleasman, is now manufactured by Zexel-Gleason Inc. It is very successful in the high performance OEM market and has been used with success in racing. Shown in FIGURE 57, it is a gearing based differential. It operates on the fact that worm gears can "efficiently" transmit torque in one direction only - in the other direction they generate huge amounts of friction. The function is complex and difficult to understand.

TORSEN DIFF

FIGURE 57

Like most differentials, the Torsen is fitted with side gears which are splined to the drive axles and free to rotate in the housing. Unlike most differentials, however, there are no bevel gears. Instead the side gears are "invex" or worm gears driven by (usually) three sets of planetary worms (termed element gears) attached to and rotating both with and on the differential case.

Drive torque on the ring gear is transmitted through the housing to the element gears to the side gears and finally to the drive axles. The axial forces imposed on the element gears are converted by the "invex" or worm gear mesh to axial thrust components acting on the side gears and their mating thrust washers.

When a torque imbalance at the tires tries to rotate the end gears at different speeds, because worm gears are capable of efficiently transmitting torque in one direction only, the frictional resistance in the worm gears resists the differential rotation. The unit thus senses the traction available at each wheel and splits the drive torque proportionally.

Like the Weismann, the Torsen is a torque sensing diff - it will react to unequal traction conditions and bias the input torque toward the laden wheel before the unladen wheel exceeds its limit of traction. Unlike the Weismann it does not fully lock under power. The bias ratio of the Torsen can be altered from about 2.5:1 to 6:1 by altering the design features. The bias ratio between drive and over-run can also be modified in the design phase. It is not field adjustable.

The major disadvantages of the Torsen, aside from availability, are its mass and the friction involved. There are a lot of gears in there. They are, of necessity, located at the periphery of the unit. The result is a high moment of rotational inertia and the flywheel effect is noticeable - especially in relatively low powered cars. Given enough money, some of this could be relieved by using a heavily heat treated high alloy steel or titanium casing.

The unit functions by dynamic friction. When the diff is differentiating under load, friction between all those gear surfaces generates a lot of heat and can result in a significant power loss during part of the corner exit phase. Again, these are problems only with racing cars featuring relatively low power - when there is enough torque to effectively lock the unit there is no loss. They are not problems at all in high performance street cars.

In the original Torsens, the friction led to heavy and premature wear. Improved gear design and metallurgy, courtesy of Gleason, and the advent of sophisticated synthetic gear oils has cured that. A very specific set of directions must be followed for disassembly and assembly.

The major loads on the worm gears in the Torsen are spreading loads. The OEM units are manufactured with a ductile iron case. Cast iron is strong in compression. It is relatively weak in tension. The ductile iron case Torsen diff, as produced by Gleason, while perfectly suitable for passenger car applications, is a basic fragmentation grenade in many racing cars - especially those featuring big tires and lots of aerodynamic download.

The steel cased units produced for a time by Richard Pare at Indianapolis Competition Parts are excellent units but did not use Gleason's latest technology and are no longer manufactured. Zexel-Gleason has indicated some willingness to work with racers - especially manufacturers.

The production Torsen has achieved great success as the splitter or transfer diff in four wheel drive street cars - notably the Audi line. Peugeot uses it at the rear of the 405 while Toyota uses it on the Turbo Supra - as does Porsche on the 968. Even the U.S. Military uses them - on the Hummer. More to our point, it seems probable that the Torsen could have a lot to with the impeccable handling of my favorite affordable road car - the Mazda RX-7 Turbo.

Zexel-Gleason has recently introduced the Torsen II, a simplified, less expensive and lighter parallel axis design featuring state of the art gear design, metallurgy and heat treating. The Torsen II is compatible with automatic transmission fluids and is designed specifically for relatively low torque biasing applications such as front wheel drive passenger cars and four wheel drive transfer cases.

THE DETROIT LOCKER

The Detroit Locker, shown in FIGURE 60, has been the diff of choice in American sedan racing forever. Mandated by NASCAR and in 1995 by Trans Am, it is a somewhat crude device - noisy and upsetting as it cycles between "on" and "off" at partial or changing throttle. It is, however, effective, cheap, reliable and available.

FIGURE 59 – DETROIT LOCKER

The unit consists of a central trunnioned spider with dog teeth on each side. On either side of the spyder - and interlocking with it through matching dogs - are clutch rings. Each clutch ring is splined to a side gear which is in turn splined to an axle shaft. Holdout rings supposedly prevent the dogs from ratcheting in and out.

Under power the spyder dogs engage the clutch dogs and the unit is fully locked. When the car turns, the outer wheel rotational speed increases and the outer dogs unlock. When the vehicle is decelerating or under neutral throttle in a turn, it is driven by the inside wheel only. Under full power, in a straight line or on cor-

ner exit, it locks. The Detroit Locker, and its close cousin the No-Spin, senses and reacts to differential wheel speed, not to differential torque. There is a lot of necessary backlash in the Detroit Locker - it is a truly noisy and clanksome device. This is, in itself, not a problem in racing cars. What is a problem is that, when the thing cycles from locked to unlocked and back, the car goes from two wheel drive to one wheel drive on corner entry and back to two wheel drive when the power is applied. This makes the car jump around in a fairly inconsistent pattern and makes it impossible to place the car with the sort of precision that one would prefer.

The transition from one wheel to two wheel drive can be particularly upsetting if the driver decides to play with the throttle on corner exit. Not an optimum device - but reliable and cheap, it is available to fit most U.S. and some Japanese differential housings.

THE OPEN DIFFERENTIAL

If we could guarantee that wheelspin would not be a problem, the open differential has several advantages over any of the limited slips, torque sensing diffs and/or lockers. With the open diff there is no tire drag caused corner entry understeer. There is no transition from one wheel to two wheel drive. The units are inherently reliable and easy on the rest of the drive train. Should a half shaft failure occur the open diff will not put the car into the wall. It will also not get the car back to the pits.

Of course, it is often a bit difficult to guarantee that there will be no wheelspin - it can always, for instance, rain, or the track can get dirty. In the dry, however, with a well balanced car - in other words a purpose built and properly designed racing car (as opposed to a sedan based vehicle) - wheelspin should not be a problem. In fact, several Formula One teams are rumored to be running open diffs.

In the States we do not race in the wet on oval tracks. With Indy Cars, Indy Lights and Formula Atlantic, there is enough download on ovals to preclude the possibility of wheelspin. The benign characteristics of the open diff make it attractive on the ovals. Of course tire stagger is less effective with the open diff - but there is no tire drag on the straights and there are other ways to encourage a car to turn left.

In road racing, if the weather is good, if there are no really slow corners and the car features a lot of download and not an overabundance of horsepower, I would like to try it. Unfortunately most of the circuits on this side of the water feature both slow corners and bumps. Perhaps best practical solution for many tracks would be an 80/80 Salisbury or Powr Flow with enough preload to deal with the one wheel off the ground situation.

THE ACTIVE DIFFS AND TRACTION CONTROL

There are "active" plate diffs around. There is no reason why viscous diffs cannot be made active.

In 1993 and 1994 virtually every Formula One team (and Penske in CART) used traction control - to the immense detriment of the sport (and to the sound of racing). These were not active diffs but wheelspin detecting sensors and electronic control loops which cut spark, spark advance or fuel to the engine at the onset of wheelspin.

The torque sensing diff is the obvious mate to electronic traction control. Since all of the traction control feedback loops sense differential wheel speed, theoretically at least, the use of a torque sensing diff would put off the onset of power interruption and allow more efficient use of total available tire traction. Matching the Torsen to sophisticated traction control software should produce the optimum result.

DIFFERENTIAL STEER

Bump steer and roll steer are well known phenomena. The steering action of the various types of differential is less well known - but equally frustrating. If we view the racing (or passenger) car from above and represent driving torque by vector arrows at the rear tires it is apparent that an excess of torque on either rear tire will create a rotational moment about the polar center of the vehicle.

This moment will tend to steer the car in the direction away from the tire with the most torque. Excess torque on the inside tire will cause understeer and excess torque on the outside tire will cause oversteer. The reverse is true in the off throttle or over-run mode - excess drag on the outside tire will tend toward understeer. You can demonstrate this with by pushing or pulling on one corner of a model car - or, for that matter, of a block of wood. FIGURE 59 illustrates.

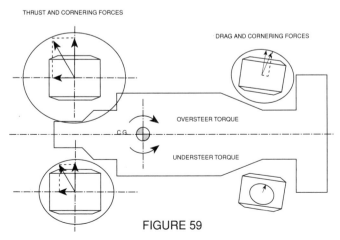

THRUST AND CORNERING FORCES

DRAG AND CORNERING FORCES

OVERSTEER TORQUE

C.G.

UNDERSTEER TORQUE

FIGURE 59

TIRE FORCES COTRIBUTING TO CONDITIONS OF OVERSTEER AND UNDERSTEER

In the case of the open differential, the driving torque on each wheel is normally equal and no steering effect is present. When noticeable wheelspin occurs, the driving tire strongly steers the car towards the spinning tire. For a graphic example, do a fierce standing start in a rear drive street car in damp conditions - or watch the start of a Formula One, Formula 3000 or Formula Atlantic race.

In the case of the locked differential (assuming equal tire diameters) the outside tire in a corner is trying to rotate faster than it would in a straight line while the inner is trying to rotate slower. The neutral and part throttle longitudinal forces on the tires are therefore forward on the inner tire and rearward on the outer tire - causing an understeer moment about the center of mass. This, of course, is what tire stagger in oval track racing is all about.

The Detroit Locker and its cousins incorporate over-run clutches so that, in the over-run or off throttle condition, the effect is that of an open differential. When significant driving torque is applied the diff locks. Under mid corner conditions, because the outer wheel has a greater rotational speed, all of the tractive force is applied to the inside tire, causing an understeer moment about the polar center. When the throttle is opened the diff locks, adding to the understeer. We should also note that, when one wheel attached to a locking diff slips in a straight line, all of the driving torque is immediately applied to the other tire - the well known if not beloved ratchet effect.

HORSES FOR COURSES

There is an old saying from the time when the beer halls offered a free snack table that goes, "There ain't no free lunch!" This is just as true of the automotive differential as it is of life in general - every type of differential has its drawbacks.

The open diff, while simple, reliable and benign in operation, allows wheelspin in conditions of reduced traction and or excess torque. The locking and limited slip units, while smooth under ideal (equilibrium) conditions may be unstable under real world conditions - locking and unlocking in rapid sequence (ratcheting). This gives rise to erratic and uncomfortable vehicle response.

This sort of thing doesn't bother the real racing driver (it is usually effectively cured by a bootfull of throttle - so long as the hammer is kept down.) It can, however, be most disconcerting to the unwary and unpracticed highway driver. It is also hard on the rear tires of the racing sedan.

The torque sensing diffs, on the other hand, should split the torque in proportion to the traction available from each tire (generally in proportion to the instantaneous normal load on the tire). They are therefore more linear and consistent in action and much more pleasant to drive - which is why the "Torsen" has found wide acceptance in high performance road cars and four wheel drive. They are, however, virtually unavailable for the racing car and the Torsen is a bit power hungry on corner exit.

Basically, at low accelerative force values, in a straight line on smooth pavement, all of the diffs work well. Under full throttle conditions, in a straight line, all of them except the open diff work well - and the open diff may be the answer on the big ovals where download and roadspeed ensure that wheelspin cannot be a problem. Decelerating into a corner, balancing the car on the throttle and accelerating out of corners (in other words under transient conditions of load transfer and throttle application) the limitations of each type make themselves known - except for the torque sensing diffs which have no unfortunate operational characteristics,

So which is best? Probably the viscous coupling. For those of us who do not have access to a developed viscous, as usual it's different horses for different courses. In the current environment, given a limited budget and a reasonable amount of horsepower, a steel cased Torsen would be my choice, simply because the unit is so effective, so benign in operation and so reliable - one less variable. Given a testing budget I would do a back to back comparison between the Emco, the Xtrac Viscous and either the Xtrac Salisbury or the Hewland Powr Flow.

I would not be at all surprised to find that I ended up running different diffs for different types of course. For sure I would be tailoring the Salisbury or Powr Flow to the type of circuit. With a severely limited budget and/or an inexperienced driver I would probably elect to use a cam and pawl - no surprises. As always with any question having to do with vehicle dynamics, I reserve the right to change my mind without notice.

CONCLUSION

Writing 101, which I have not attended, states that every piece of writing should have a definite beginning, a body and a definite conclusion. I wrote an introduction. God knows that I have written a body of work. I feel that conclusions are the responsibility of the readers. I will, however, offer a few closing observations.

The late Ken Purdy (who wrote about this sport as well as anyone ever has) once said that to be considered great at anything one had first to last a long time. Motor racing has had its fair share of shooting stars - drivers who burst upon the scene, shone brightly for a brief time, and then, for various reasons, disappeared. Those who lasted - the great multi-champions - have been, almost without exception, astute and serious students of the game.

By way of example I give you, in Formula One, Juan Manuel Fangio, Emerson Fittipaldi, Jackie Stewart, Niki Lauda, Alain Prost (not for nothing is he nicknamed "the professor ") and Ayrton Senna. Between them Prost and Senna won 92 Grands Prix and seven World Championships.

In Indy Cars Mario Andretti and Rick Mears come to mind, as does - believe it or not - A.J. Foyt (you had to work with him in his great days to appreciate how good he was and how much he knew). Sprint Cars have given us Steve Kinser, Sammy Swindell, Doug Wolfgang and, way back when, the greatest of then all, Tommy Hinnershitz. The list of Stock Car drivers is headed by Richard Petty but there is no shortage of drivers who have stayed at the top of that heap for decades.

Each of these men was blessed with extraordinary talents. None of them depended on natural talent to take him to greatness. Each learned how to make his cars work under varying conditions, how to get the most out of his car without abusing it or its tires.

Not just astute students, but astute politicians and psychologists, every one of them. They wound up in the best cars - and they got the most out of not only their cars, but their crews. As I said, at the higher levels and in the long run, it's a thinking man's game. If that is imprinted on your brain and you have learned nothing else from this book, I have succeeded.

APPENDIX: BOOKS

A large number of books have been written about the twin subjects of driving the racing car and how to become a racing driver. Most have been written by men with valid credentials. Most are entertaining. Few are of any real use to the aspiring racing driver - perhaps because the actual driving is only a small part of achieving success and perhaps because few of the successful drivers have really analyzed either their driving or their success. Nevertheless you should read every one you can get your hands on.

As teaching manuals few of the driving books are worth buying. A couple that are were written by World Champions. THE ART OF MOTOR RACING by Emerson Fittipaldi and Gordon Kirby (1987, Nutmeg Productions, New Haven, CT 1-800-847-4741) contains, in Fittipaldi's words, "no bullshit". There is no time wasted on the obvious nor in "how great I am". This is the work of a man who has been there, done it all and knows exactly how he got there and why he has remained there.

The other must-buy is AYRTON SENNA'S PRINCIPLES OF RACE DRIVING. The worst that can be said of Senna is that he was the best racing driver of his time. He was also the most serious student of the art of all time. Read the book.

Niki Lauda's two books, THE ART AND SCIENCE OF GRAND PRIX DRIVING and MEINE STORY are very good and should be read. Alain Prost has a book out with Pierre-Francois Rousselot - COMPETITION DRIVING - which has the best graphics of cornering lines I have yet seen. Prost's own comments are trenchant and valuable. Rousselot did most of the book and his portion is a lot less valuable.

I have always maintained that racing is racing. To prove my point some of the very best instructional books on driving the racing car are actually about riding racing motorcycles.

Keith Code, the originator and chief instructor of the legendary Super Bike School, has written A TWIST OF THE WRIST and it is required reading by anyone who wants to conduct any sort of vehicle at or near the fringes of its (or his/her) performance envelope. It is available at bike shops, from California Superbike School, Inc., P.O. Box 3743, Manhatten Beach, CA 90266 or from Acrobat Books, P.O. Box 480820, Los Angeles, CA 90048.

While you're at it, get Keith's SOFT SCIENCE OF MOTORCYCLE RACING. If you are only going to buy two books (other than mine) these are the two.

While on the subject of bikes, the legendary Kenny Roberts has also written a book. TECHNIQUES OF MOTORCYCLE ROAD RACING is also a must read, not for the techniques described but for its insight into the character and determination that make a champion.

I have always maintained that, after a certain level of skill and experience has been attained, success at racing is about 98% mental. That being the case, it stands to reason that each of us should devote a large portion of our training time to mental training. Great idea, heh? The trouble is that we don't know how.

An ex touring tennis pro named James E. Loehr has spent decades learning how to mentally prepare oneself for combat, and preaching his gospel to notable athletes. His book, MENTAL TOUGHNESS TRAINING FOR SPORTS, subtitled ACHIEVING ATHLETIC EXCELLENCE (The Stephen Greene Press, 1982) is a must for anyone seriously considering any sort of competitive life.

Perhaps the most important lesson that Loehr has to teach is that mental toughness is not inborn in anyone - it is acquired and it can be learned. If you really want to progress beyond the, "He had a lot of talent, but didn't get the breaks" stage, you had better learn mental toughness. Loehr's book is an excellent first step.

An army travels on its stomach and we are what we eat - old saws, but true ones. Sports nutrition is relatively new - when I was young, the experts all agreed that red meat and proteins in general were the diet of champions. We enjoyed our food more, but our performance suffered. Fortunately none of us knew any better so nobody got an advantage.

Every serious athlete in this generation knows more about sports nutrition than the experts did a few decades ago. Every successful professional athlete pays a lot of attention to his diet. I don't think that it is necessary to eat only Willi Dungel's baby-food-like ground up stuff (read Niki Lauda). The plan that makes sense to me is outlined in Dr.Robert Haas' EAT TO WIN (New American Library, 1983 - available in Signet paper back).

Haas' plan works for Martina Navratilova (who gets my vote as athlete of the century) and it is not at all unpleasant. It is also eminently practical. The good doctor even includes advice on how to eat well on the road. Most libraries carry this one. Try it.

It has been said that what matters in life is not how many times you get knocked down but how many times you get up again. Dennis Conner, of America's Cup fame, has been knocked down about as hard as anyone. He has also gotten up again and carried on to more and bigger triumphs. We are all going to be knocked down. If you contemplate getting up again you should read his book (THE ART OF WINNING, St Martin's Press, New York, 1989).

I have stated that Racing Drivers and Fighter Pilots are the same people. Everyone who intends to be either should read THE ACE FACTOR by Mike Spick (The Naval Institute Press, 1988). My favorite race driving book of all time is THE RACING DRIVER by Denis Jenkinson - which has just been reissued. It should be purchased.

Recent publications include INSIDE RACING TECHNOLOGY by my good friend Paul Haney, in cooperation with another good friend (and damned good racing engineer) Jeff Braun. It is good. It is readable. While it does not deal with the driving of the racing car, its extensive interviews with racing engineers (including yours truly) make it a must-read for drivers, and would be drivers.

Just about everything learned about racing car vehicle dynamics in the past century has been compiled into one volume by the much respected Bill Milliken (of Calspan fame) and his son Douglas. Comprehensive and highly technical, this SAE-published book contains previously unpublished work on stability and control at high force levels. It is a "must have" reference work for any serious automotive engineer.

The total cost of all the recommended purchases is less than a set of tires. I submit that you would gain more performance from the books. Most are available from

Motorbooks International, P.O. Box 2, Osceola, WI 54020   1-800-458-0454.

Anyone interested in the art of driving racing cars should subscribe to two English magazines, each of which is published six times a year. RACE TECH, under the Editorship of Ian Bamsey, who edited this book, provides in-depth coverage of racing techniques and racing car technology and as such is essential reading for both drivers and engineers.

Subscriptions are available direct from the UK (call 011-44-1935-415000 for details) or via its North American distributor Eric Waiter Associates, 369 Springfield Avenue, Berkeley Heights, New Jersey 07922 (tel 908-665-7811, fax 665-7814).

RACE CAR ENGINEERING, under the editorship of Quentin Spurring, is slightly less technical, with more general content. Credit card subscriptions can be faxed to: 011-44-181-760-5117.

ORDER FORM

Carroll Smith Consulting, Inc.
1236 Via Landeta
Palos Verdes Estates, CA 90274   Date: _____
Enclosed please find my check for $ _____. Please send, postpaid.
_____ Copies of   DRIVE TO WIN @ $24.95 ea. ($27.00 in California)
_____ Copies of   PREPARE TO WIN @ $19.95 ea. ($21.60 in California)
_____ Copies of   TUNE TO WIN @ $19.95 ea. ($21.60 in California)
_____ Copies of   ENGINEER TO WIN @ $19.95 ea. ($21.60 in California)
_____ Copies of   SCREW TO WIN @ $19.95 ea. ($21.60 in California)
SHIP TO:
NAME _____
ADDRESS _____
CITY _____ STATE _____ ZIP _____

- -

ORDER FORM

Carroll Smith Consulting, Inc.
1236 Via Landeta
Palos Verdes Estates, CA 90274   Date: _____
Enclosed please find my check for $ _____. Please send, postpaid.
_____ Copies of   DRIVE TO WIN @ $24.95 ea. ($27.00 in California)
_____ Copies of   PREPARE TO WIN @ $19.95 ea. ($21.60 in California)
_____ Copies of   TUNE TO WIN @ $19.95 ea. ($21.60 in California)
_____ Copies of   ENGINEER TO WIN @ $19.95 ea. ($21.60 in California)
_____ Copies of   SCREW TO WIN @ $19.95 ea. ($21.60 in California)
SHIP TO:
NAME _____
ADDRESS _____
CITY _____ STATE _____ ZIP _____

- -

ORDER FORM

Carroll Smith Consulting, Inc.
1236 Via Landeta
Palos Verdes Estates, CA 90274   Date: _____
Enclosed please find my check for $ _____. Please send, postpaid.
_____ Copies of   DRIVE TO WIN @ $24.95 ea. ($27.00 in California)
_____ Copies of   PREPARE TO WIN @ $19.95 ea. ($21.60 in California)
_____ Copies of   TUNE TO WIN @ $19.95 ea. ($21.60 in California)
_____ Copies of   ENGINEER TO WIN @ $19.95 ea. ($21.60 in California)
_____ Copies of   SCREW TO WIN @ $19.95 ea. ($21.60 in California)
SHIP TO:
NAME _____
ADDRESS _____
CITY _____ STATE _____ ZIP _____